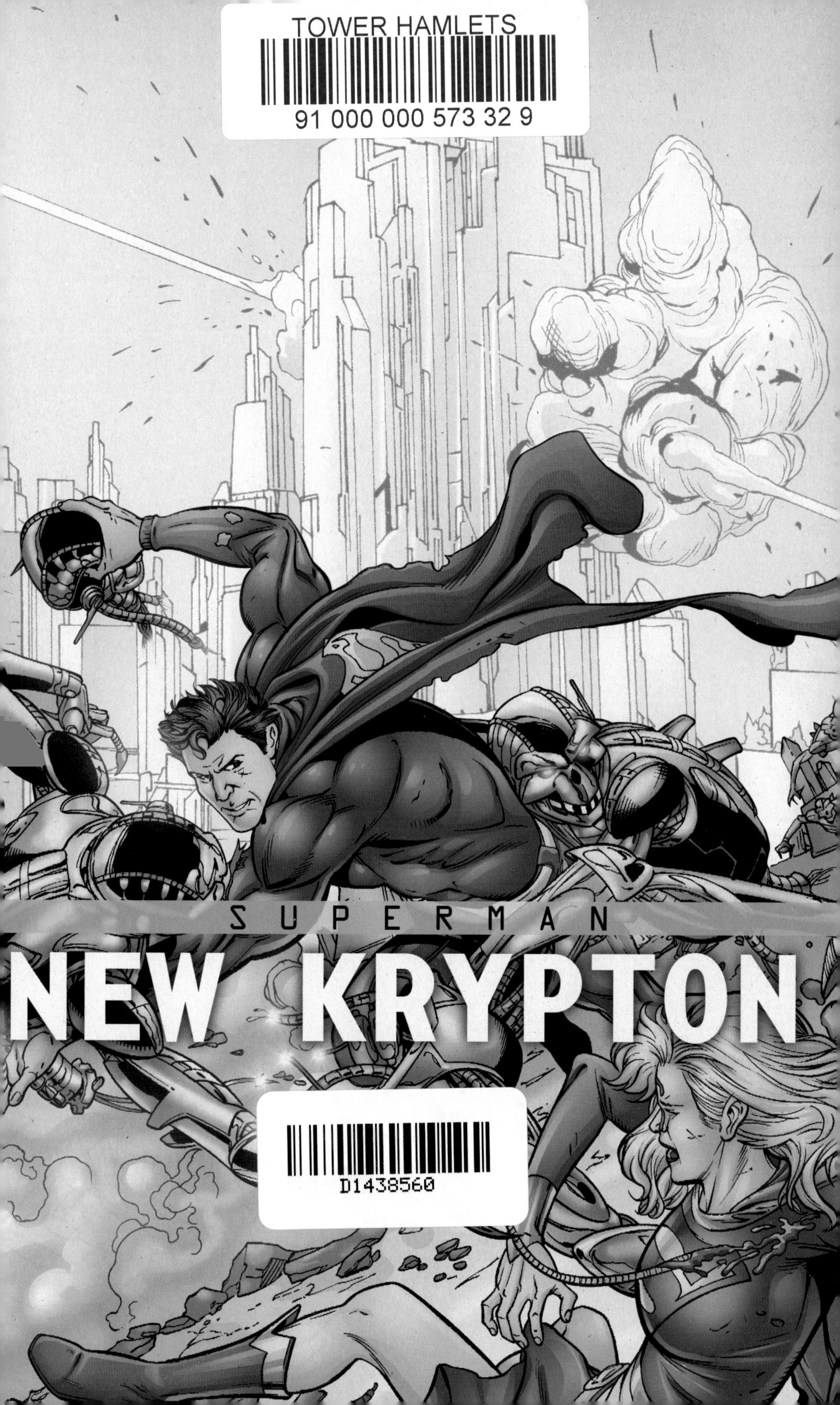

# SUPERMAN
# NEW KRYPTON

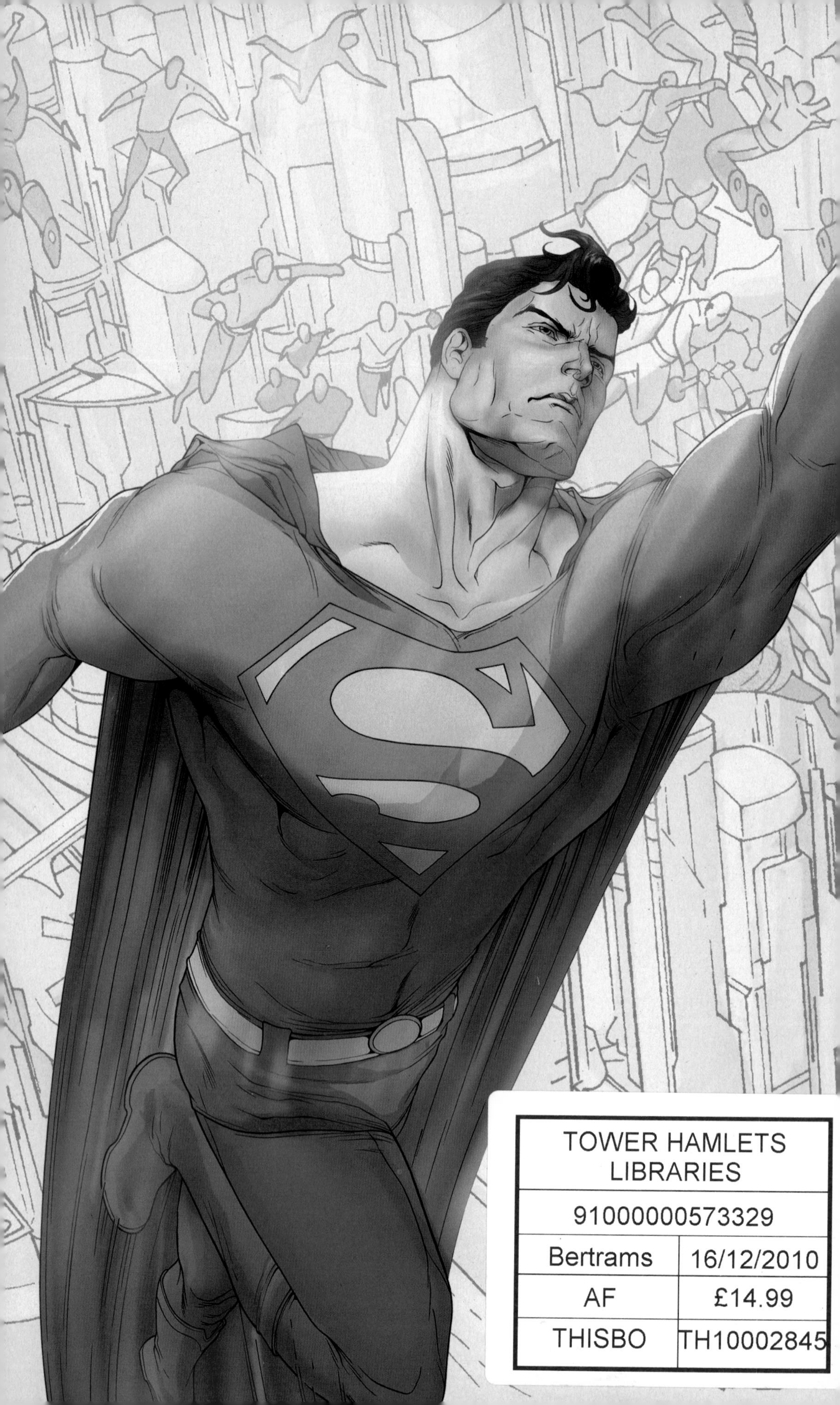

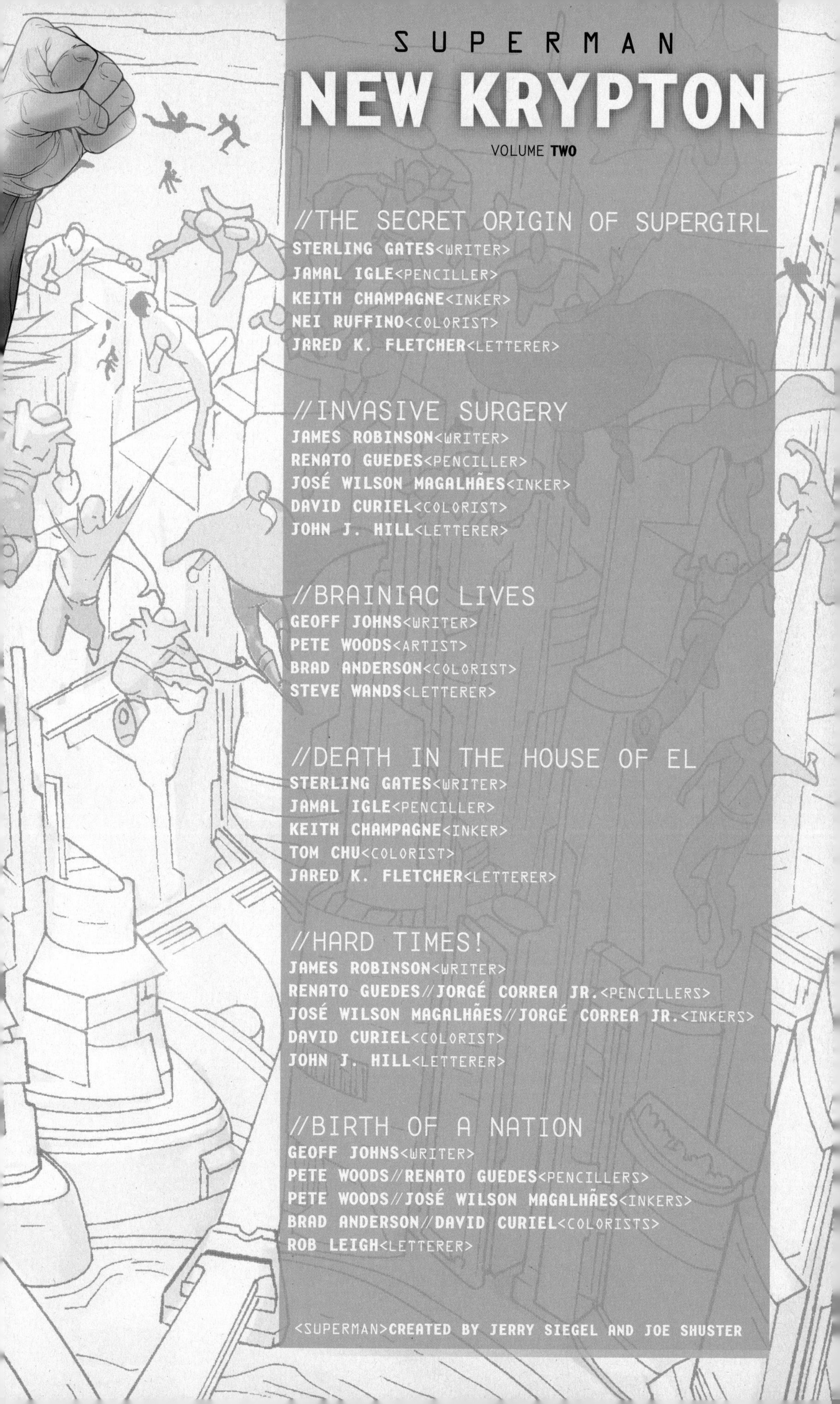

# SUPERMAN
# NEW KRYPTON
VOLUME **TWO**

## //THE SECRET ORIGIN OF SUPERGIRL
**STERLING GATES**<WRITER>
**JAMAL IGLE**<PENCILLER>
**KEITH CHAMPAGNE**<INKER>
**NEI RUFFINO**<COLORIST>
**JARED K. FLETCHER**<LETTERER>

## //INVASIVE SURGERY
**JAMES ROBINSON**<WRITER>
**RENATO GUEDES**<PENCILLER>
**JOSÉ WILSON MAGALHÃES**<INKER>
**DAVID CURIEL**<COLORIST>
**JOHN J. HILL**<LETTERER>

## //BRAINIAC LIVES
**GEOFF JOHNS**<WRITER>
**PETE WOODS**<ARTIST>
**BRAD ANDERSON**<COLORIST>
**STEVE WANDS**<LETTERER>

## //DEATH IN THE HOUSE OF EL
**STERLING GATES**<WRITER>
**JAMAL IGLE**<PENCILLER>
**KEITH CHAMPAGNE**<INKER>
**TOM CHU**<COLORIST>
**JARED K. FLETCHER**<LETTERER>

## //HARD TIMES!
**JAMES ROBINSON**<WRITER>
**RENATO GUEDES**//**JORGÉ CORREA JR.**<PENCILLERS>
**JOSÉ WILSON MAGALHÃES**//**JORGÉ CORREA JR.**<INKERS>
**DAVID CURIEL**<COLORIST>
**JOHN J. HILL**<LETTERER>

## //BIRTH OF A NATION
**GEOFF JOHNS**<WRITER>
**PETE WOODS**//**RENATO GUEDES**<PENCILLERS>
**PETE WOODS**//**JOSÉ WILSON MAGALHÃES**<INKERS>
**BRAD ANDERSON**//**DAVID CURIEL**<COLORISTS>
**ROB LEIGH**<LETTERER>

<SUPERMAN>**CREATED BY JERRY SIEGEL AND JOE SHUSTER**

Cover by Alex Ross
Publication design by ROBBIE BIEDERMAN

SUPERMAN: NEW KRYPTON Volume 2
Published by DC Comics. Cover and compilation Copyright © 2009
DC Comics. All Rights Reserved.

Originally published in single magazine form in SUPERGIRL 35, 36,
SUPERMAN 682, 683, ACTION COMICS 872, 873 Copyright © 2008, 2009
DC Comics. All Rights Reserved. All characters, their distinctive
likenesses and related elements featured in this publication are
trademarks of DC Comics. The stories, characters and incidents
featured in this publication are entirely fictional. DC Comics
does not read or accept unsolicited submissions of ideas,
stories or artwork.

DC Comics, 1700 Broadway, New York, NY 10019
A Warner Bros. Entertainment Company
Printed by RR Donnelley, Salem, VA, USA. 8/11/10
ISBN: 978-1-4012-2320-5

SUSTAINABLE
FORESTRY
INITIATIVE
Certified Chain of Custody
Promoting Sustainable
Forest Management
www.sfiprogram.org

Fiber used in this product line meets the
sourcing requirements of the SFI program.
www.sfiprogram.org NFS-SPICOC-C0001801

<THE SECRET ORIGIN OF SUPERGIRL> SUPERGIRL 35 COVER ART BY **ALEX ROSS**

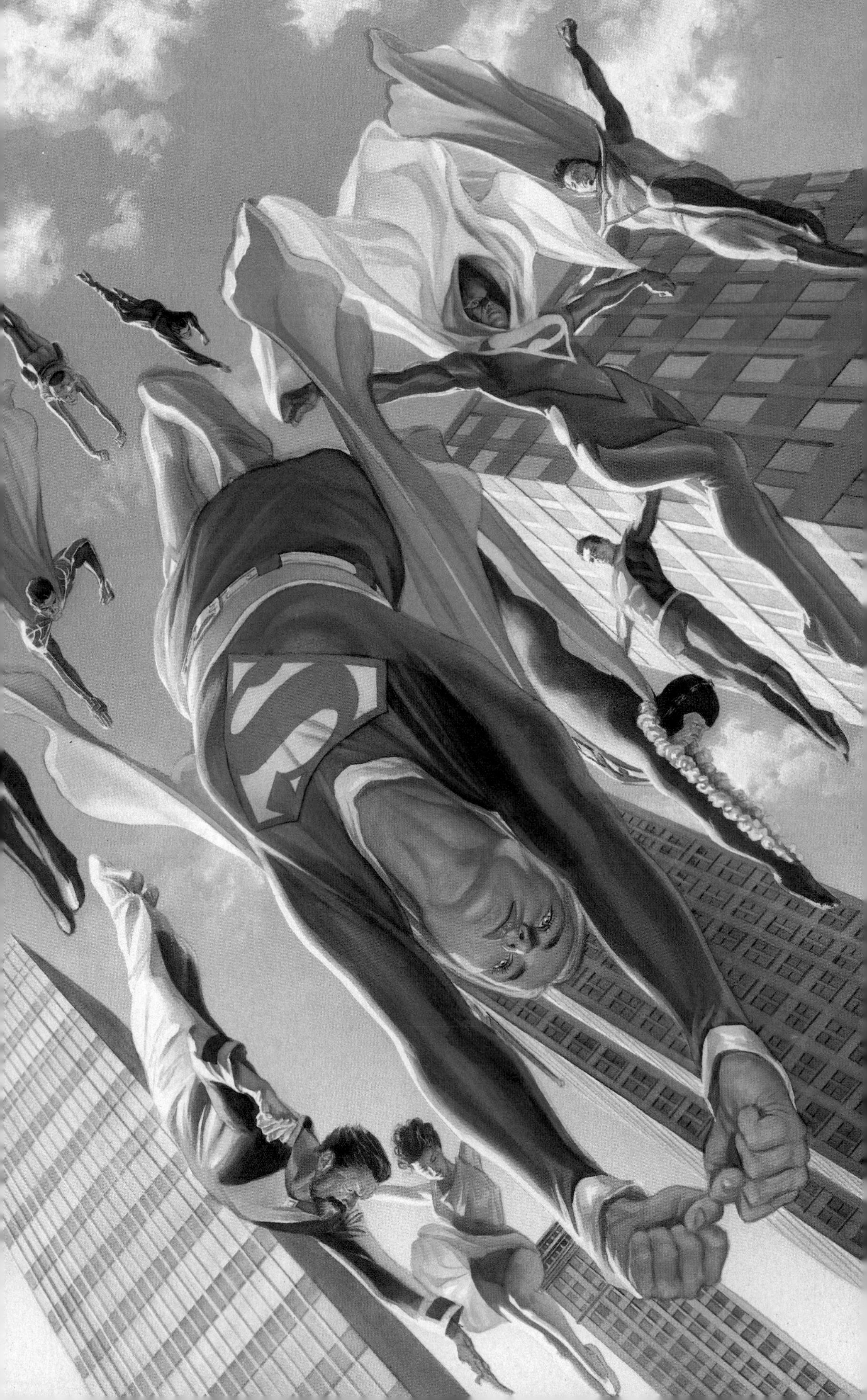

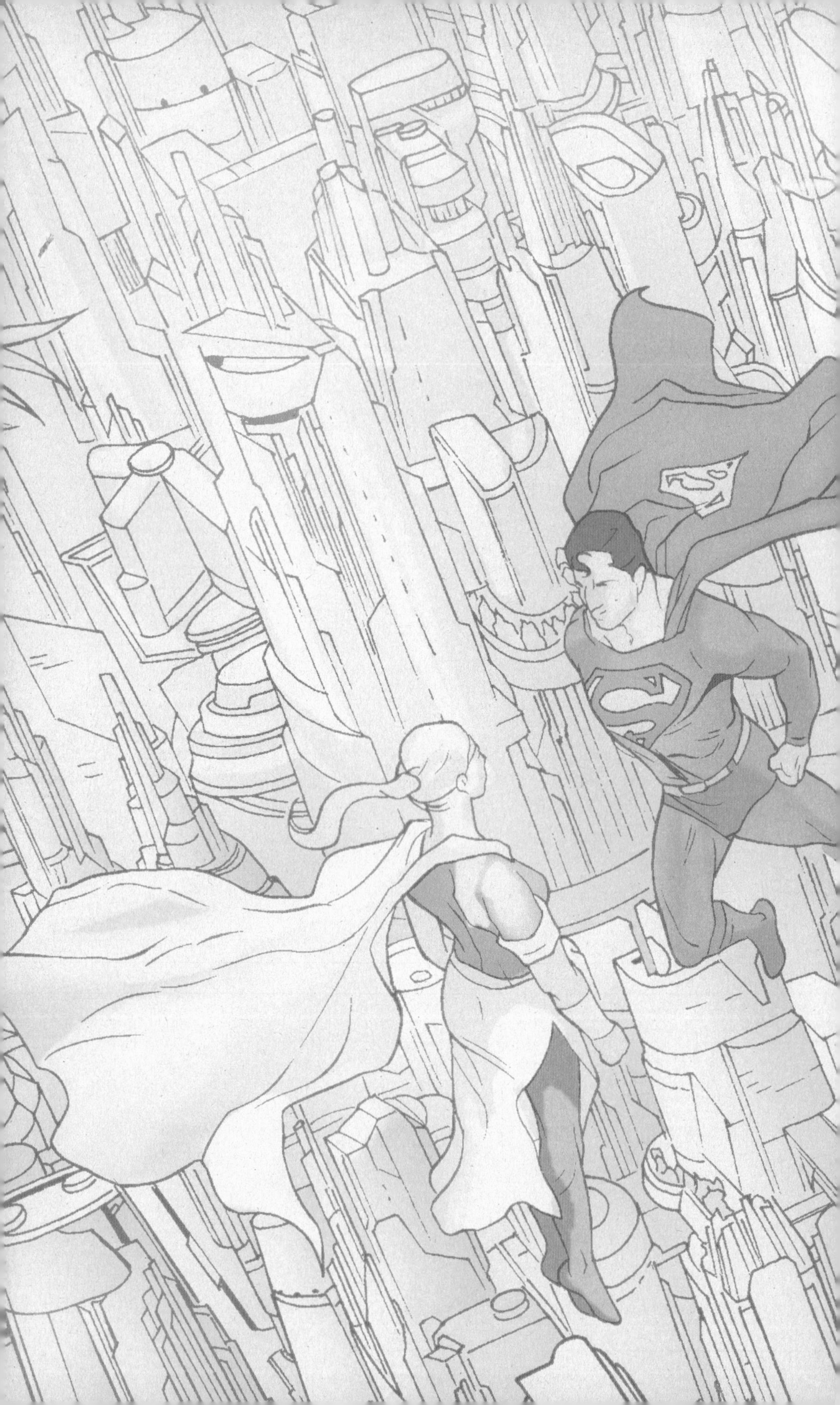

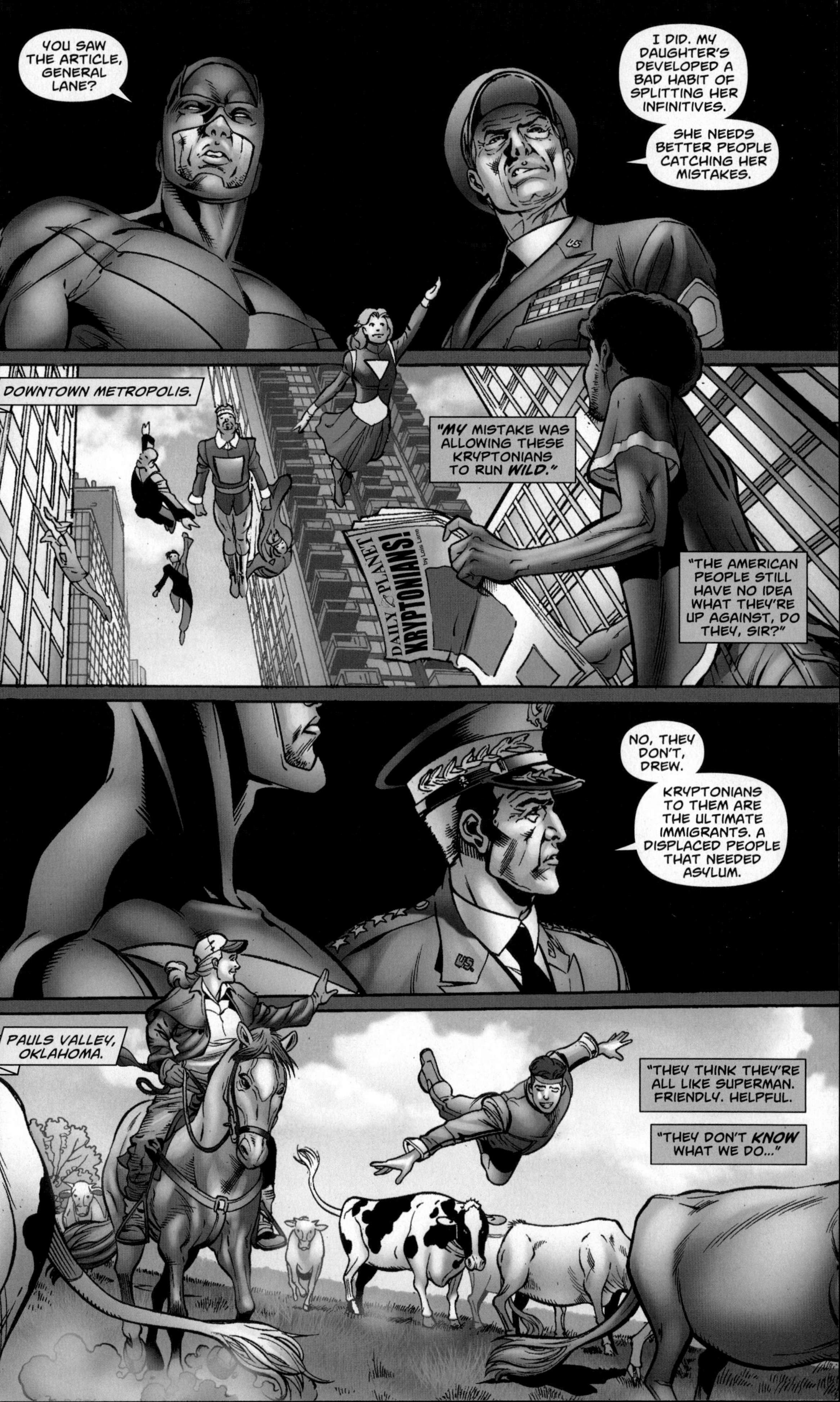

YOU SAW THE ARTICLE, GENERAL LANE?
I DID. MY DAUGHTER'S DEVELOPED A BAD HABIT OF SPLITTING HER INFINITIVES.
SHE NEEDS BETTER PEOPLE CATCHING HER MISTAKES.
DOWNTOWN METROPOLIS.
"MY MISTAKE WAS ALLOWING THESE KRYPTONIANS TO RUN WILD."
DAILY PLANET
KRYPTONIANS!
by Lois Lane
"THE AMERICAN PEOPLE STILL HAVE NO IDEA WHAT THEY'RE UP AGAINST, DO THEY, SIR?"
NO, THEY DON'T, DREW.
KRYPTONIANS TO THEM ARE THE ULTIMATE IMMIGRANTS. A DISPLACED PEOPLE THAT NEEDED ASYLUM.
PAULS VALLEY, OKLAHOMA.
"THEY THINK THEY'RE ALL LIKE SUPERMAN. FRIENDLY. HELPFUL.
"THEY DON'T KNOW WHAT WE DO..."

**DC COMICS** *proudly presents*

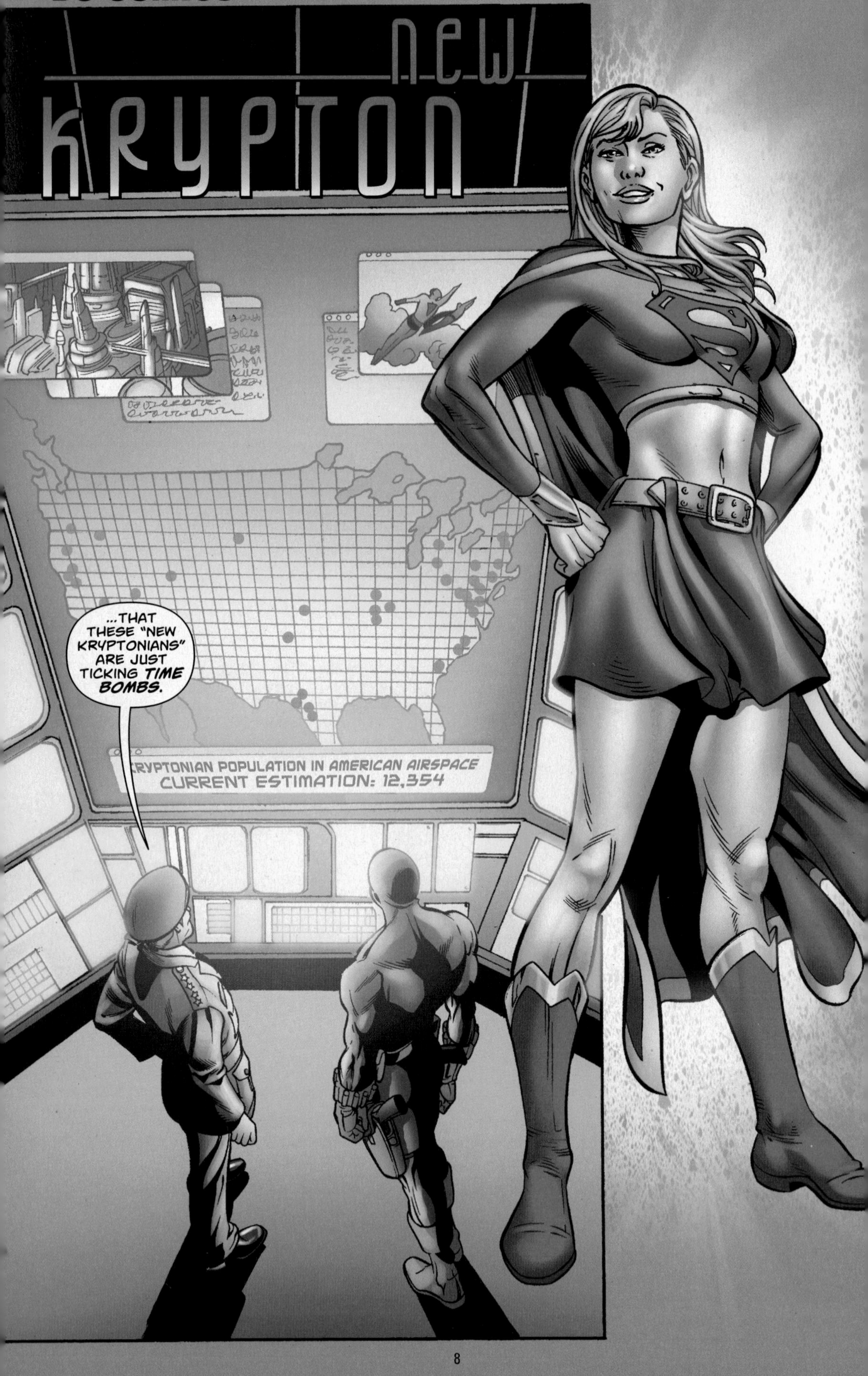

NEW KRYPTON
...THAT THESE "NEW KRYPTONIANS" ARE JUST TICKING TIME BOMBS.
KRYPTONIAN POPULATION IN AMERICAN AIRSPACE
CURRENT ESTIMATION: 12,354

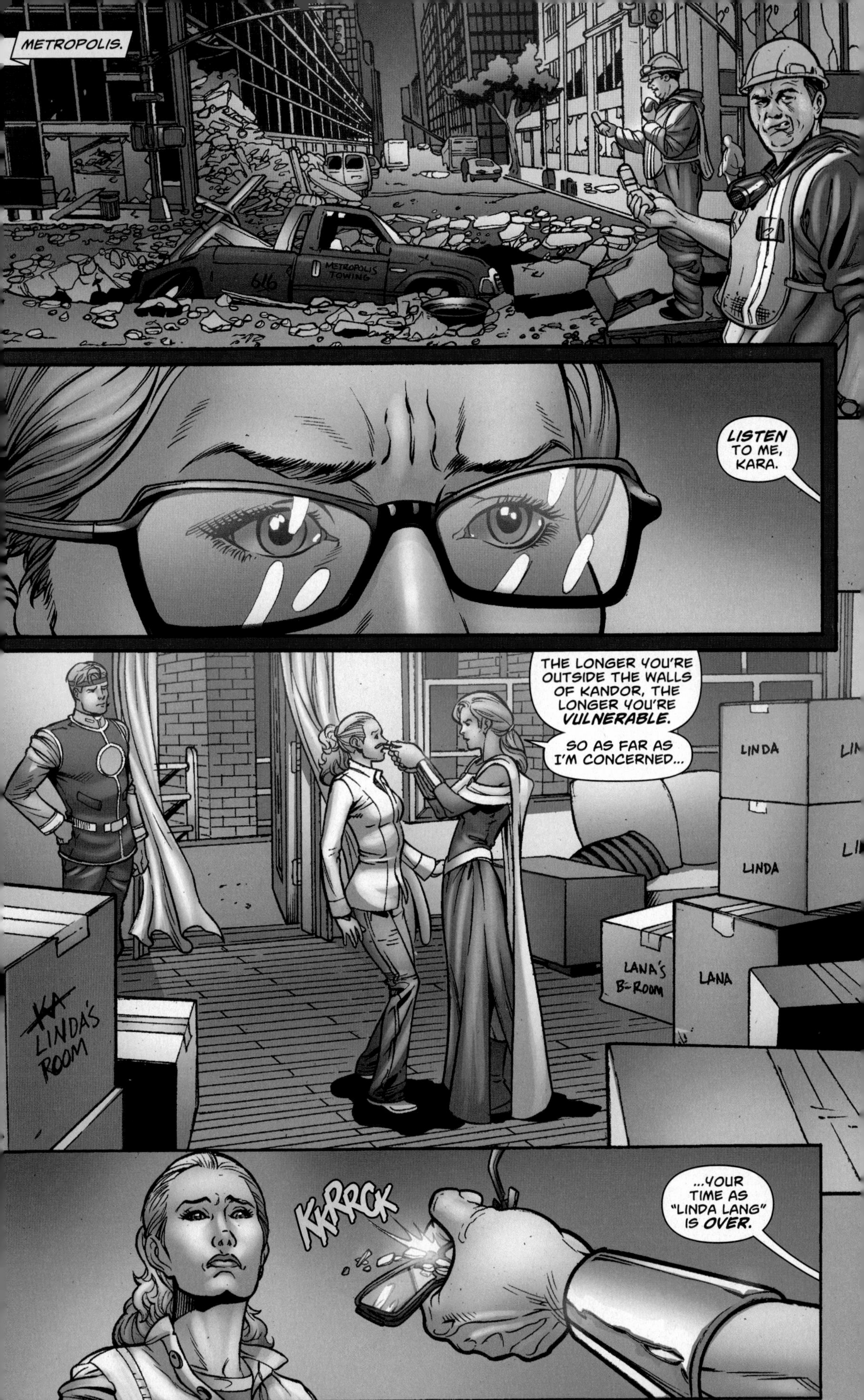

METROPOLIS.
METROPOLIS TOWING
616
LISTEN TO ME, KARA.
THE LONGER YOU'RE OUTSIDE THE WALLS OF KANDOR, THE LONGER YOU'RE VULNERABLE.
SO AS FAR AS I'M CONCERNED...
LINDA
LINDA
LANA'S B-ROOM
LANA
LINDA'S ROOM
KKRRCK
...YOUR TIME AS "LINDA LANG" IS OVER.

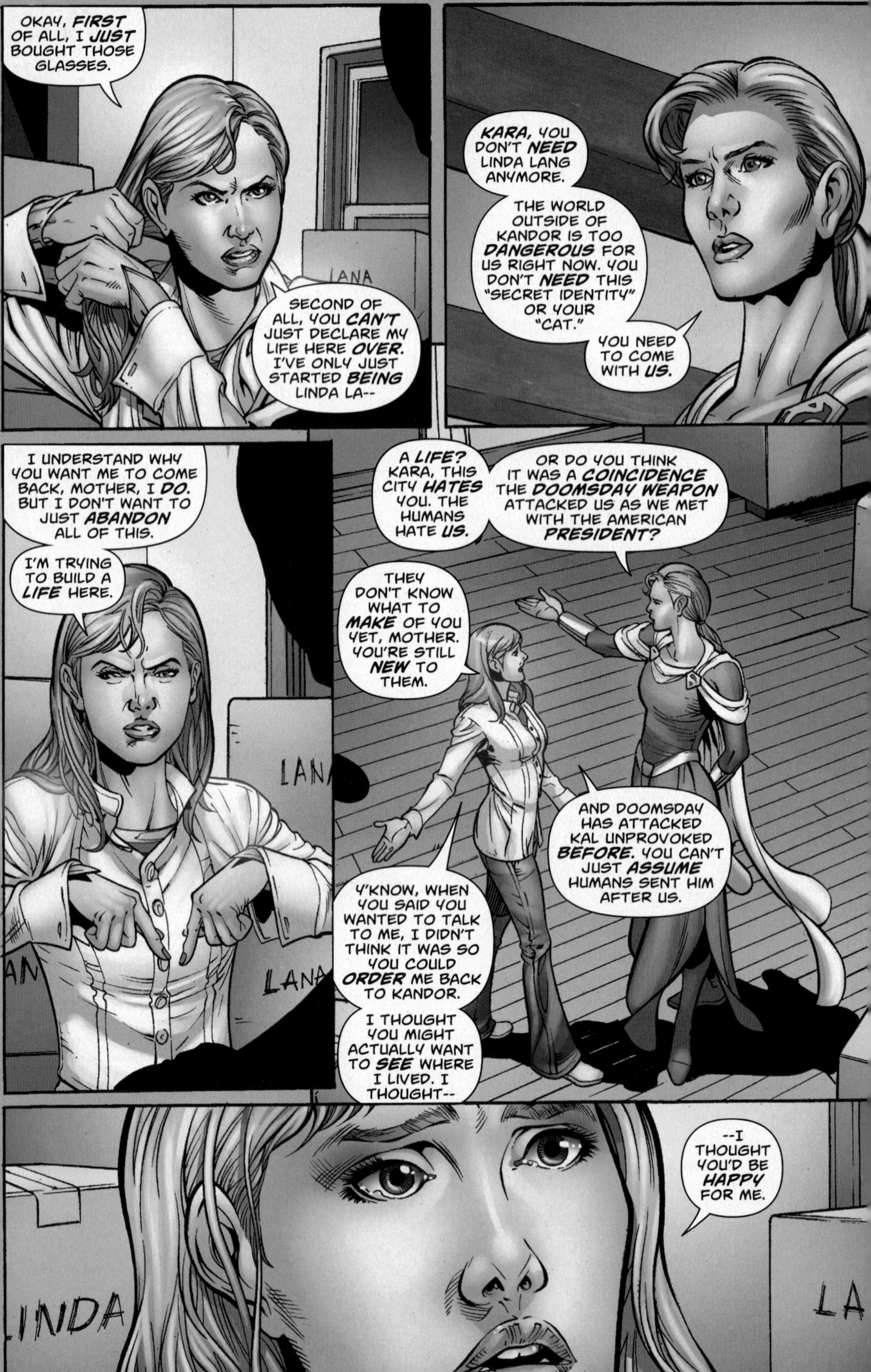
OKAY, FIRST OF ALL, I JUST BOUGHT THOSE GLASSES.
LANA
SECOND OF ALL, YOU CAN'T JUST DECLARE MY LIFE HERE OVER. I'VE ONLY JUST STARTED BEING LINDA LA--
KARA, YOU DON'T NEED LINDA LANG ANYMORE.
THE WORLD OUTSIDE OF KANDOR IS TOO DANGEROUS FOR US RIGHT NOW. YOU DON'T NEED THIS "SECRET IDENTITY" OR YOUR "CAT."
YOU NEED TO COME WITH US.
I UNDERSTAND WHY YOU WANT ME TO COME BACK, MOTHER, I DO. BUT I DON'T WANT TO JUST ABANDON ALL OF THIS.
I'M TRYING TO BUILD A LIFE HERE.
A LIFE? KARA, THIS CITY HATES YOU. THE HUMANS HATE US.
OR DO YOU THINK IT WAS A COINCIDENCE THE DOOMSDAY WEAPON ATTACKED US AS WE MET WITH THE AMERICAN PRESIDENT?
THEY DON'T KNOW WHAT TO MAKE OF YOU YET, MOTHER. YOU'RE STILL NEW TO THEM.
AND DOOMSDAY HAS ATTACKED KAL UNPROVOKED BEFORE. YOU CAN'T JUST ASSUME HUMANS SENT HIM AFTER US.
Y'KNOW, WHEN YOU SAID YOU WANTED TO TALK TO ME, I DIDN'T THINK IT WAS SO YOU COULD ORDER ME BACK TO KANDOR.
I THOUGHT YOU MIGHT ACTUALLY WANT TO SEE WHERE I LIVED. I THOUGHT--
--I THOUGHT YOU'D BE HAPPY FOR ME.
LINDA

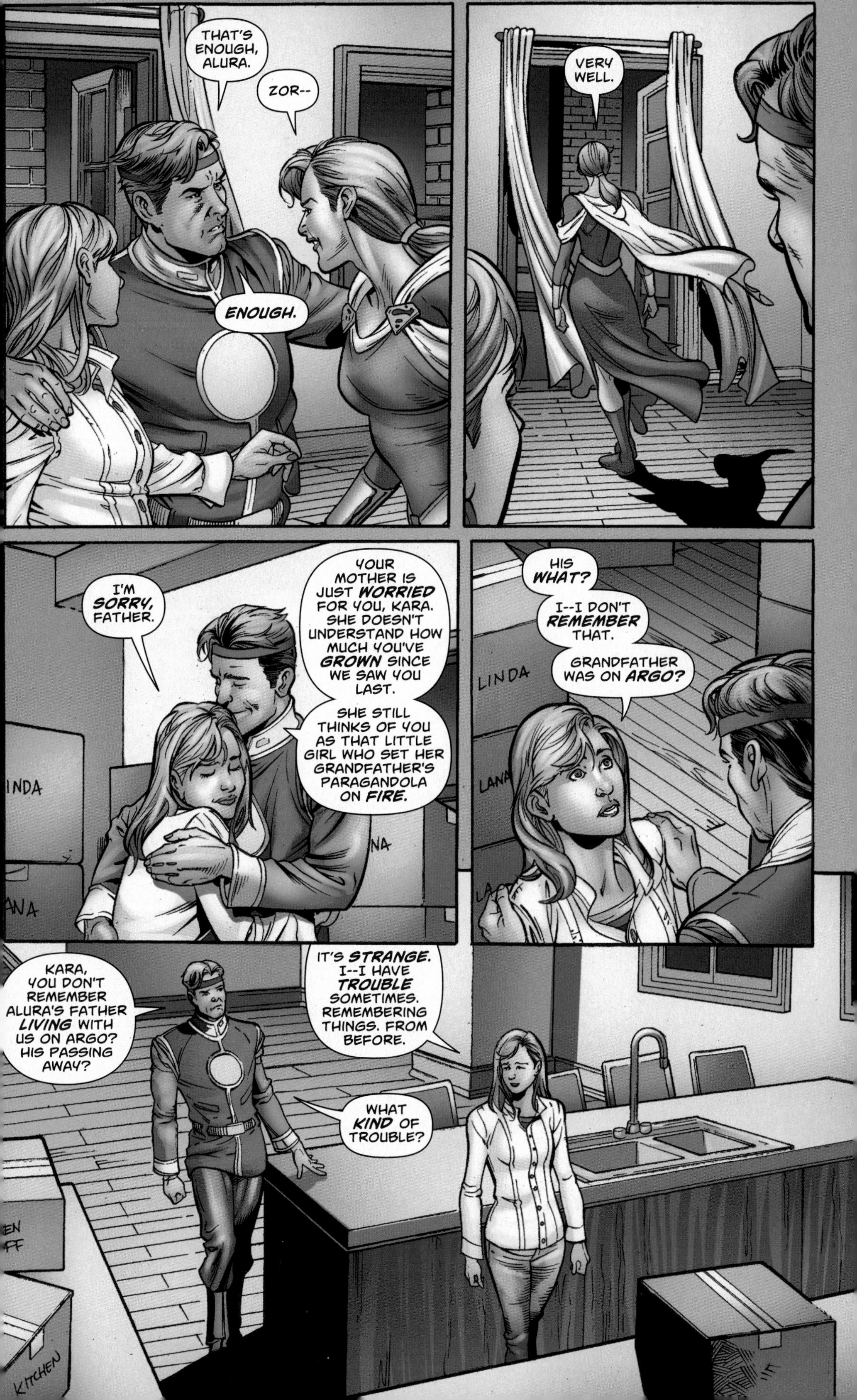
THAT'S ENOUGH, ALURA.
ZOR--
ENOUGH.
VERY WELL.
I'M SORRY, FATHER.
YOUR MOTHER IS JUST WORRIED FOR YOU, KARA. SHE DOESN'T UNDERSTAND HOW MUCH YOU'VE GROWN SINCE WE SAW YOU LAST.
SHE STILL THINKS OF YOU AS THAT LITTLE GIRL WHO SET HER GRANDFATHER'S PARAGANDOLA ON FIRE.
LINDA
HIS WHAT?
I--I DON'T REMEMBER THAT.
GRANDFATHER WAS ON ARGO?
LINDA
KARA, YOU DON'T REMEMBER ALURA'S FATHER LIVING WITH US ON ARGO? HIS PASSING AWAY?
IT'S STRANGE. I--I HAVE TROUBLE SOMETIMES. REMEMBERING THINGS. FROM BEFORE.
WHAT KIND OF TROUBLE?
KITCHEN

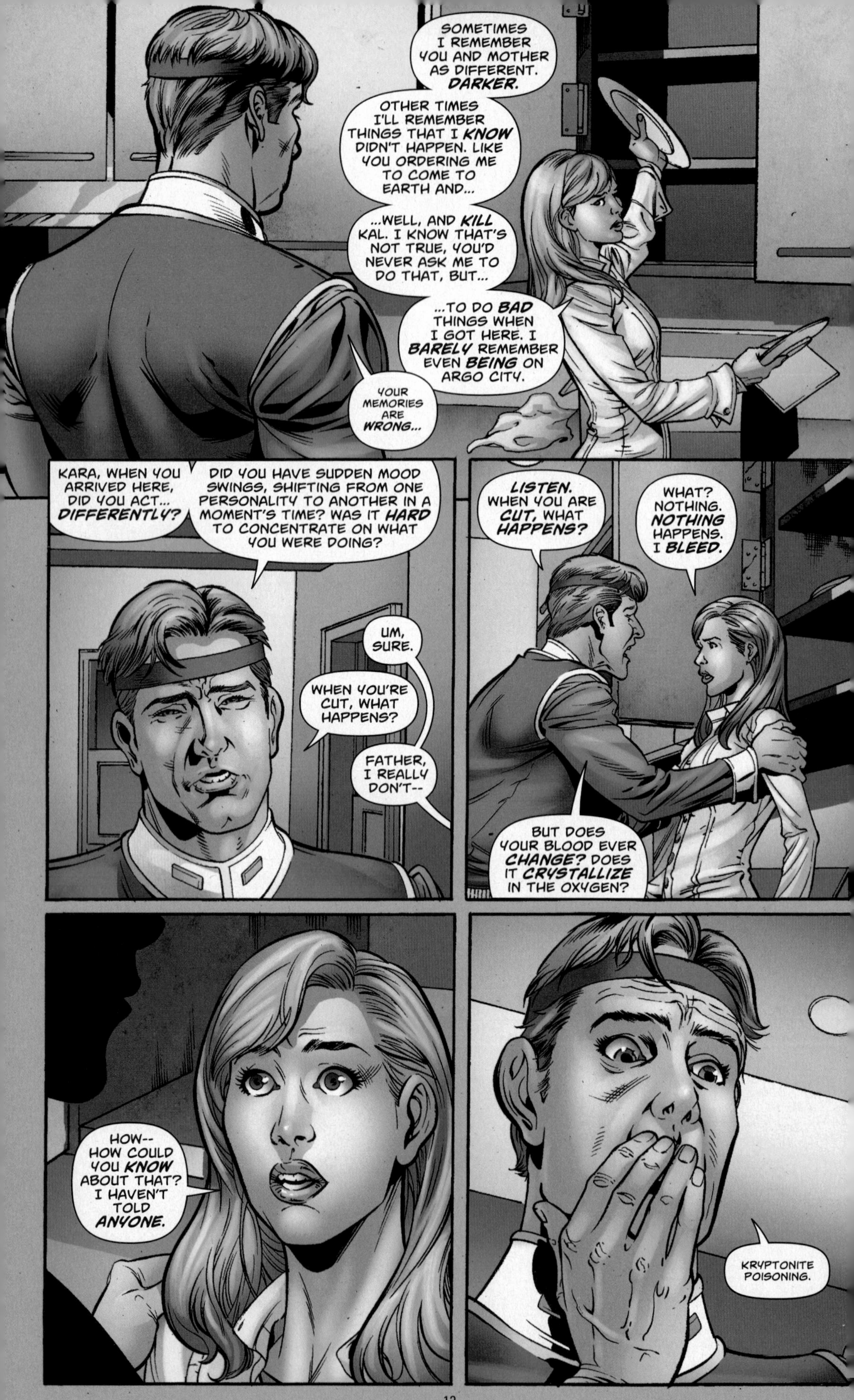
SOMETIMES I REMEMBER YOU AND MOTHER AS DIFFERENT. DARKER.
OTHER TIMES I'LL REMEMBER THINGS THAT I KNOW DIDN'T HAPPEN. LIKE YOU ORDERING ME TO COME TO EARTH AND...
...WELL, AND KILL KAL. I KNOW THAT'S NOT TRUE, YOU'D NEVER ASK ME TO DO THAT, BUT...
...TO DO BAD THINGS WHEN I GOT HERE. I BARELY REMEMBER EVEN BEING ON ARGO CITY.
YOUR MEMORIES ARE WRONG...
KARA, WHEN YOU ARRIVED HERE, DID YOU ACT... DIFFERENTLY?
DID YOU HAVE SUDDEN MOOD SWINGS, SHIFTING FROM ONE PERSONALITY TO ANOTHER IN A MOMENT'S TIME? WAS IT HARD TO CONCENTRATE ON WHAT YOU WERE DOING?
UM, SURE.
WHEN YOU'RE CUT, WHAT HAPPENS?
FATHER, I REALLY DON'T--
LISTEN. WHEN YOU ARE CUT, WHAT HAPPENS?
WHAT? NOTHING. NOTHING HAPPENS. I BLEED.
BUT DOES YOUR BLOOD EVER CHANGE? DOES IT CRYSTALLIZE IN THE OXYGEN?
HOW-- HOW COULD YOU KNOW ABOUT THAT? I HAVEN'T TOLD ANYONE.
KRYPTONITE POISONING.

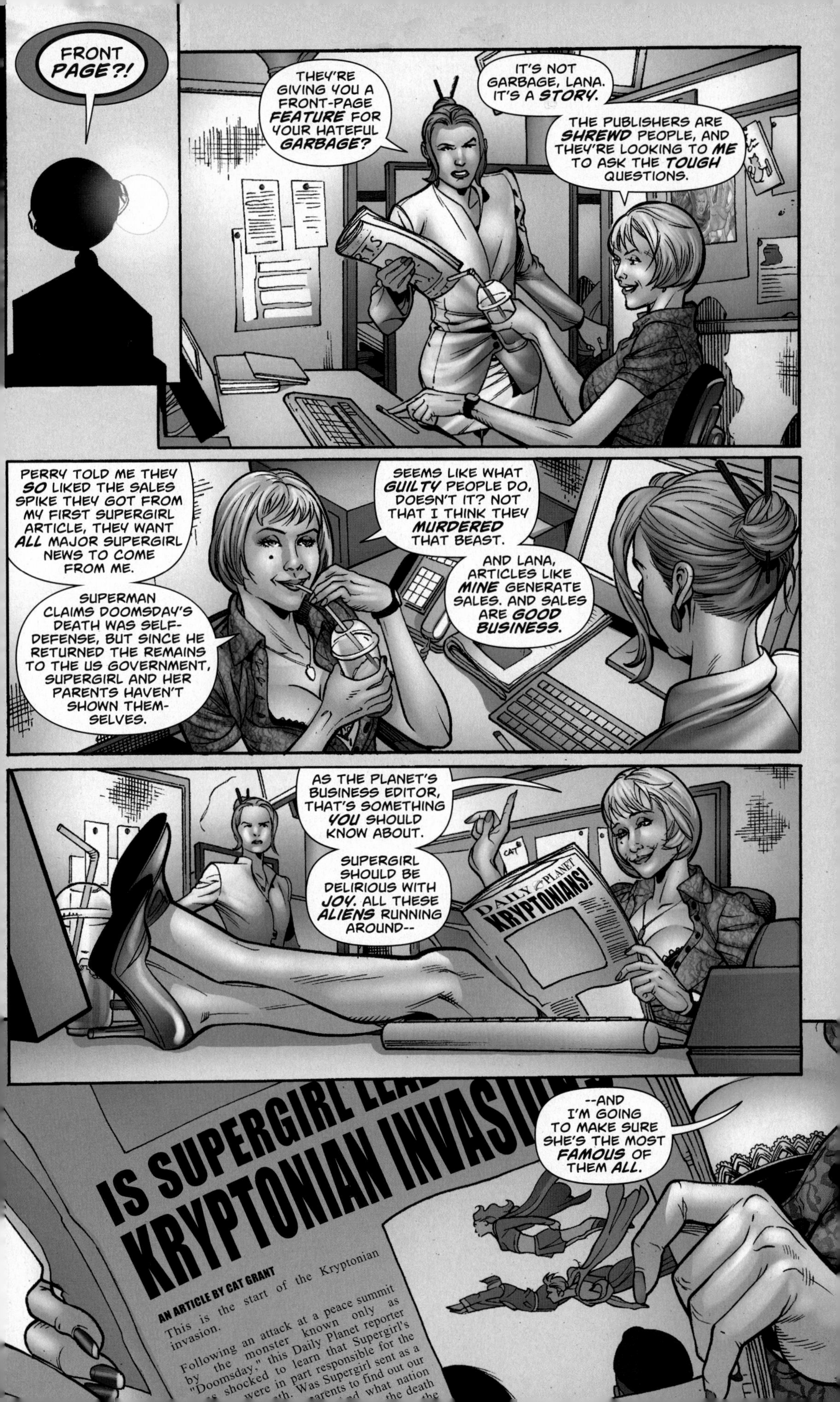
FRONT PAGE?!
THEY'RE GIVING YOU A FRONT-PAGE FEATURE FOR YOUR HATEFUL GARBAGE?
IT'S NOT GARBAGE, LANA. IT'S A STORY.
THE PUBLISHERS ARE SHREWD PEOPLE, AND THEY'RE LOOKING TO ME TO ASK THE TOUGH QUESTIONS.
PERRY TOLD ME THEY SO LIKED THE SALES SPIKE THEY GOT FROM MY FIRST SUPERGIRL ARTICLE, THEY WANT ALL MAJOR SUPERGIRL NEWS TO COME FROM ME.
SUPERMAN CLAIMS DOOMSDAY'S DEATH WAS SELF-DEFENSE, BUT SINCE HE RETURNED THE REMAINS TO THE US GOVERNMENT, SUPERGIRL AND HER PARENTS HAVEN'T SHOWN THEMSELVES.
SEEMS LIKE WHAT GUILTY PEOPLE DO, DOESN'T IT? NOT THAT I THINK THEY MURDERED THAT BEAST.
AND LANA, ARTICLES LIKE MINE GENERATE SALES. AND SALES ARE GOOD BUSINESS.
AS THE PLANET'S BUSINESS EDITOR, THAT'S SOMETHING YOU SHOULD KNOW ABOUT.
SUPERGIRL SHOULD BE DELIRIOUS WITH JOY. ALL THESE ALIENS RUNNING AROUND--
DAILY PLANET
KRYPTONIANS!
--AND I'M GOING TO MAKE SURE SHE'S THE MOST FAMOUS OF THEM ALL.
IS SUPERGIRL LEA
KRYPTONIAN INVASI
AN ARTICLE BY CAT GRANT
This is the start of the Kryptonian invasion.
Following an attack at a peace summit by the monster known only as "Doomsday," this Daily Planet reporter was shocked to learn that Supergirl's were in part responsible for the th. Was Supergirl sent as a parents to find out our and what nation the death

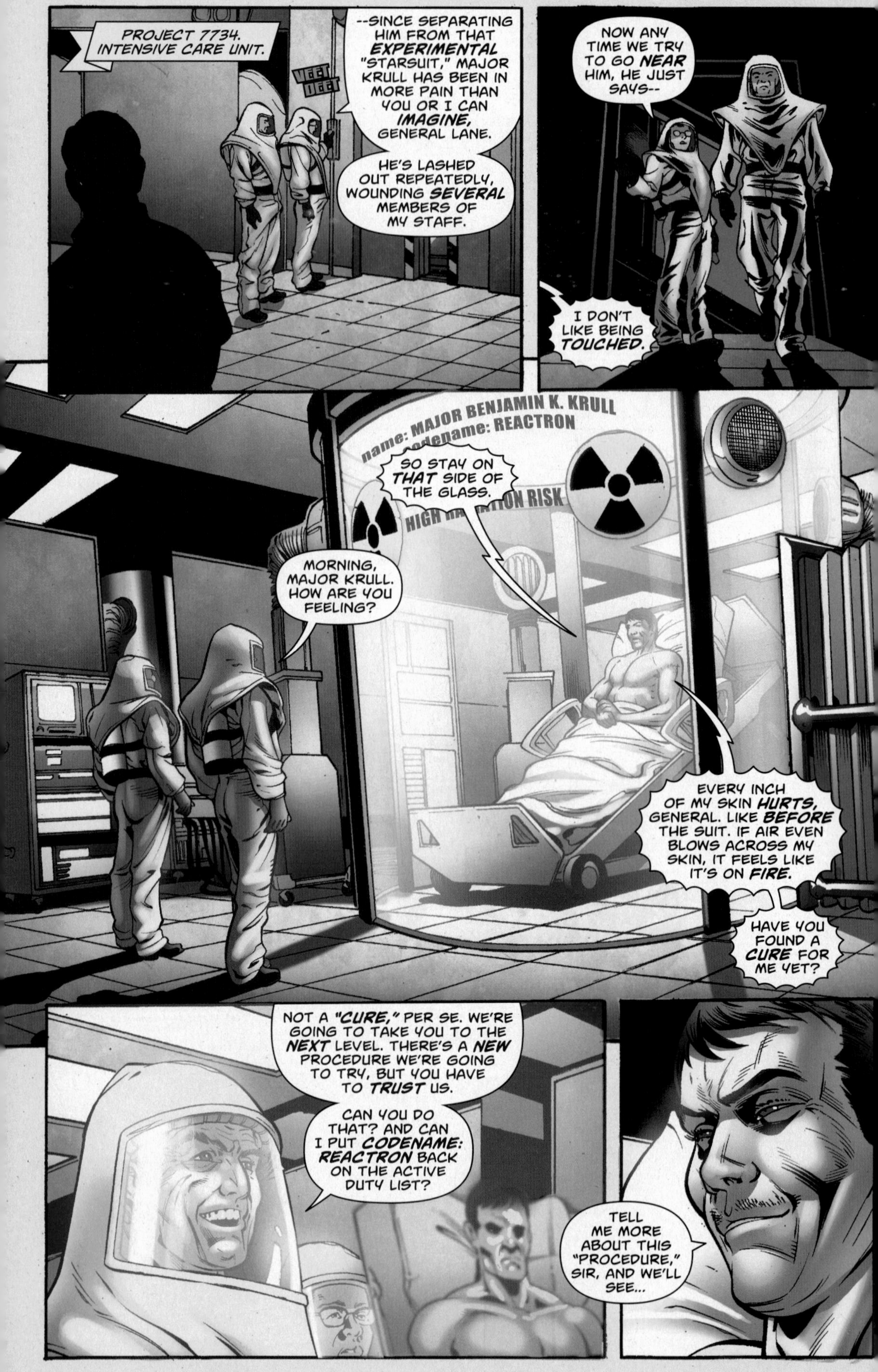

PROJECT 7734. INTENSIVE CARE UNIT.
BEEEP BEEEP
--SINCE SEPARATING HIM FROM THAT EXPERIMENTAL "STARSUIT," MAJOR KRULL HAS BEEN IN MORE PAIN THAN YOU OR I CAN IMAGINE, GENERAL LANE.
HE'S LASHED OUT REPEATEDLY, WOUNDING SEVERAL MEMBERS OF MY STAFF.
NOW ANY TIME WE TRY TO GO NEAR HIM, HE JUST SAYS--
I DON'T LIKE BEING TOUCHED.
name: MAJOR BENJAMIN K. KRULL
codename: REACTRON
HIGH RADIATION RISK
SO STAY ON THAT SIDE OF THE GLASS.
MORNING, MAJOR KRULL. HOW ARE YOU FEELING?
EVERY INCH OF MY SKIN HURTS, GENERAL. LIKE BEFORE THE SUIT. IF AIR EVEN BLOWS ACROSS MY SKIN, IT FEELS LIKE IT'S ON FIRE.
HAVE YOU FOUND A CURE FOR ME YET?
NOT A "CURE," PER SE. WE'RE GOING TO TAKE YOU TO THE NEXT LEVEL. THERE'S A NEW PROCEDURE WE'RE GOING TO TRY, BUT YOU HAVE TO TRUST US.
CAN YOU DO THAT? AND CAN I PUT CODENAME: REACTRON BACK ON THE ACTIVE DUTY LIST?
TELL ME MORE ABOUT THIS "PROCEDURE," SIR, AND WE'LL SEE...

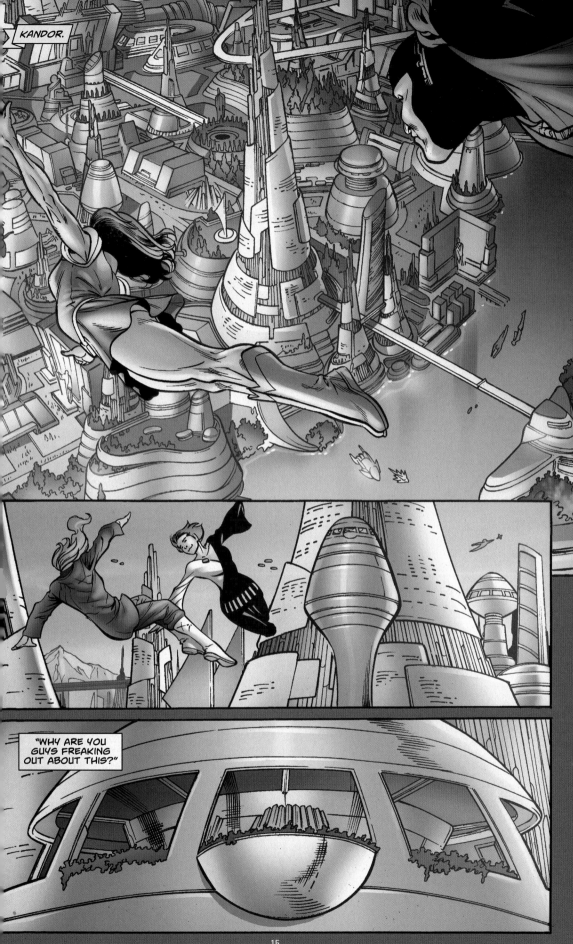

KANDOR.

"WHY ARE YOU GUYS FREAKING OUT ABOUT THIS?"

15

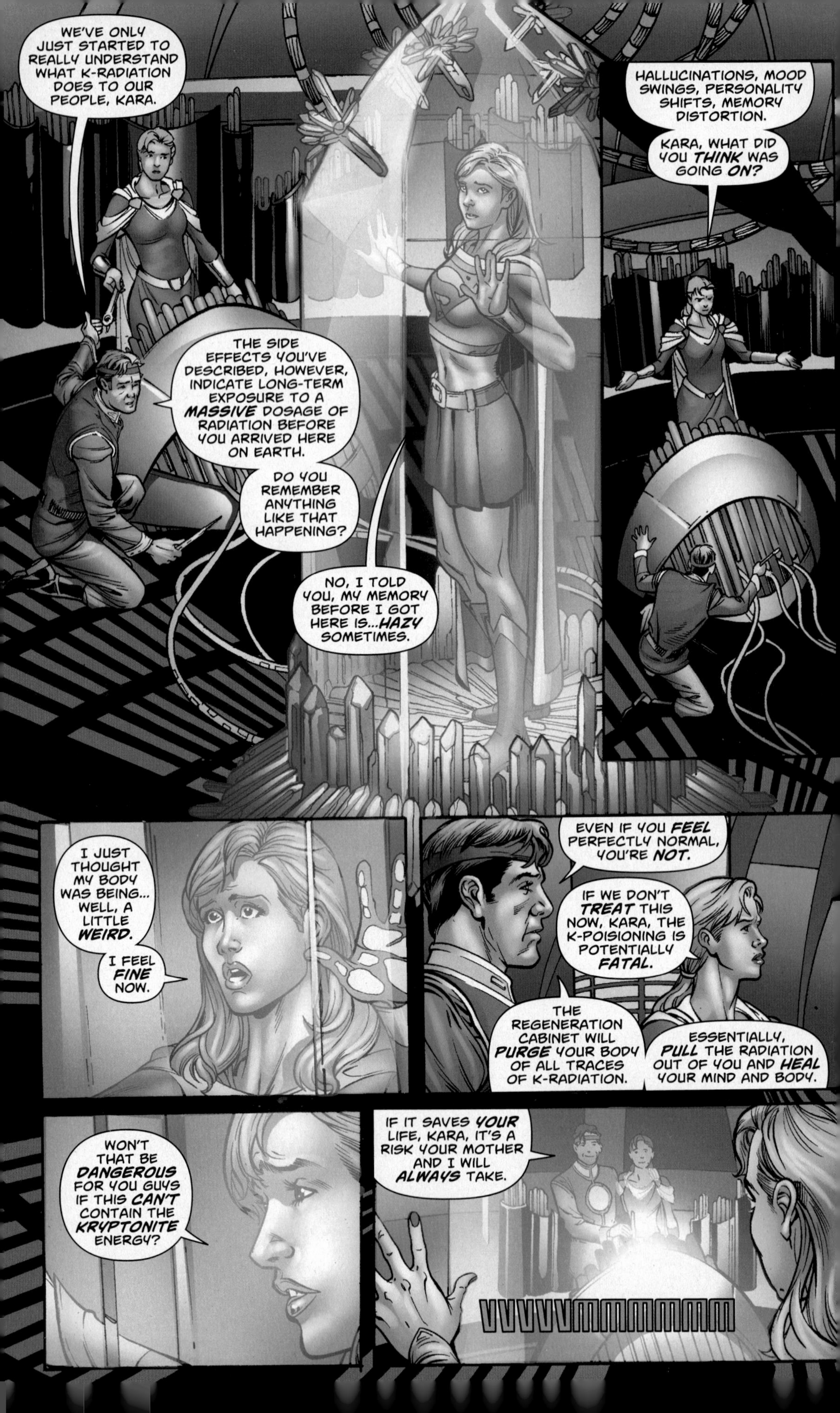
WE'VE ONLY JUST STARTED TO REALLY UNDERSTAND WHAT K-RADIATION DOES TO OUR PEOPLE, KARA.
THE SIDE EFFECTS YOU'VE DESCRIBED, HOWEVER, INDICATE LONG-TERM EXPOSURE TO A MASSIVE DOSAGE OF RADIATION BEFORE YOU ARRIVED HERE ON EARTH.
DO YOU REMEMBER ANYTHING LIKE THAT HAPPENING?
NO, I TOLD YOU, MY MEMORY BEFORE I GOT HERE IS...HAZY SOMETIMES.
HALLUCINATIONS, MOOD SWINGS, PERSONALITY SHIFTS, MEMORY DISTORTION.
KARA, WHAT DID YOU THINK WAS GOING ON?
I JUST THOUGHT MY BODY WAS BEING... WELL, A LITTLE WEIRD.
I FEEL FINE NOW.
EVEN IF YOU FEEL PERFECTLY NORMAL, YOU'RE NOT.
IF WE DON'T TREAT THIS NOW, KARA, THE K-POISONING IS POTENTIALLY FATAL.
THE REGENERATION CABINET WILL PURGE YOUR BODY OF ALL TRACES OF K-RADIATION.
ESSENTIALLY, PULL THE RADIATION OUT OF YOU AND HEAL YOUR MIND AND BODY.
WON'T THAT BE DANGEROUS FOR YOU GUYS IF THIS CAN'T CONTAIN THE KRYPTONITE ENERGY?
IF IT SAVES YOUR LIFE, KARA, IT'S A RISK YOUR MOTHER AND I WILL ALWAYS TAKE.
VVVVVMMMMMMM

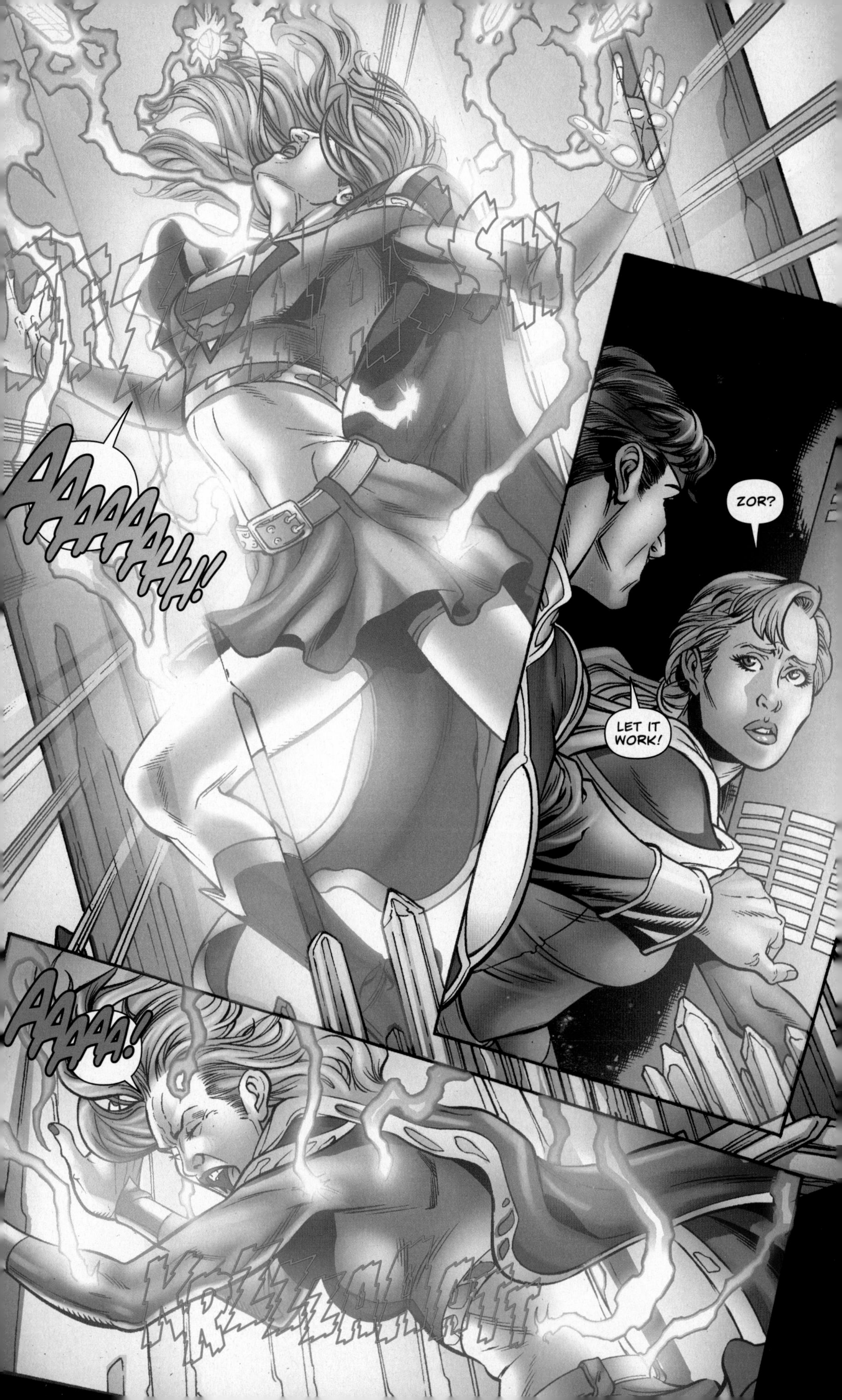

AAAAAAHH!
ZOR?
LET IT WORK!
AAAAA!

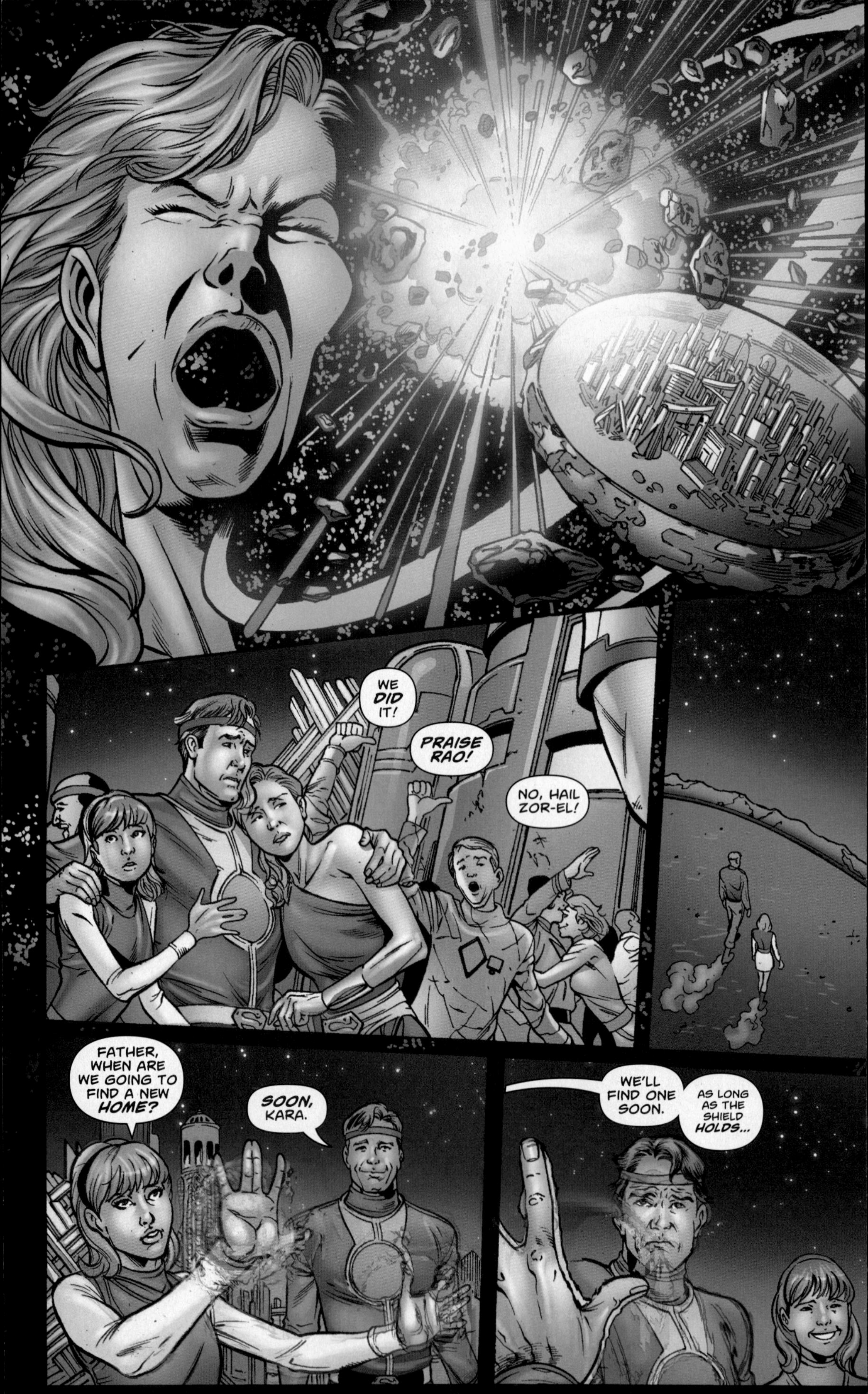
WE DID IT!
PRAISE RAO!
NO, HAIL ZOR-EL!
FATHER, WHEN ARE WE GOING TO FIND A NEW HOME?
SOON, KARA.
WE'LL FIND ONE SOON.
AS LONG AS THE SHIELD HOLDS...

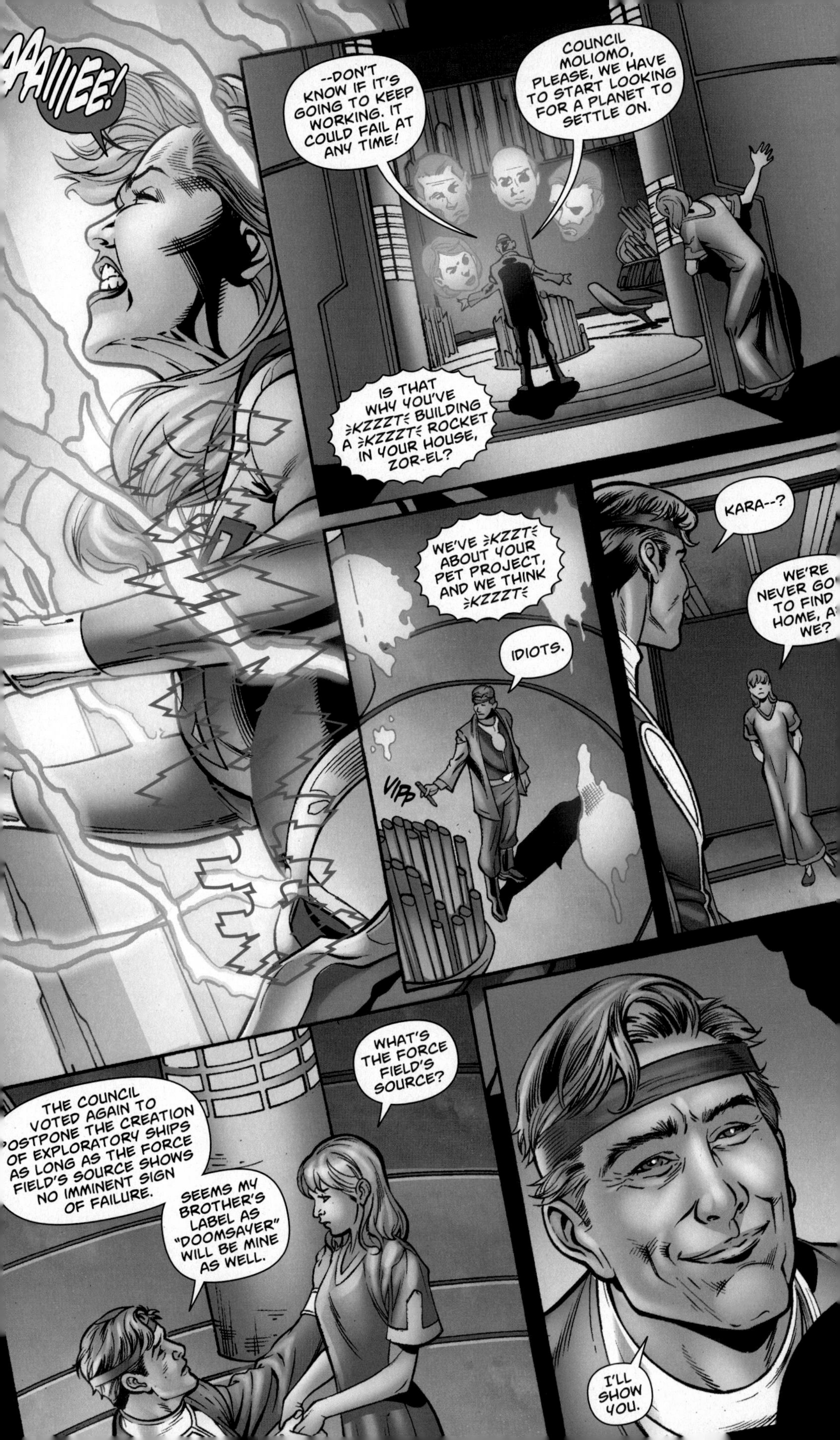
AAAIIIEE!
--DON'T KNOW IF IT'S GOING TO KEEP WORKING. IT COULD FAIL AT ANY TIME!
COUNCIL MOLIOMO, PLEASE, WE HAVE TO START LOOKING FOR A PLANET TO SETTLE ON.
IS THAT WHY YOU'VE ≷KZZZT≷ BUILDING A ≷KZZZT≷ ROCKET IN YOUR HOUSE, ZOR-EL?
WE'VE ≷KZZT≷ ABOUT YOUR PET PROJECT, AND WE THINK ≷KZZZT≷
IDIOTS.
VIPP
KARA--?
WE'RE NEVER GO TO FIND HOME, A WE?
THE COUNCIL VOTED AGAIN TO POSTPONE THE CREATION OF EXPLORATORY SHIPS AS LONG AS THE FORCE FIELD'S SOURCE SHOWS NO IMMINENT SIGN OF FAILURE.
SEEMS MY BROTHER'S LABEL AS "DOOMSAYER" WILL BE MINE AS WELL.
WHAT'S THE FORCE FIELD'S SOURCE?
I'LL SHOW YOU.

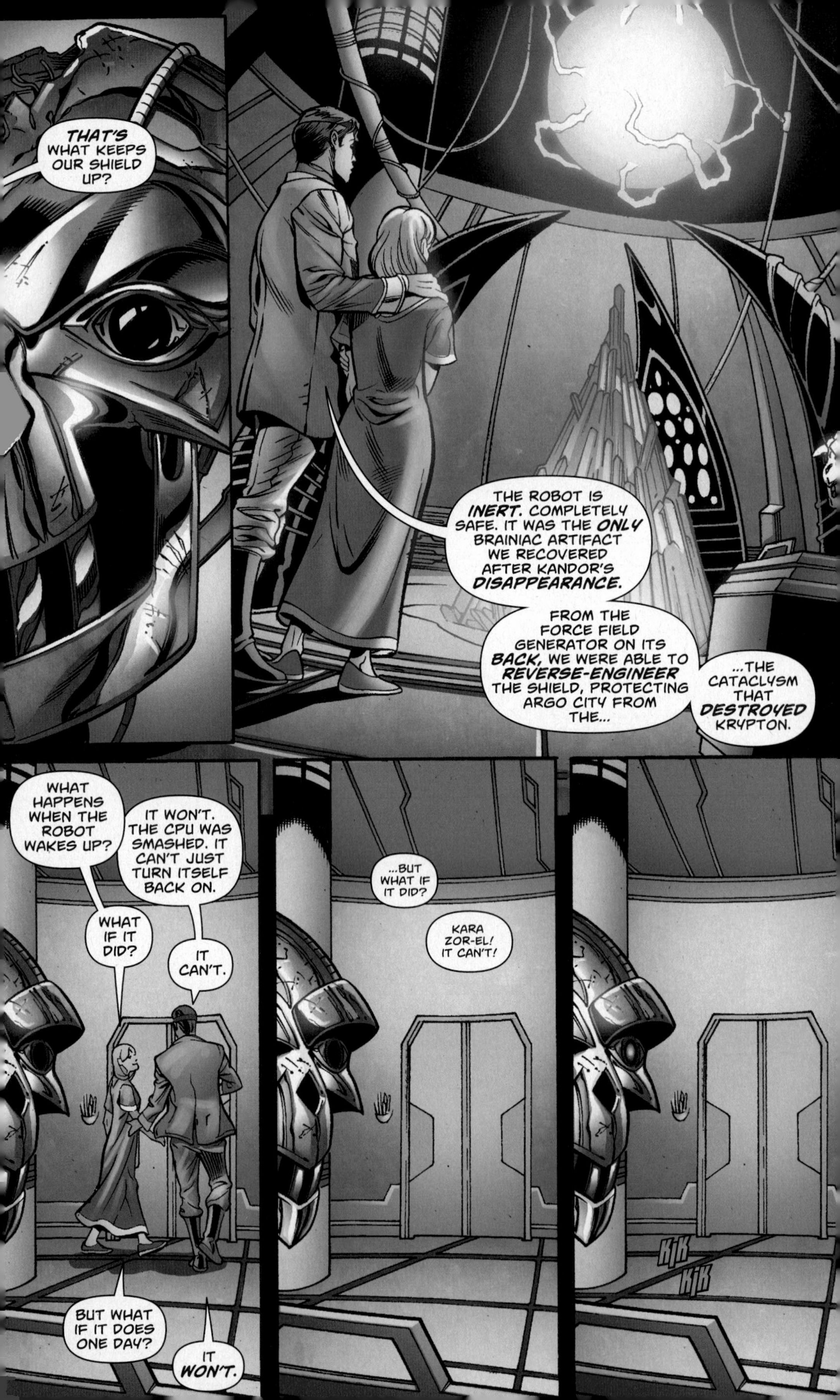
THAT'S WHAT KEEPS OUR SHIELD UP?
THE ROBOT IS INERT. COMPLETELY SAFE. IT WAS THE ONLY BRAINIAC ARTIFACT WE RECOVERED AFTER KANDOR'S DISAPPEARANCE.
FROM THE FORCE FIELD GENERATOR ON ITS BACK, WE WERE ABLE TO REVERSE-ENGINEER THE SHIELD, PROTECTING ARGO CITY FROM THE...
...THE CATACLYSM THAT DESTROYED KRYPTON.
WHAT HAPPENS WHEN THE ROBOT WAKES UP?
IT WON'T. THE CPU WAS SMASHED. IT CAN'T JUST TURN ITSELF BACK ON.
WHAT IF IT DID?
IT CAN'T.
BUT WHAT IF IT DOES ONE DAY?
IT WON'T.
...BUT WHAT IF IT DID?
KARA ZOR-EL! IT CAN'T!
KIK
KIK

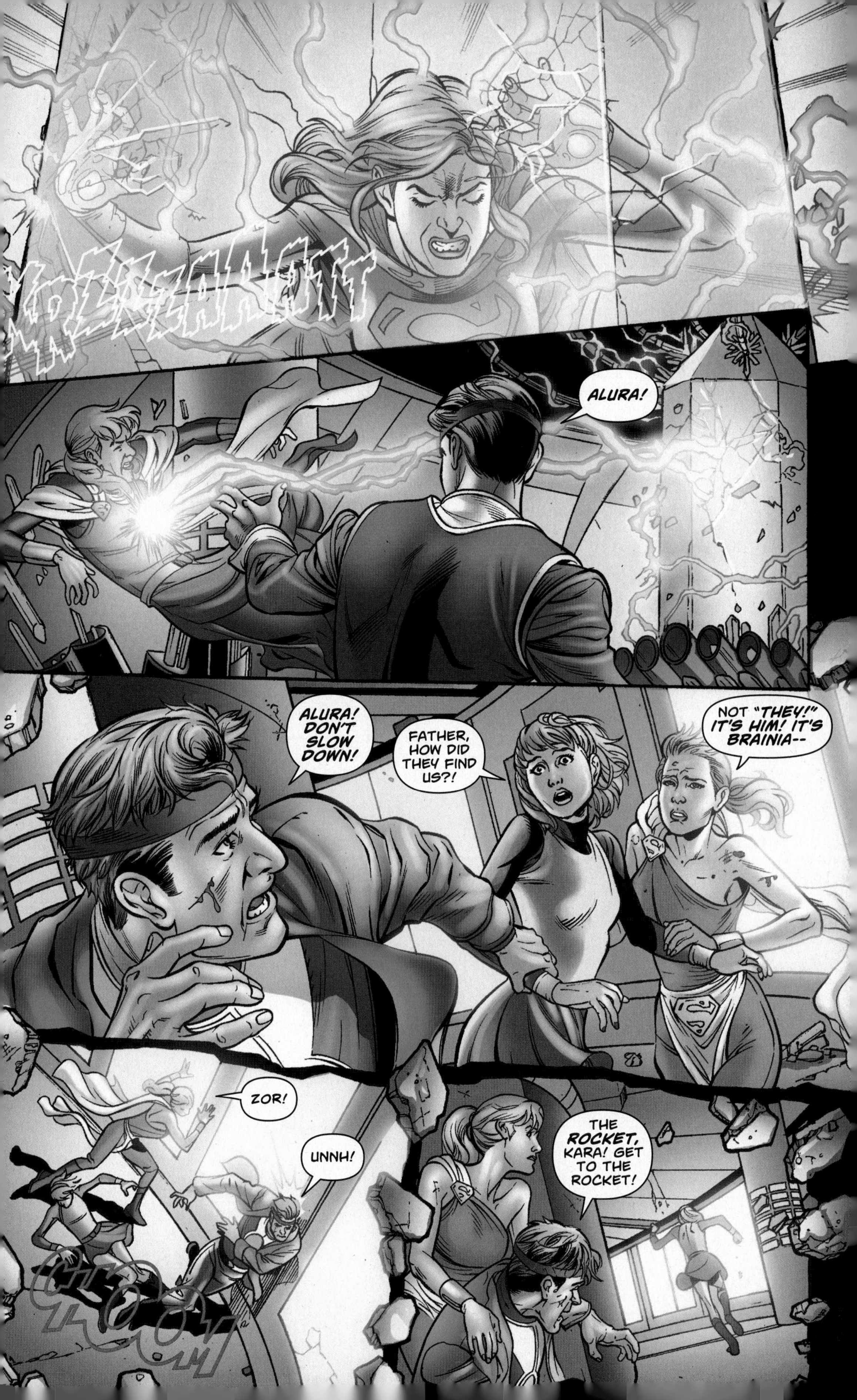
ALURA!
ALURA! DON'T SLOW DOWN!
FATHER, HOW DID THEY FIND US?!
NOT "THEY!" IT'S HIM! IT'S BRAINIA--
ZOR!
UNNH!
THE ROCKET, KARA! GET TO THE ROCKET!

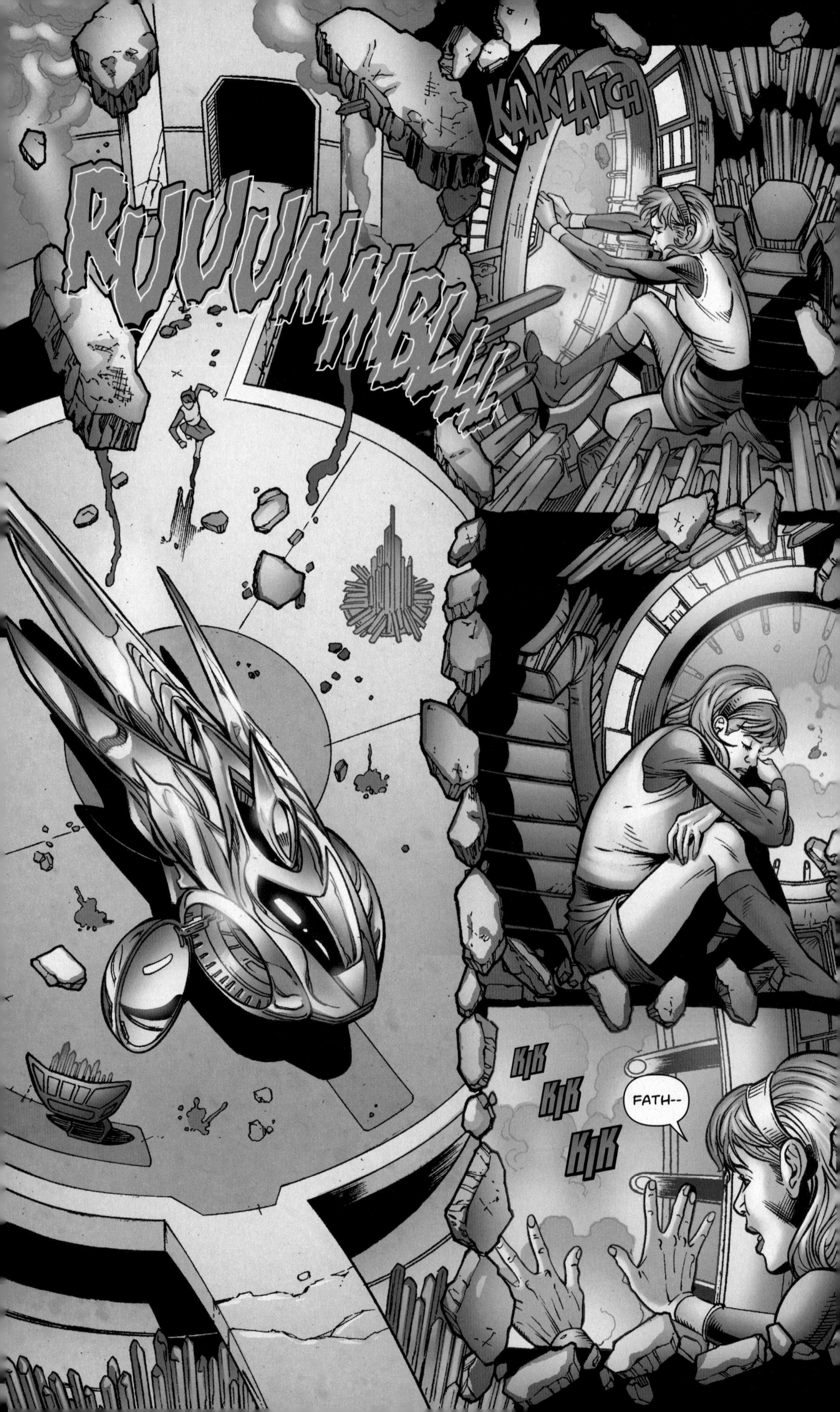
RUUUMMBLLL
KAAKLATCH
KIK
KIK
KIK
FATH--

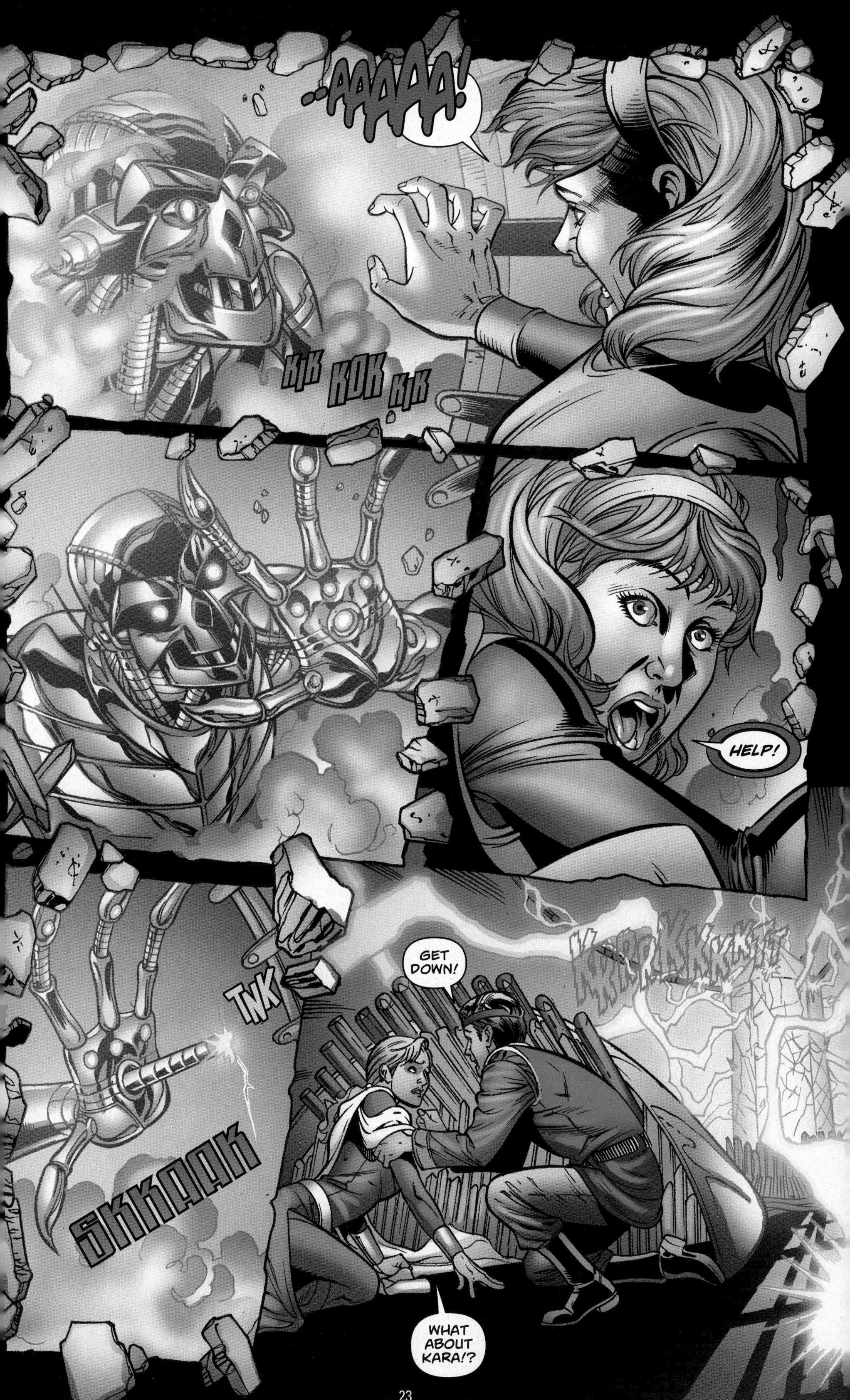
--AAAAA!
KIK KOK KIK
HELP!
TNK
SKRAAK
GET DOWN!
WHAT ABOUT KARA!?

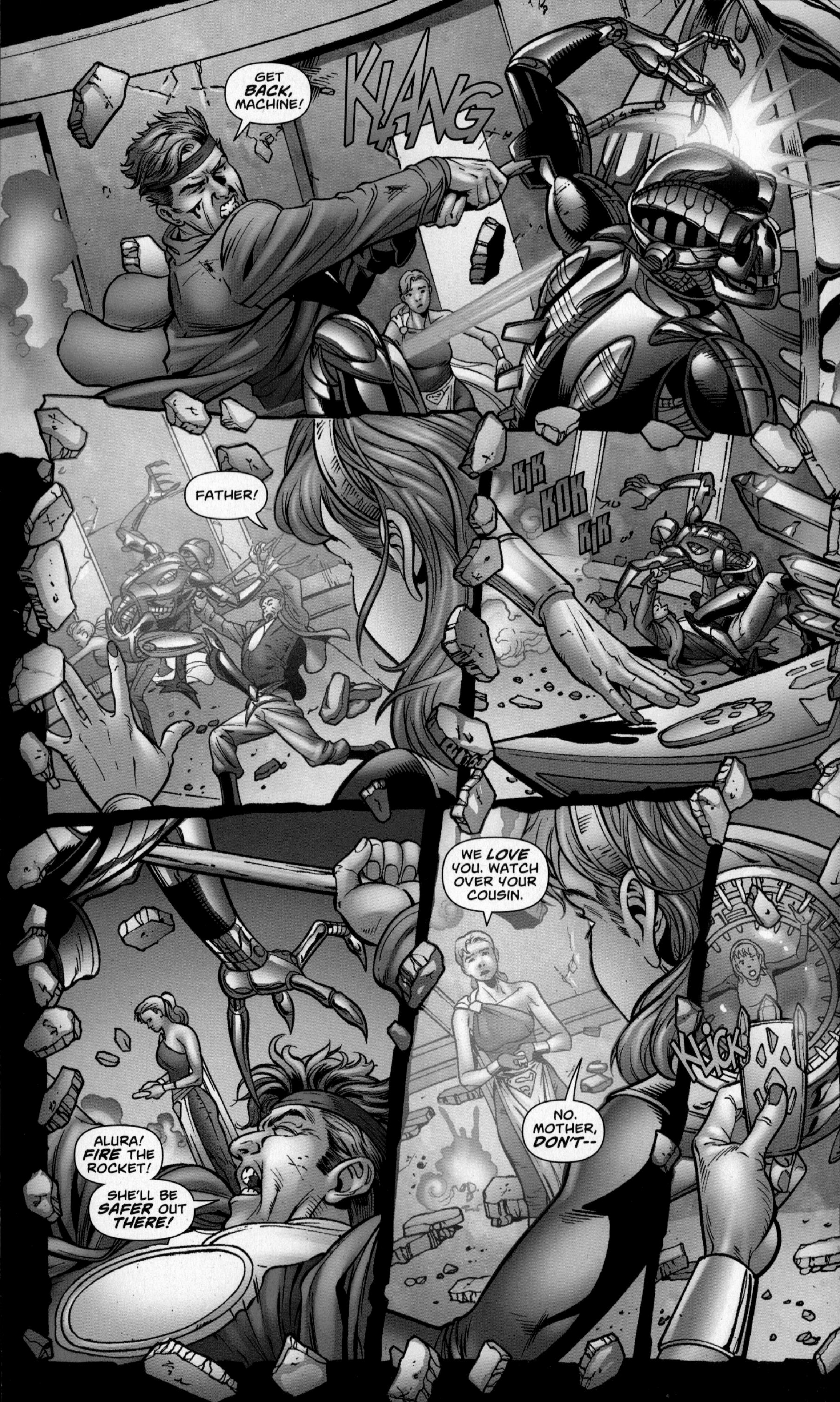
GET BACK, MACHINE!
KLANG
FATHER!
KIK KOK KIK
WE LOVE YOU. WATCH OVER YOUR COUSIN.
ALURA! FIRE THE ROCKET!
SHE'LL BE SAFER OUT THERE!
KLICK
NO. MOTHER, DON'T--

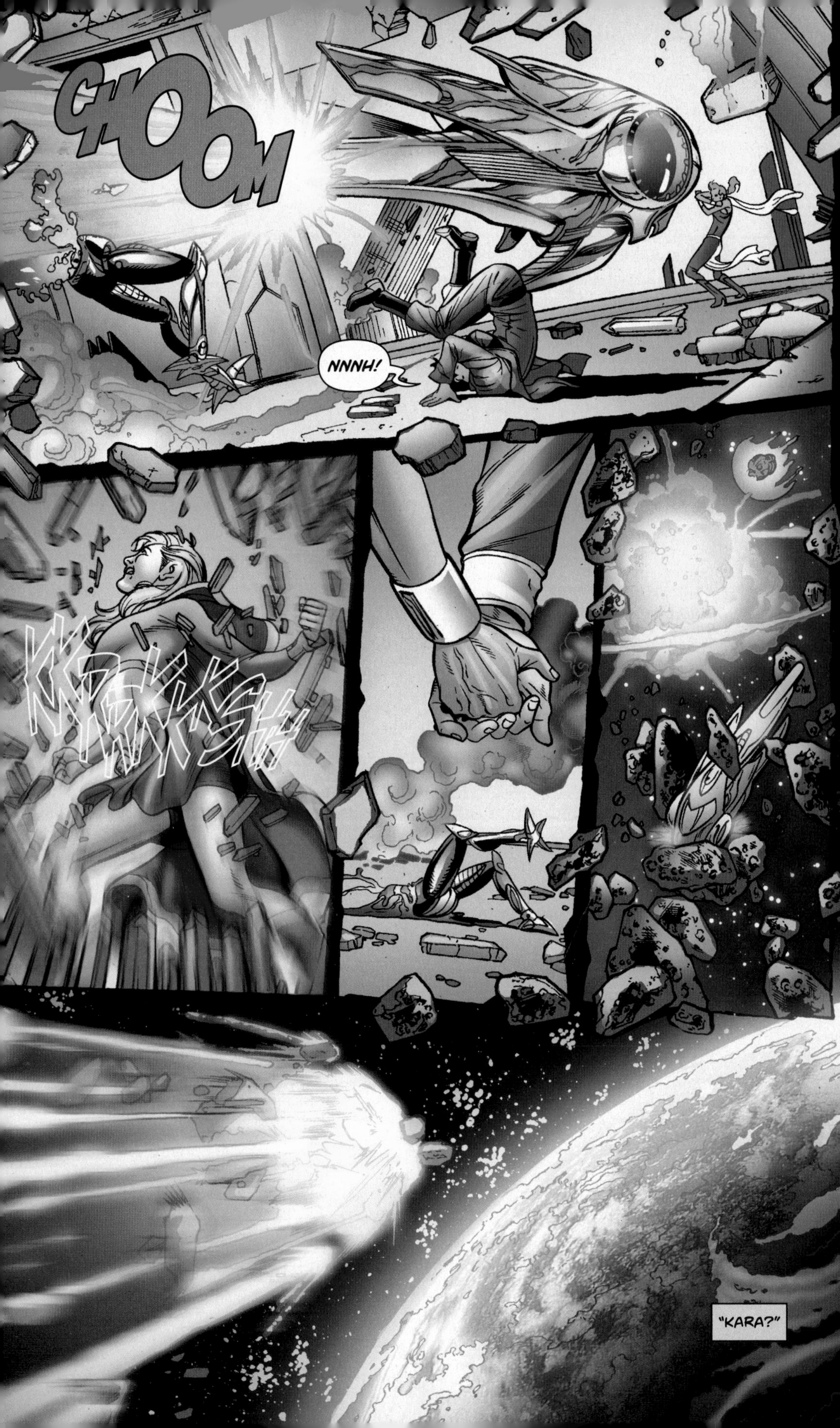
CHOOM
NNNH!
KKRKKKSH
"KARA?"

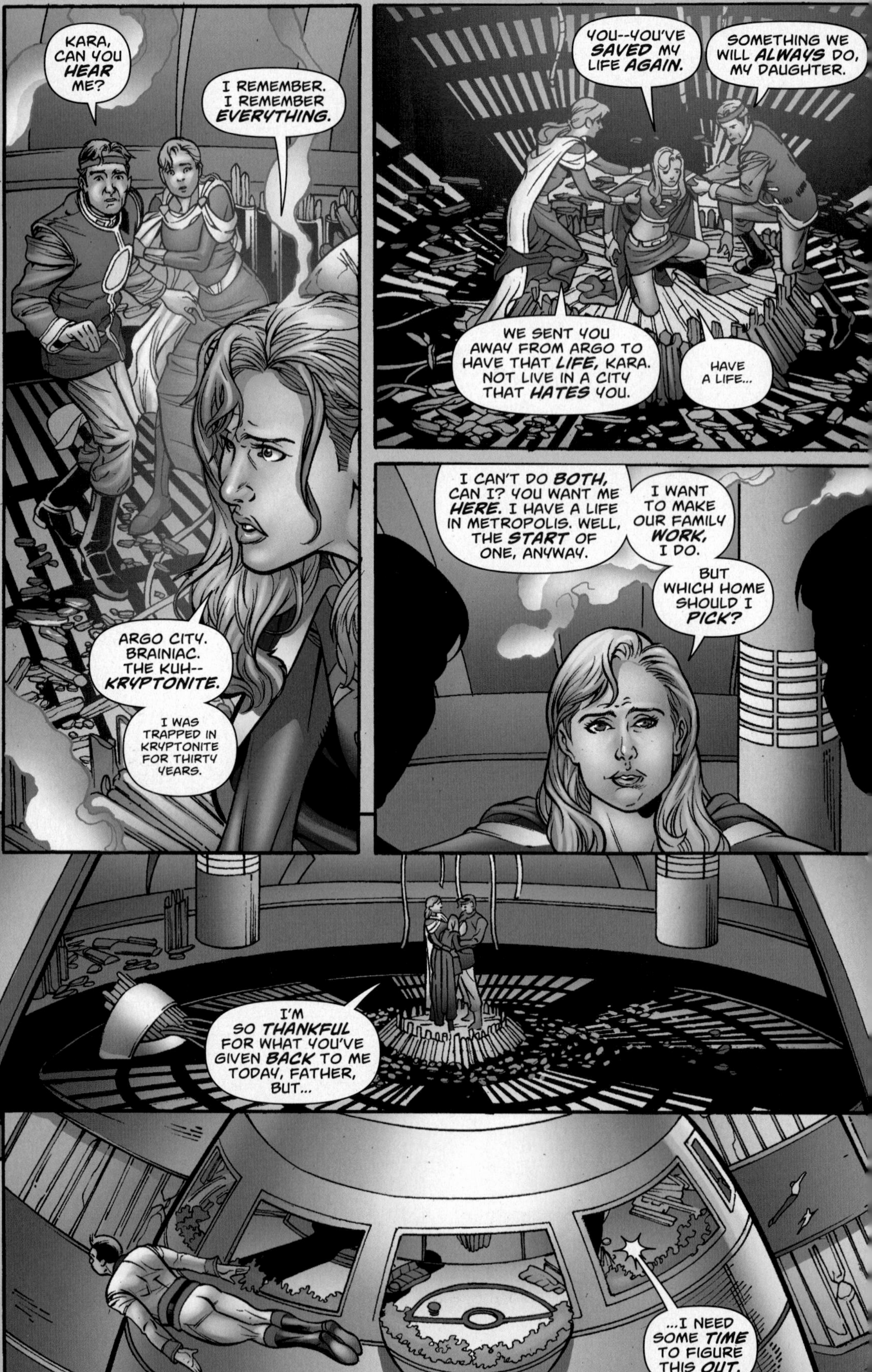
KARA, CAN YOU HEAR ME?
I REMEMBER. I REMEMBER EVERYTHING.
ARGO CITY. BRAINIAC. THE KUH-- KRYPTONITE.
I WAS TRAPPED IN KRYPTONITE FOR THIRTY YEARS.
YOU--YOU'VE SAVED MY LIFE AGAIN.
SOMETHING WE WILL ALWAYS DO, MY DAUGHTER.
WE SENT YOU AWAY FROM ARGO TO HAVE THAT LIFE, KARA. NOT LIVE IN A CITY THAT HATES YOU.
HAVE A LIFE...
I CAN'T DO BOTH, CAN I? YOU WANT ME HERE. I HAVE A LIFE IN METROPOLIS. WELL, THE START OF ONE, ANYWAY.
I WANT TO MAKE OUR FAMILY WORK, I DO.
BUT WHICH HOME SHOULD I PICK?
I'M SO THANKFUL FOR WHAT YOU'VE GIVEN BACK TO ME TODAY, FATHER, BUT...
...I NEED SOME TIME TO FIGURE THIS OUT.

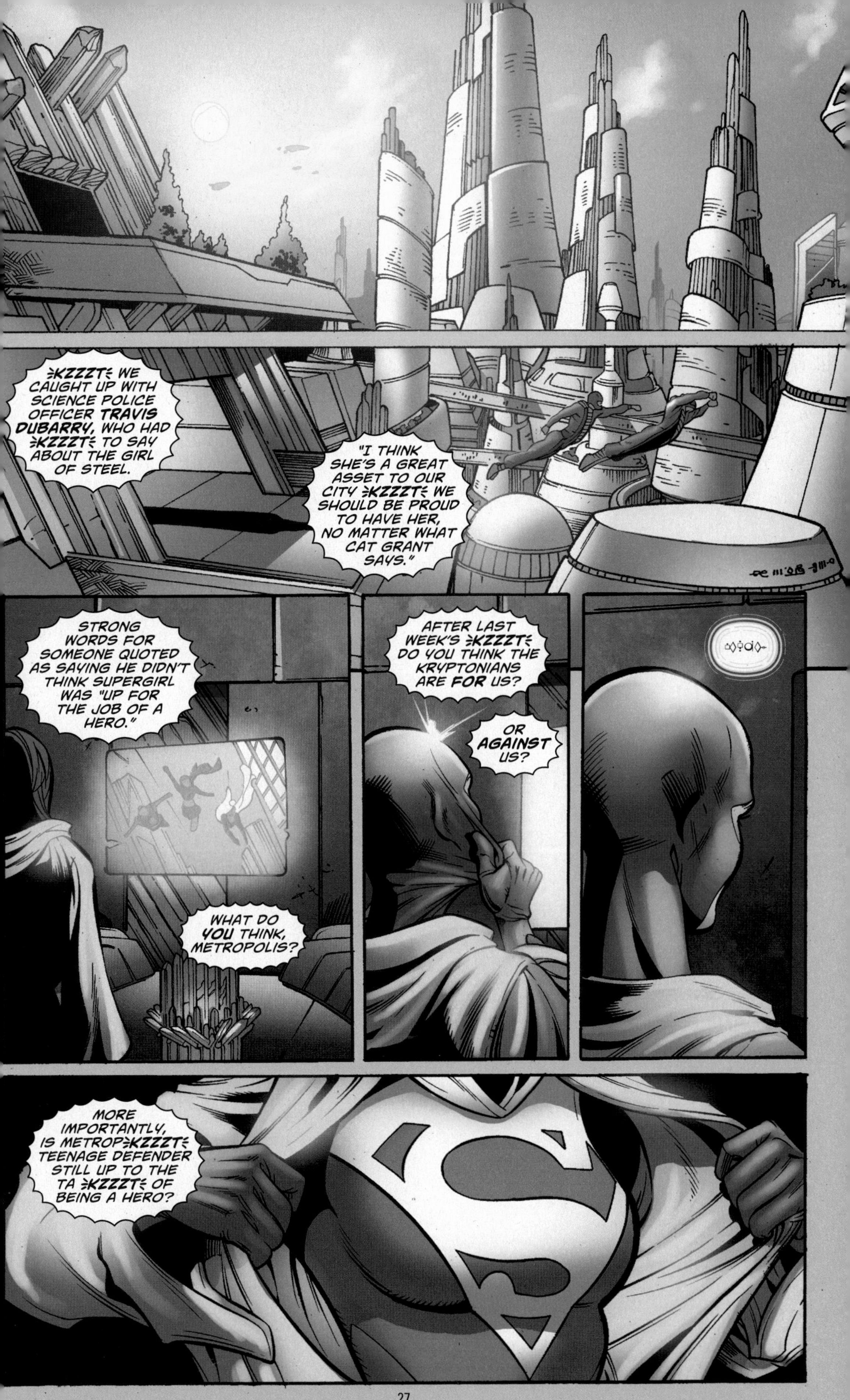
≷KZZZT≶ WE CAUGHT UP WITH SCIENCE POLICE OFFICER TRAVIS DUBARRY, WHO HAD ≷KZZZT≶ TO SAY ABOUT THE GIRL OF STEEL.
"I THINK SHE'S A GREAT ASSET TO OUR CITY ≷KZZZT≶ WE SHOULD BE PROUD TO HAVE HER, NO MATTER WHAT CAT GRANT SAYS."
STRONG WORDS FOR SOMEONE QUOTED AS SAYING HE DIDN'T THINK SUPERGIRL WAS "UP FOR THE JOB OF A HERO."
WHAT DO YOU THINK, METROPOLIS?
AFTER LAST WEEK'S ≷KZZZT≶ DO YOU THINK THE KRYPTONIANS ARE FOR US?
OR AGAINST US?
MORE IMPORTANTLY, IS METROP≷KZZZT≶ TEENAGE DEFENDER STILL UP TO THE TA ≷KZZZT≶ OF BEING A HERO?

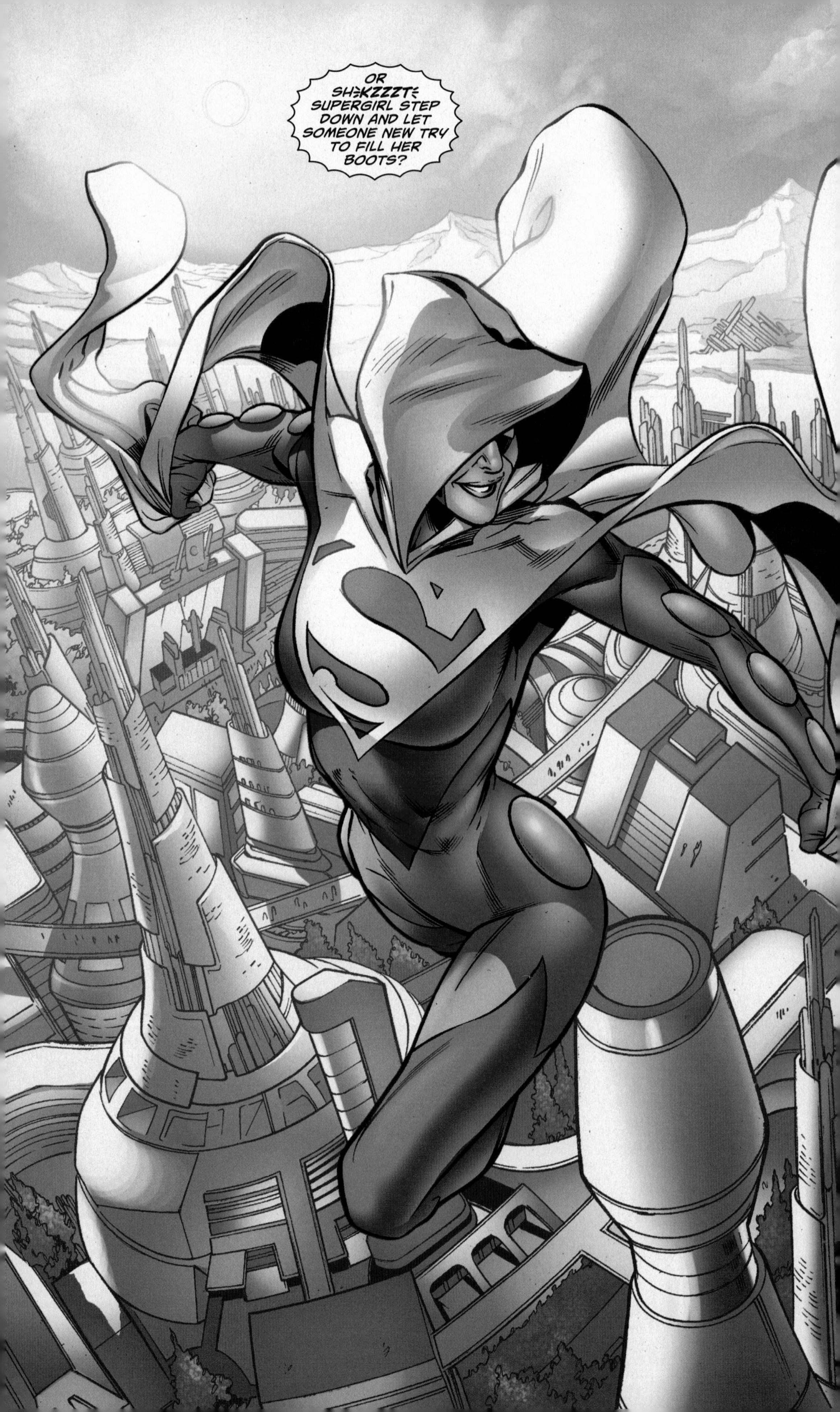
OR SH-KZZZT- SUPERGIRL STEP DOWN AND LET SOMEONE NEW TRY TO FILL HER BOOTS?

<INVASIVE SURGERY> SUPERMAN 682 COVER ART BY **ALEX ROSS**

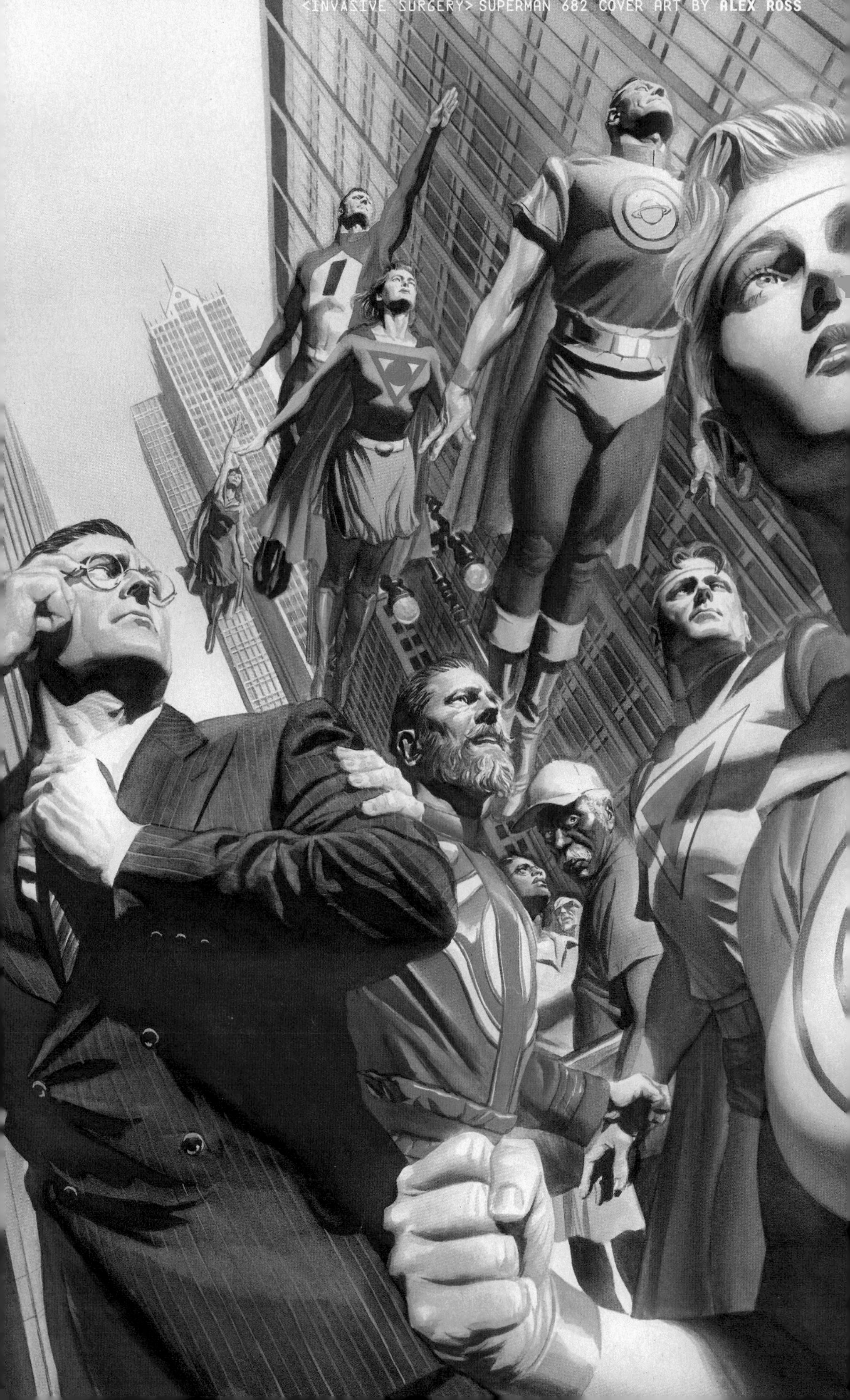

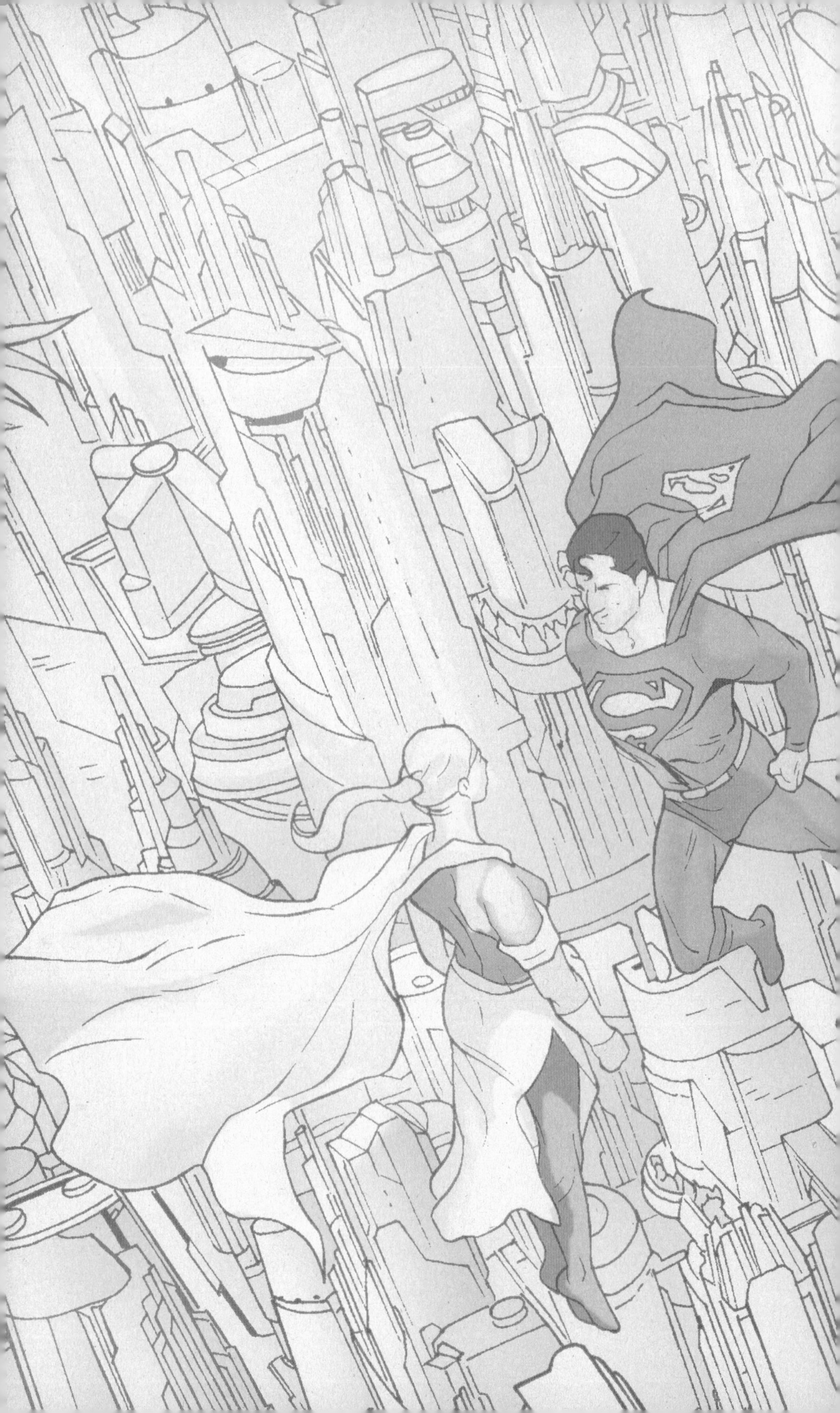

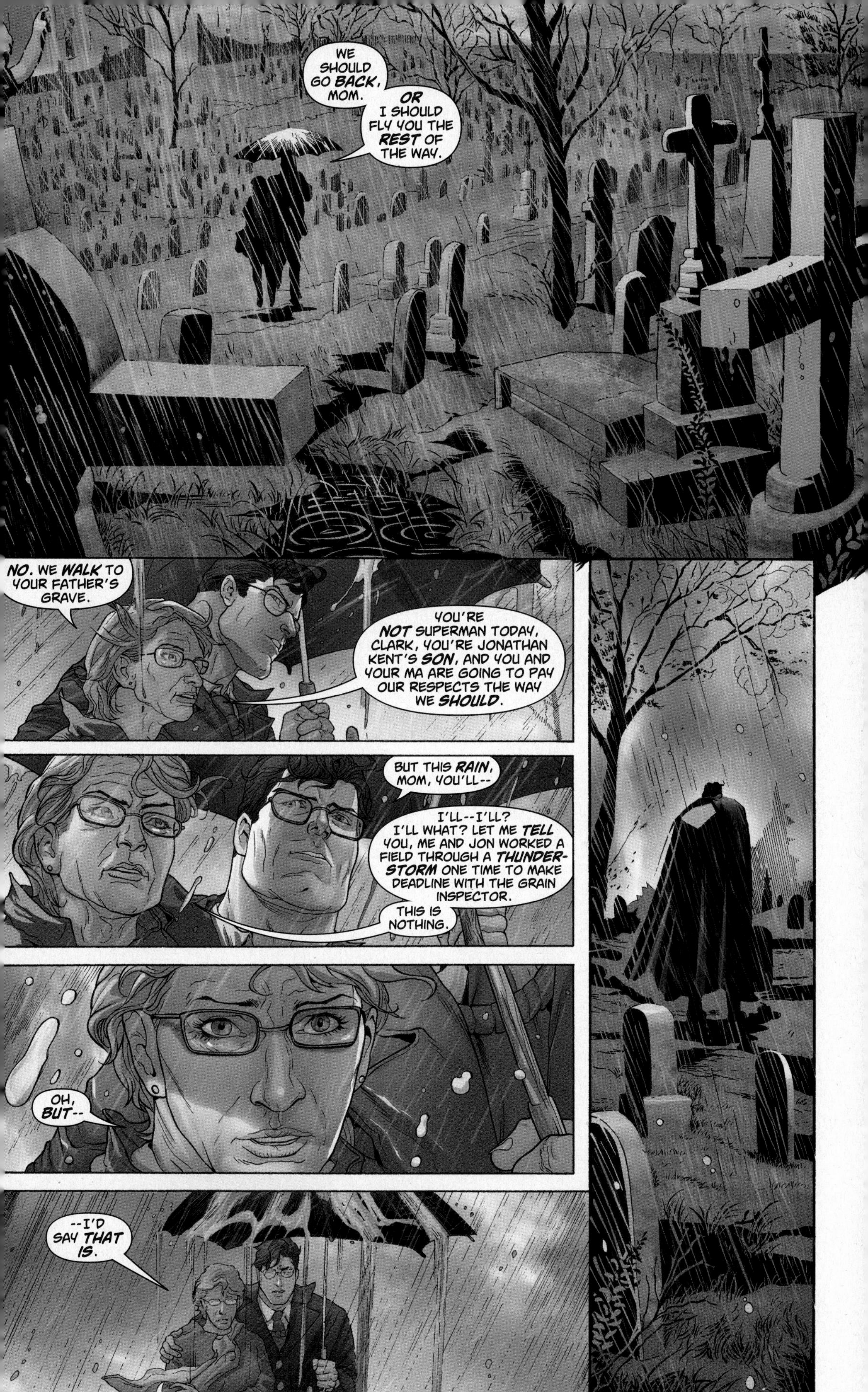
WE SHOULD GO BACK, MOM.
OR I SHOULD FLY YOU THE REST OF THE WAY.
NO. WE WALK TO YOUR FATHER'S GRAVE.
YOU'RE NOT SUPERMAN TODAY, CLARK, YOU'RE JONATHAN KENT'S SON, AND YOU AND YOUR MA ARE GOING TO PAY OUR RESPECTS THE WAY WE SHOULD.
BUT THIS RAIN, MOM, YOU'LL--
I'LL--I'LL? I'LL WHAT? LET ME TELL YOU, ME AND JON WORKED A FIELD THROUGH A THUNDER-STORM ONE TIME TO MAKE DEADLINE WITH THE GRAIN INSPECTOR.
THIS IS NOTHING.
OH, BUT--
--I'D SAY THAT IS.

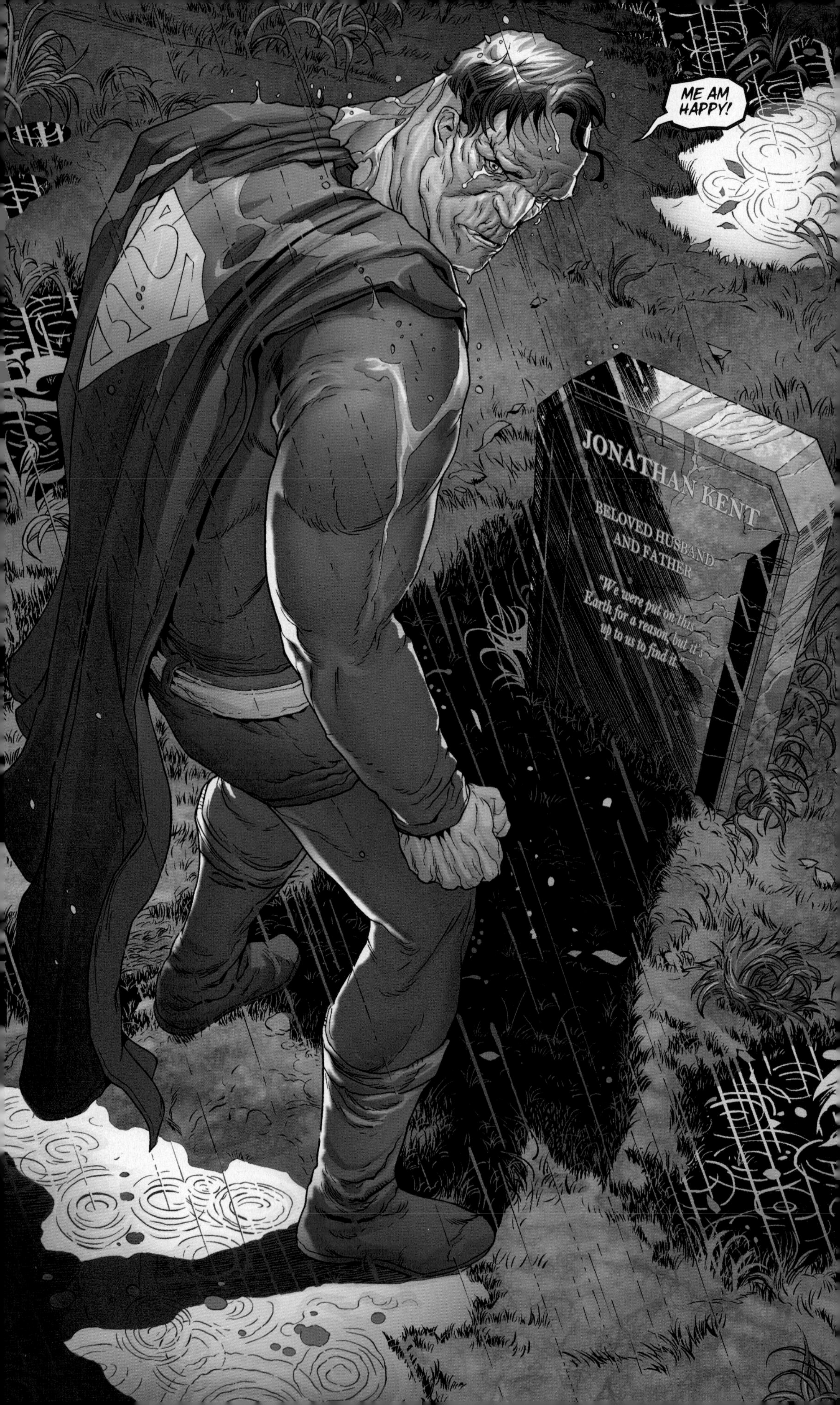

ME AM HAPPY!
JONATHAN KENT
BELOVED HUSBAND AND FATHER
"We were put on this Earth for a reason, but it's up to us to find it."

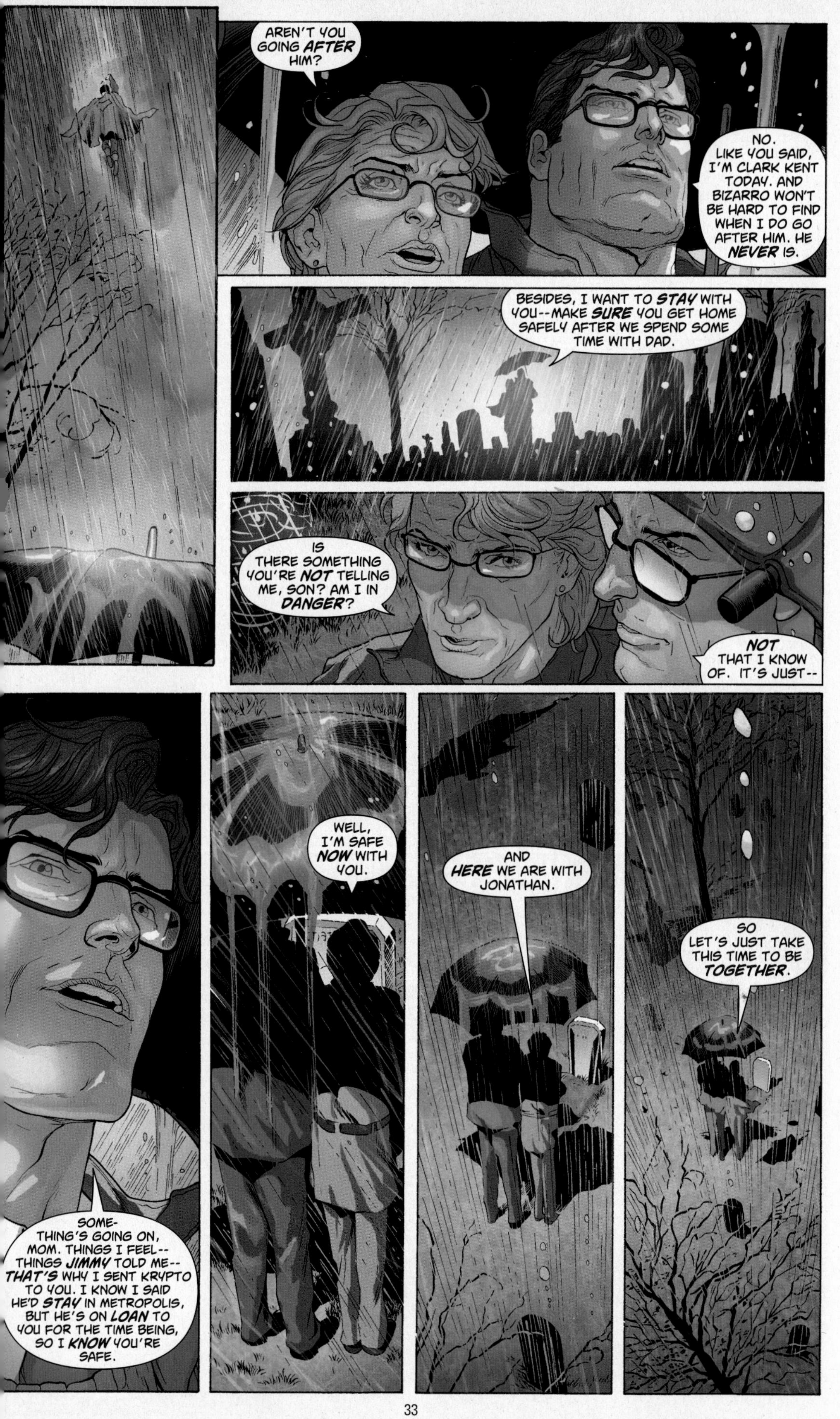

AREN'T YOU GOING AFTER HIM?
NO. LIKE YOU SAID, I'M CLARK KENT TODAY. AND BIZARRO WON'T BE HARD TO FIND WHEN I DO GO AFTER HIM. HE NEVER IS.
BESIDES, I WANT TO STAY WITH YOU--MAKE SURE YOU GET HOME SAFELY AFTER WE SPEND SOME TIME WITH DAD.
IS THERE SOMETHING YOU'RE NOT TELLING ME, SON? AM I IN DANGER?
NOT THAT I KNOW OF. IT'S JUST--
SOME-THING'S GOING ON, MOM. THINGS I FEEL--THINGS JIMMY TOLD ME--THAT'S WHY I SENT KRYPTO TO YOU. I KNOW I SAID HE'D STAY IN METROPOLIS, BUT HE'S ON LOAN TO YOU FOR THE TIME BEING, SO I KNOW YOU'RE SAFE.
WELL, I'M SAFE NOW WITH YOU.
AND HERE WE ARE WITH JONATHAN.
SO LET'S JUST TAKE THIS TIME TO BE TOGETHER.

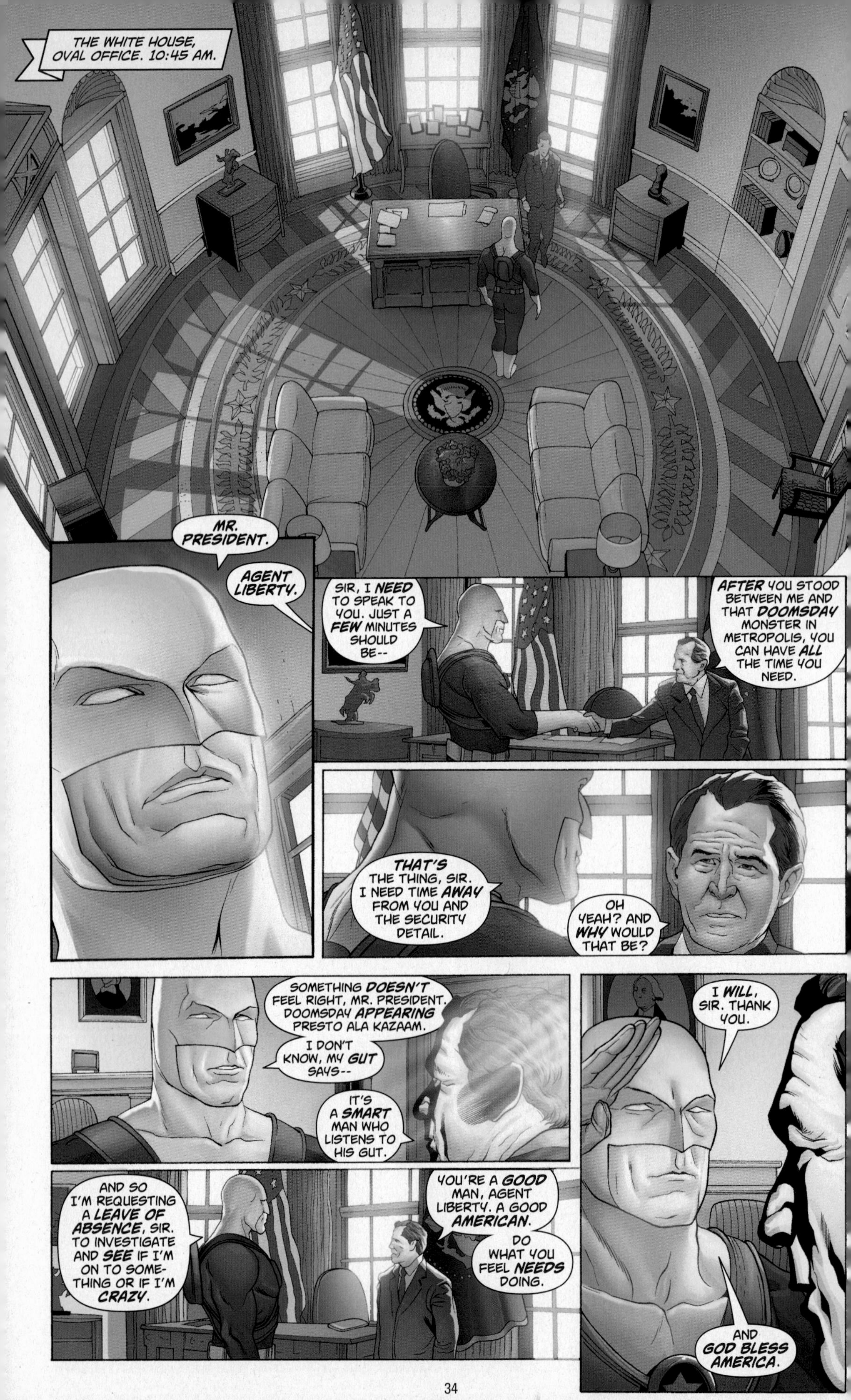
THE WHITE HOUSE, OVAL OFFICE. 10:45 AM.
MR. PRESIDENT.
AGENT LIBERTY.
SIR, I NEED TO SPEAK TO YOU. JUST A FEW MINUTES SHOULD BE--
AFTER YOU STOOD BETWEEN ME AND THAT DOOMSDAY MONSTER IN METROPOLIS, YOU CAN HAVE ALL THE TIME YOU NEED.
THAT'S THE THING, SIR. I NEED TIME AWAY FROM YOU AND THE SECURITY DETAIL.
OH YEAH? AND WHY WOULD THAT BE?
SOMETHING DOESN'T FEEL RIGHT, MR. PRESIDENT. DOOMSDAY APPEARING PRESTO ALA KAZAAM.
I DON'T KNOW, MY GUT SAYS--
IT'S A SMART MAN WHO LISTENS TO HIS GUT.
AND SO I'M REQUESTING A LEAVE OF ABSENCE, SIR. TO INVESTIGATE AND SEE IF I'M ON TO SOME-THING OR IF I'M CRAZY.
YOU'RE A GOOD MAN, AGENT LIBERTY. A GOOD AMERICAN.
DO WHAT YOU FEEL NEEDS DOING.
I WILL, SIR. THANK YOU.
AND GOD BLESS AMERICA.

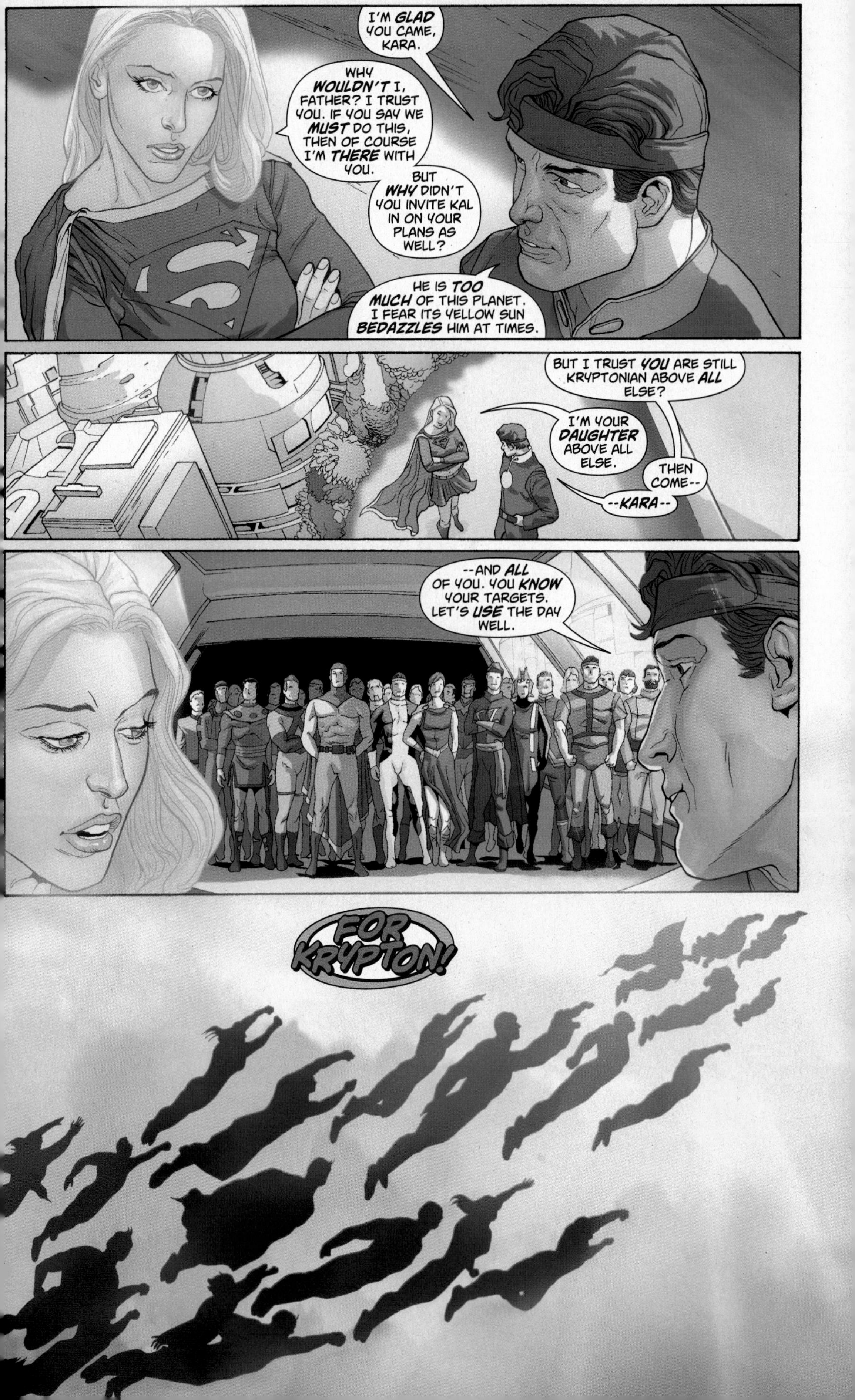
I'M GLAD YOU CAME, KARA.
WHY WOULDN'T I, FATHER? I TRUST YOU. IF YOU SAY WE MUST DO THIS, THEN OF COURSE I'M THERE WITH YOU.
BUT WHY DIDN'T YOU INVITE KAL IN ON YOUR PLANS AS WELL?
HE IS TOO MUCH OF THIS PLANET. I FEAR ITS YELLOW SUN BEDAZZLES HIM AT TIMES.
BUT I TRUST YOU ARE STILL KRYPTONIAN ABOVE ALL ELSE?
I'M YOUR DAUGHTER ABOVE ALL ELSE.
THEN COME--
--KARA--
--AND ALL OF YOU. YOU KNOW YOUR TARGETS. LET'S USE THE DAY WELL.
FOR KRYPTON!

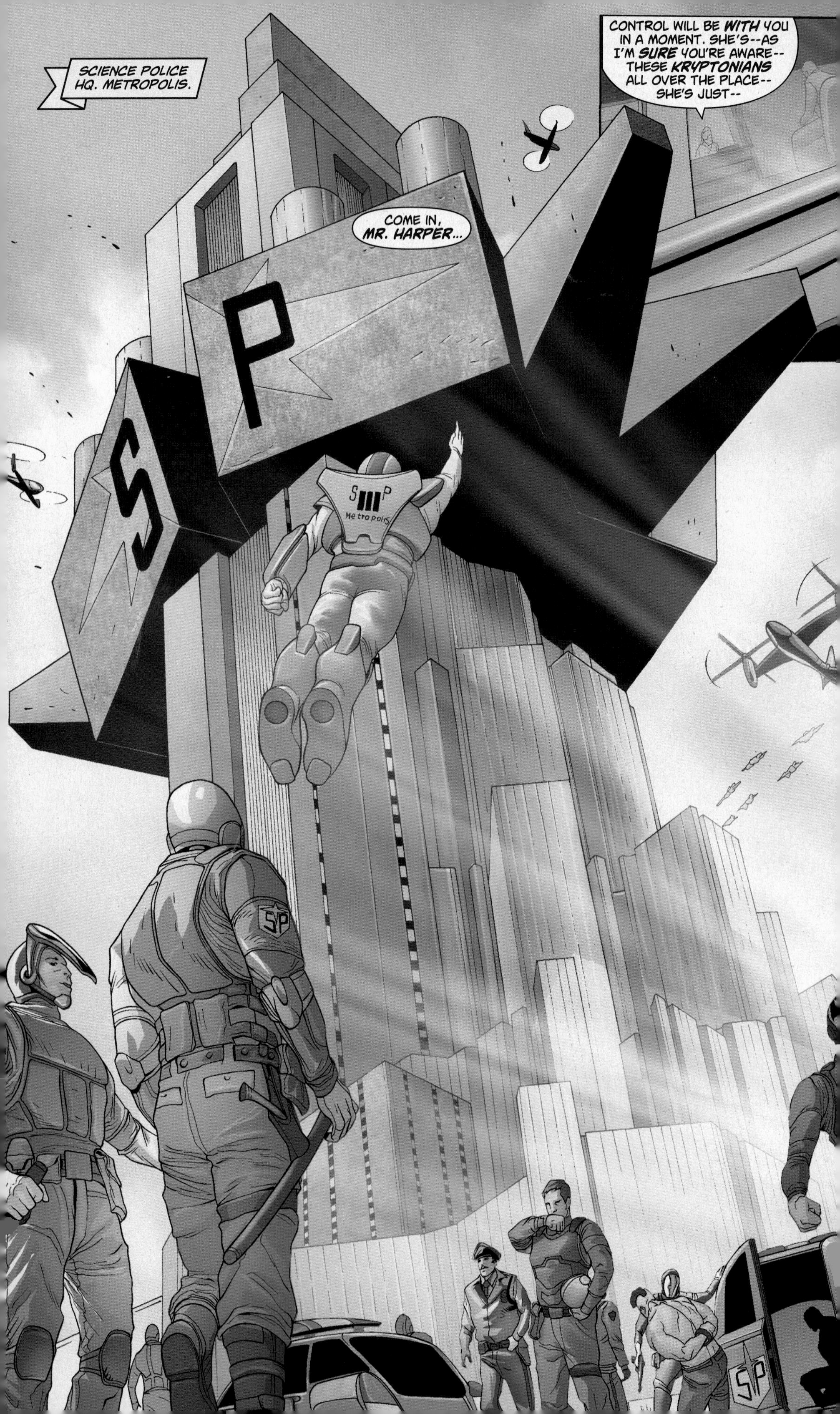
SCIENCE POLICE HQ. METROPOLIS.
CONTROL WILL BE WITH YOU IN A MOMENT. SHE'S--AS I'M SURE YOU'RE AWARE--THESE KRYPTONIANS ALL OVER THE PLACE--SHE'S JUST--
COME IN, MR. HARPER...
SP
SP Metropolis
SP
SP

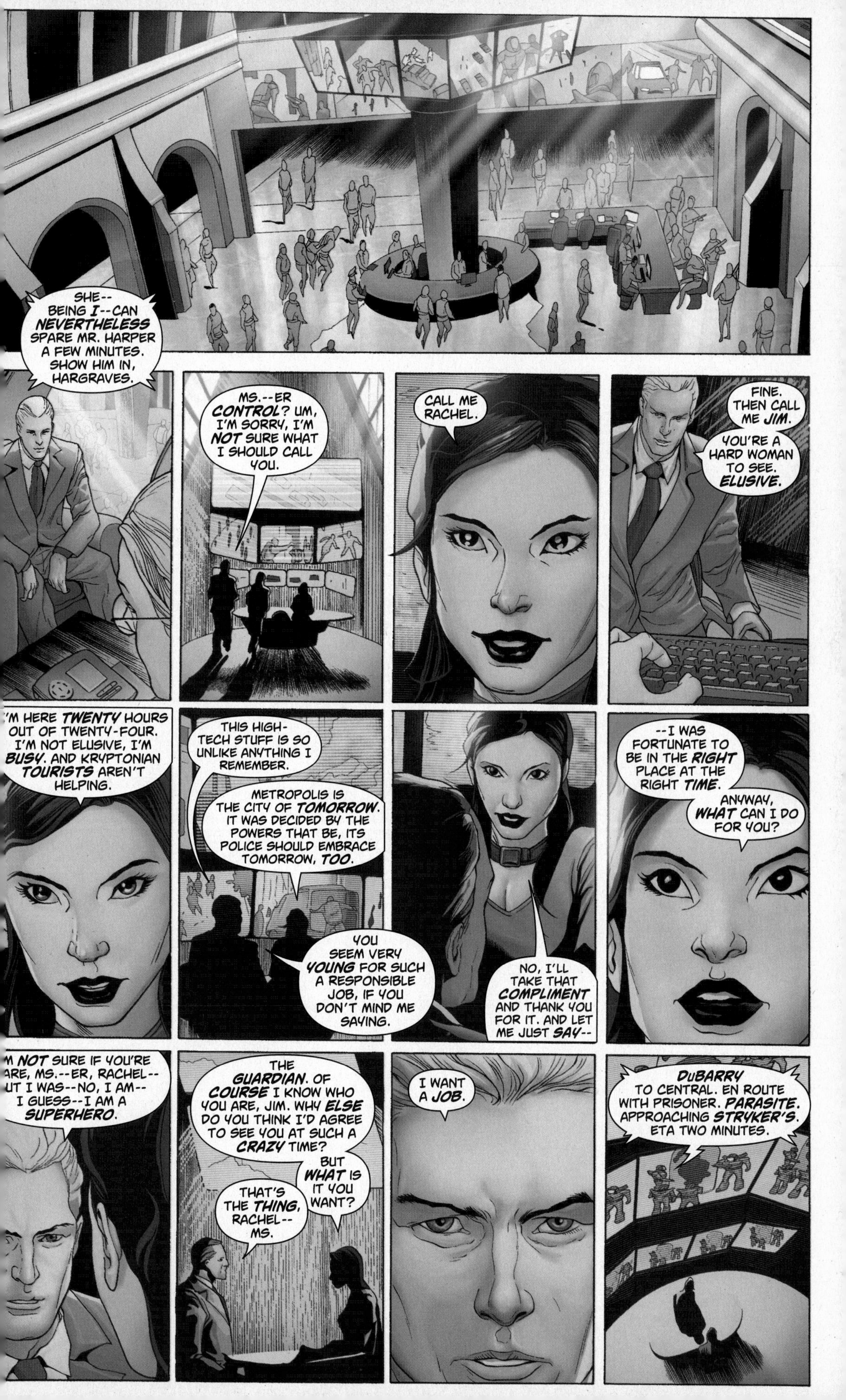
SHE-- BEING I--CAN NEVERTHELESS SPARE MR. HARPER A FEW MINUTES. SHOW HIM IN, HARGRAVES.
MS.--ER CONTROL? UM, I'M SORRY, I'M NOT SURE WHAT I SHOULD CALL YOU.
CALL ME RACHEL.
FINE. THEN CALL ME JIM.
YOU'RE A HARD WOMAN TO SEE. ELUSIVE.
I'M HERE TWENTY HOURS OUT OF TWENTY-FOUR. I'M NOT ELUSIVE, I'M BUSY. AND KRYPTONIAN TOURISTS AREN'T HELPING.
THIS HIGH-TECH STUFF IS SO UNLIKE ANYTHING I REMEMBER.
METROPOLIS IS THE CITY OF TOMORROW. IT WAS DECIDED BY THE POWERS THAT BE, ITS POLICE SHOULD EMBRACE TOMORROW, TOO.
YOU SEEM VERY YOUNG FOR SUCH A RESPONSIBLE JOB, IF YOU DON'T MIND ME SAYING.
NO, I'LL TAKE THAT COMPLIMENT AND THANK YOU FOR IT. AND LET ME JUST SAY--
--I WAS FORTUNATE TO BE IN THE RIGHT PLACE AT THE RIGHT TIME.
ANYWAY, WHAT CAN I DO FOR YOU?
M NOT SURE IF YOU'RE ARE, MS.--ER, RACHEL-- UT I WAS--NO, I AM-- I GUESS--I AM A SUPERHERO.
THE GUARDIAN. OF COURSE I KNOW WHO YOU ARE, JIM. WHY ELSE DO YOU THINK I'D AGREE TO SEE YOU AT SUCH A CRAZY TIME?
BUT WHAT IS IT YOU WANT?
THAT'S THE THING, RACHEL-- MS.
I WANT A JOB.
DUBARRY TO CENTRAL. EN ROUTE WITH PRISONER. PARASITE. APPROACHING STRYKER'S. ETA TWO MINUTES.

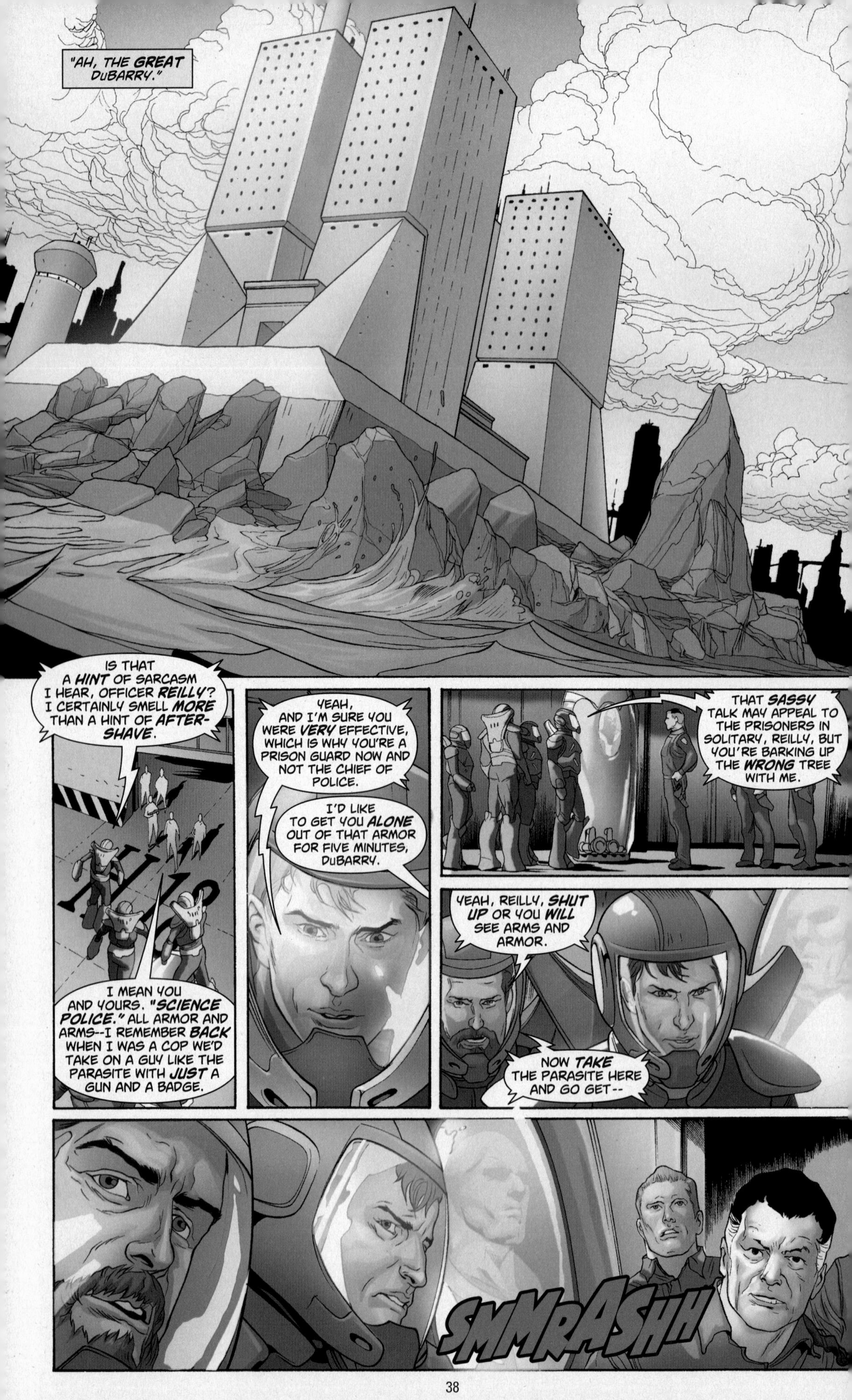
"AH, THE GREAT DuBARRY."
IS THAT A HINT OF SARCASM I HEAR, OFFICER REILLY? I CERTAINLY SMELL MORE THAN A HINT OF AFTER-SHAVE.
I MEAN YOU AND YOURS. "SCIENCE POLICE." ALL ARMOR AND ARMS--I REMEMBER BACK WHEN I WAS A COP WE'D TAKE ON A GUY LIKE THE PARASITE WITH JUST A GUN AND A BADGE.
YEAH, AND I'M SURE YOU WERE VERY EFFECTIVE, WHICH IS WHY YOU'RE A PRISON GUARD NOW AND NOT THE CHIEF OF POLICE.
I'D LIKE TO GET YOU ALONE OUT OF THAT ARMOR FOR FIVE MINUTES, DuBARRY.
THAT SASSY TALK MAY APPEAL TO THE PRISONERS IN SOLITARY, REILLY, BUT YOU'RE BARKING UP THE WRONG TREE WITH ME.
YEAH, REILLY, SHUT UP OR YOU WILL SEE ARMS AND ARMOR.
NOW TAKE THE PARASITE HERE AND GO GET--
SMMRASHH

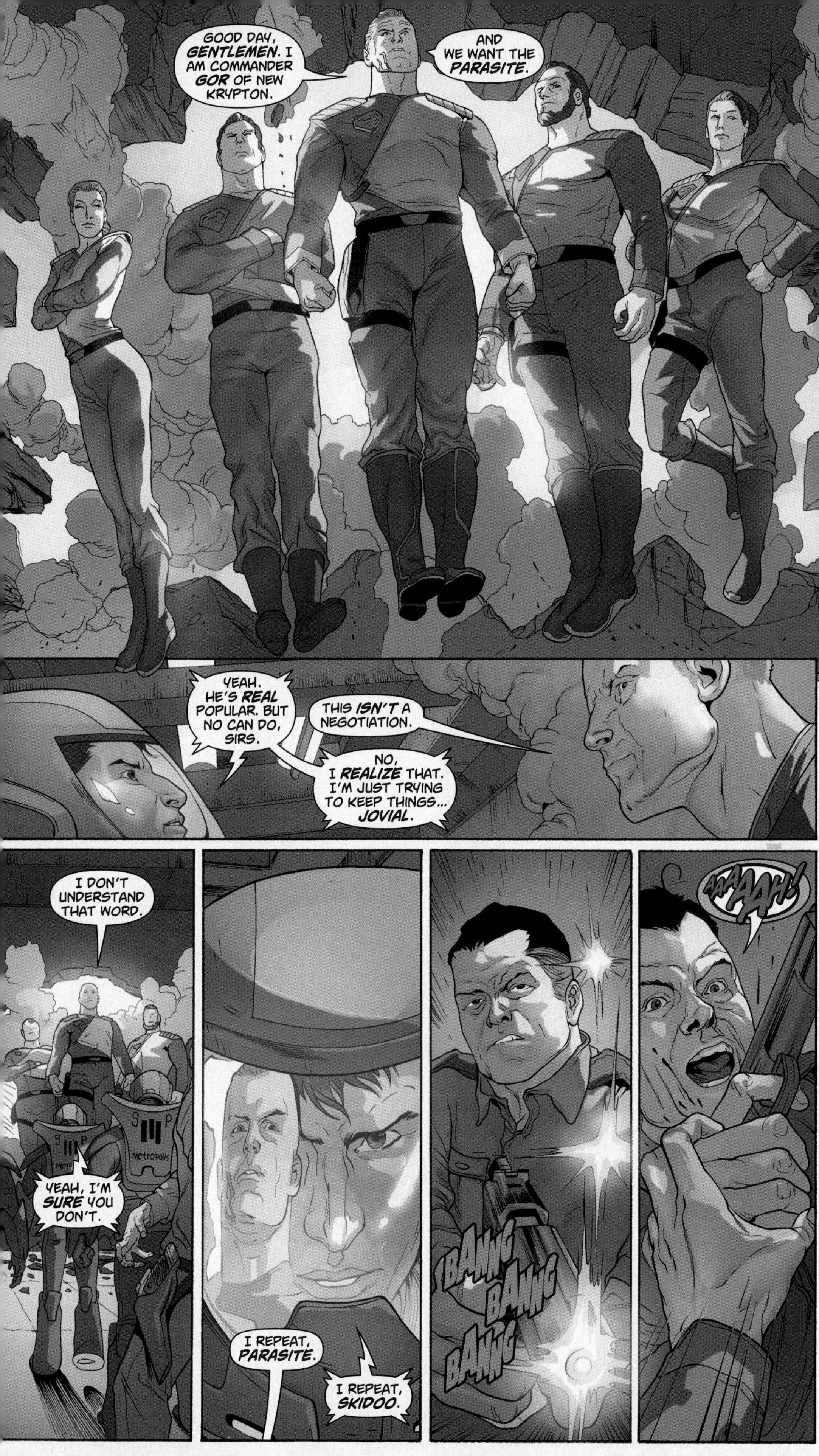
GOOD DAY, GENTLEMEN. I AM COMMANDER GOR OF NEW KRYPTON.
AND WE WANT THE PARASITE.
YEAH. HE'S REAL POPULAR. BUT NO CAN DO, SIRS.
THIS ISN'T A NEGOTIATION.
NO, I REALIZE THAT. I'M JUST TRYING TO KEEP THINGS... JOVIAL.
I DON'T UNDERSTAND THAT WORD.
YEAH, I'M SURE YOU DON'T.
I REPEAT, PARASITE.
I REPEAT, SKIDOO.
BANNG BANNG BANNG
AAAAAH!

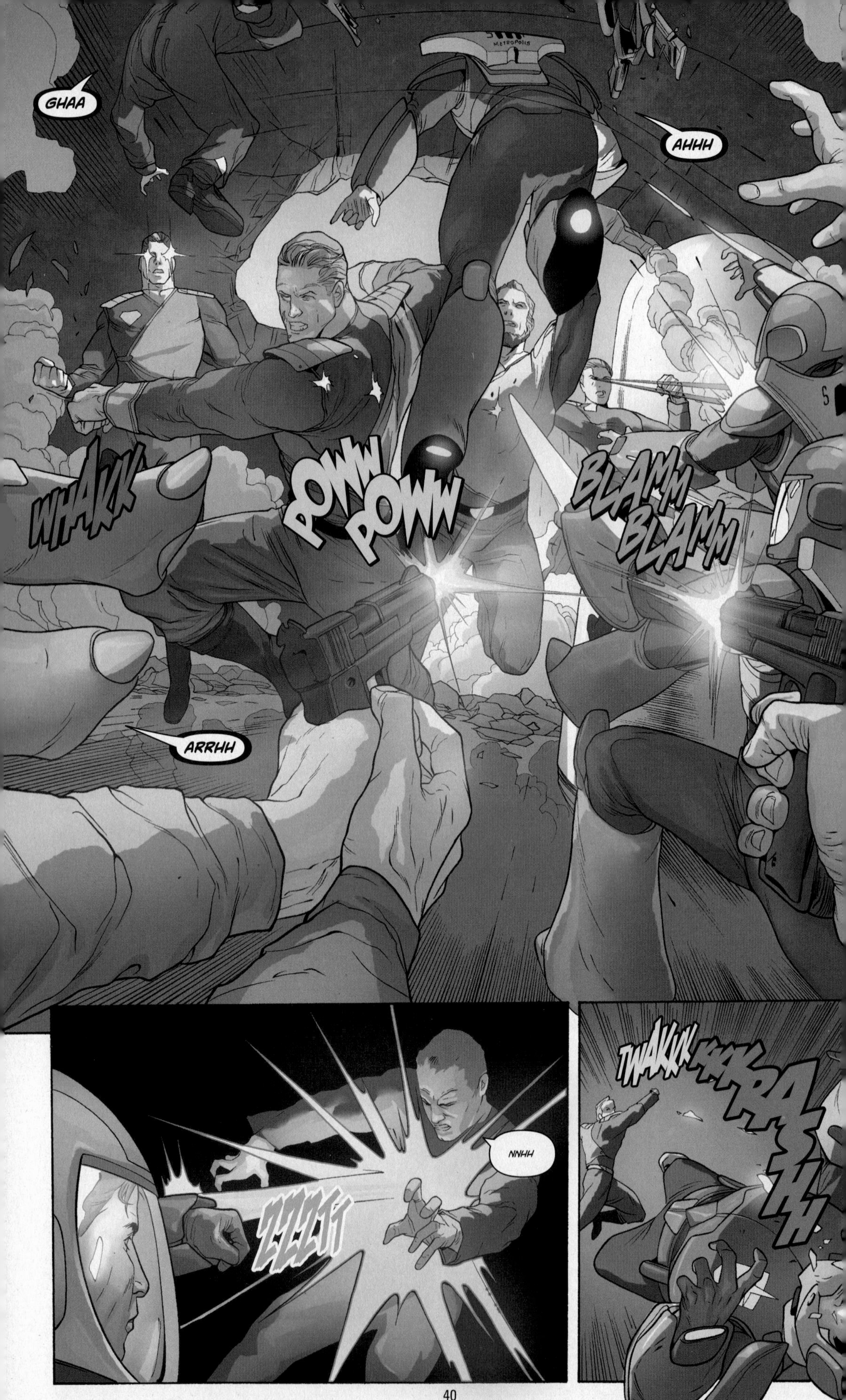
GHAA
AHHH
WHAKK
POWW POWW
BLAMM BLAMM
ARRHH
NNHH
ZZZTT
TWAKKK KKRASH

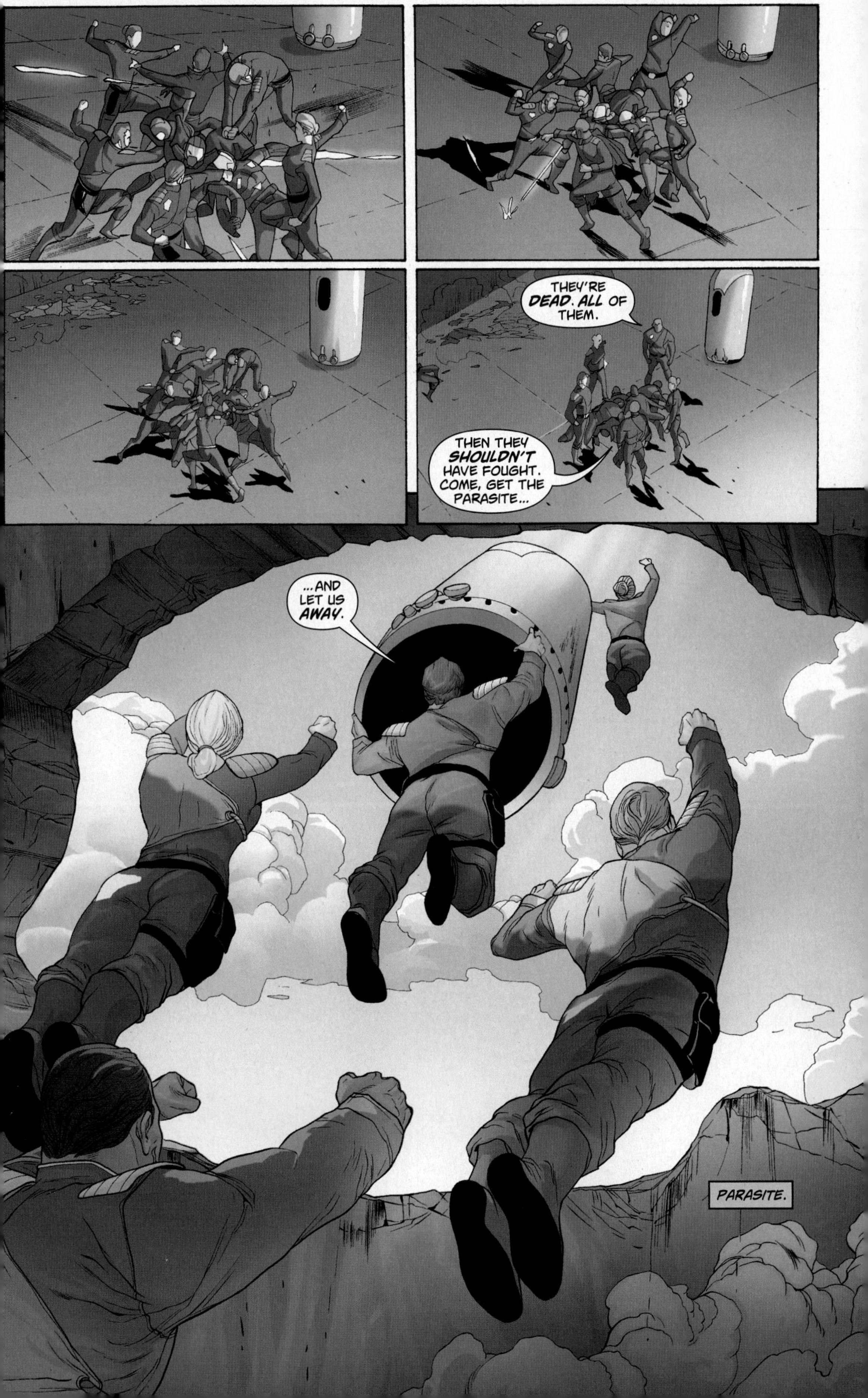
THEY'RE DEAD. ALL OF THEM.
THEN THEY SHOULDN'T HAVE FOUGHT. COME, GET THE PARASITE...
...AND LET US AWAY.
PARASITE.

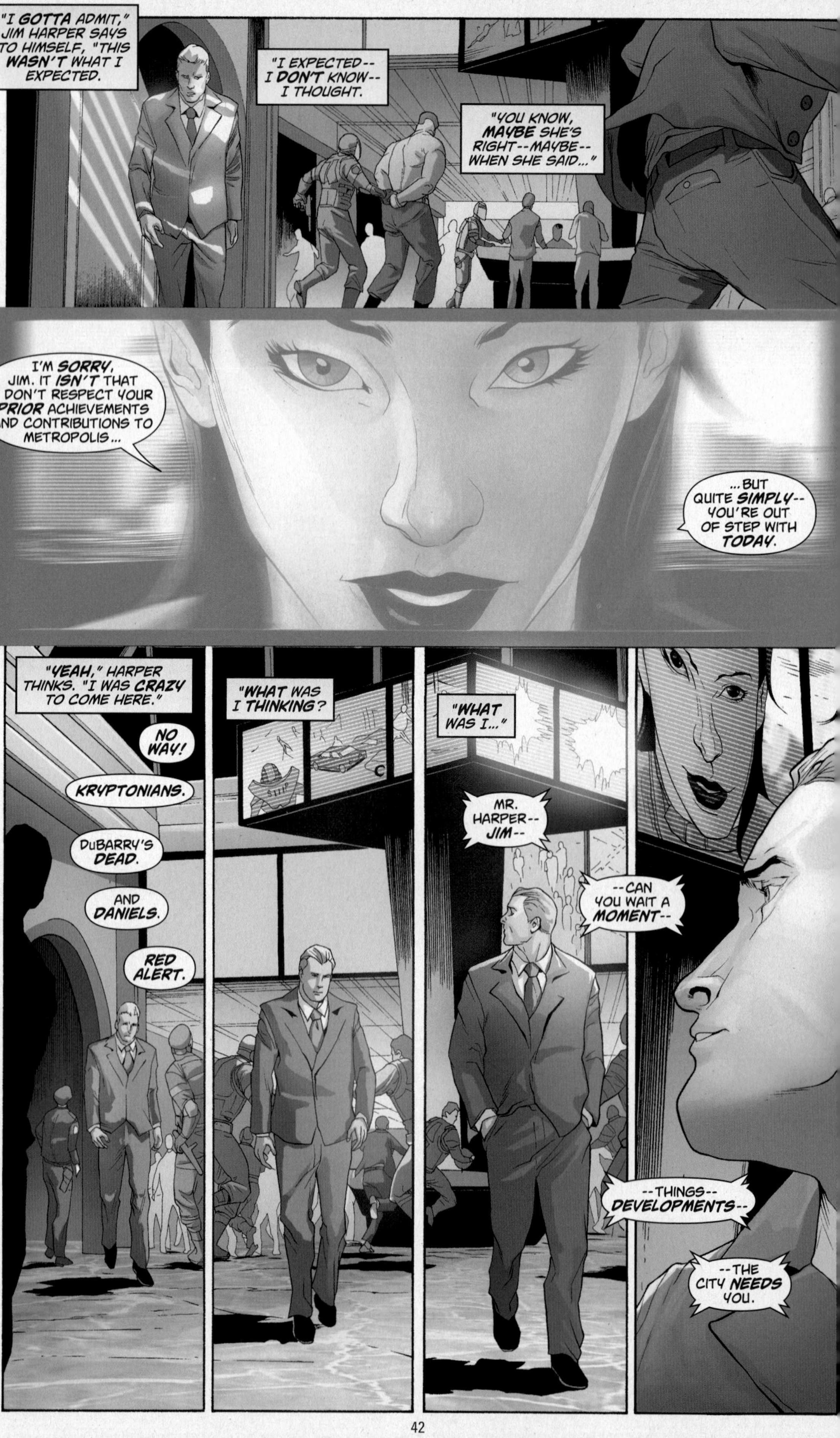

"I GOTTA ADMIT," JIM HARPER SAYS TO HIMSELF, "THIS WASN'T WHAT I EXPECTED.
"I EXPECTED-- I DON'T KNOW-- I THOUGHT.
"YOU KNOW, MAYBE SHE'S RIGHT--MAYBE-- WHEN SHE SAID..."
I'M SORRY, JIM. IT ISN'T THAT I DON'T RESPECT YOUR PRIOR ACHIEVEMENTS AND CONTRIBUTIONS TO METROPOLIS...
...BUT QUITE SIMPLY-- YOU'RE OUT OF STEP WITH TODAY.
"YEAH," HARPER THINKS. "I WAS CRAZY TO COME HERE."
NO WAY!
KRYPTONIANS.
DuBARRY'S DEAD.
AND DANIELS.
RED ALERT.
"WHAT WAS I THINKING?
"WHAT WAS I..."
MR. HARPER-- JIM--
--CAN YOU WAIT A MOMENT--
--THINGS-- DEVELOPMENTS--
--THE CITY NEEDS YOU.

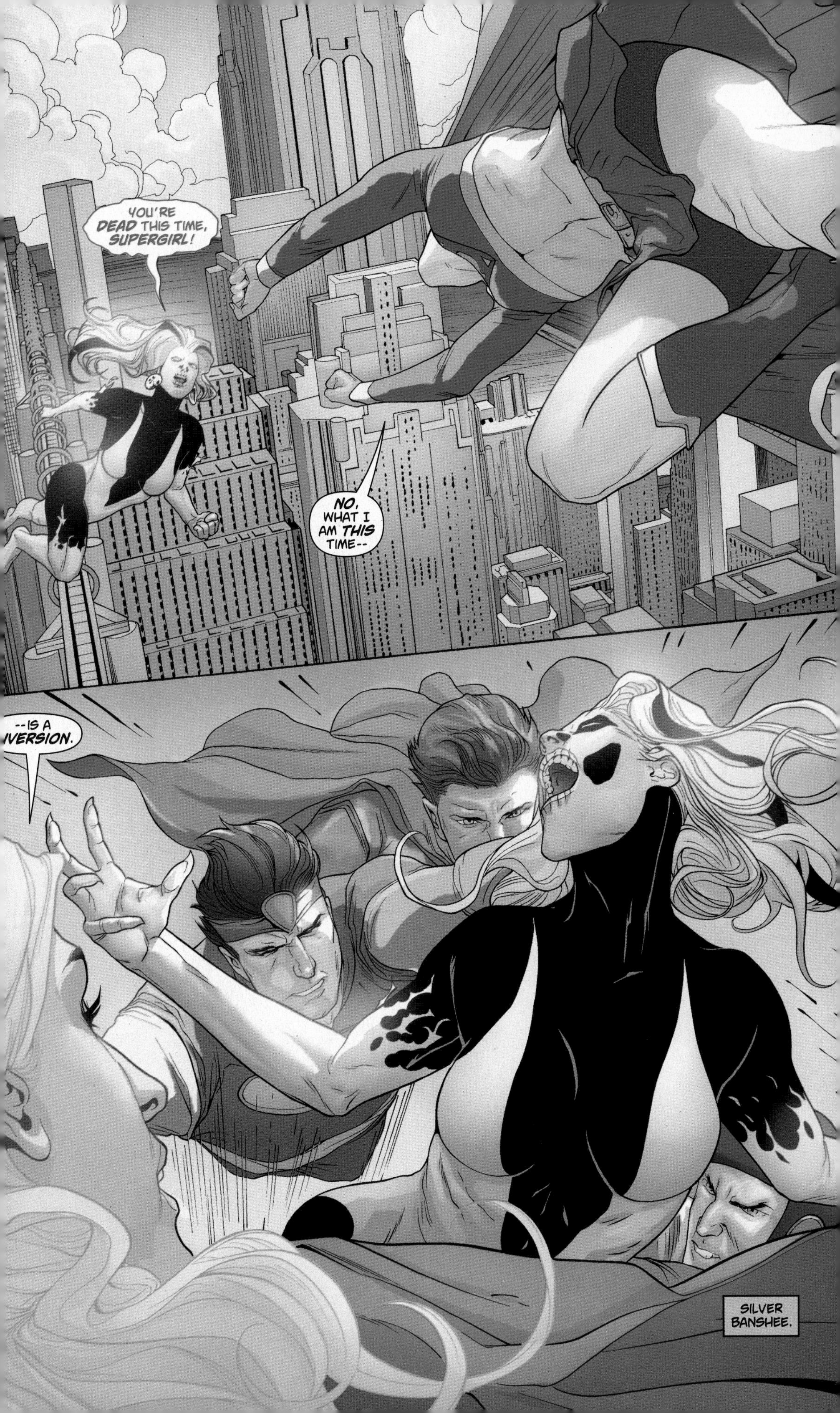
YOU'RE DEAD THIS TIME, SUPERGIRL!
NO, WHAT I AM THIS TIME--
--IS A IVERSION.
SILVER BANSHEE.

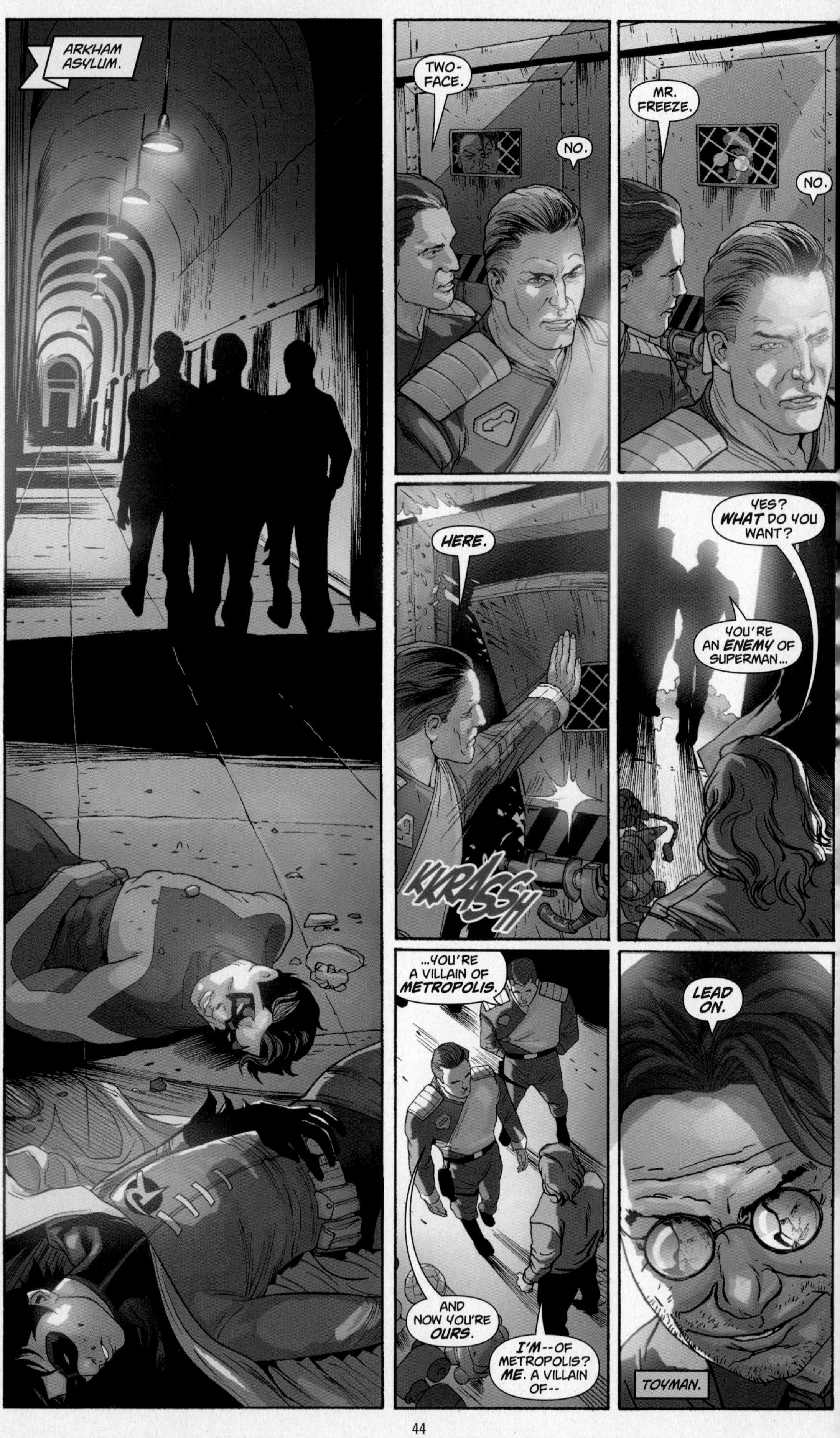

ARKHAM ASYLUM.
TWO-FACE.
NO.
MR. FREEZE.
NO.
HERE.
KKRASSH
YES? WHAT DO YOU WANT?
YOU'RE AN ENEMY OF SUPERMAN...
...YOU'RE A VILLAIN OF METROPOLIS.
AND NOW YOU'RE OURS.
I'M--OF METROPOLIS? ME. A VILLAIN OF--
LEAD ON.
TOYMAN.

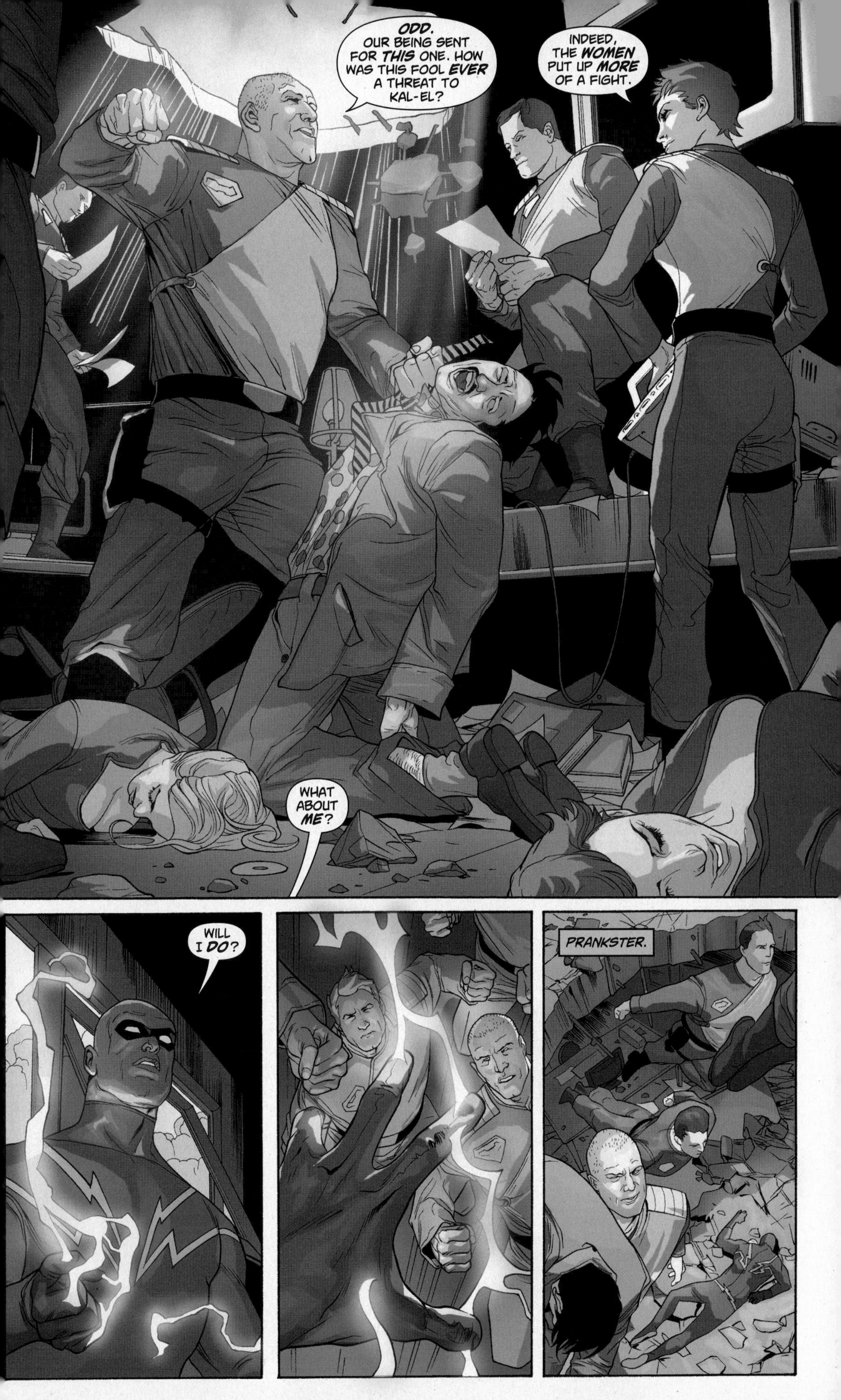
ODD. OUR BEING SENT FOR THIS ONE. HOW WAS THIS FOOL EVER A THREAT TO KAL-EL?
INDEED, THE WOMEN PUT UP MORE OF A FIGHT.
WHAT ABOUT ME?
WILL I DO?
PRANKSTER.

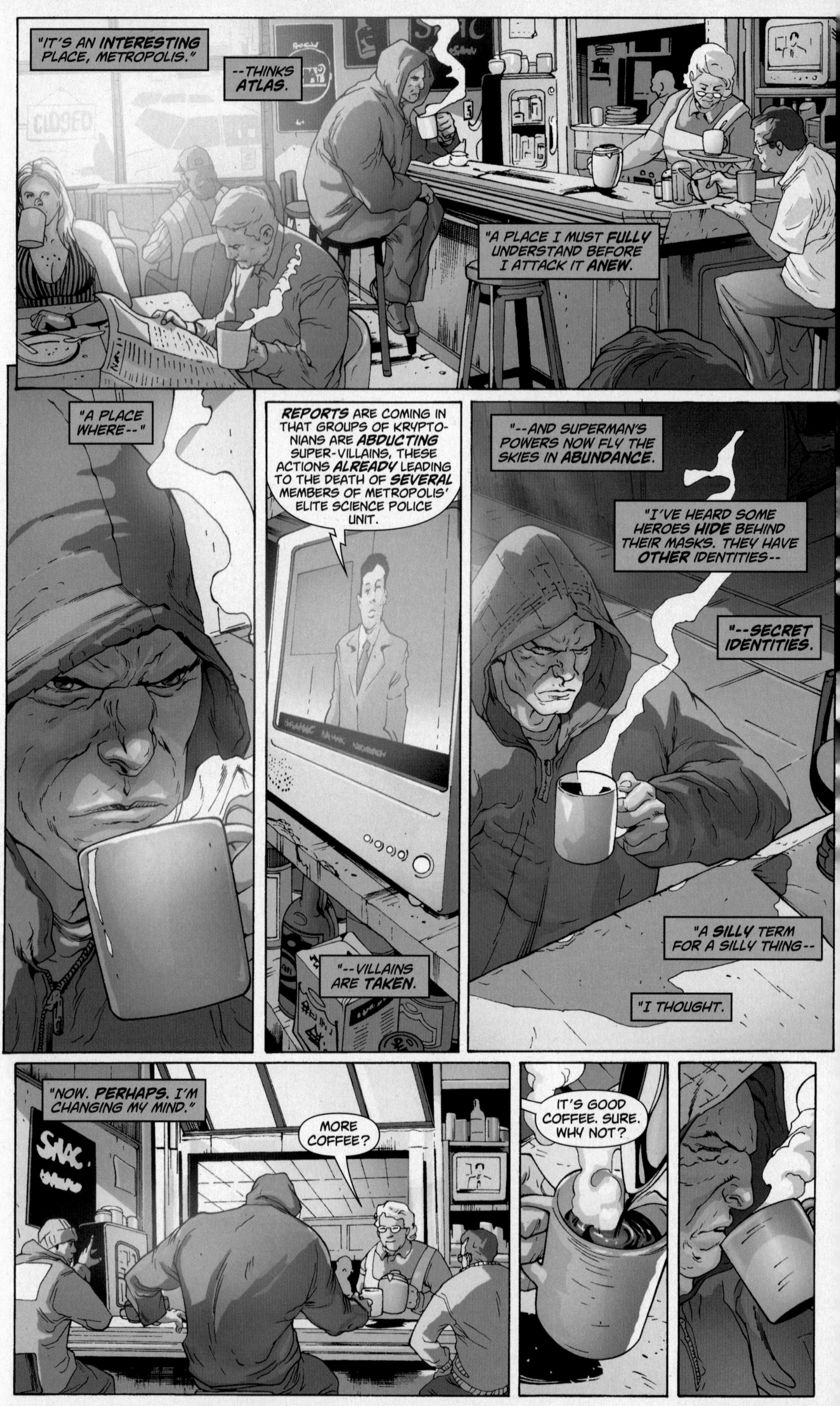

"IT'S AN INTERESTING PLACE, METROPOLIS."
--THINKS ATLAS.
CLOSED
"A PLACE I MUST FULLY UNDERSTAND BEFORE I ATTACK IT ANEW.
"A PLACE WHERE--"
REPORTS ARE COMING IN THAT GROUPS OF KRYPTO-NIANS ARE ABDUCTING SUPER-VILLAINS, THESE ACTIONS ALREADY LEADING TO THE DEATH OF SEVERAL MEMBERS OF METROPOLIS' ELITE SCIENCE POLICE UNIT.
"--VILLAINS ARE TAKEN.
"--AND SUPERMAN'S POWERS NOW FLY THE SKIES IN ABUNDANCE.
"I'VE HEARD SOME HEROES HIDE BEHIND THEIR MASKS. THEY HAVE OTHER IDENTITIES--
"--SECRET IDENTITIES.
"A SILLY TERM FOR A SILLY THING--
"I THOUGHT.
"NOW. PERHAPS. I'M CHANGING MY MIND."
MORE COFFEE?
IT'S GOOD COFFEE. SURE. WHY NOT?

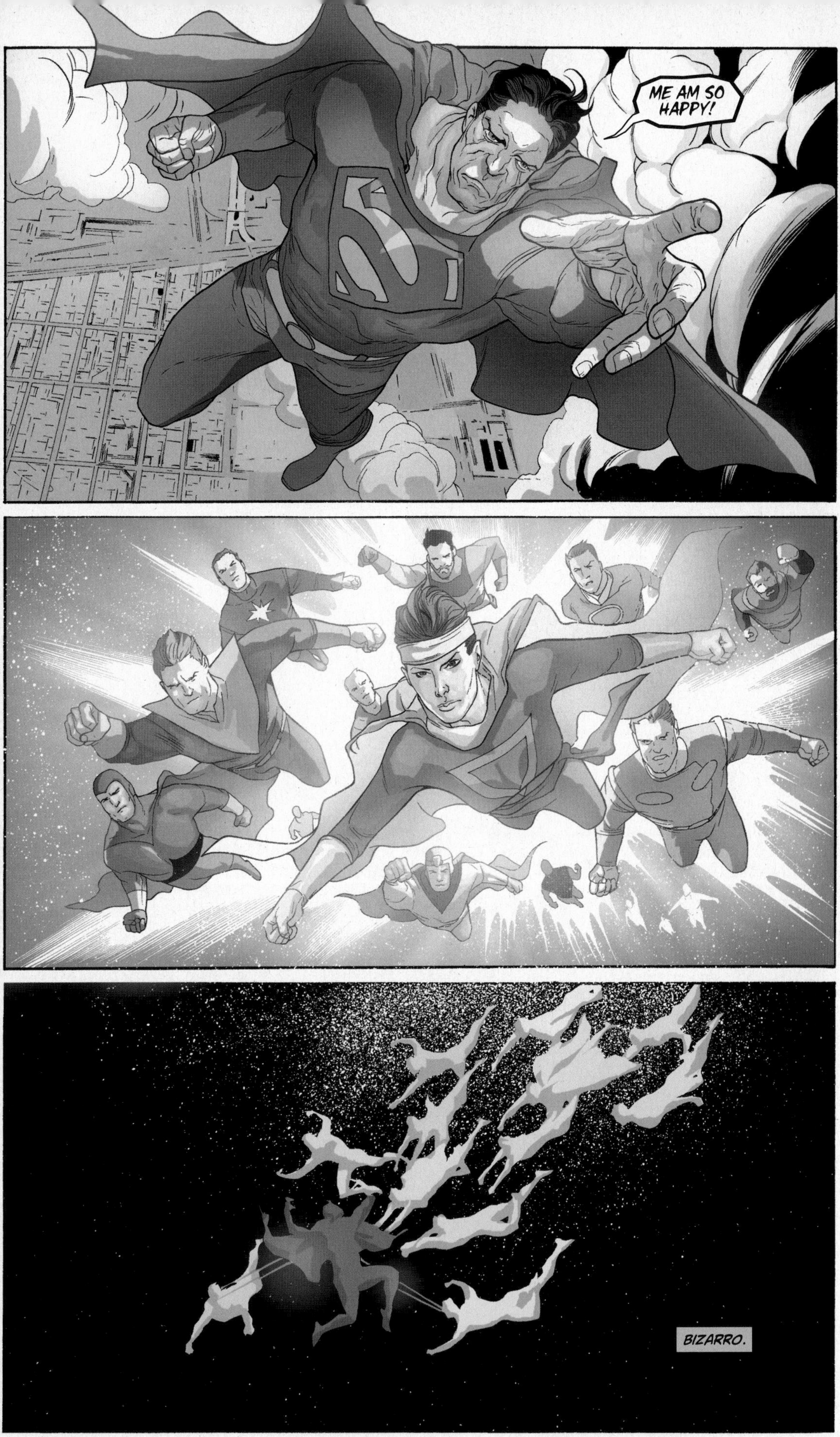
ME AM SO HAPPY!
BIZARRO.

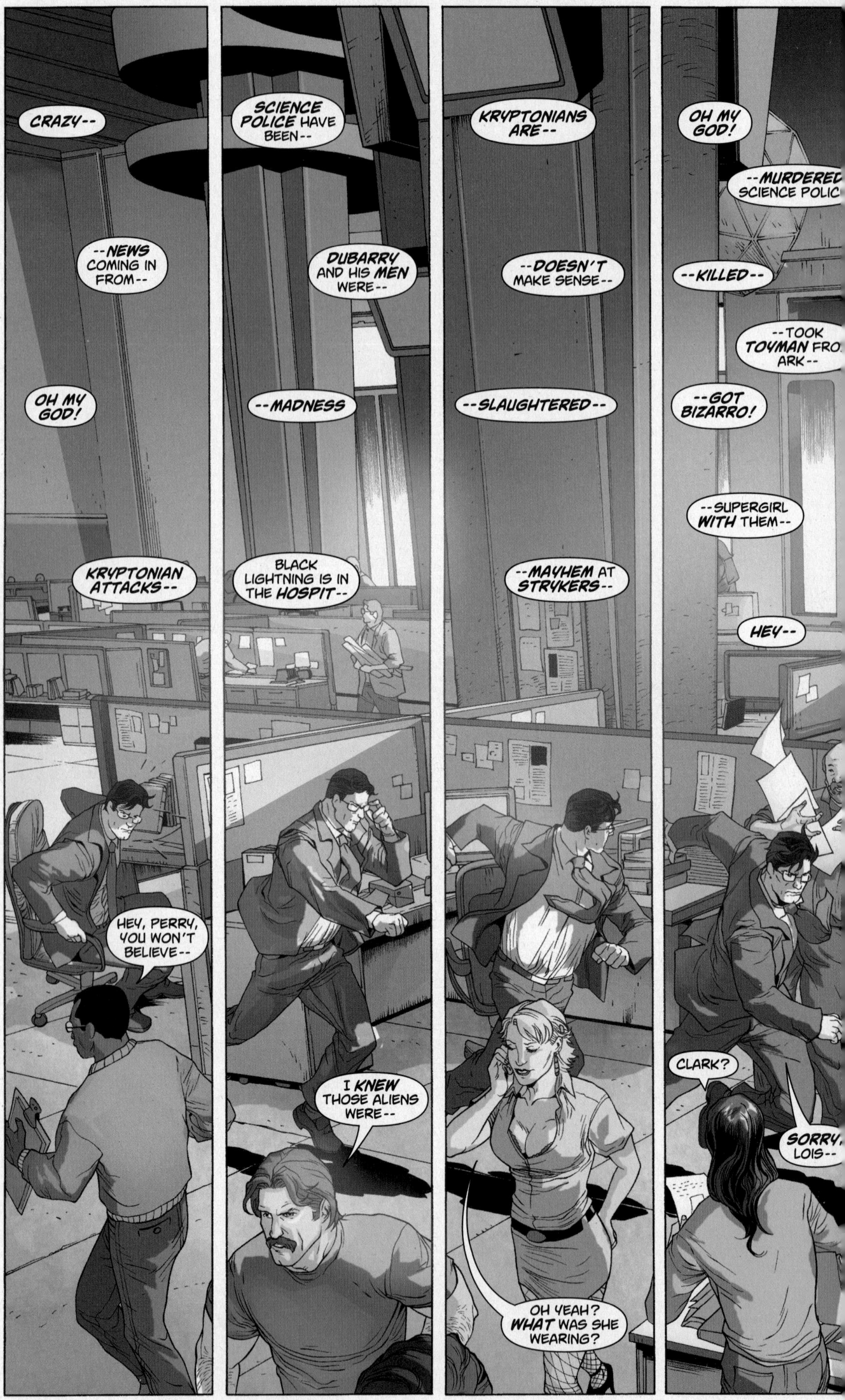

CRAZY--
--NEWS COMING IN FROM--
OH MY GOD!
KRYPTONIAN ATTACKS--
HEY, PERRY, YOU WON'T BELIEVE--
SCIENCE POLICE HAVE BEEN--
DUBARRY AND HIS MEN WERE--
--MADNESS
BLACK LIGHTNING IS IN THE HOSPIT--
I KNEW THOSE ALIENS WERE--
KRYPTONIANS ARE--
--DOESN'T MAKE SENSE--
--SLAUGHTERED--
--MAYHEM AT STRYKERS--
OH YEAH? WHAT WAS SHE WEARING?
OH MY GOD!
--MURDERED SCIENCE POLIC
--KILLED--
--TOOK TOYMAN FRO ARK--
--GOT BIZARRO!
--SUPERGIRL WITH THEM--
HEY--
CLARK?
SORRY, LOIS--

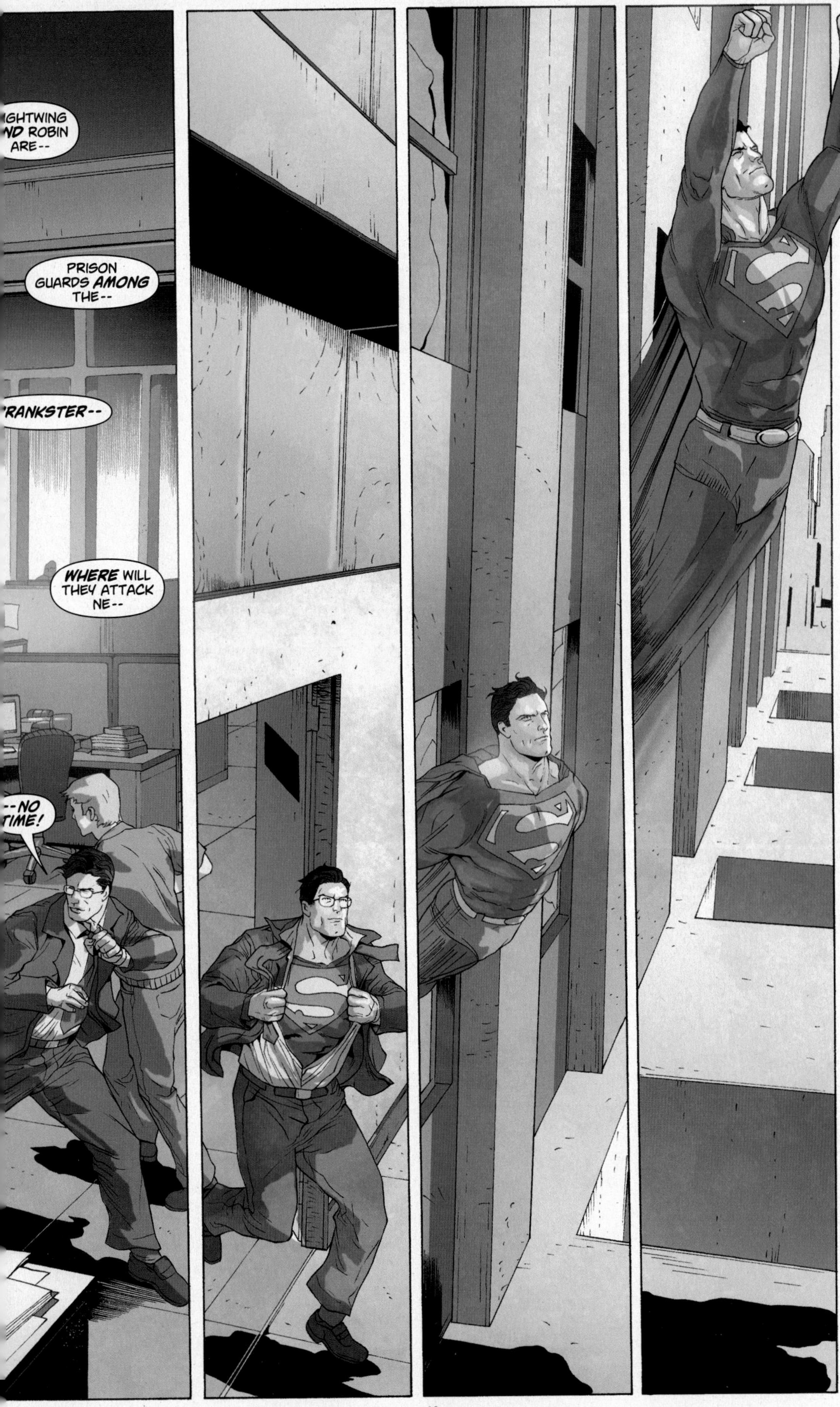

...IGHTWING ...ND ROBIN ARE--
PRISON GUARDS AMONG THE--
...RANKSTER--
WHERE WILL THEY ATTACK NE--
--NO TIME!

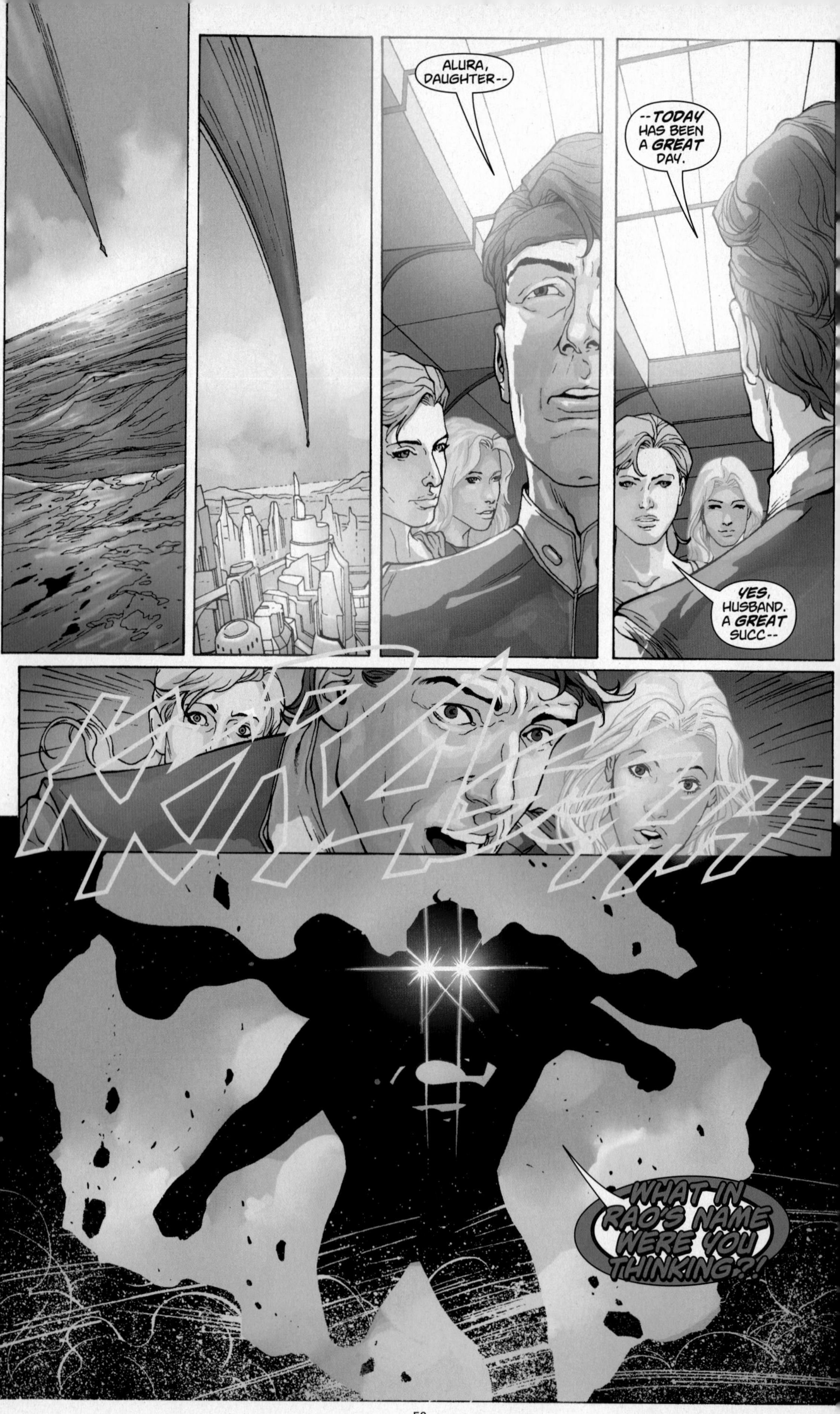
ALURA, DAUGHTER--
--TODAY HAS BEEN A GREAT DAY.
YES, HUSBAND. A GREAT SUCC--
WHAT IN RAO'S NAME WERE YOU THINKING?!

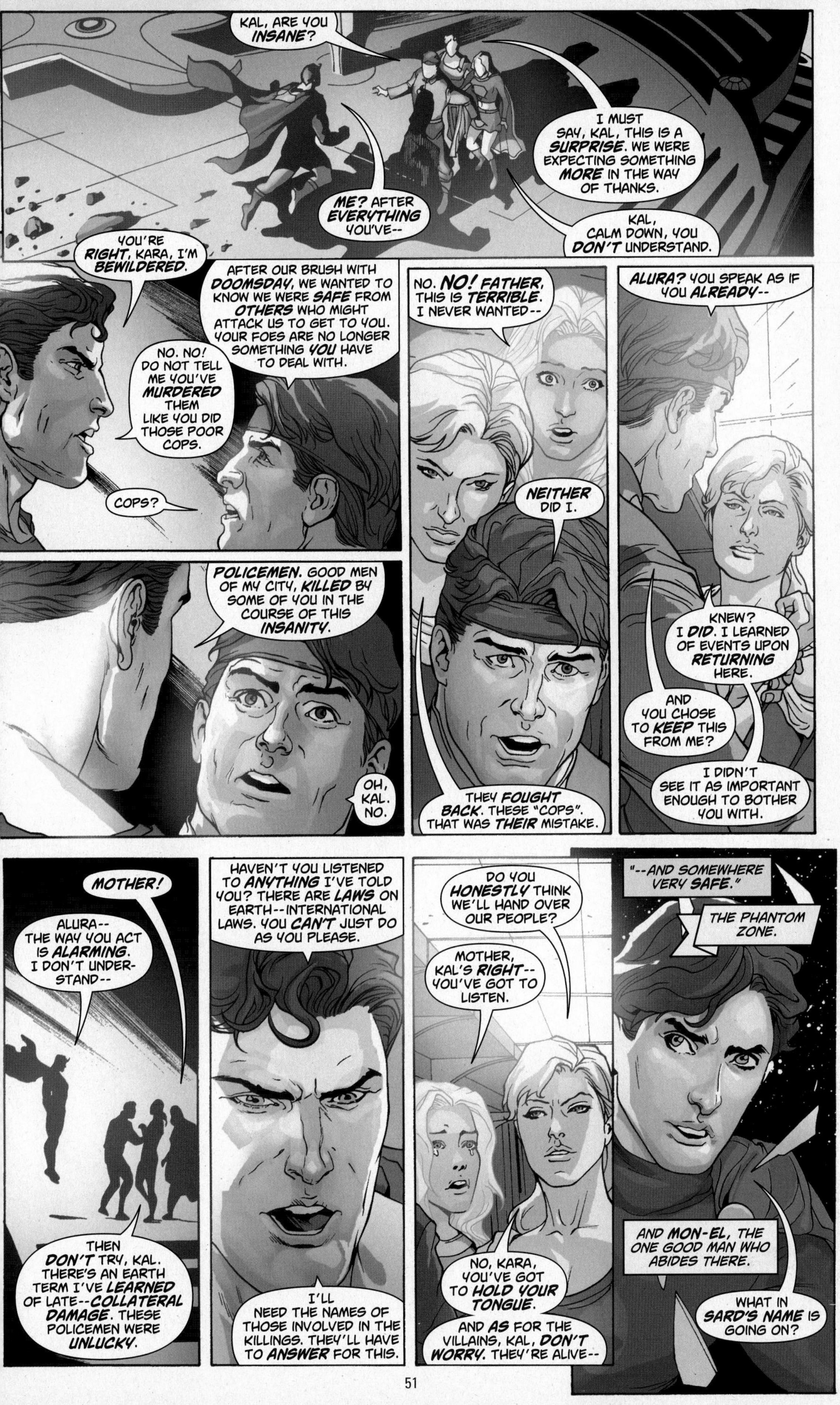
KAL, ARE YOU INSANE?
ME? AFTER EVERYTHING YOU'VE--
I MUST SAY, KAL, THIS IS A SURPRISE. WE WERE EXPECTING SOMETHING MORE IN THE WAY OF THANKS.
KAL, CALM DOWN, YOU DON'T UNDERSTAND.
YOU'RE RIGHT, KARA, I'M BEWILDERED.
AFTER OUR BRUSH WITH DOOMSDAY, WE WANTED TO KNOW WE WERE SAFE FROM OTHERS WHO MIGHT ATTACK US TO GET TO YOU. YOUR FOES ARE NO LONGER SOMETHING YOU HAVE TO DEAL WITH.
NO. NO! DO NOT TELL ME YOU'VE MURDERED THEM LIKE YOU DID THOSE POOR COPS.
COPS?
POLICEMEN. GOOD MEN OF MY CITY, KILLED BY SOME OF YOU IN THE COURSE OF THIS INSANITY.
OH, KAL. NO.
NO. NO! FATHER, THIS IS TERRIBLE. I NEVER WANTED--
NEITHER DID I.
THEY FOUGHT BACK. THESE "COPS". THAT WAS THEIR MISTAKE.
ALURA? YOU SPEAK AS IF YOU ALREADY--
KNEW? I DID. I LEARNED OF EVENTS UPON RETURNING HERE.
AND YOU CHOSE TO KEEP THIS FROM ME?
I DIDN'T SEE IT AS IMPORTANT ENOUGH TO BOTHER YOU WITH.
MOTHER!
ALURA-- THE WAY YOU ACT IS ALARMING. I DON'T UNDER-STAND--
THEN DON'T TRY, KAL. THERE'S AN EARTH TERM I'VE LEARNED OF LATE--COLLATERAL DAMAGE. THESE POLICEMEN WERE UNLUCKY.
HAVEN'T YOU LISTENED TO ANYTHING I'VE TOLD YOU? THERE ARE LAWS ON EARTH--INTERNATIONAL LAWS. YOU CAN'T JUST DO AS YOU PLEASE.
I'LL NEED THE NAMES OF THOSE INVOLVED IN THE KILLINGS. THEY'LL HAVE TO ANSWER FOR THIS.
DO YOU HONESTLY THINK WE'LL HAND OVER OUR PEOPLE?
MOTHER, KAL'S RIGHT-- YOU'VE GOT TO LISTEN.
NO, KARA, YOU'VE GOT TO HOLD YOUR TONGUE.
AND AS FOR THE VILLAINS, KAL, DON'T WORRY. THEY'RE ALIVE--
"--AND SOMEWHERE VERY SAFE."
THE PHANTOM ZONE.
AND MON-EL, THE ONE GOOD MAN WHO ABIDES THERE.
WHAT IN SARD'S NAME IS GOING ON?

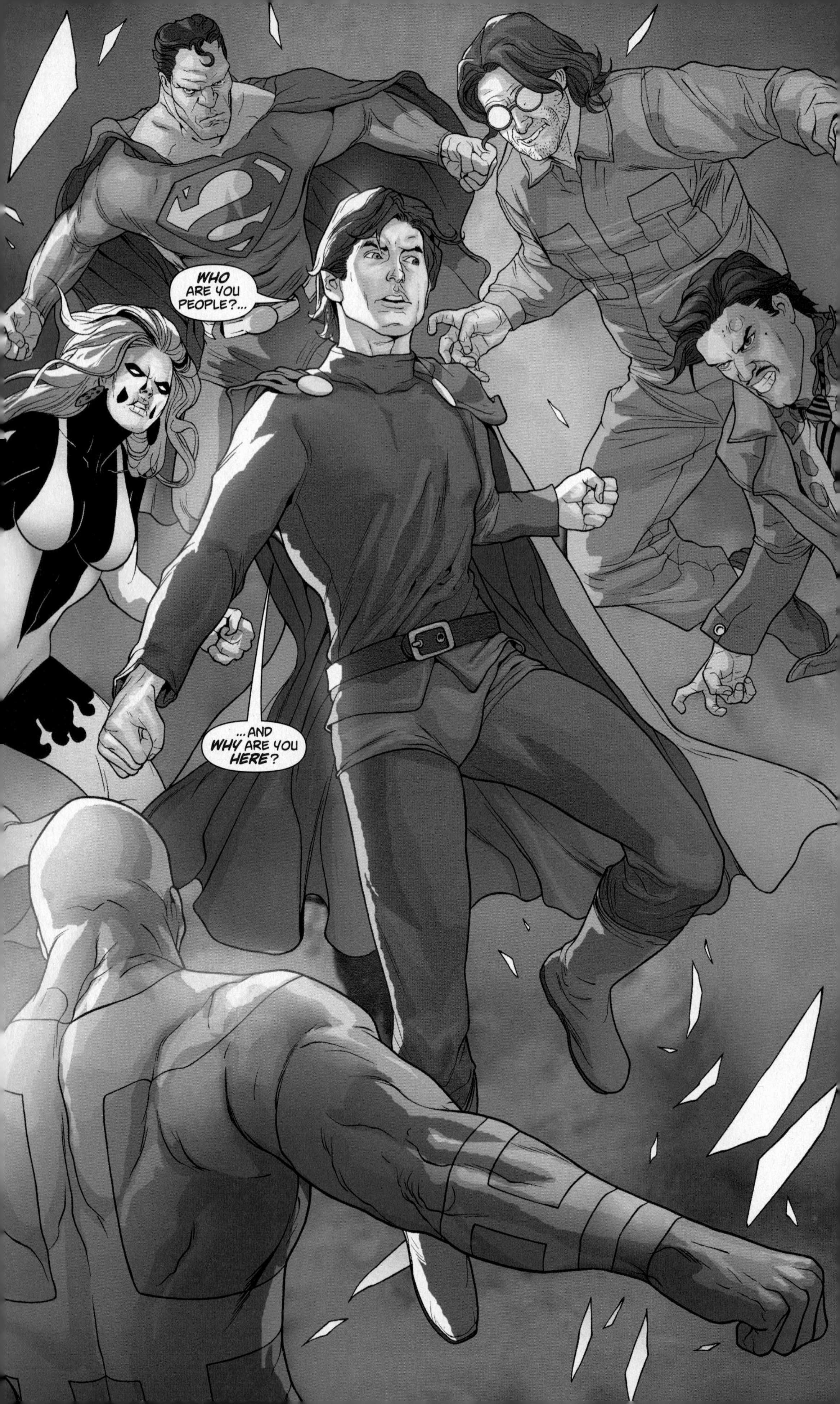
WHO ARE YOU PEOPLE?...
...AND WHY ARE YOU HERE?

<BRAINIAC LIVES> ACTION COMICS 872 COVER ART BY **GARY FRANK** WITH **BRAD ANDERSON**

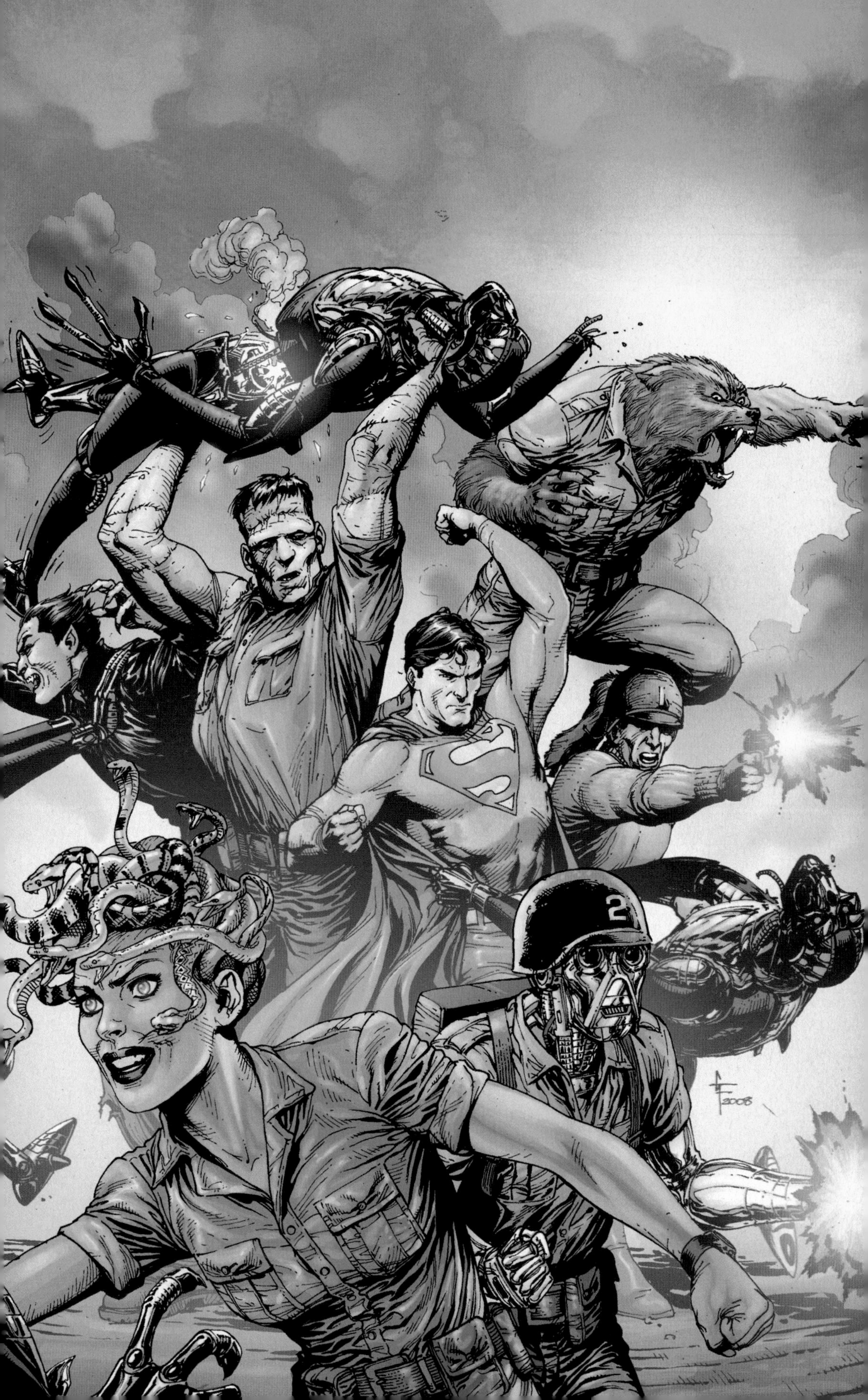

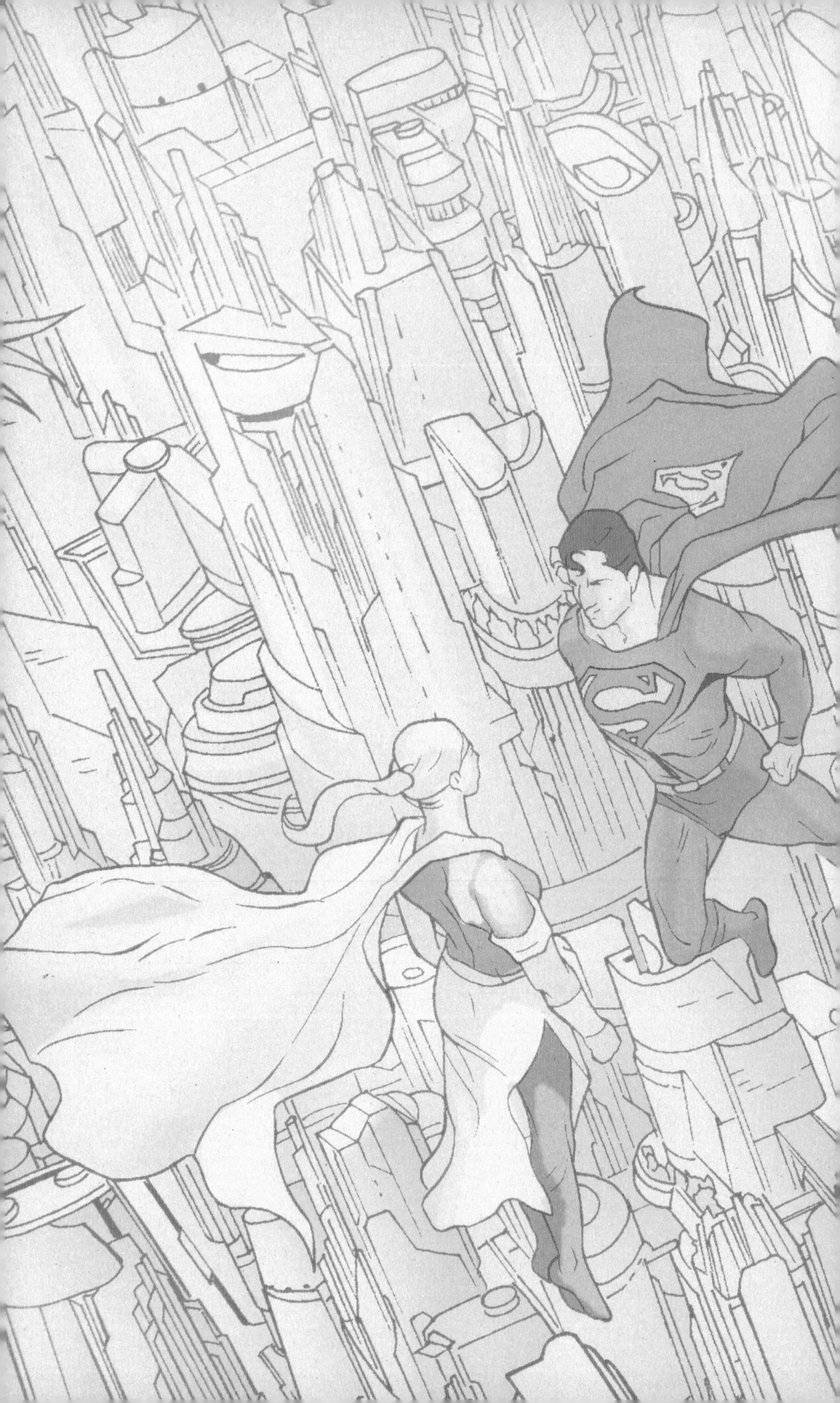

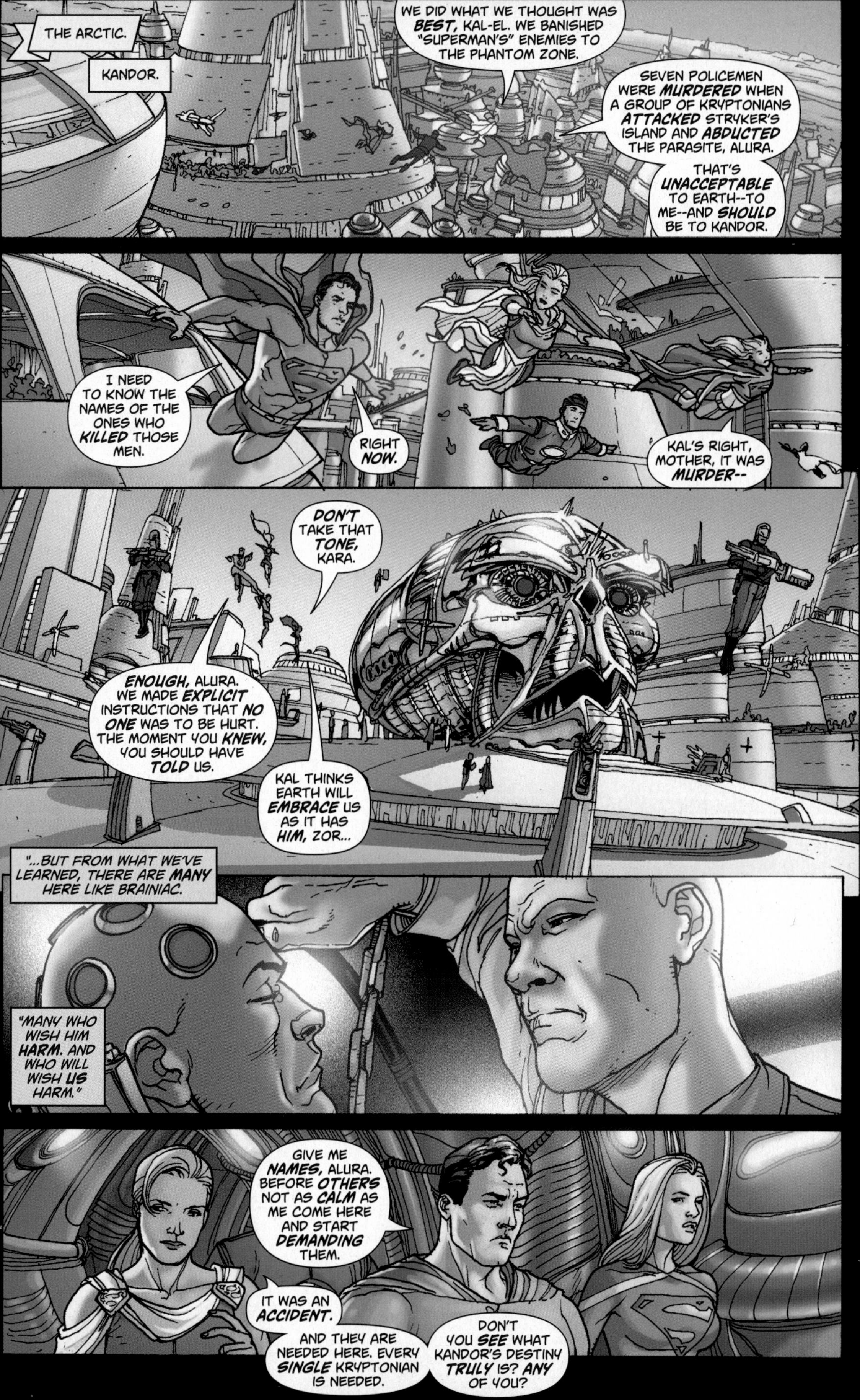
THE ARCTIC.
KANDOR.
WE DID WHAT WE THOUGHT WAS BEST, KAL-EL. WE BANISHED "SUPERMAN'S" ENEMIES TO THE PHANTOM ZONE.
SEVEN POLICEMEN WERE MURDERED WHEN A GROUP OF KRYPTONIANS ATTACKED STRYKER'S ISLAND AND ABDUCTED THE PARASITE, ALURA.
THAT'S UNACCEPTABLE TO EARTH--TO ME--AND SHOULD BE TO KANDOR.
I NEED TO KNOW THE NAMES OF THE ONES WHO KILLED THOSE MEN.
RIGHT NOW.
KAL'S RIGHT, MOTHER, IT WAS MURDER--
DON'T TAKE THAT TONE, KARA.
ENOUGH, ALURA. WE MADE EXPLICIT INSTRUCTIONS THAT NO ONE WAS TO BE HURT. THE MOMENT YOU KNEW, YOU SHOULD HAVE TOLD US.
KAL THINKS EARTH WILL EMBRACE US AS IT HAS HIM, ZOR...
"...BUT FROM WHAT WE'VE LEARNED, THERE ARE MANY HERE LIKE BRAINIAC.
"MANY WHO WISH HIM HARM. AND WHO WILL WISH US HARM."
GIVE ME NAMES, ALURA. BEFORE OTHERS NOT AS CALM AS ME COME HERE AND START DEMANDING THEM.
IT WAS AN ACCIDENT.
AND THEY ARE NEEDED HERE. EVERY SINGLE KRYPTONIAN IS NEEDED.
DON'T YOU SEE WHAT KANDOR'S DESTINY TRULY IS? ANY OF YOU?

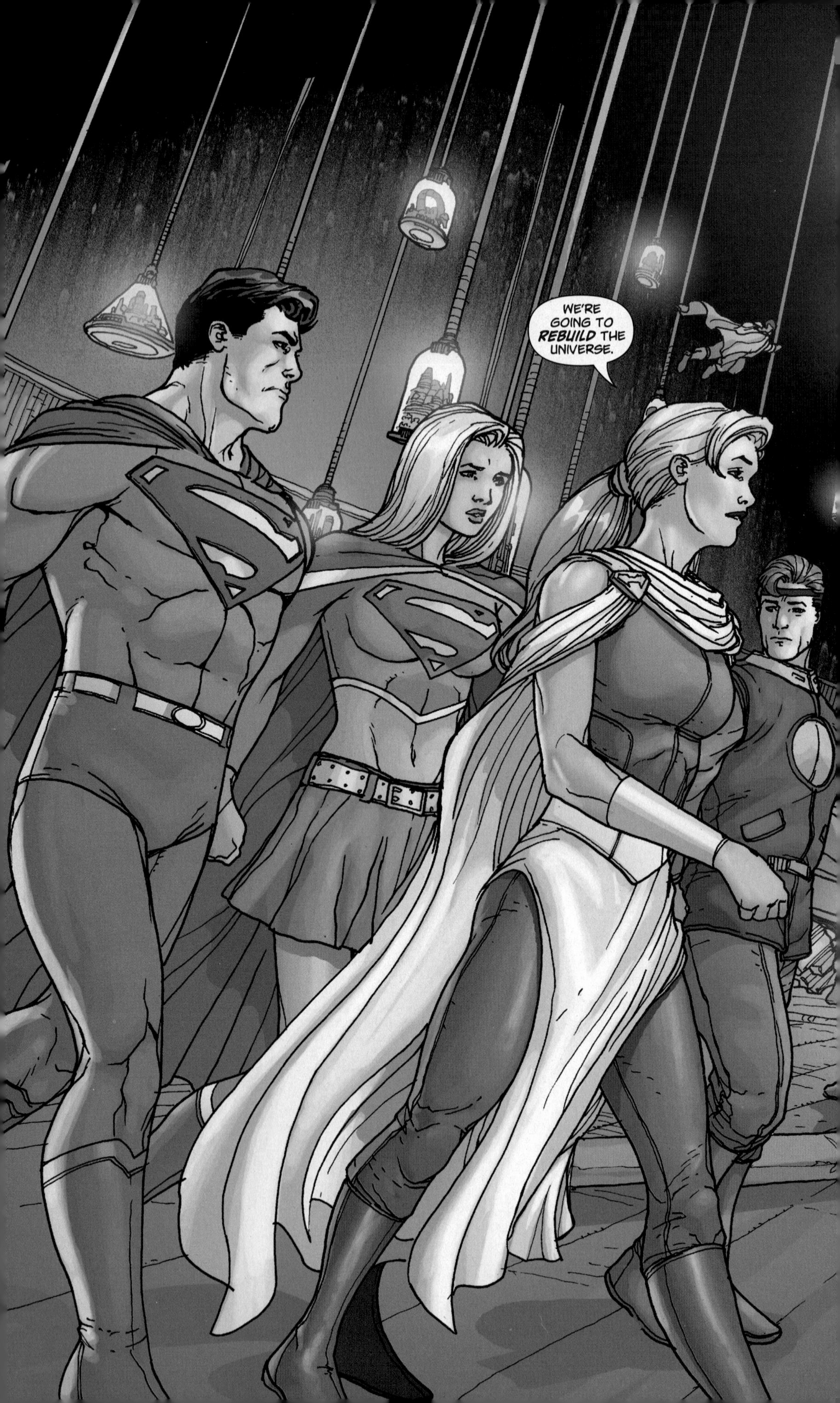
WE'RE GOING TO REBUILD THE UNIVERSE.

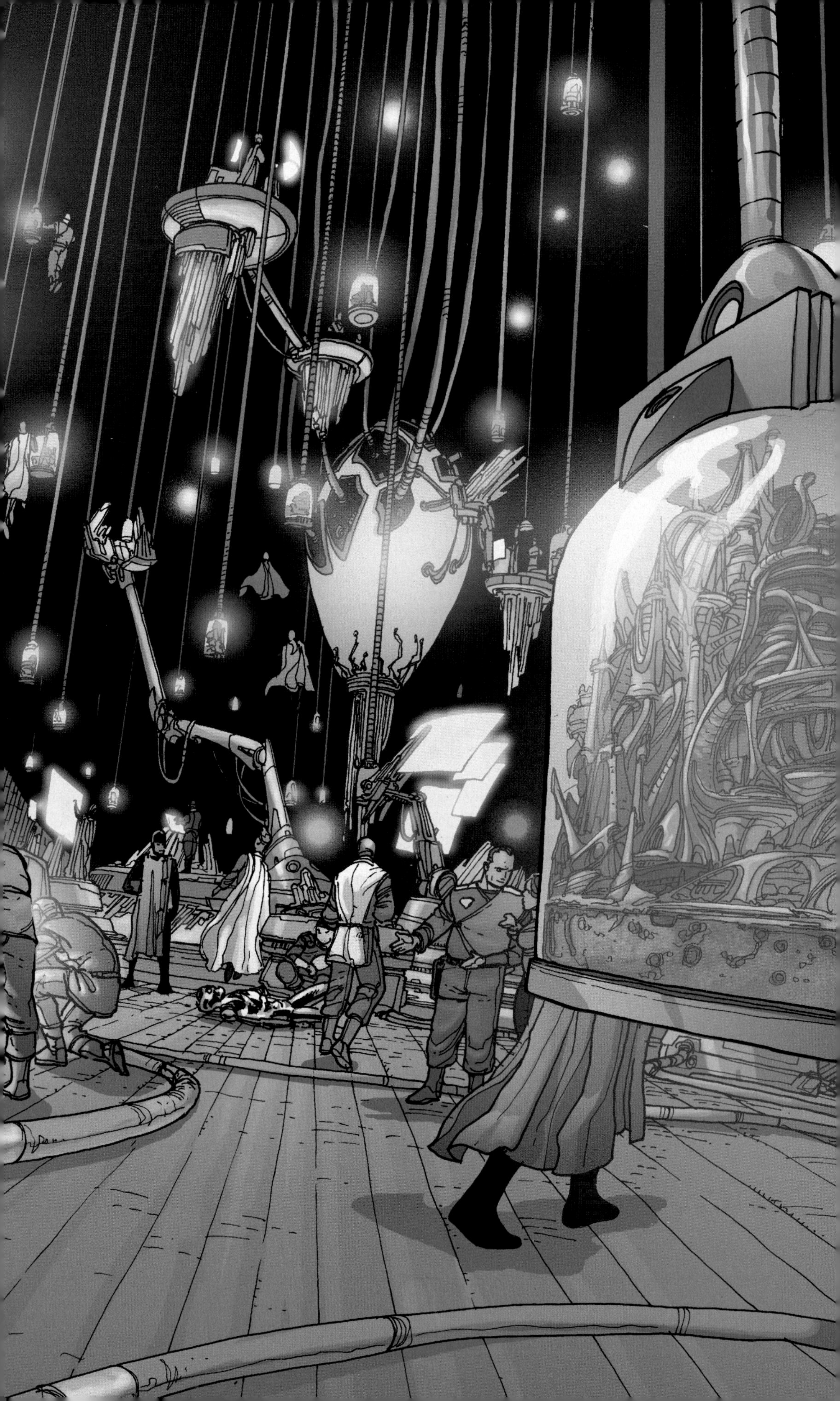

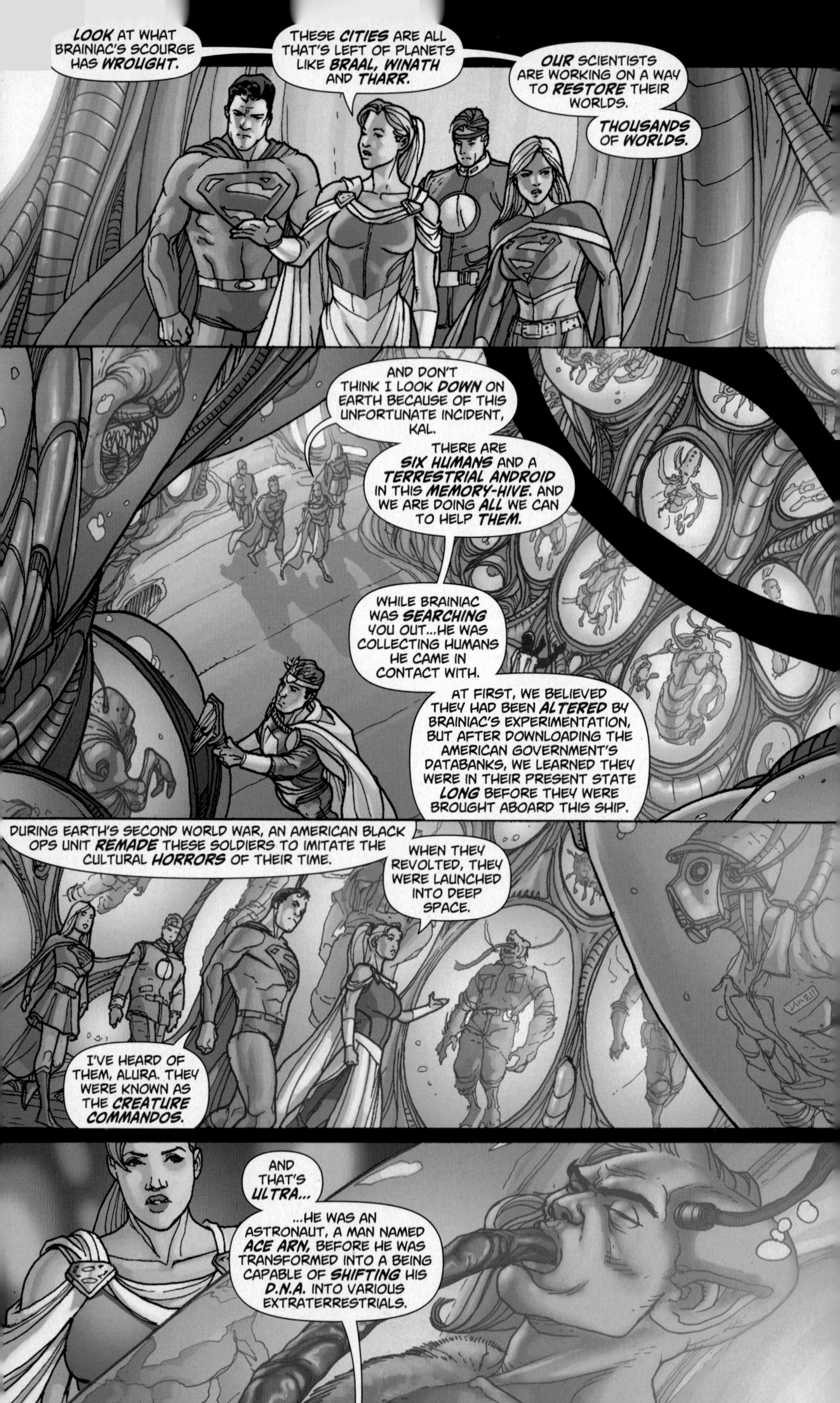
LOOK AT WHAT BRAINIAC'S SCOURGE HAS WROUGHT.
THESE CITIES ARE ALL THAT'S LEFT OF PLANETS LIKE BRAAL, WINATH AND THARR.
OUR SCIENTISTS ARE WORKING ON A WAY TO RESTORE THEIR WORLDS.
THOUSANDS OF WORLDS.
AND DON'T THINK I LOOK DOWN ON EARTH BECAUSE OF THIS UNFORTUNATE INCIDENT, KAL.
THERE ARE SIX HUMANS AND A TERRESTRIAL ANDROID IN THIS MEMORY-HIVE. AND WE ARE DOING ALL WE CAN TO HELP THEM.
WHILE BRAINIAC WAS SEARCHING YOU OUT...HE WAS COLLECTING HUMANS HE CAME IN CONTACT WITH.
AT FIRST, WE BELIEVED THEY HAD BEEN ALTERED BY BRAINIAC'S EXPERIMENTATION, BUT AFTER DOWNLOADING THE AMERICAN GOVERNMENT'S DATABANKS, WE LEARNED THEY WERE IN THEIR PRESENT STATE LONG BEFORE THEY WERE BROUGHT ABOARD THIS SHIP.
DURING EARTH'S SECOND WORLD WAR, AN AMERICAN BLACK OPS UNIT REMADE THESE SOLDIERS TO IMITATE THE CULTURAL HORRORS OF THEIR TIME.
WHEN THEY REVOLTED, THEY WERE LAUNCHED INTO DEEP SPACE.
I'VE HEARD OF THEM, ALURA. THEY WERE KNOWN AS THE CREATURE COMMANDOS.
AND THAT'S ULTRA...
...HE WAS AN ASTRONAUT, A MAN NAMED ACE ARN, BEFORE HE WAS TRANSFORMED INTO A BEING CAPABLE OF SHIFTING HIS D.N.A. INTO VARIOUS EXTRATERRESTRIALS.

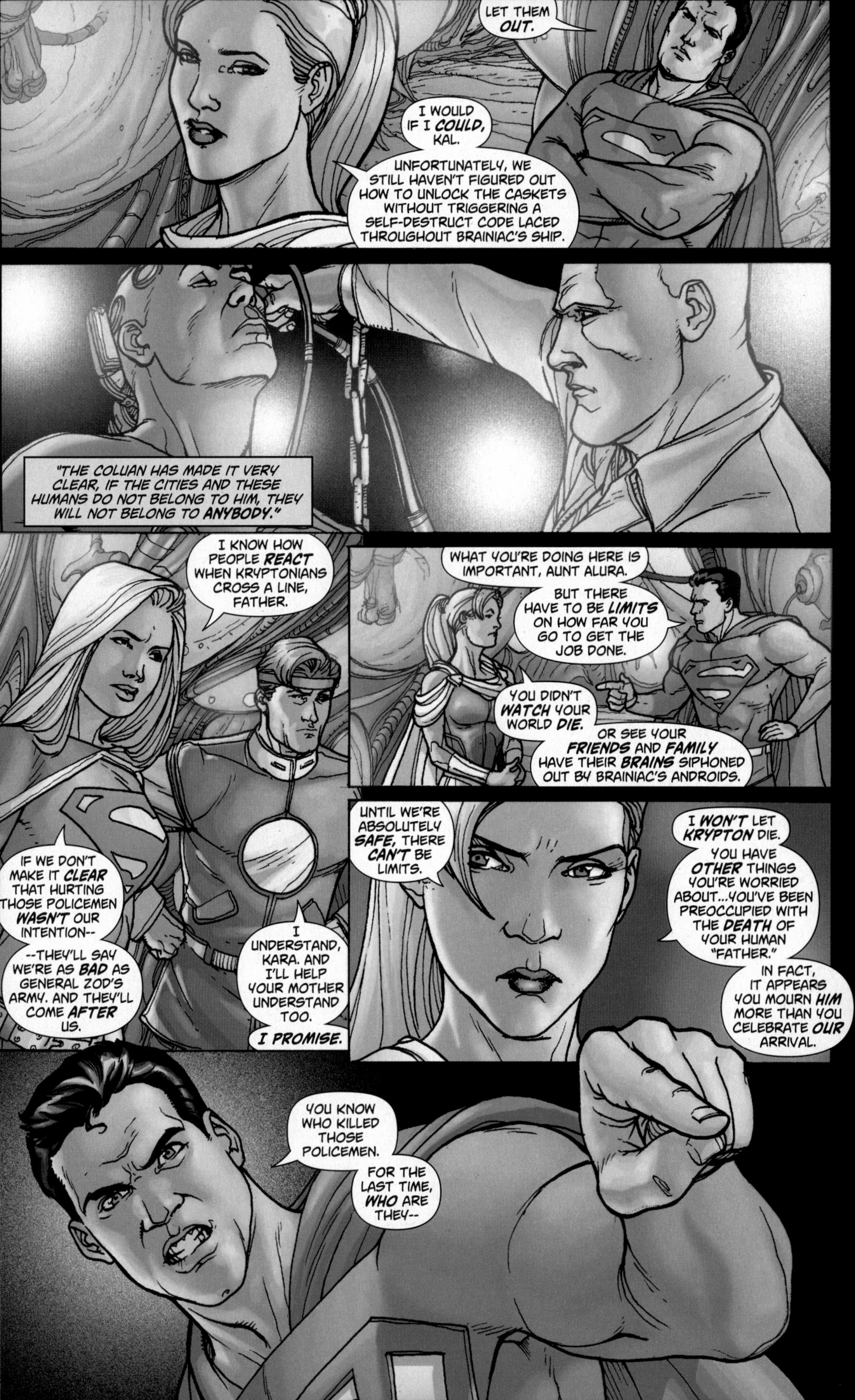
LET THEM OUT.
I WOULD IF I COULD, KAL.
UNFORTUNATELY, WE STILL HAVEN'T FIGURED OUT HOW TO UNLOCK THE CASKETS WITHOUT TRIGGERING A SELF-DESTRUCT CODE LACED THROUGHOUT BRAINIAC'S SHIP.
"THE COLUAN HAS MADE IT VERY CLEAR, IF THE CITIES AND THESE HUMANS DO NOT BELONG TO HIM, THEY WILL NOT BELONG TO ANYBODY."
I KNOW HOW PEOPLE REACT WHEN KRYPTONIANS CROSS A LINE, FATHER.
IF WE DON'T MAKE IT CLEAR THAT HURTING THOSE POLICEMEN WASN'T OUR INTENTION--
--THEY'LL SAY WE'RE AS BAD AS GENERAL ZOD'S ARMY. AND THEY'LL COME AFTER US.
I UNDERSTAND, KARA. AND I'LL HELP YOUR MOTHER UNDERSTAND TOO.
I PROMISE.
WHAT YOU'RE DOING HERE IS IMPORTANT, AUNT ALURA.
BUT THERE HAVE TO BE LIMITS ON HOW FAR YOU GO TO GET THE JOB DONE.
YOU DIDN'T WATCH YOUR WORLD DIE.
OR SEE YOUR FRIENDS AND FAMILY HAVE THEIR BRAINS SIPHONED OUT BY BRAINIAC'S ANDROIDS.
UNTIL WE'RE ABSOLUTELY SAFE, THERE CAN'T BE LIMITS.
I WON'T LET KRYPTON DIE.
YOU HAVE OTHER THINGS YOU'RE WORRIED ABOUT...YOU'VE BEEN PREOCCUPIED WITH THE DEATH OF YOUR HUMAN "FATHER."
IN FACT, IT APPEARS YOU MOURN HIM MORE THAN YOU CELEBRATE OUR ARRIVAL.
YOU KNOW WHO KILLED THOSE POLICEMEN.
FOR THE LAST TIME, WHO ARE THEY--

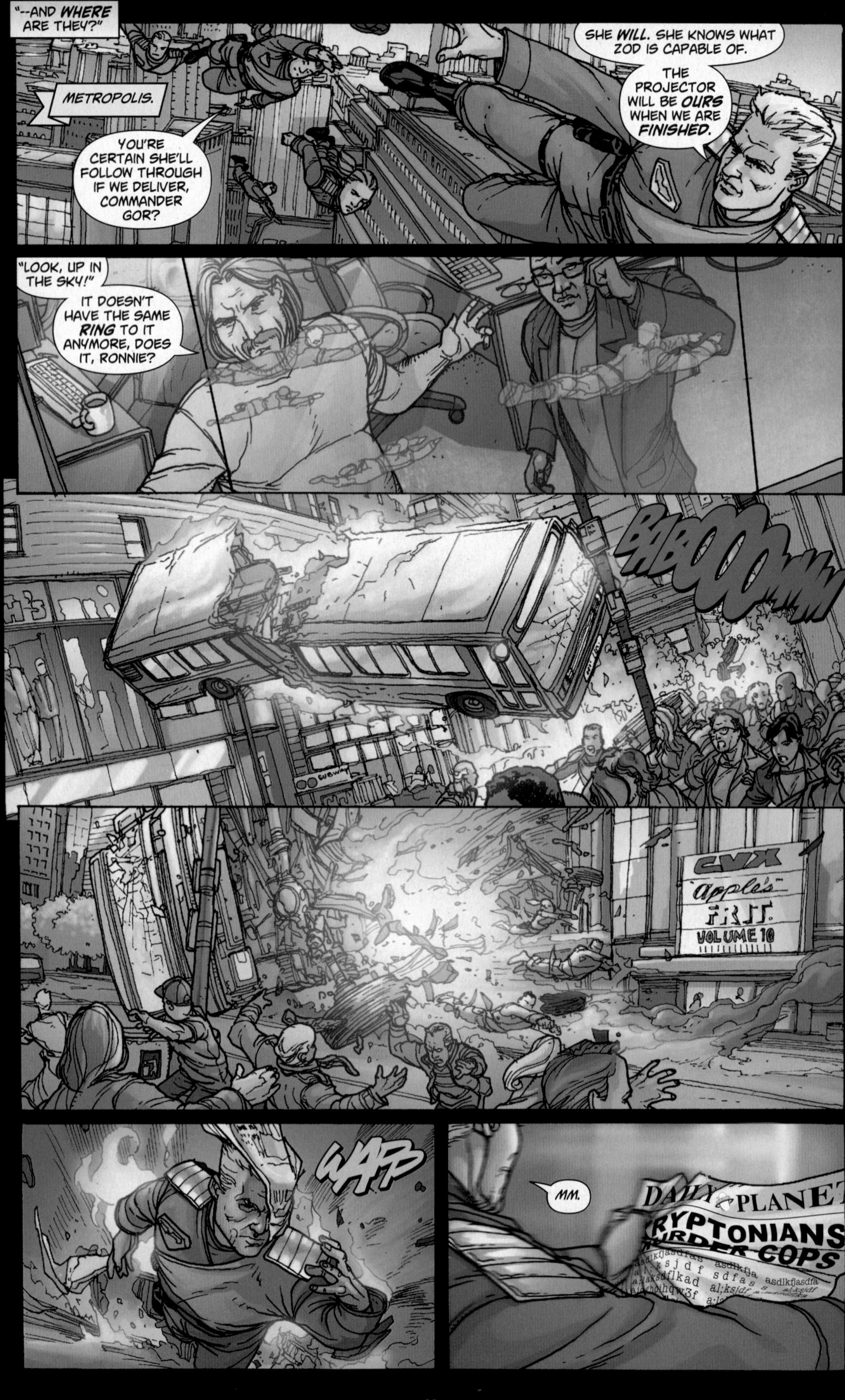

"--AND WHERE ARE THEY?"
METROPOLIS.
YOU'RE CERTAIN SHE'LL FOLLOW THROUGH IF WE DELIVER, COMMANDER GOR?
SHE WILL. SHE KNOWS WHAT ZOD IS CAPABLE OF.
THE PROJECTOR WILL BE OURS WHEN WE ARE FINISHED.
"LOOK, UP IN THE SKY!"
IT DOESN'T HAVE THE SAME RING TO IT ANYMORE, DOES IT, RONNIE?
BABOOOMM
SUBWAY
CVX
apple's
VOLUME 10
WAP
MM.
DAILY PLANET
KRYPTONIANS
COPS

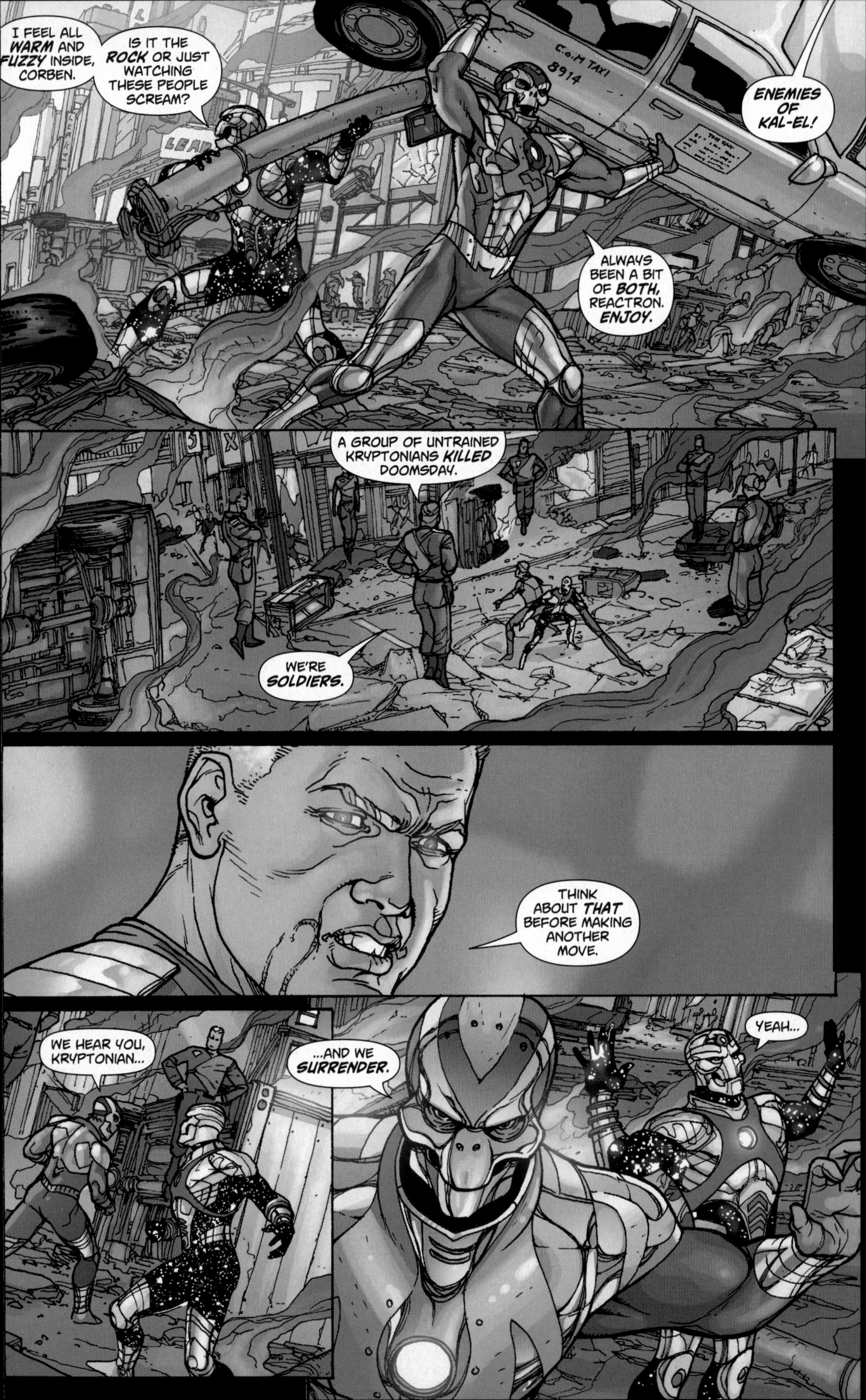

I FEEL ALL WARM AND FUZZY INSIDE, CORBEN.
IS IT THE ROCK OR JUST WATCHING THESE PEOPLE SCREAM?
C.o.M TAXI 8914
ENEMIES OF KAL-EL!
ALWAYS BEEN A BIT OF BOTH, REACTRON. ENJOY.
A GROUP OF UNTRAINED KRYPTONIANS KILLED DOOMSDAY.
WE'RE SOLDIERS.
THINK ABOUT THAT BEFORE MAKING ANOTHER MOVE.
WE HEAR YOU, KRYPTONIAN...
...AND WE SURRENDER.
YEAH...

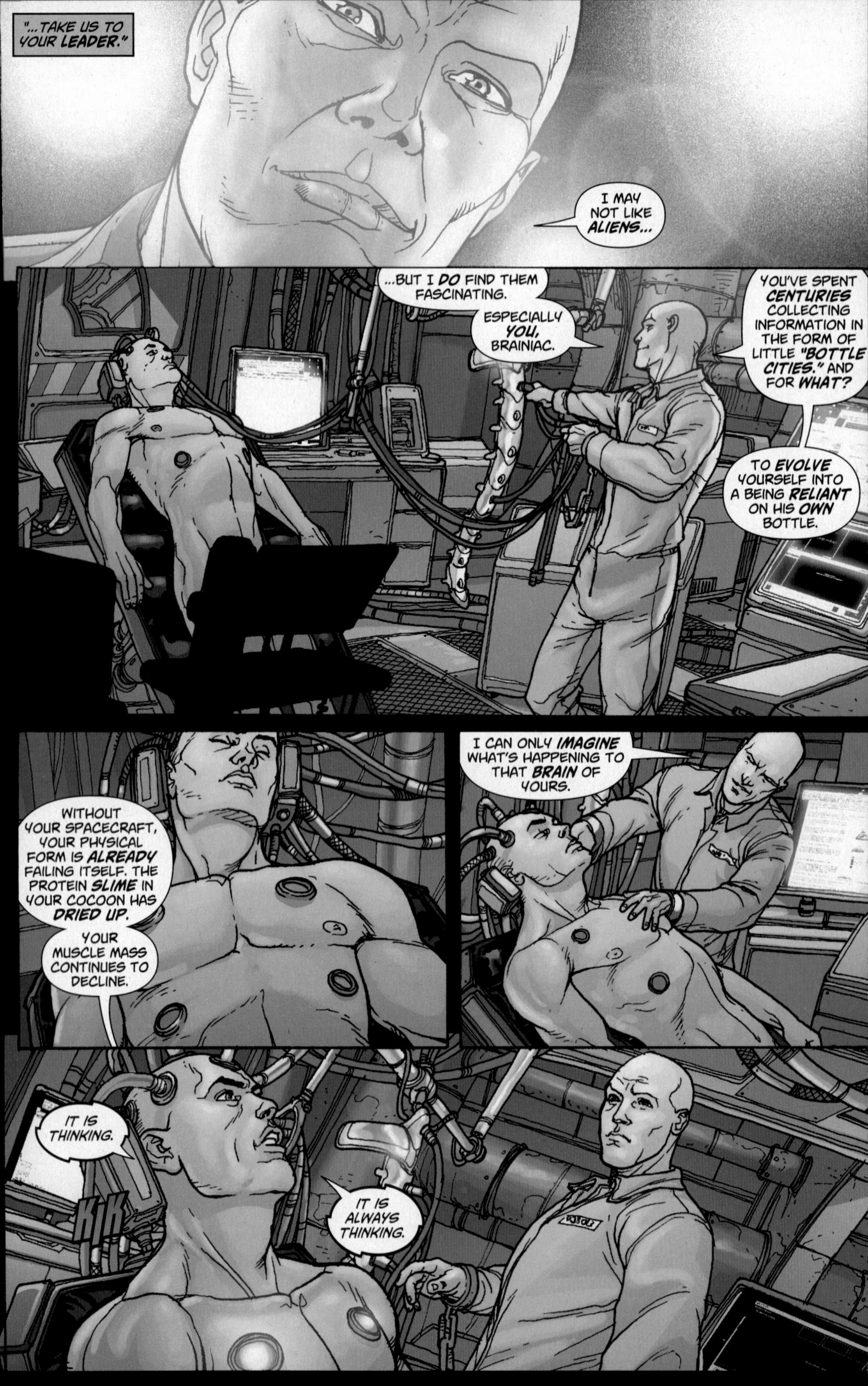

"...TAKE US TO YOUR LEADER."
I MAY NOT LIKE ALIENS...
...BUT I DO FIND THEM FASCINATING.
ESPECIALLY YOU, BRAINIAC.
YOU'VE SPENT CENTURIES COLLECTING INFORMATION IN THE FORM OF LITTLE "BOTTLE CITIES." AND FOR WHAT?
TO EVOLVE YOURSELF INTO A BEING RELIANT ON HIS OWN BOTTLE.
WITHOUT YOUR SPACECRAFT, YOUR PHYSICAL FORM IS ALREADY FAILING ITSELF. THE PROTEIN SLIME IN YOUR COCOON HAS DRIED UP.
YOUR MUSCLE MASS CONTINUES TO DECLINE.
I CAN ONLY IMAGINE WHAT'S HAPPENING TO THAT BRAIN OF YOURS.
IT IS THINKING.
KIK
IT IS ALWAYS THINKING.

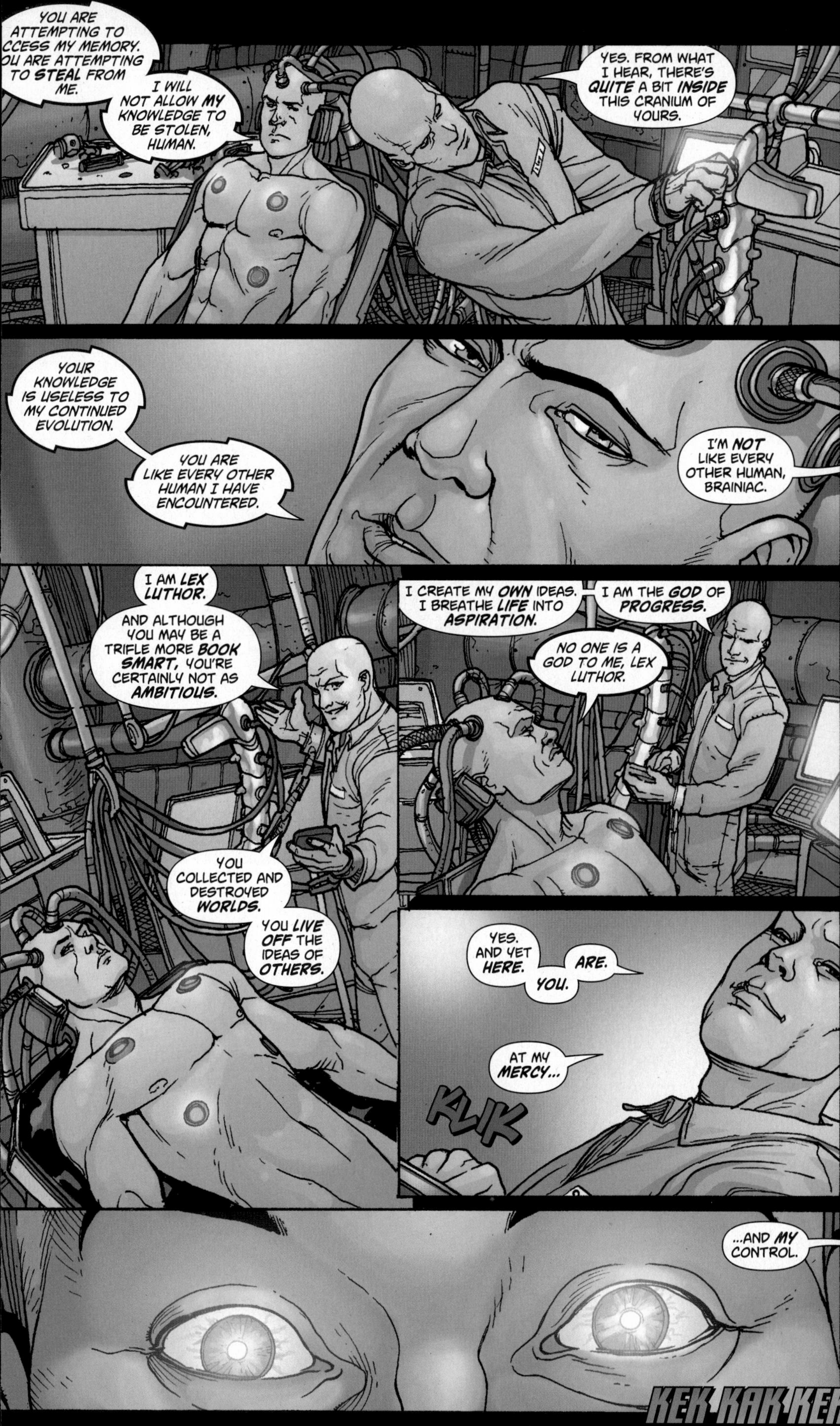
YOU ARE ATTEMPTING TO CCESS MY MEMORY. OU ARE ATTEMPTING TO STEAL FROM ME.
I WILL NOT ALLOW MY KNOWLEDGE TO BE STOLEN, HUMAN.
YES. FROM WHAT I HEAR, THERE'S QUITE A BIT INSIDE THIS CRANIUM OF YOURS.
YOUR KNOWLEDGE IS USELESS TO MY CONTINUED EVOLUTION.
YOU ARE LIKE EVERY OTHER HUMAN I HAVE ENCOUNTERED.
I'M NOT LIKE EVERY OTHER HUMAN, BRAINIAC.
I AM LEX LUTHOR.
AND ALTHOUGH YOU MAY BE A TRIFLE MORE BOOK SMART, YOU'RE CERTAINLY NOT AS AMBITIOUS.
YOU COLLECTED AND DESTROYED WORLDS.
YOU LIVE OFF THE IDEAS OF OTHERS.
I CREATE MY OWN IDEAS. I BREATHE LIFE INTO ASPIRATION.
I AM THE GOD OF PROGRESS.
NO ONE IS A GOD TO ME, LEX LUTHOR.
YES. AND YET HERE.
YOU.
ARE.
AT MY MERCY...
KLIK
...AND MY CONTROL.
KEK KAK KEK

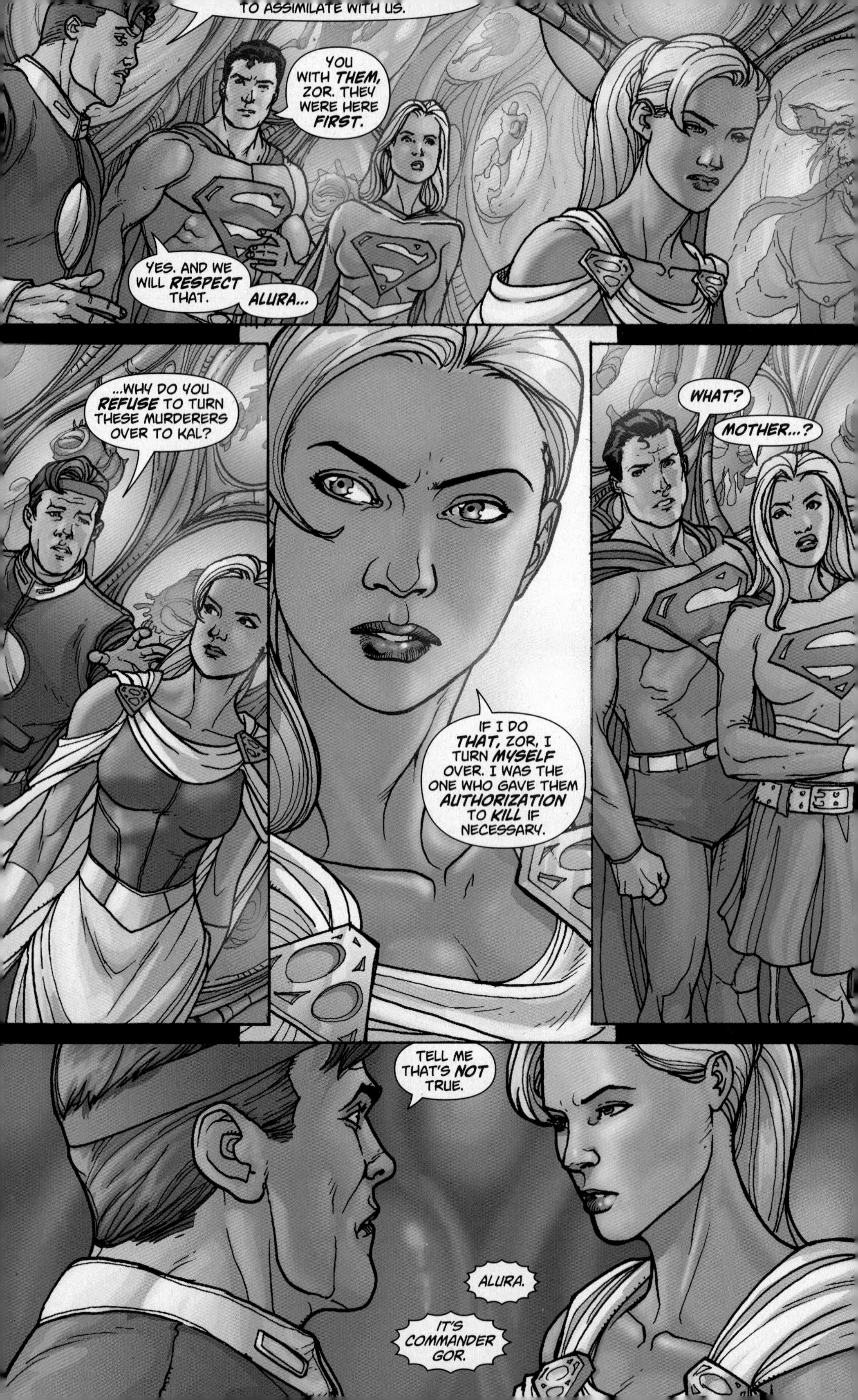

TO ASSIMILATE WITH US.
YOU WITH THEM, ZOR. THEY WERE HERE FIRST.
YES. AND WE WILL RESPECT THAT.
ALURA...
...WHY DO YOU REFUSE TO TURN THESE MURDERERS OVER TO KAL?
IF I DO THAT, ZOR, I TURN MYSELF OVER. I WAS THE ONE WHO GAVE THEM AUTHORIZATION TO KILL IF NECESSARY.
WHAT?
MOTHER...?
TELL ME THAT'S NOT TRUE.
ALURA.
IT'S COMMANDER GOR.

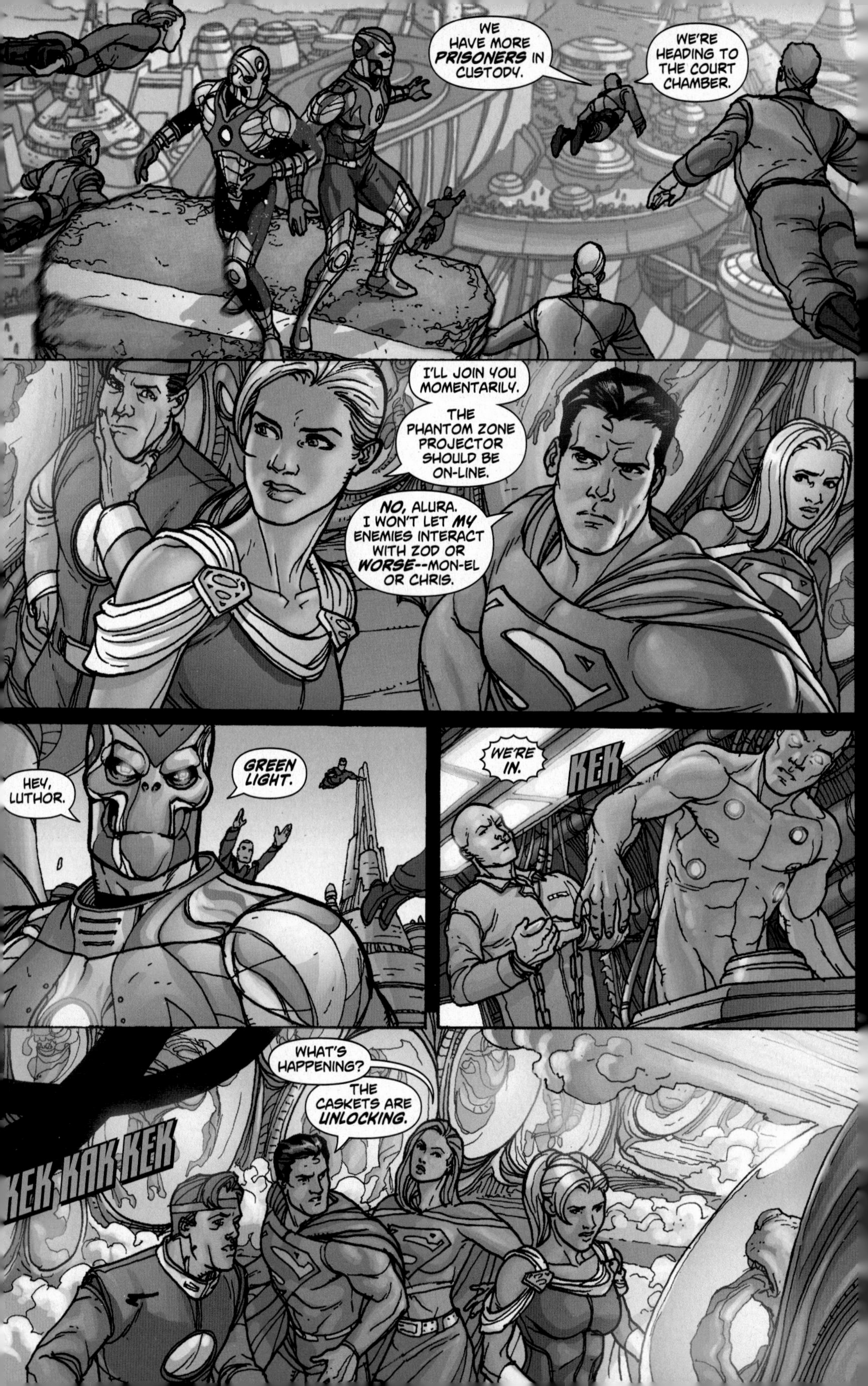
WE HAVE MORE PRISONERS IN CUSTODY.
WE'RE HEADING TO THE COURT CHAMBER.
I'LL JOIN YOU MOMENTARILY.
THE PHANTOM ZONE PROJECTOR SHOULD BE ON-LINE.
NO, ALURA. I WON'T LET MY ENEMIES INTERACT WITH ZOD OR WORSE--MON-EL OR CHRIS.
HEY, LUTHOR.
GREEN LIGHT.
WE'RE IN.
KEK
WHAT'S HAPPENING?
THE CASKETS ARE UNLOCKING.
KEK KAK KEK

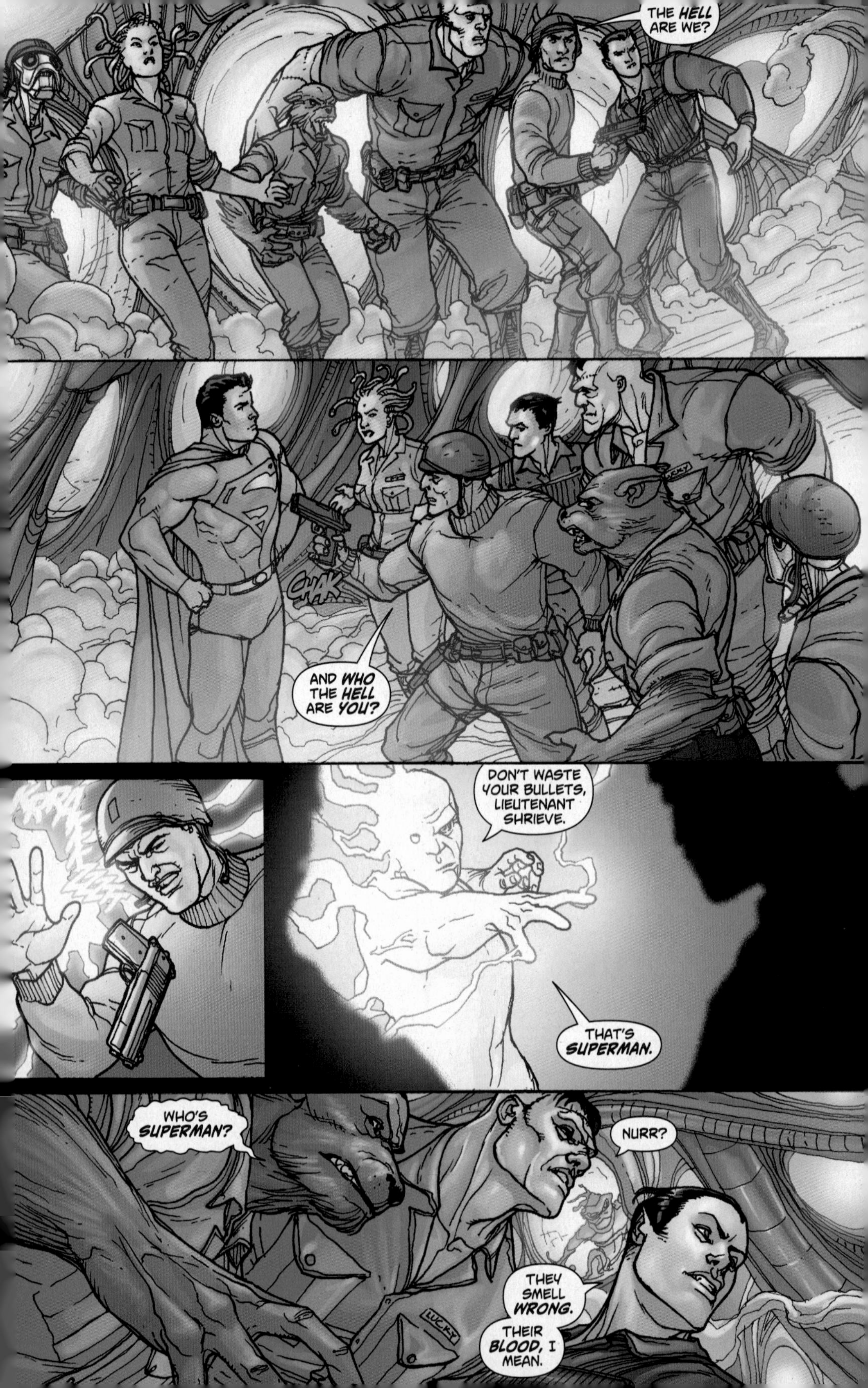
THE HELL ARE WE?
CHAK
AND WHO THE HELL ARE YOU?
DON'T WASTE YOUR BULLETS, LIEUTENANT SHRIEVE.
THAT'S SUPERMAN.
WHO'S SUPERMAN?
NURR?
THEY SMELL WRONG.
THEIR BLOOD, I MEAN.

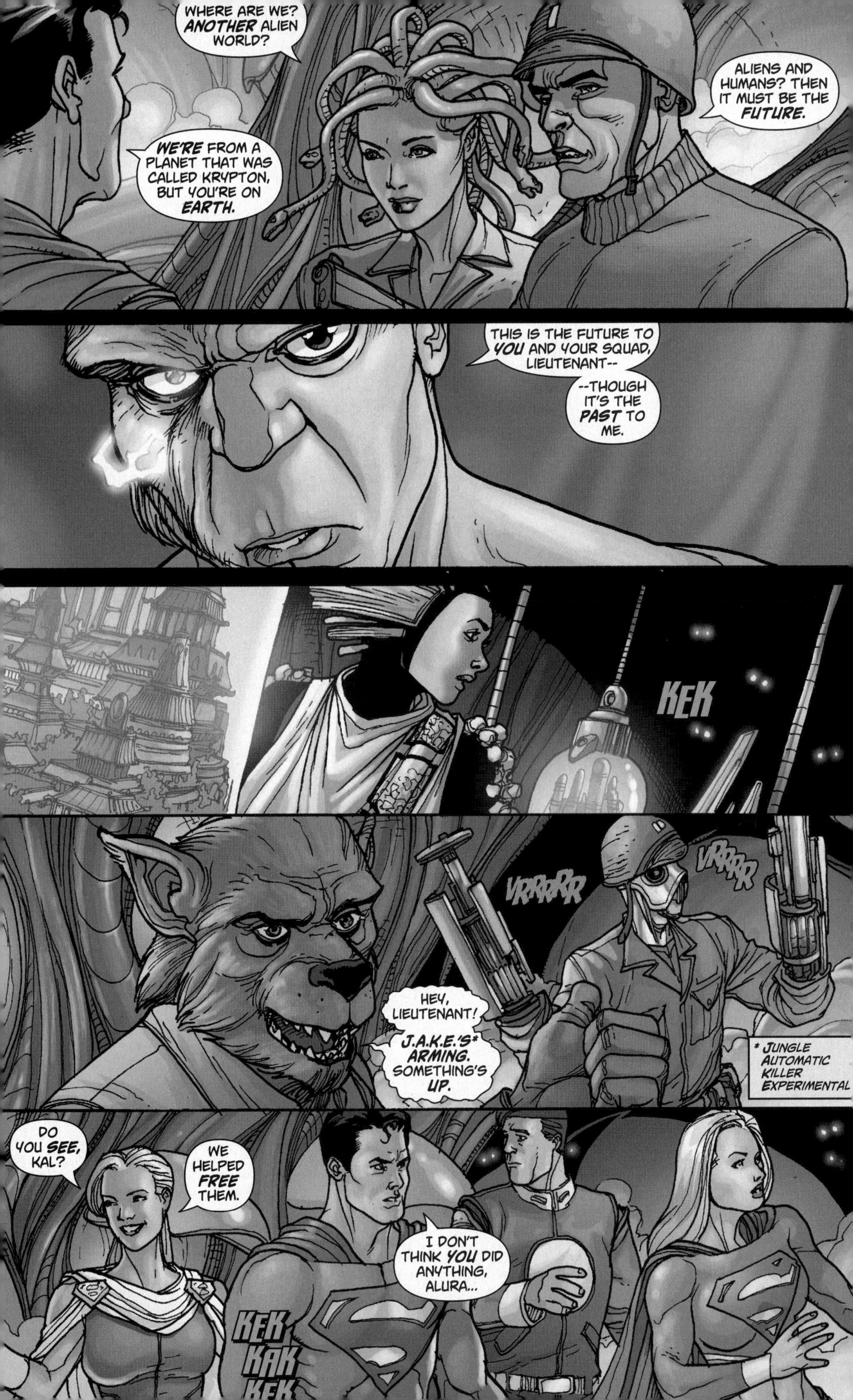
WHERE ARE WE? ANOTHER ALIEN WORLD?
WE'RE FROM A PLANET THAT WAS CALLED KRYPTON, BUT YOU'RE ON EARTH.
ALIENS AND HUMANS? THEN IT MUST BE THE FUTURE.
THIS IS THE FUTURE TO YOU AND YOUR SQUAD, LIEUTENANT--
--THOUGH IT'S THE PAST TO ME.
KEK
VRRRRR
VRRRR
HEY, LIEUTENANT!
J.A.K.E.'S* ARMING. SOMETHING'S UP.
* JUNGLE AUTOMATIC KILLER EXPERIMENTAL
DO YOU SEE, KAL?
WE HELPED FREE THEM.
I DON'T THINK YOU DID ANYTHING, ALURA...
KEK
KAK

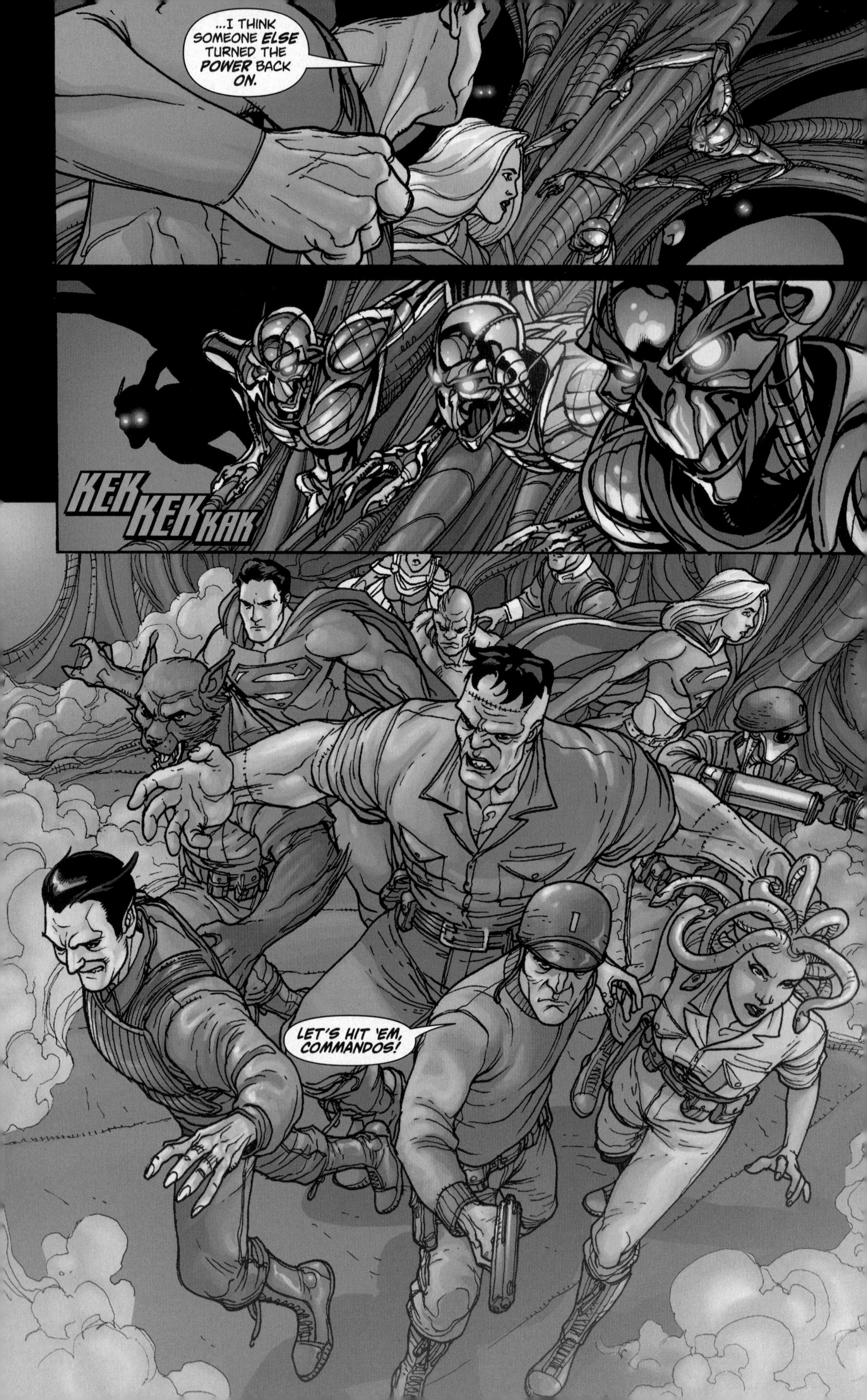
...I THINK SOMEONE ELSE TURNED THE POWER BACK ON.
KEK KEK KAK
LET'S HIT 'EM, COMMANDOS!

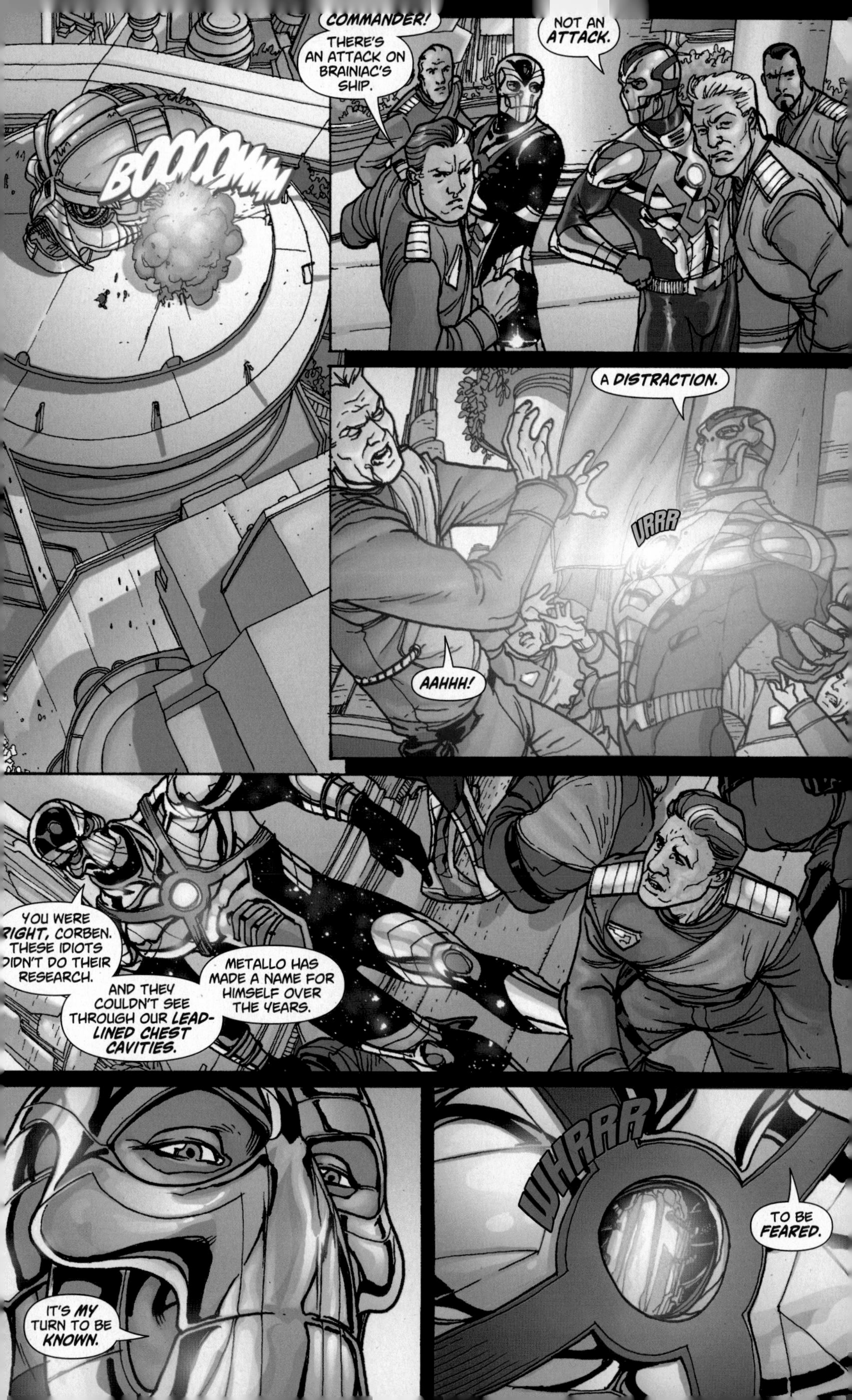
BOOOOOMM
COMMANDER! THERE'S AN ATTACK ON BRAINIAC'S SHIP.
NOT AN ATTACK.
A DISTRACTION.
URRR
AAHHH!
YOU WERE RIGHT, CORBEN. THESE IDIOTS DIDN'T DO THEIR RESEARCH.
AND THEY COULDN'T SEE THROUGH OUR LEAD-LINED CHEST CAVITIES.
METALLO HAS MADE A NAME FOR HIMSELF OVER THE YEARS.
IT'S MY TURN TO BE KNOWN.
WHRRR
TO BE FEARED.

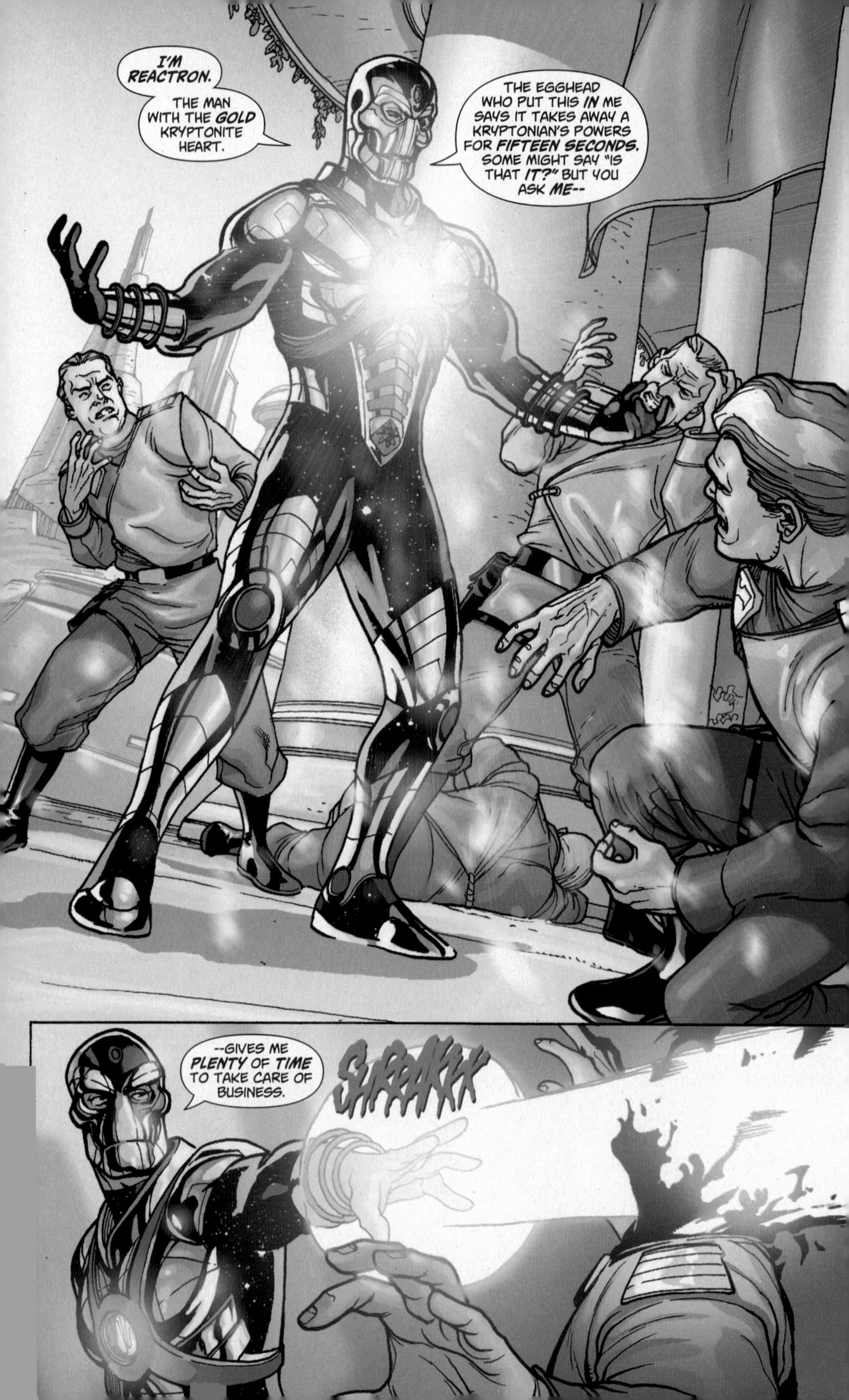
I'M REACTRON.
THE MAN WITH THE GOLD KRYPTONITE HEART.
THE EGGHEAD WHO PUT THIS IN ME SAYS IT TAKES AWAY A KRYPTONIAN'S POWERS FOR FIFTEEN SECONDS. SOME MIGHT SAY "IS THAT IT?" BUT YOU ASK ME--
--GIVES ME PLENTY OF TIME TO TAKE CARE OF BUSINESS.
SHRAKKK

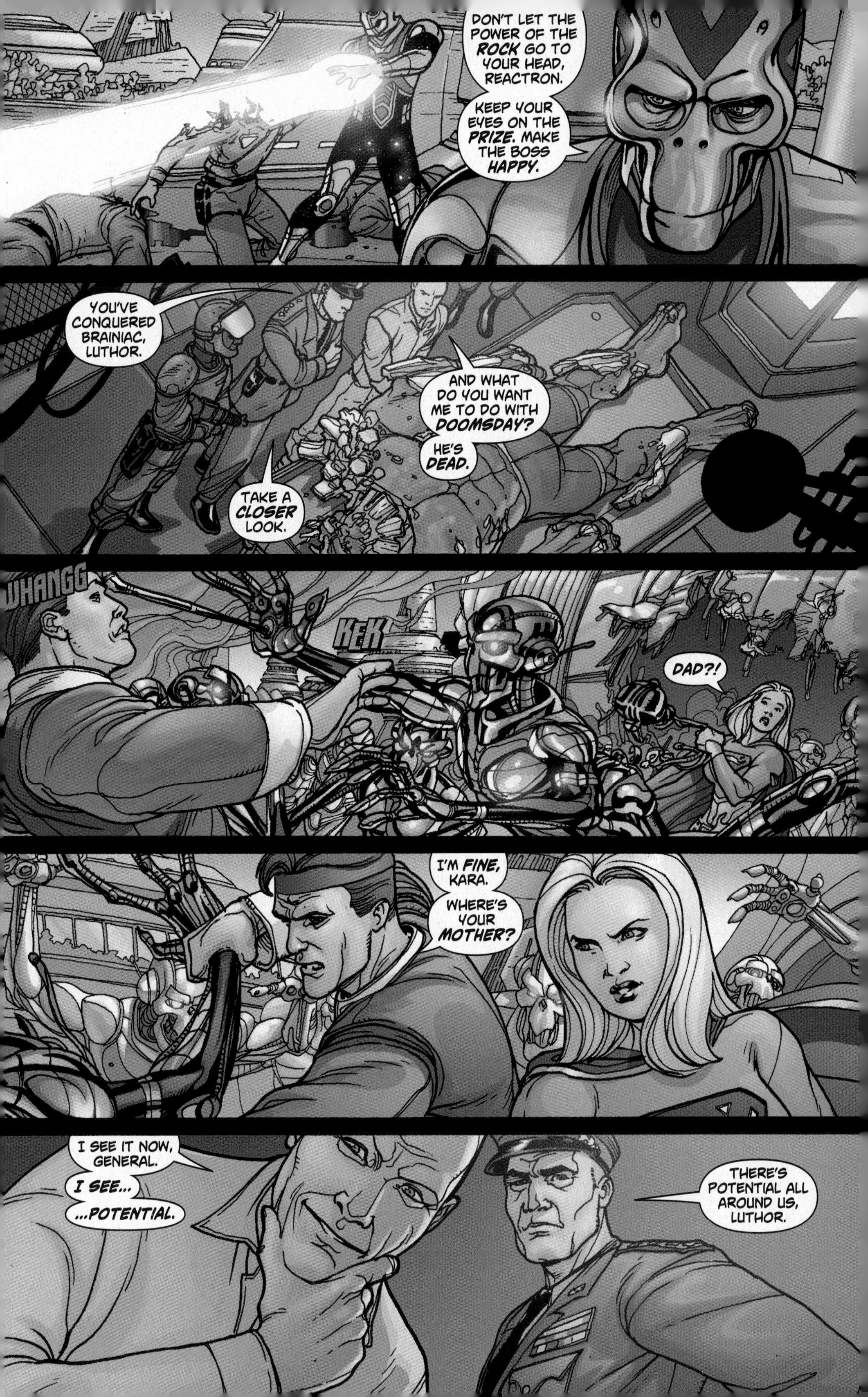
DON'T LET THE POWER OF THE ROCK GO TO YOUR HEAD, REACTRON.
KEEP YOUR EYES ON THE PRIZE. MAKE THE BOSS HAPPY.
YOU'VE CONQUERED BRAINIAC, LUTHOR.
AND WHAT DO YOU WANT ME TO DO WITH DOOMSDAY?
HE'S DEAD.
TAKE A CLOSER LOOK.
WHANGG
KEK
DAD?!
I'M FINE, KARA.
WHERE'S YOUR MOTHER?
I SEE IT NOW, GENERAL.
I SEE...
...POTENTIAL.
THERE'S POTENTIAL ALL AROUND US, LUTHOR.

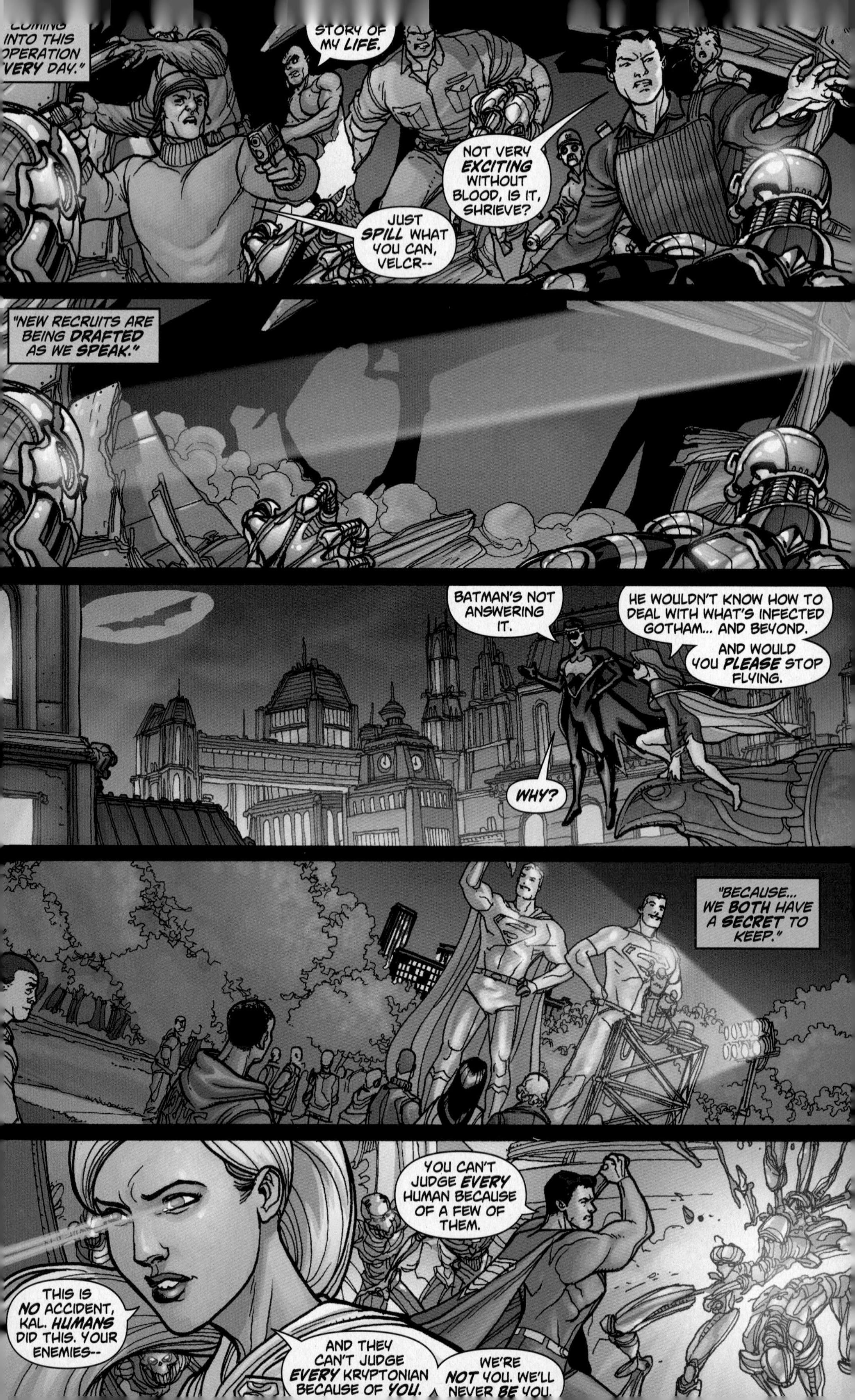
"COMING INTO THIS OPERATION EVERY DAY."
STORY OF MY LIFE.
NOT VERY EXCITING WITHOUT BLOOD, IS IT, SHRIEVE?
JUST SPILL WHAT YOU CAN, VELCR--
"NEW RECRUITS ARE BEING DRAFTED AS WE SPEAK."
BATMAN'S NOT ANSWERING IT.
HE WOULDN'T KNOW HOW TO DEAL WITH WHAT'S INFECTED GOTHAM... AND BEYOND.
AND WOULD YOU PLEASE STOP FLYING.
WHY?
"BECAUSE... WE BOTH HAVE A SECRET TO KEEP."
YOU CAN'T JUDGE EVERY HUMAN BECAUSE OF A FEW OF THEM.
THIS IS NO ACCIDENT, KAL. HUMANS DID THIS. YOUR ENEMIES--
AND THEY CAN'T JUDGE EVERY KRYPTONIAN BECAUSE OF YOU.
WE'RE NOT YOU. WE'LL NEVER BE YOU.

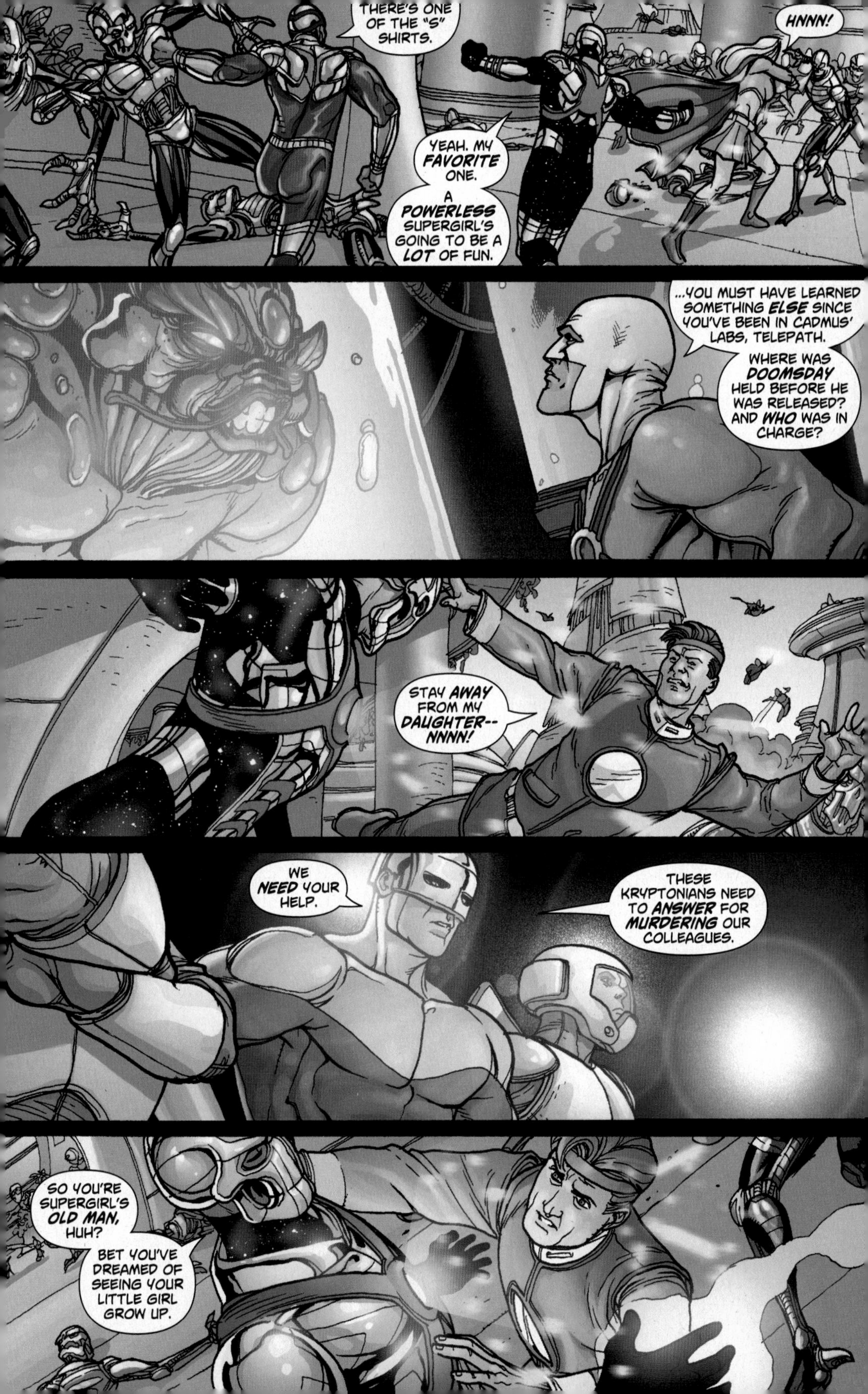
THERE'S ONE OF THE "S" SHIRTS.
YEAH. MY FAVORITE ONE.
A POWERLESS SUPERGIRL'S GOING TO BE A LOT OF FUN.
HNNN!
...YOU MUST HAVE LEARNED SOMETHING ELSE SINCE YOU'VE BEEN IN CADMUS' LABS, TELEPATH.
WHERE WAS DOOMSDAY HELD BEFORE HE WAS RELEASED? AND WHO WAS IN CHARGE?
STAY AWAY FROM MY DAUGHTER-- NNNN!
WE NEED YOUR HELP.
THESE KRYPTONIANS NEED TO ANSWER FOR MURDERING OUR COLLEAGUES.
SO YOU'RE SUPERGIRL'S OLD MAN, HUH?
BET YOU'VE DREAMED OF SEEING YOUR LITTLE GIRL GROW UP.

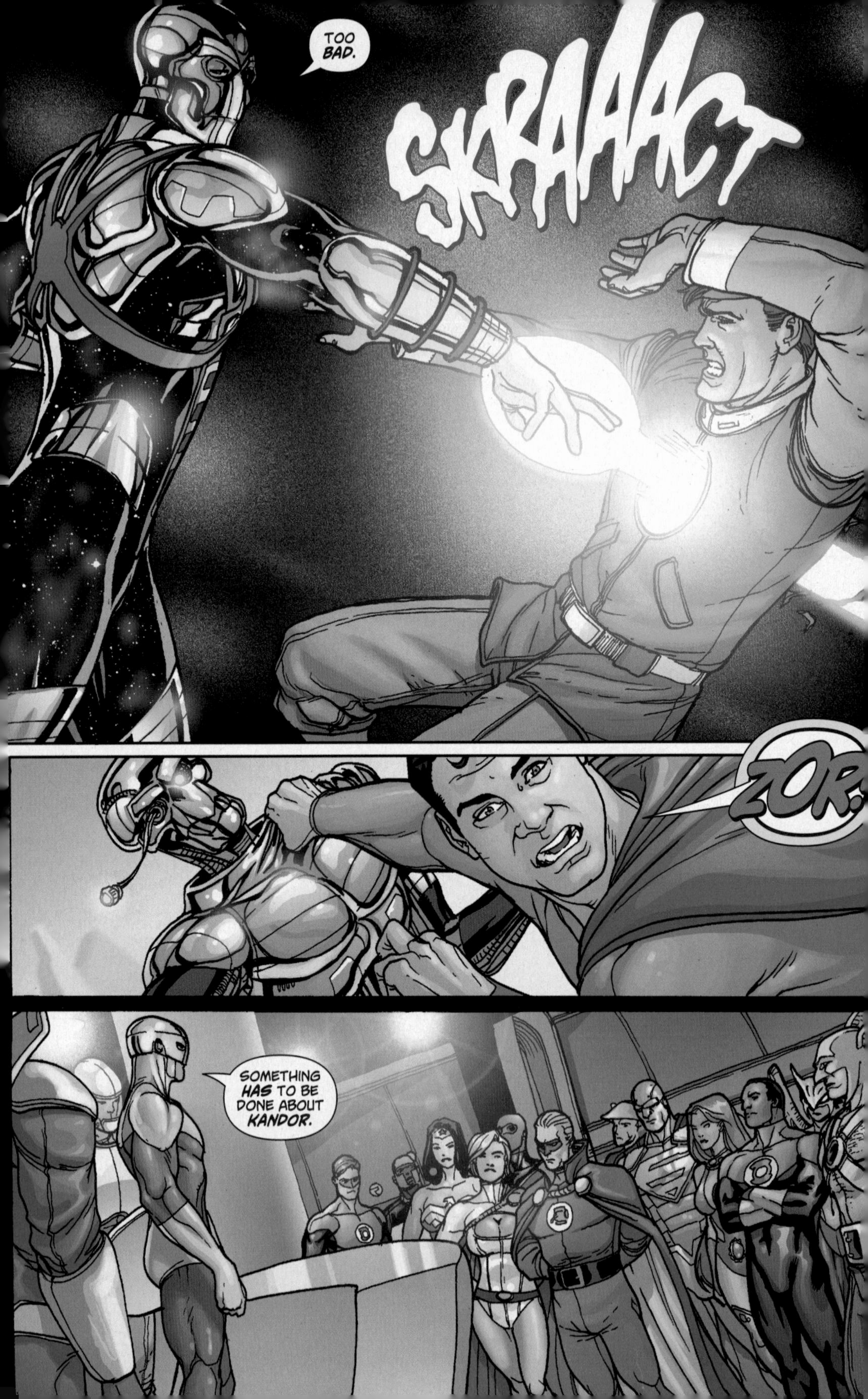
TOO BAD.
SKRAAACT
ZOR!
SOMETHING *HAS* TO BE DONE ABOUT *KANDOR*.

<DEATH IN THE HOUSE OF EL> SUPERGIRL 36 COVER ART BY **JOSHUA MIDDLETON**

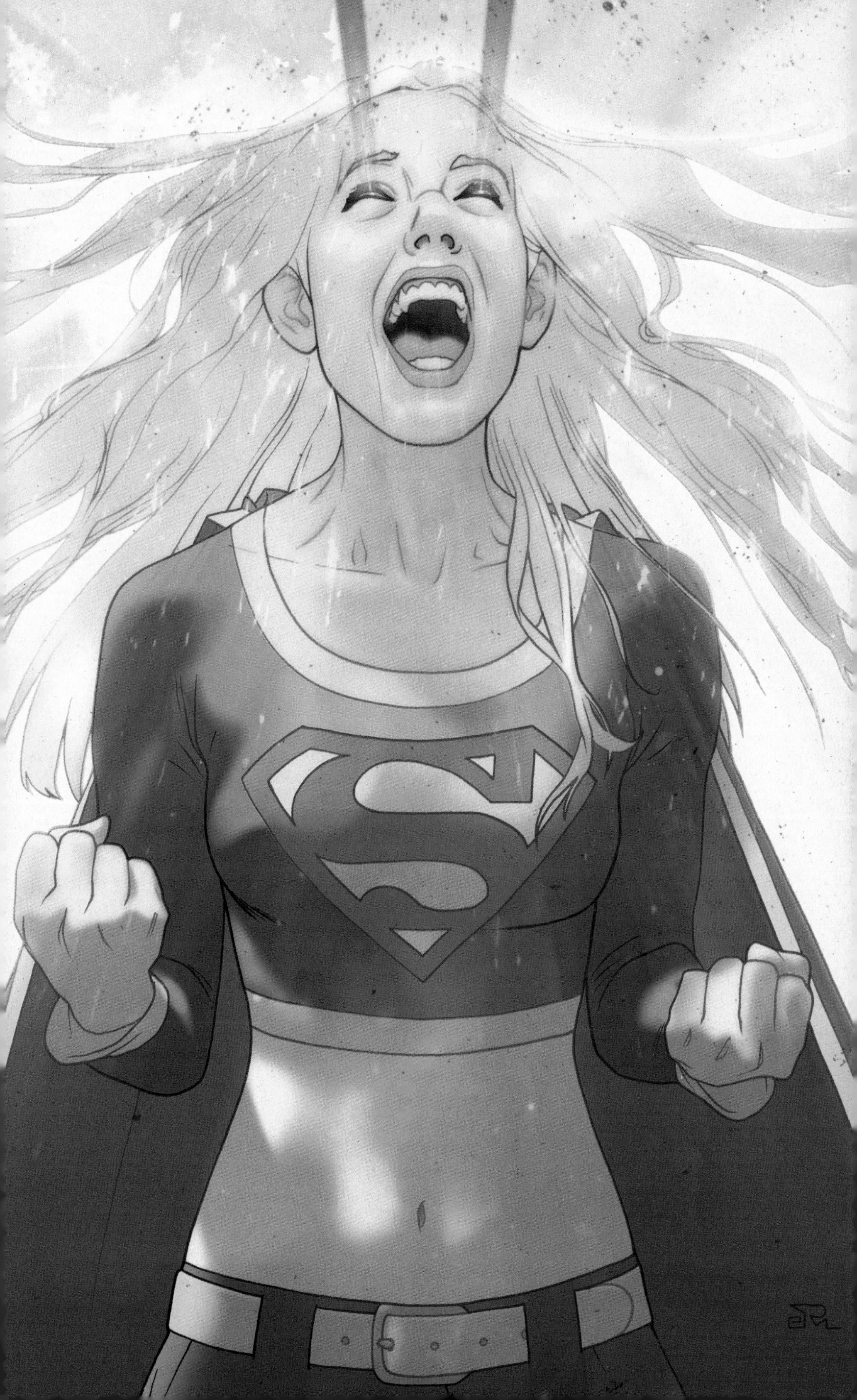

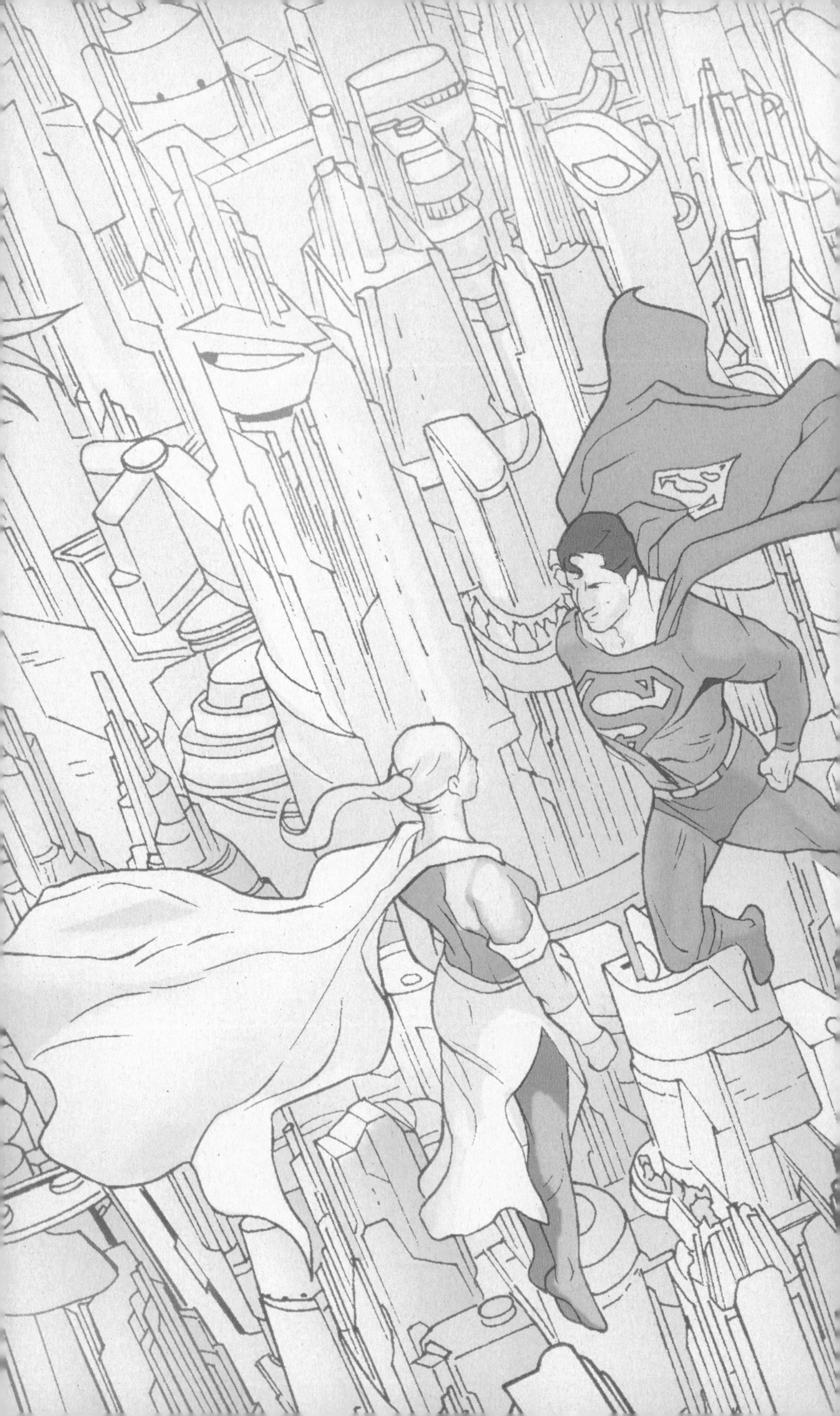

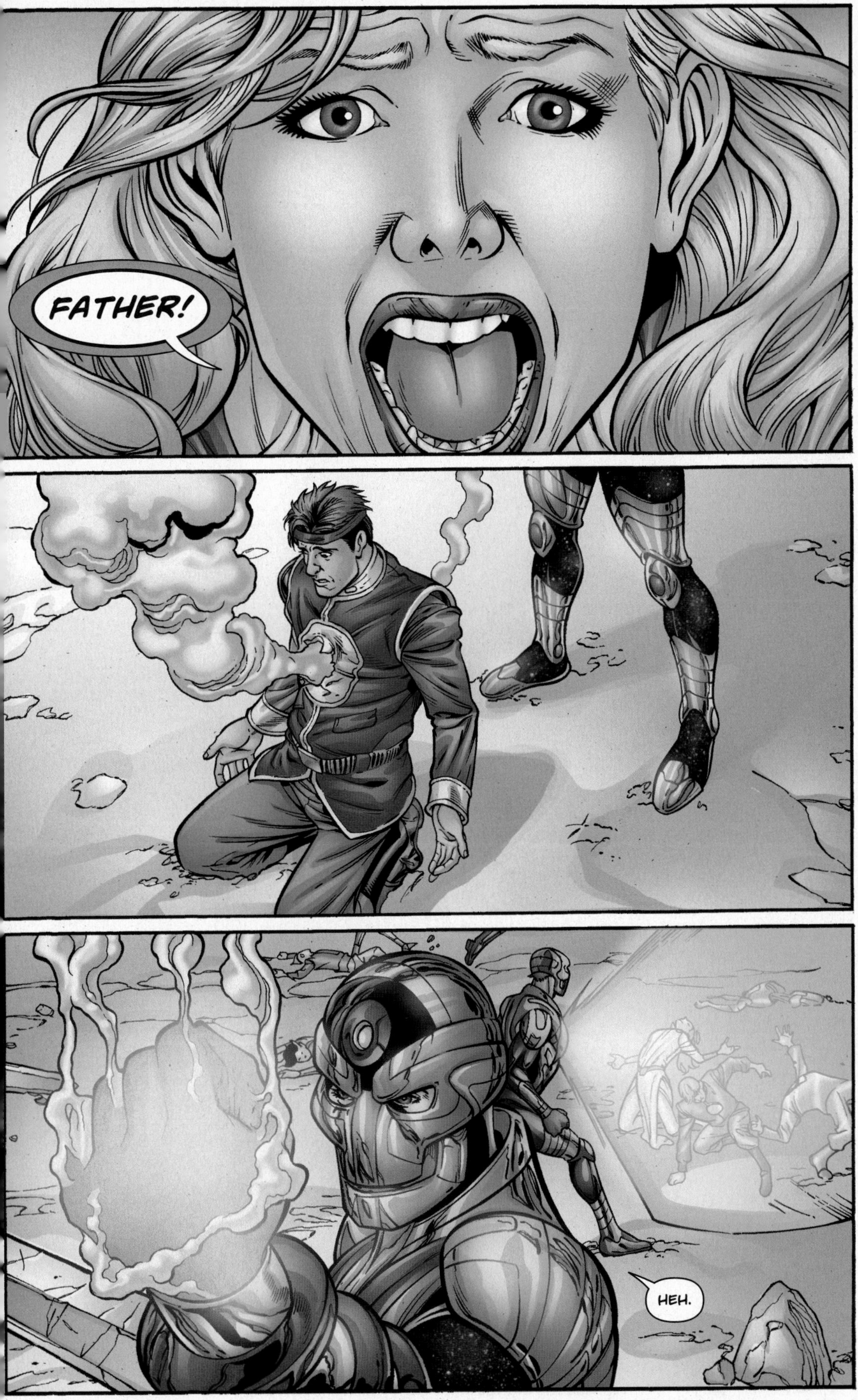
FATHER!
HEH.

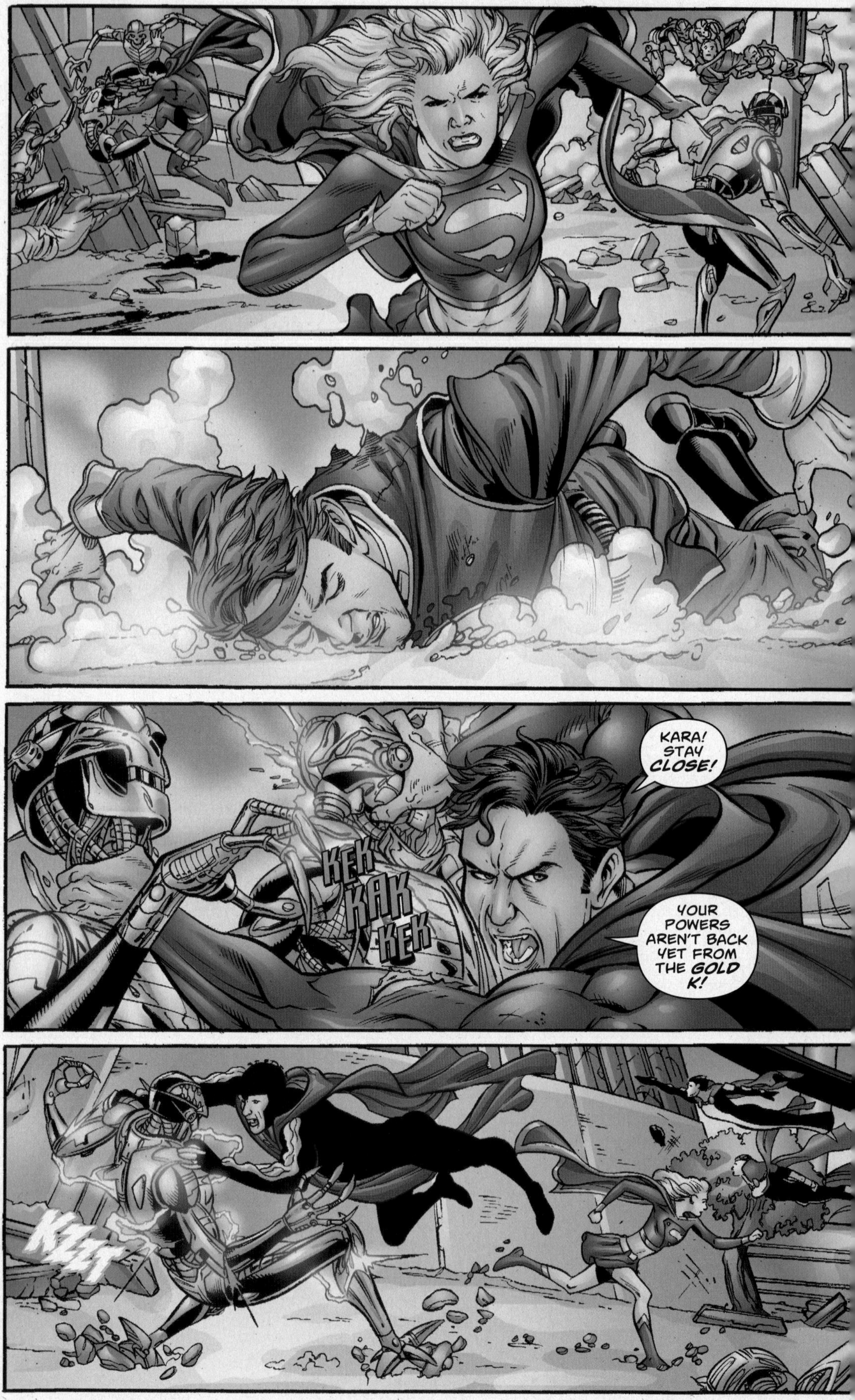
KARA! STAY CLOSE!
YOUR POWERS AREN'T BACK YET FROM THE GOLD K!
KEK KAK KEK
KZZZT

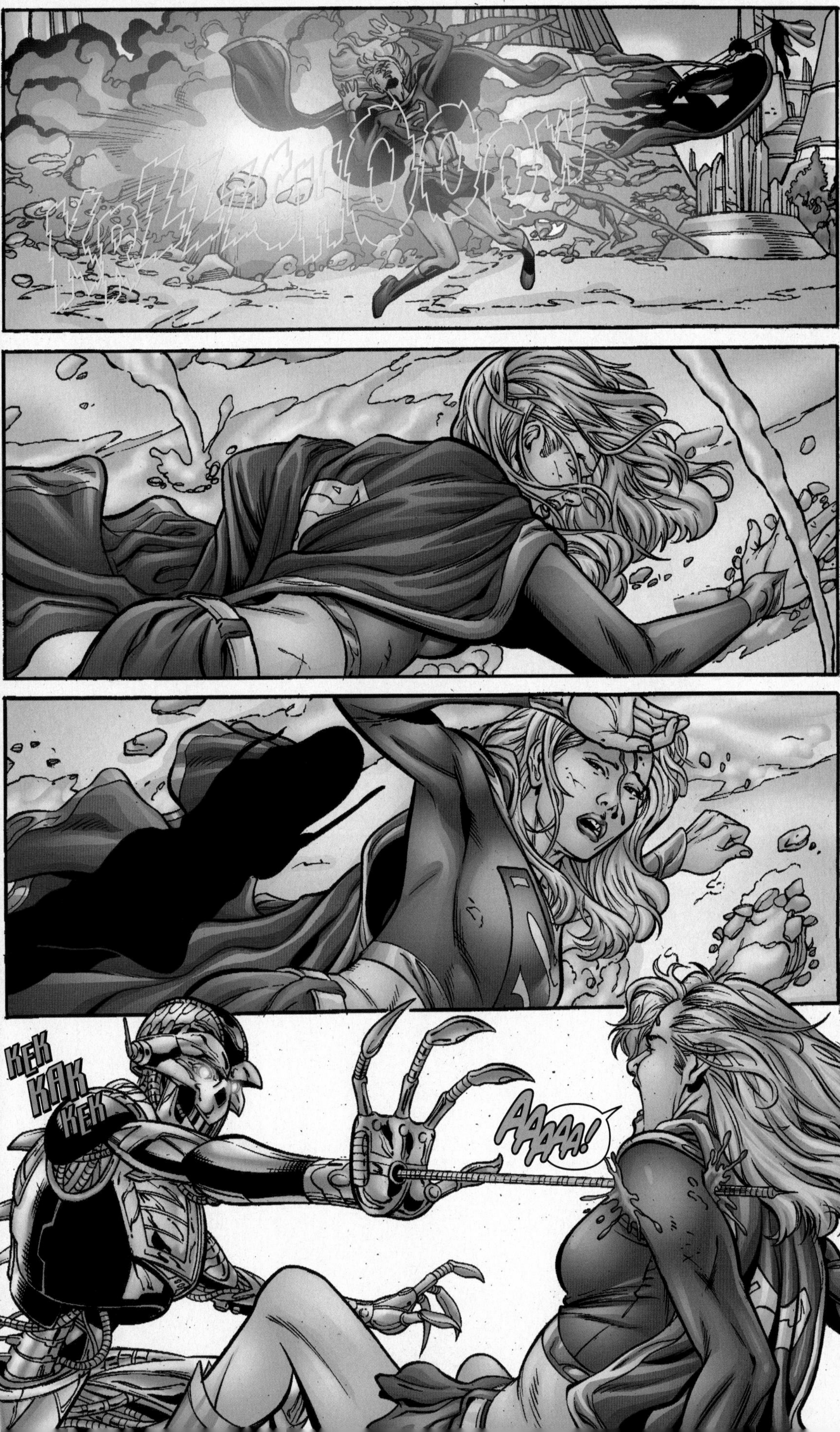
KEK
KAK
KEK
AAAAA!

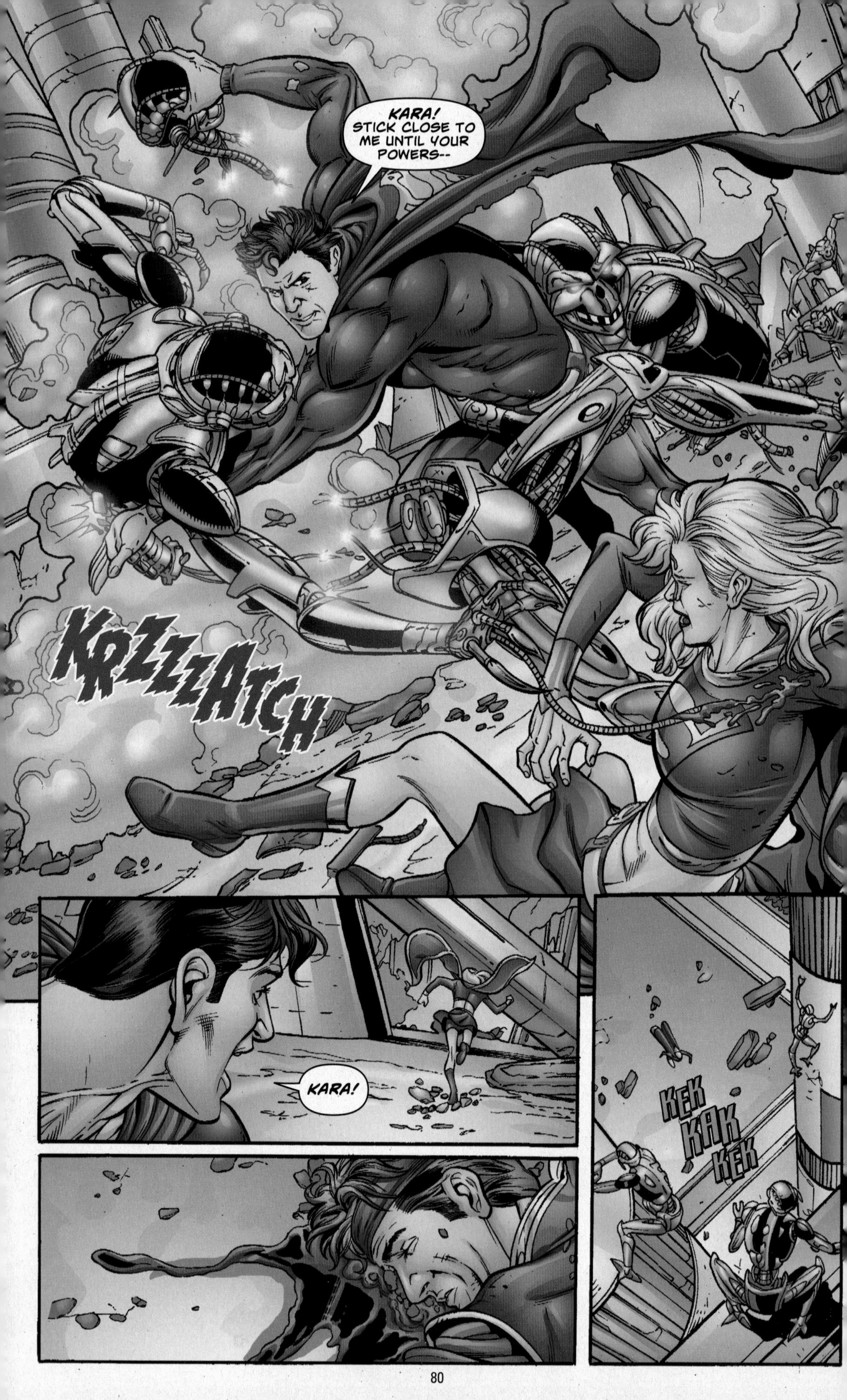
KARA! STICK CLOSE TO ME UNTIL YOUR POWERS--
KRZZZZATCH
KARA!
KEK KAK KEK

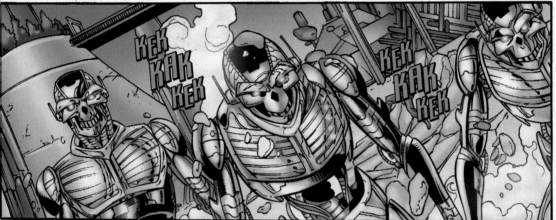

KEK KAK KEK

KEK KAK KEK

FZZ

MOVE.

KEK KA—

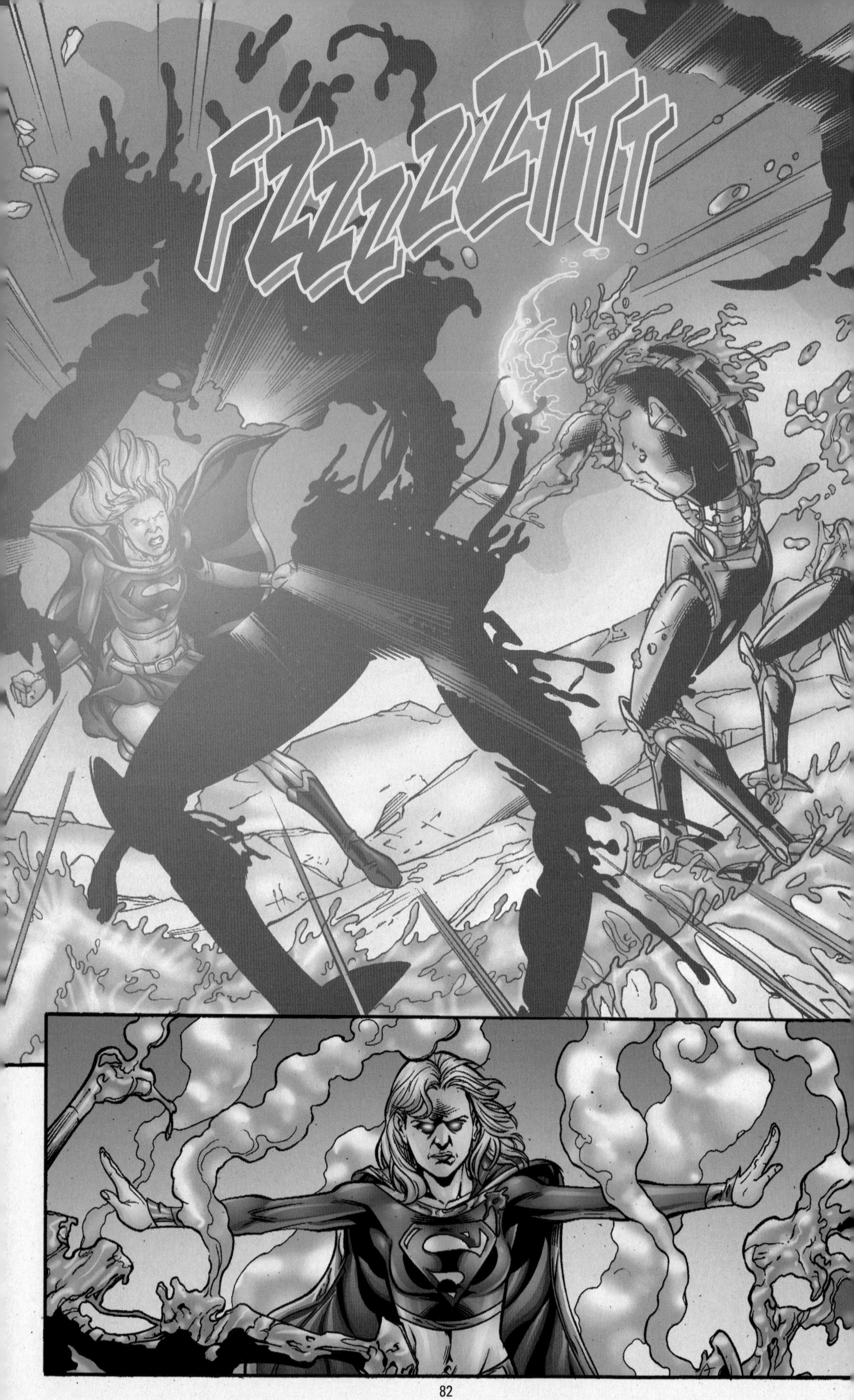
FZZZZZTTT

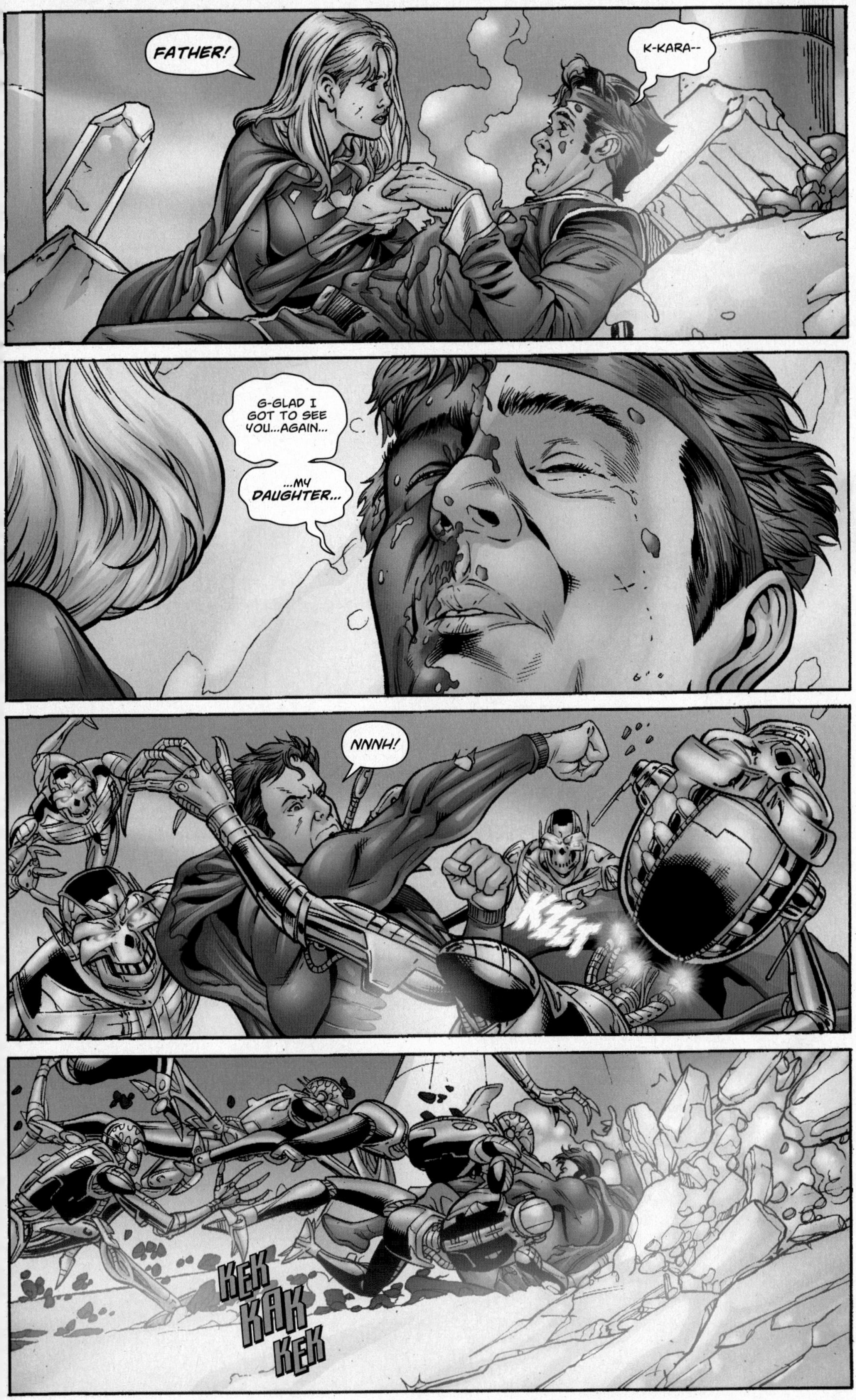
FATHER!
K-KARA--
G-GLAD I GOT TO SEE YOU...AGAIN...
...MY DAUGHTER...
NNNH!
KZZT
KEK KAK KEK

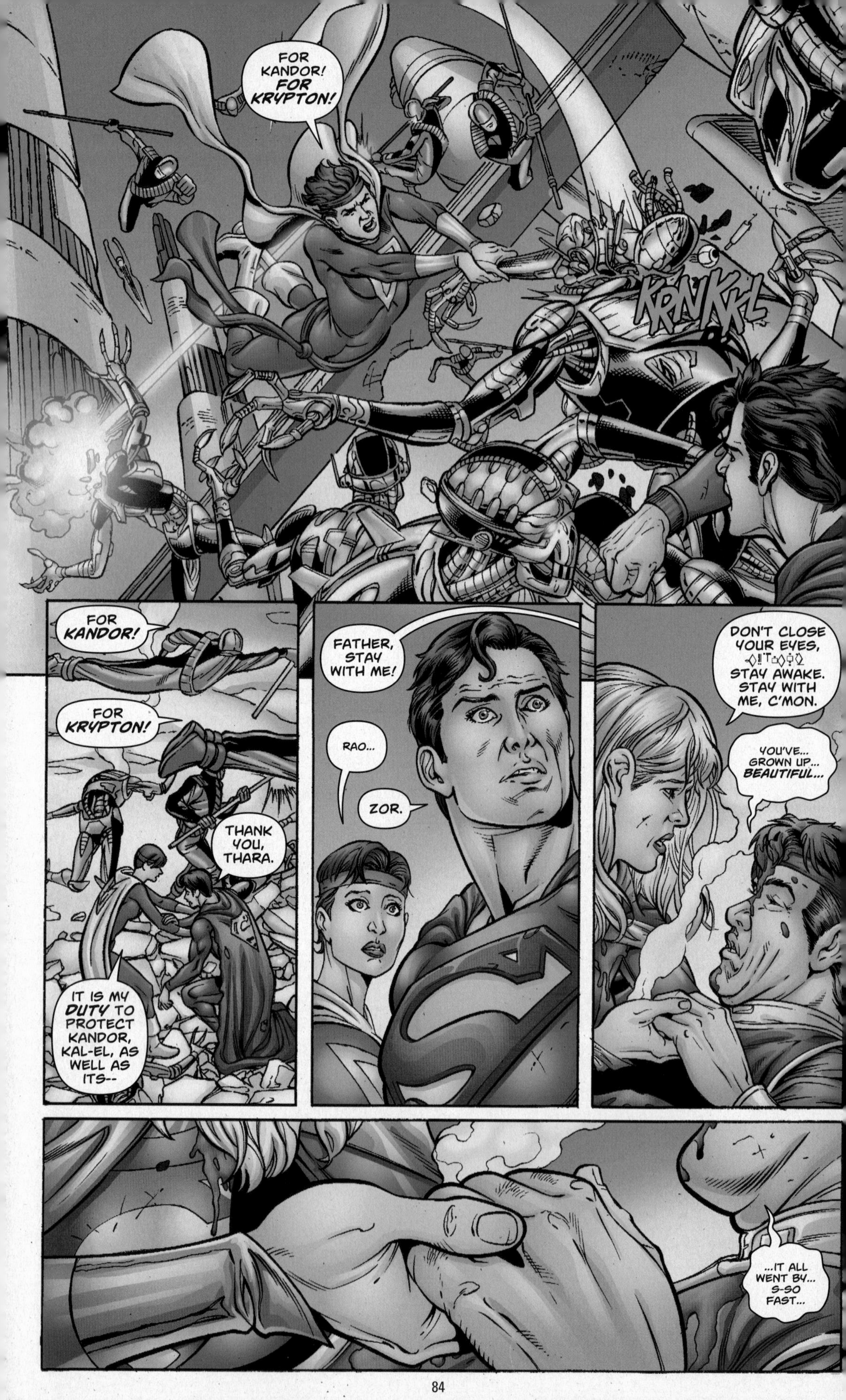
FOR KANDOR! FOR KRYPTON!
KRNKKL
FOR KANDOR!
FOR KRYPTON!
THANK YOU, THARA.
IT IS MY DUTY TO PROTECT KANDOR, KAL-EL, AS WELL AS ITS--
FATHER, STAY WITH ME!
RAO...
ZOR.
DON'T CLOSE YOUR EYES,
STAY AWAKE. STAY WITH ME, C'MON.
YOU'VE... GROWN UP... BEAUTIFUL...
...IT ALL WENT BY... S-SO FAST...

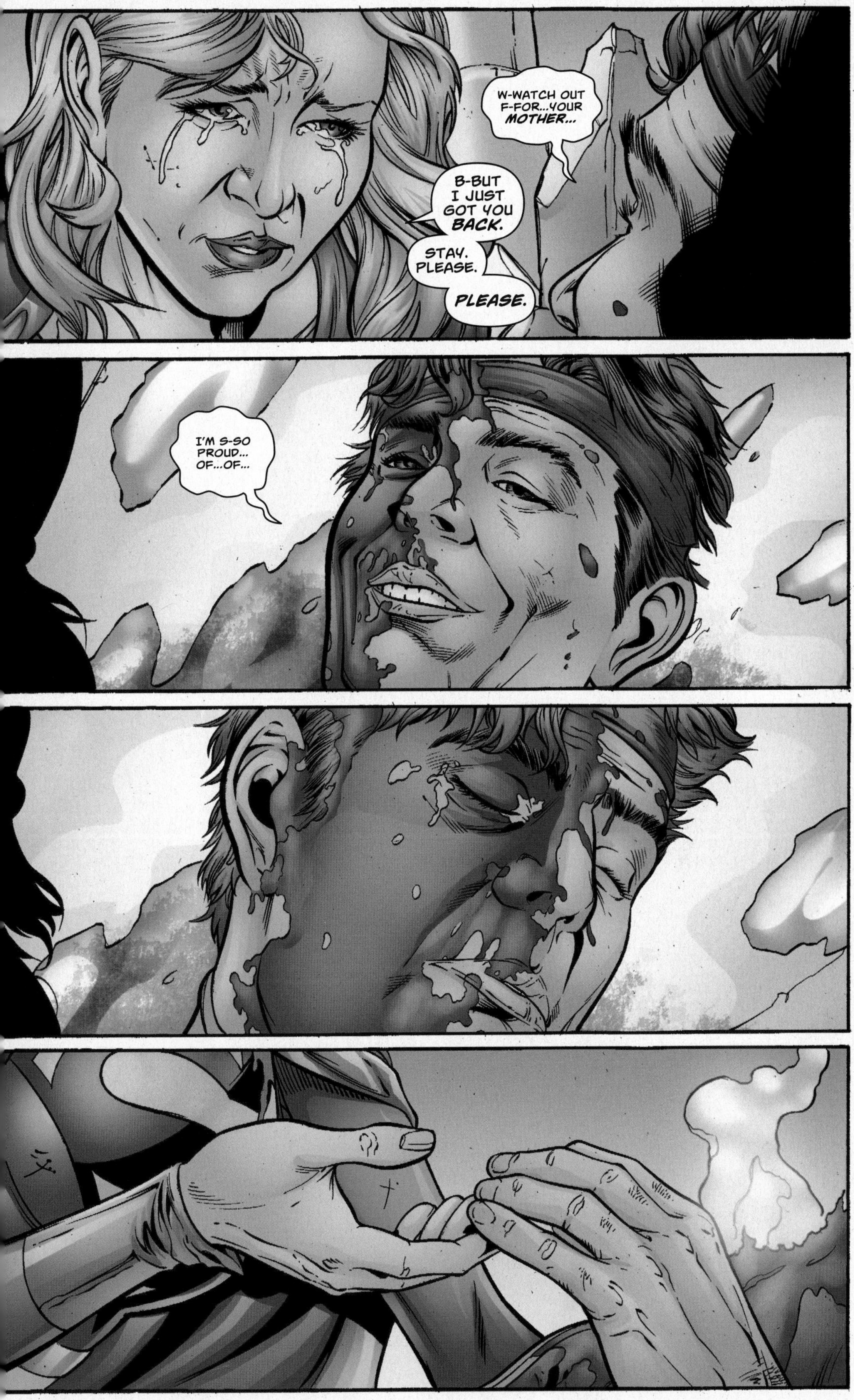
W-WATCH OUT F-FOR...YOUR MOTHER...
B-BUT I JUST GOT YOU BACK.
STAY. PLEASE.
PLEASE.
I'M S-SO PROUD... OF...OF...

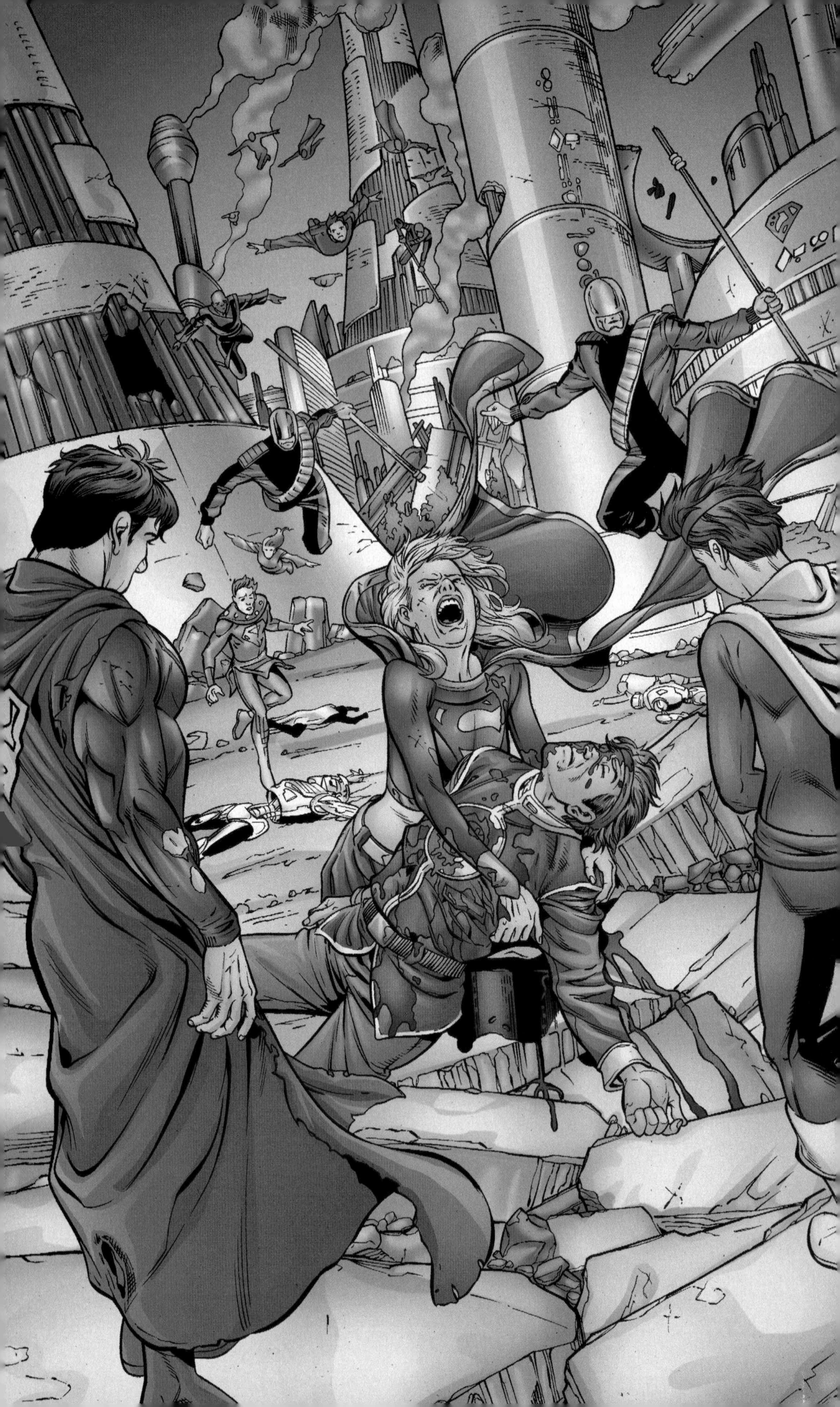

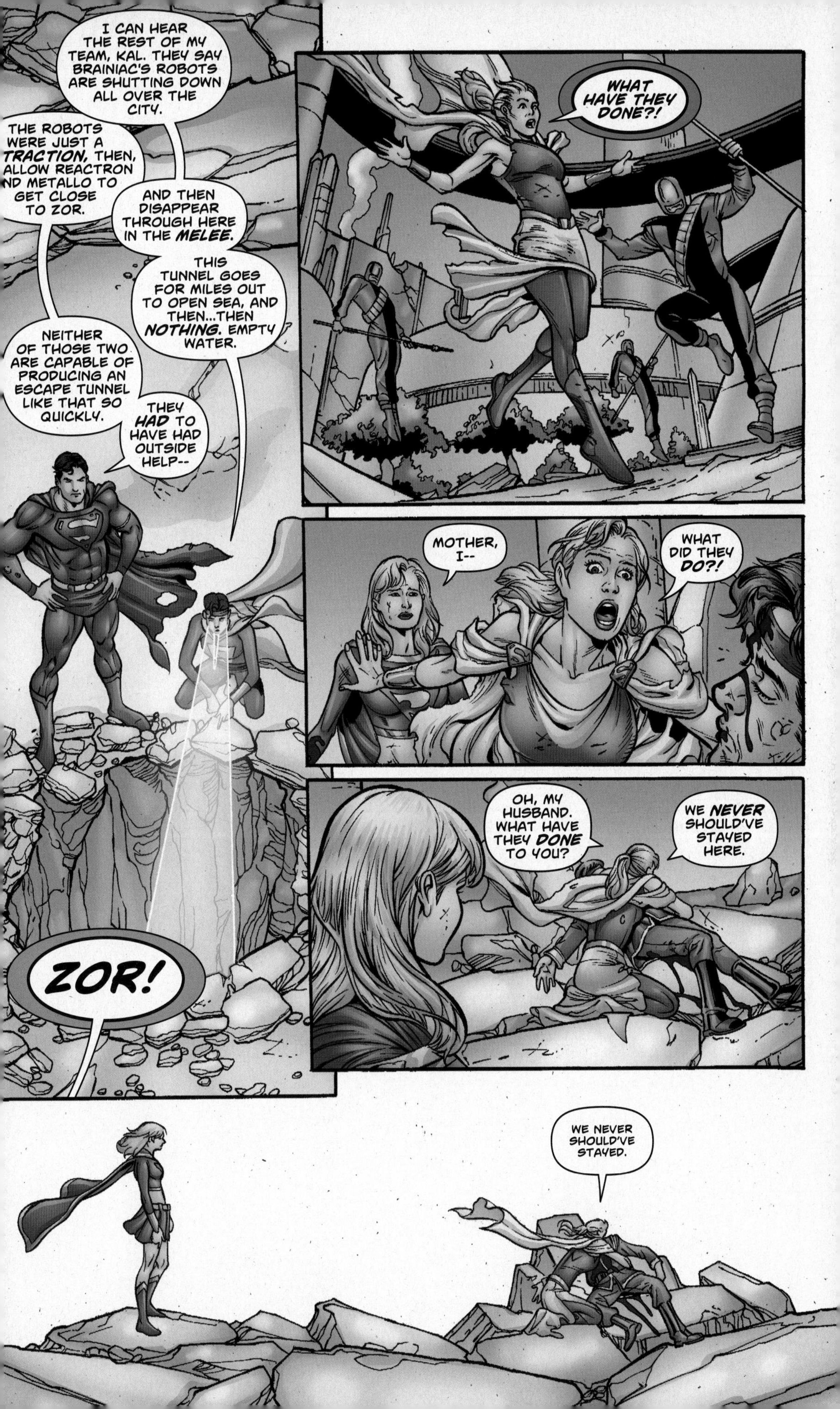

I CAN HEAR THE REST OF MY TEAM, KAL. THEY SAY BRAINIAC'S ROBOTS ARE SHUTTING DOWN ALL OVER THE CITY.
THE ROBOTS WERE JUST A TRACTION, THEN, ALLOW REACTRON ND METALLO TO GET CLOSE TO ZOR.
AND THEN DISAPPEAR THROUGH HERE IN THE MELEE.
THIS TUNNEL GOES FOR MILES OUT TO OPEN SEA, AND THEN...THEN NOTHING. EMPTY WATER.
NEITHER OF THOSE TWO ARE CAPABLE OF PRODUCING AN ESCAPE TUNNEL LIKE THAT SO QUICKLY.
THEY HAD TO HAVE HAD OUTSIDE HELP--
ZOR!
WHAT HAVE THEY DONE?!
MOTHER, I--
WHAT DID THEY DO?!
OH, MY HUSBAND. WHAT HAVE THEY DONE TO YOU?
WE NEVER SHOULD'VE STAYED HERE.
WE NEVER SHOULD'VE STAYED.

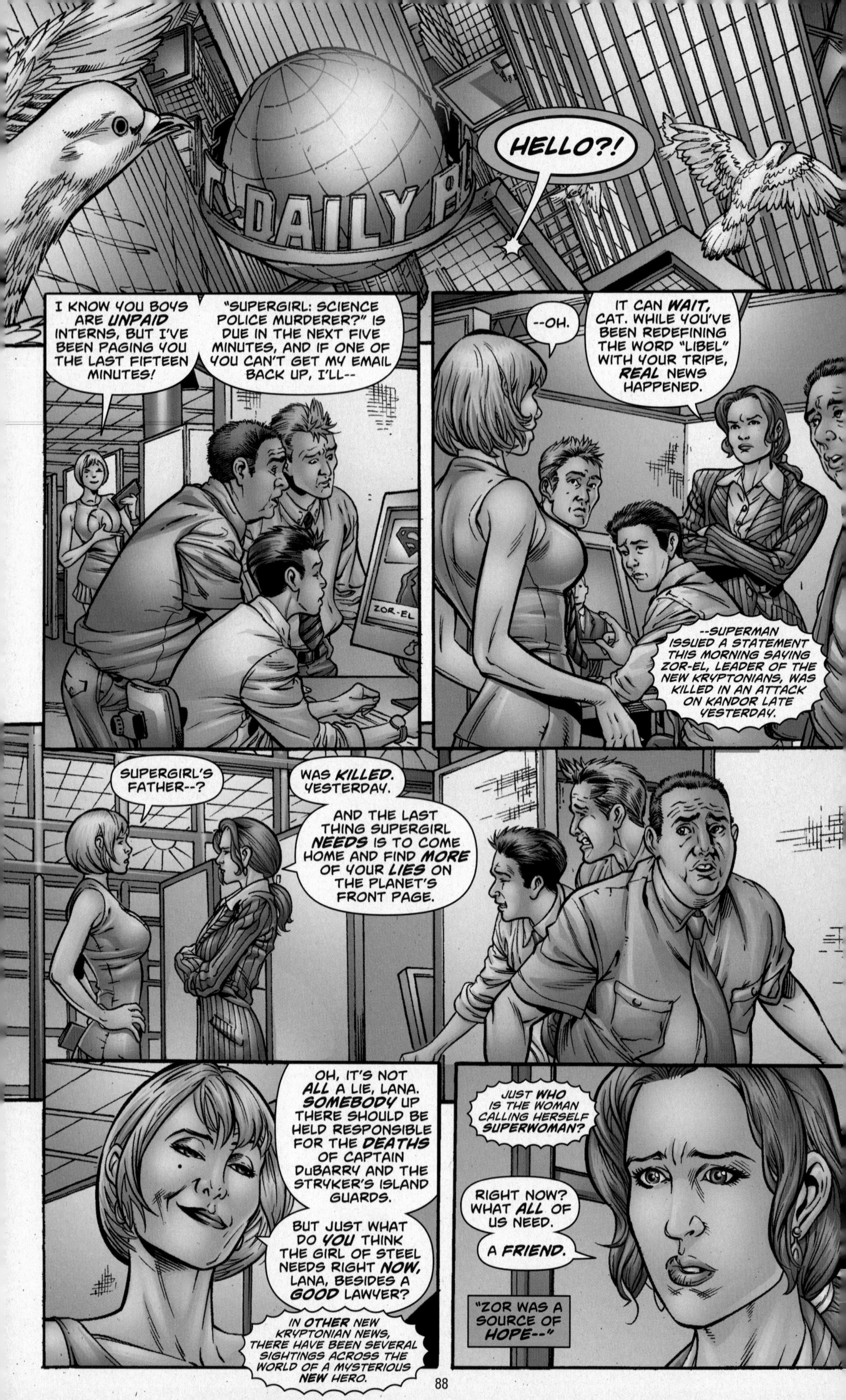
DAILY
HELLO?!
I KNOW YOU BOYS ARE UNPAID INTERNS, BUT I'VE BEEN PAGING YOU THE LAST FIFTEEN MINUTES!
"SUPERGIRL: SCIENCE POLICE MURDERER?" IS DUE IN THE NEXT FIVE MINUTES, AND IF ONE OF YOU CAN'T GET MY EMAIL BACK UP, I'LL--
ZOR-EL
--OH.
IT CAN WAIT, CAT. WHILE YOU'VE BEEN REDEFINING THE WORD "LIBEL" WITH YOUR TRIPE, REAL NEWS HAPPENED.
--SUPERMAN ISSUED A STATEMENT THIS MORNING SAYING ZOR-EL, LEADER OF THE NEW KRYPTONIANS, WAS KILLED IN AN ATTACK ON KANDOR LATE YESTERDAY.
SUPERGIRL'S FATHER--?
WAS KILLED. YESTERDAY.
AND THE LAST THING SUPERGIRL NEEDS IS TO COME HOME AND FIND MORE OF YOUR LIES ON THE PLANET'S FRONT PAGE.
OH, IT'S NOT ALL A LIE, LANA. SOMEBODY UP THERE SHOULD BE HELD RESPONSIBLE FOR THE DEATHS OF CAPTAIN DuBARRY AND THE STRYKER'S ISLAND GUARDS.
BUT JUST WHAT DO YOU THINK THE GIRL OF STEEL NEEDS RIGHT NOW, LANA, BESIDES A GOOD LAWYER?
IN OTHER NEW KRYPTONIAN NEWS, THERE HAVE BEEN SEVERAL SIGHTINGS ACROSS THE WORLD OF A MYSTERIOUS NEW HERO.
JUST WHO IS THE WOMAN CALLING HERSELF SUPERWOMAN?
RIGHT NOW? WHAT ALL OF US NEED.
A FRIEND.
"ZOR WAS A SOURCE OF HOPE--"

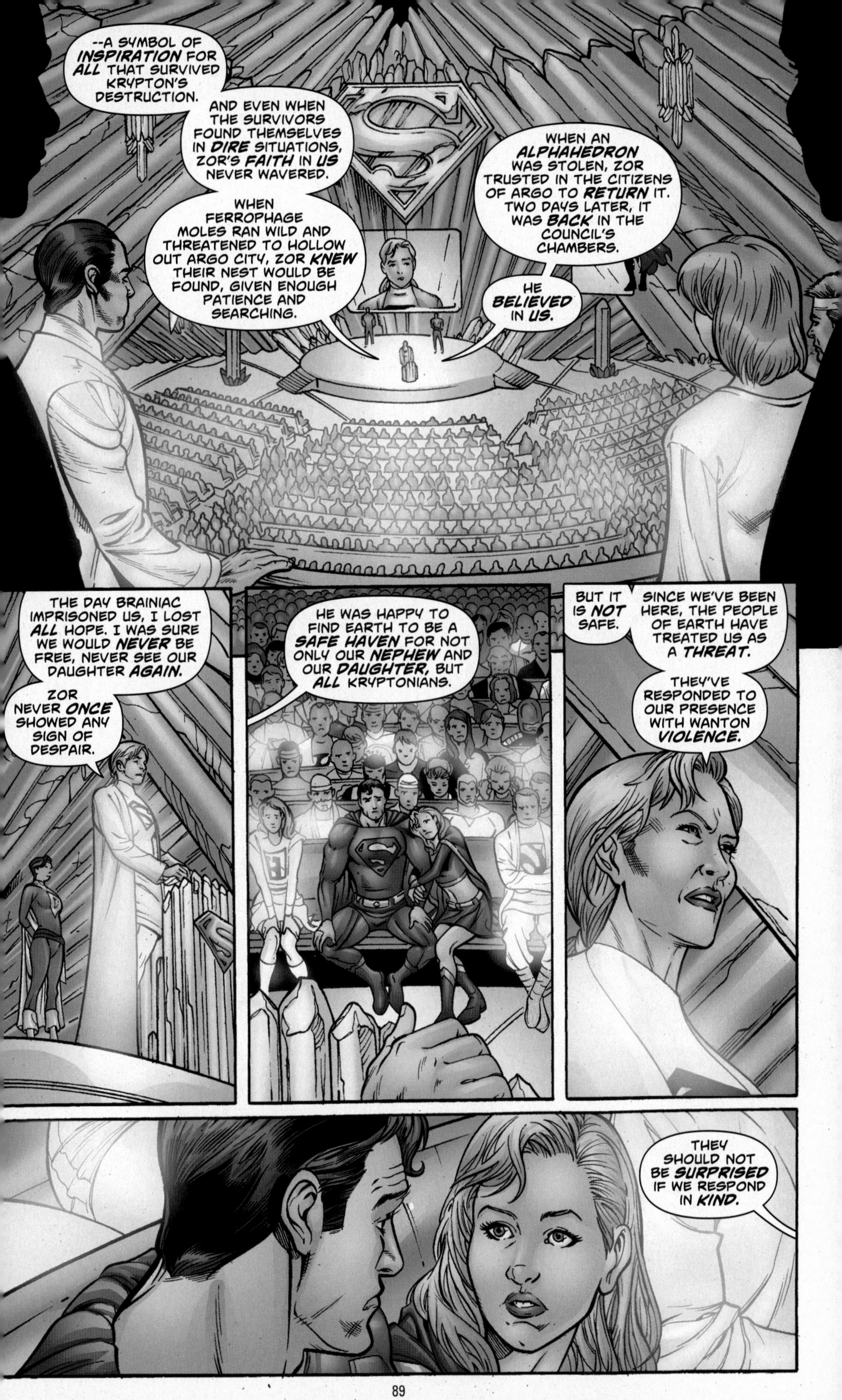
--A SYMBOL OF INSPIRATION FOR ALL THAT SURVIVED KRYPTON'S DESTRUCTION.
AND EVEN WHEN THE SURVIVORS FOUND THEMSELVES IN DIRE SITUATIONS, ZOR'S FAITH IN US NEVER WAVERED.
WHEN FERROPHAGE MOLES RAN WILD AND THREATENED TO HOLLOW OUT ARGO CITY, ZOR KNEW THEIR NEST WOULD BE FOUND, GIVEN ENOUGH PATIENCE AND SEARCHING.
WHEN AN ALPHAHEDRON WAS STOLEN, ZOR TRUSTED IN THE CITIZENS OF ARGO TO RETURN IT. TWO DAYS LATER, IT WAS BACK IN THE COUNCIL'S CHAMBERS.
HE BELIEVED IN US.
THE DAY BRAINIAC IMPRISONED US, I LOST ALL HOPE. I WAS SURE WE WOULD NEVER BE FREE, NEVER SEE OUR DAUGHTER AGAIN.
ZOR NEVER ONCE SHOWED ANY SIGN OF DESPAIR.
HE WAS HAPPY TO FIND EARTH TO BE A SAFE HAVEN FOR NOT ONLY OUR NEPHEW AND OUR DAUGHTER, BUT ALL KRYPTONIANS.
BUT IT IS NOT SAFE.
SINCE WE'VE BEEN HERE, THE PEOPLE OF EARTH HAVE TREATED US AS A THREAT.
THEY'VE RESPONDED TO OUR PRESENCE WITH WANTON VIOLENCE.
THEY SHOULD NOT BE SURPRISED IF WE RESPOND IN KIND.

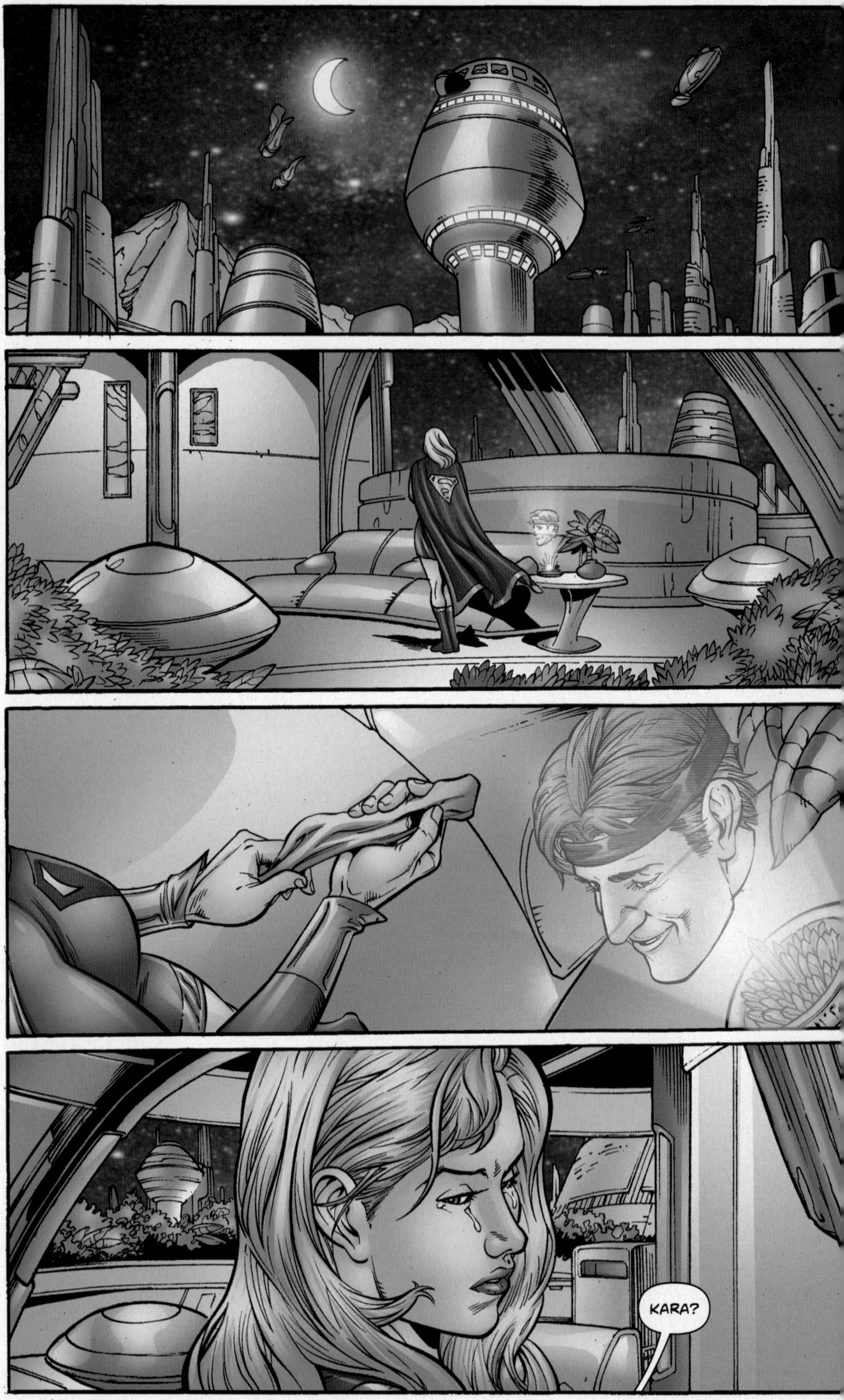
KARA?

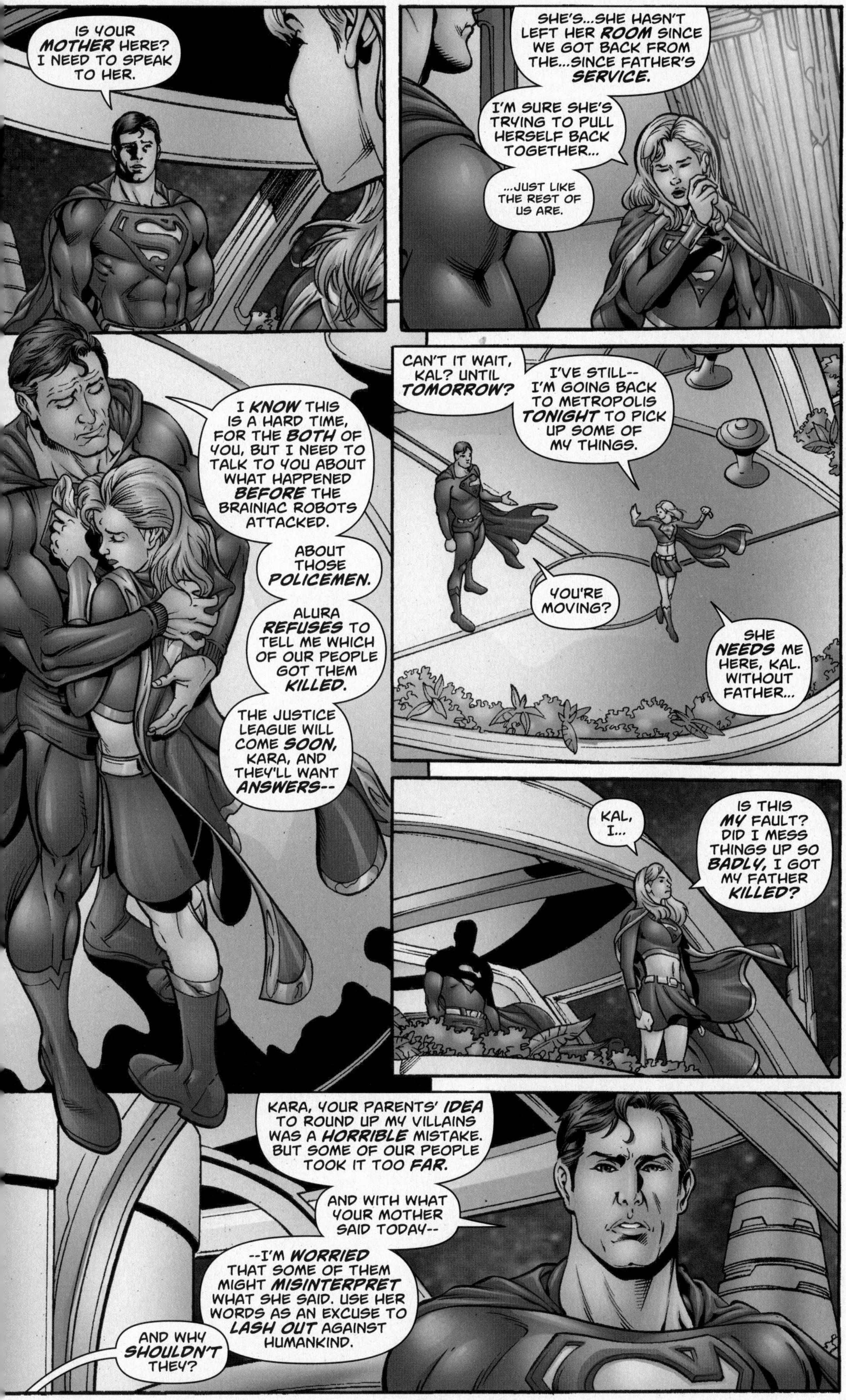
IS YOUR MOTHER HERE? I NEED TO SPEAK TO HER.
SHE'S...SHE HASN'T LEFT HER ROOM SINCE WE GOT BACK FROM THE...SINCE FATHER'S SERVICE.
I'M SURE SHE'S TRYING TO PULL HERSELF BACK TOGETHER...
...JUST LIKE THE REST OF US ARE.
I KNOW THIS IS A HARD TIME, FOR THE BOTH OF YOU, BUT I NEED TO TALK TO YOU ABOUT WHAT HAPPENED BEFORE THE BRAINIAC ROBOTS ATTACKED.
ABOUT THOSE POLICEMEN.
ALURA REFUSES TO TELL ME WHICH OF OUR PEOPLE GOT THEM KILLED.
THE JUSTICE LEAGUE WILL COME SOON, KARA, AND THEY'LL WANT ANSWERS--
CAN'T IT WAIT, KAL? UNTIL TOMORROW?
I'VE STILL-- I'M GOING BACK TO METROPOLIS TONIGHT TO PICK UP SOME OF MY THINGS.
YOU'RE MOVING?
SHE NEEDS ME HERE, KAL. WITHOUT FATHER...
KAL, I...
IS THIS MY FAULT? DID I MESS THINGS UP SO BADLY, I GOT MY FATHER KILLED?
KARA, YOUR PARENTS' IDEA TO ROUND UP MY VILLAINS WAS A HORRIBLE MISTAKE. BUT SOME OF OUR PEOPLE TOOK IT TOO FAR.
AND WITH WHAT YOUR MOTHER SAID TODAY--
--I'M WORRIED THAT SOME OF THEM MIGHT MISINTERPRET WHAT SHE SAID. USE HER WORDS AS AN EXCUSE TO LASH OUT AGAINST HUMANKIND.
AND WHY SHOULDN'T THEY?

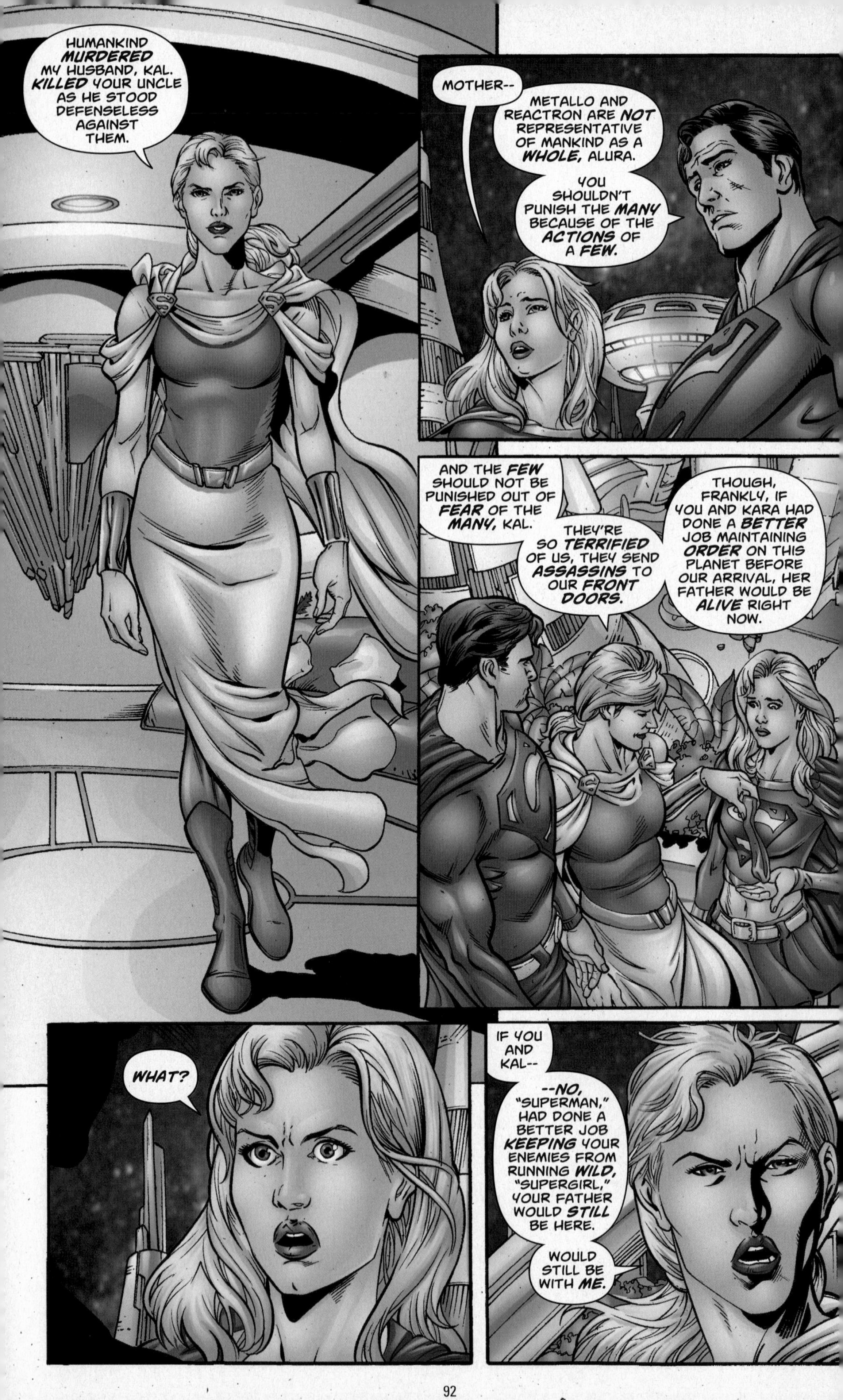
HUMANKIND MURDERED MY HUSBAND, KAL. KILLED YOUR UNCLE AS HE STOOD DEFENSELESS AGAINST THEM.
MOTHER--
METALLO AND REACTRON ARE NOT REPRESENTATIVE OF MANKIND AS A WHOLE, ALURA.
YOU SHOULDN'T PUNISH THE MANY BECAUSE OF THE ACTIONS OF A FEW.
AND THE FEW SHOULD NOT BE PUNISHED OUT OF FEAR OF THE MANY, KAL.
THEY'RE SO TERRIFIED OF US, THEY SEND ASSASSINS TO OUR FRONT DOORS.
THOUGH, FRANKLY, IF YOU AND KARA HAD DONE A BETTER JOB MAINTAINING ORDER ON THIS PLANET BEFORE OUR ARRIVAL, HER FATHER WOULD BE ALIVE RIGHT NOW.
WHAT?
IF YOU AND KAL--
--NO, "SUPERMAN," HAD DONE A BETTER JOB KEEPING YOUR ENEMIES FROM RUNNING WILD, "SUPERGIRL," YOUR FATHER WOULD STILL BE HERE.
WOULD STILL BE WITH ME.

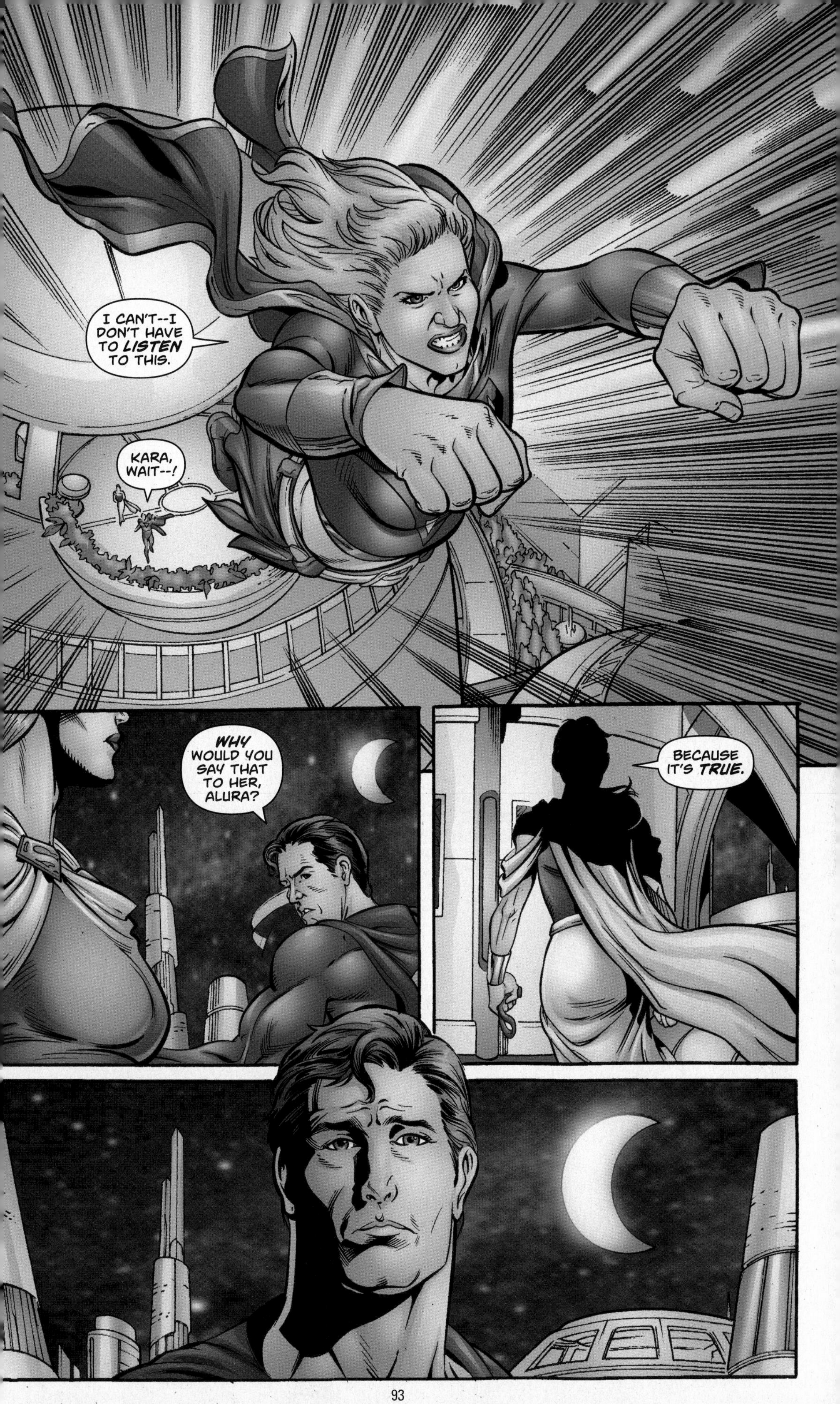

I CAN'T--I DON'T HAVE TO **LISTEN** TO THIS.
KARA, WAIT--!
**WHY** WOULD YOU SAY THAT TO HER, ALURA?
BECAUSE IT'S **TRUE**.

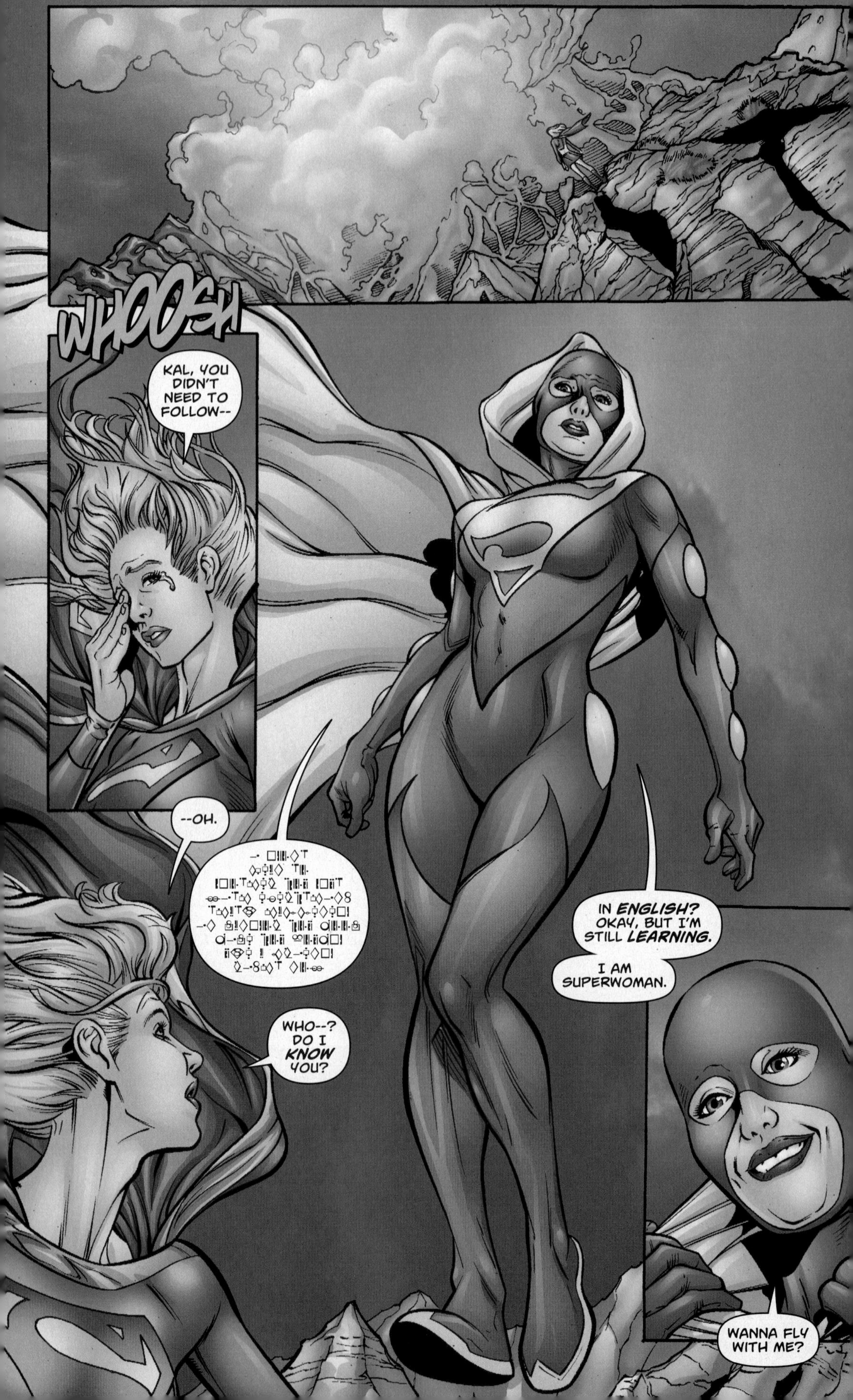
WHOOSH
KAL, YOU DIDN'T NEED TO FOLLOW--
--OH.
IN ENGLISH? OKAY, BUT I'M STILL LEARNING.
I AM SUPERWOMAN.
WHO--? DO I KNOW YOU?
WANNA FLY WITH ME?

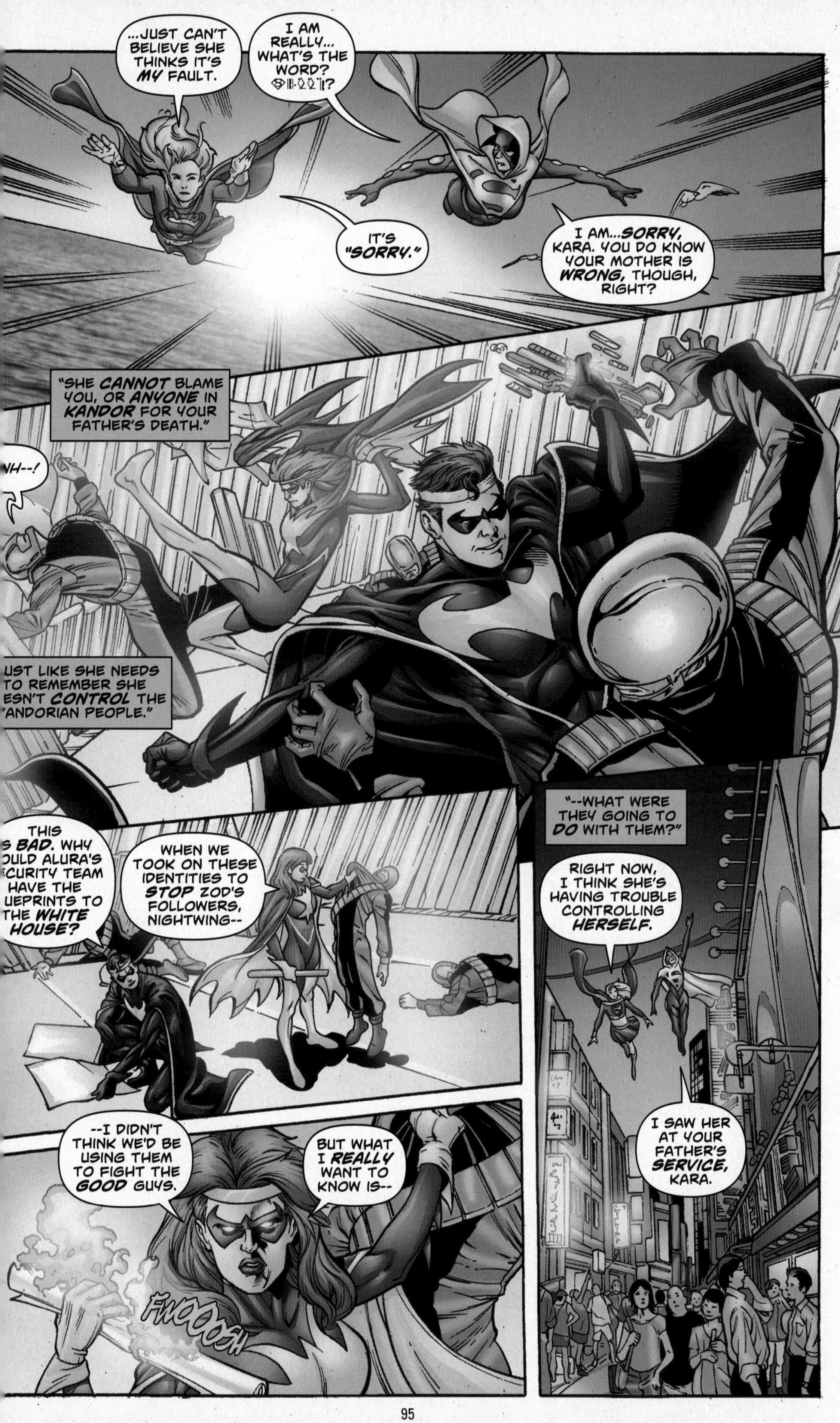

...JUST CAN'T BELIEVE SHE THINKS IT'S *MY* FAULT.
I AM REALLY... WHAT'S THE WORD?
IT'S **"SORRY."**
I AM...**SORRY,** KARA. YOU DO KNOW YOUR MOTHER IS **WRONG,** THOUGH, RIGHT?
"SHE **CANNOT** BLAME YOU, OR **ANYONE** IN **KANDOR** FOR YOUR FATHER'S DEATH."
NH--!
UST LIKE SHE NEEDS TO REMEMBER SHE ESN'T **CONTROL** THE 'ANDORIAN PEOPLE."
THIS S **BAD.** WHY OULD ALURA'S CURITY TEAM HAVE THE UEPRINTS TO THE **WHITE HOUSE?**
WHEN WE TOOK ON THESE IDENTITIES TO **STOP** ZOD'S FOLLOWERS, NIGHTWING--
--I DIDN'T THINK WE'D BE USING THEM TO FIGHT THE **GOOD** GUYS.
BUT WHAT I **REALLY** WANT TO KNOW IS--
FWOOOSH
"--WHAT WERE THEY GOING TO **DO** WITH THEM?"
RIGHT NOW, I THINK SHE'S HAVING TROUBLE CONTROLLING **HERSELF.**
I SAW HER AT YOUR FATHER'S **SERVICE,** KARA.

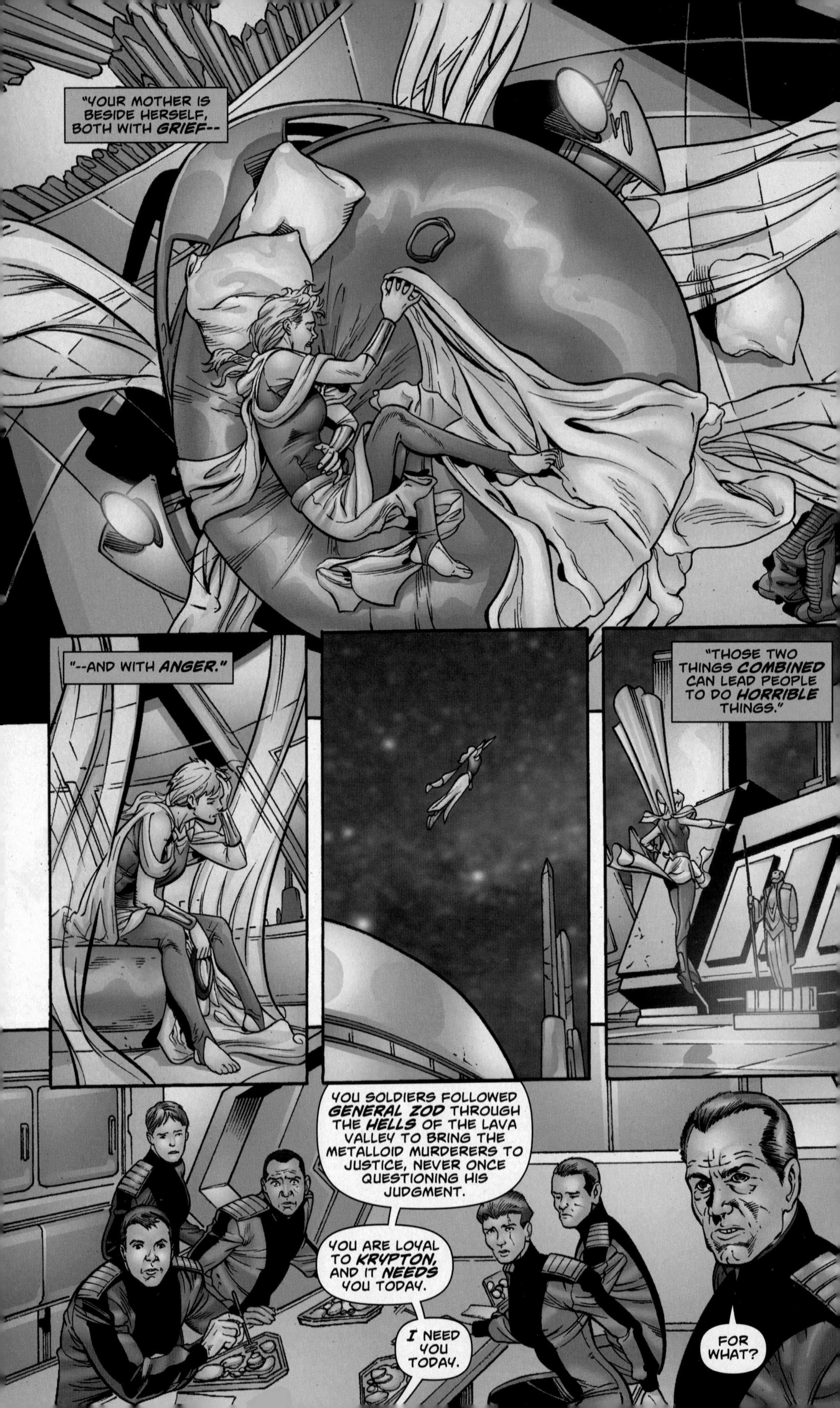
"YOUR MOTHER IS BESIDE HERSELF, BOTH WITH GRIEF--
"--AND WITH ANGER."
"THOSE TWO THINGS COMBINED CAN LEAD PEOPLE TO DO HORRIBLE THINGS."
YOU SOLDIERS FOLLOWED GENERAL ZOD THROUGH THE HELLS OF THE LAVA VALLEY TO BRING THE METALLOID MURDERERS TO JUSTICE, NEVER ONCE QUESTIONING HIS JUDGMENT.
YOU ARE LOYAL TO KRYPTON, AND IT NEEDS YOU TODAY.
I NEED YOU TODAY.
FOR WHAT?

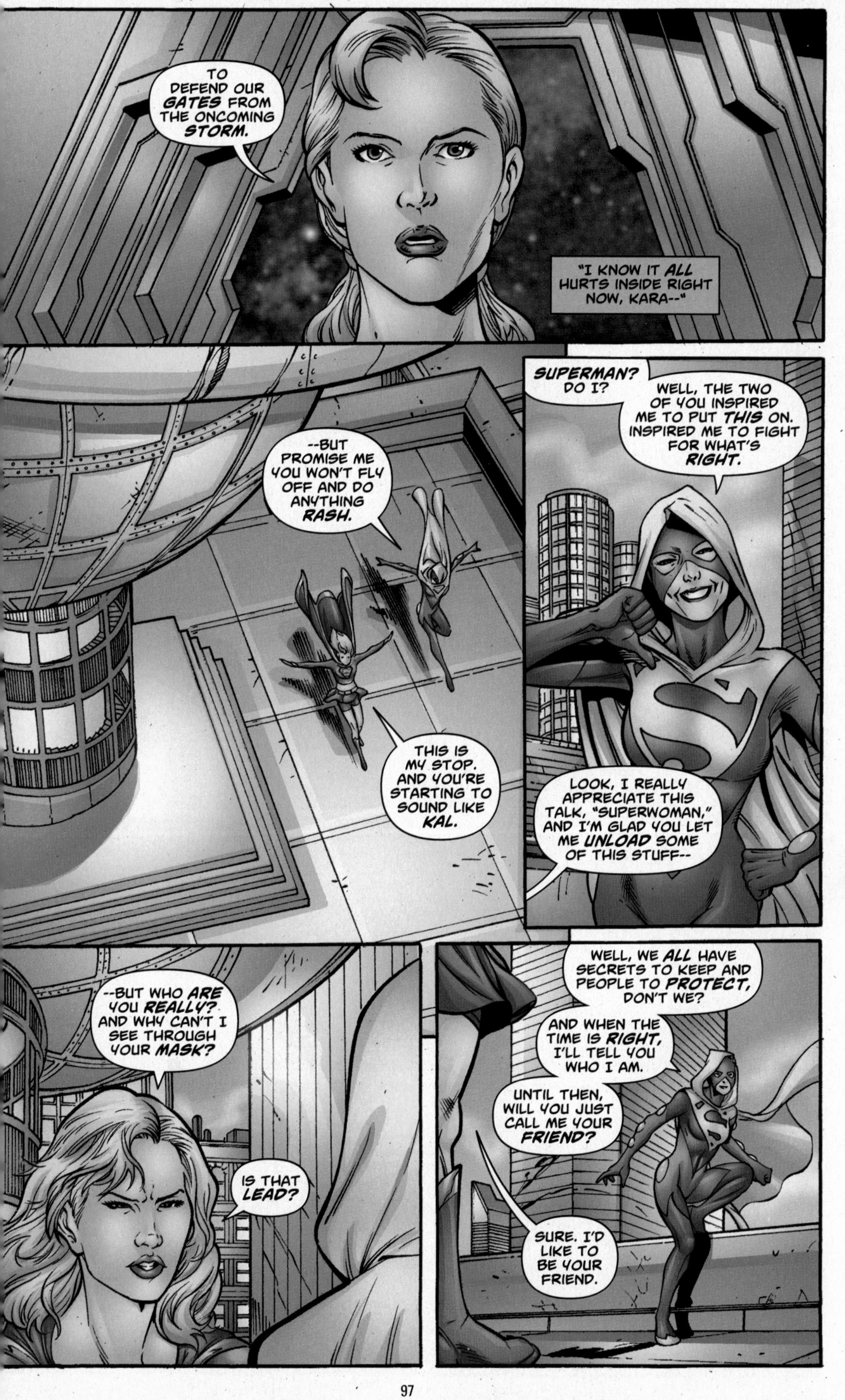
TO DEFEND OUR GATES FROM THE ONCOMING STORM.
"I KNOW IT ALL HURTS INSIDE RIGHT NOW, KARA--"
--BUT PROMISE ME YOU WON'T FLY OFF AND DO ANYTHING RASH.
THIS IS MY STOP. AND YOU'RE STARTING TO SOUND LIKE KAL.
SUPERMAN? DO I?
WELL, THE TWO OF YOU INSPIRED ME TO PUT THIS ON. INSPIRED ME TO FIGHT FOR WHAT'S RIGHT.
LOOK, I REALLY APPRECIATE THIS TALK, "SUPERWOMAN," AND I'M GLAD YOU LET ME UNLOAD SOME OF THIS STUFF--
--BUT WHO ARE YOU REALLY? AND WHY CAN'T I SEE THROUGH YOUR MASK?
IS THAT LEAD?
WELL, WE ALL HAVE SECRETS TO KEEP AND PEOPLE TO PROTECT, DON'T WE?
AND WHEN THE TIME IS RIGHT, I'LL TELL YOU WHO I AM.
UNTIL THEN, WILL YOU JUST CALL ME YOUR FRIEND?
SURE. I'D LIKE TO BE YOUR FRIEND.

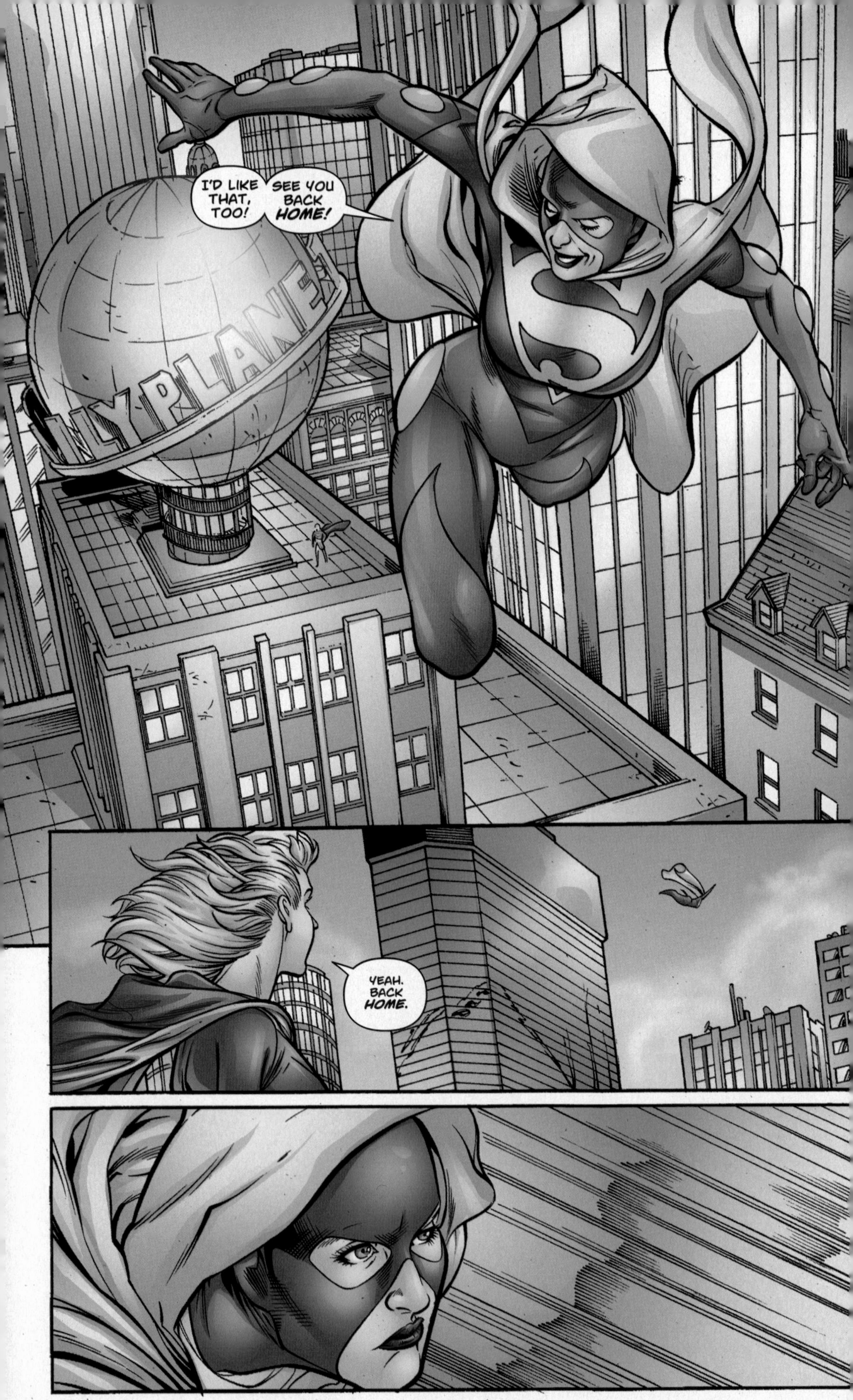
I'D LIKE THAT, TOO!
SEE YOU BACK *HOME!*
YEAH. BACK *HOME.*

<HARD TIMES!> SUPERMAN 683 COVER ART BY **ALEX ROSS**

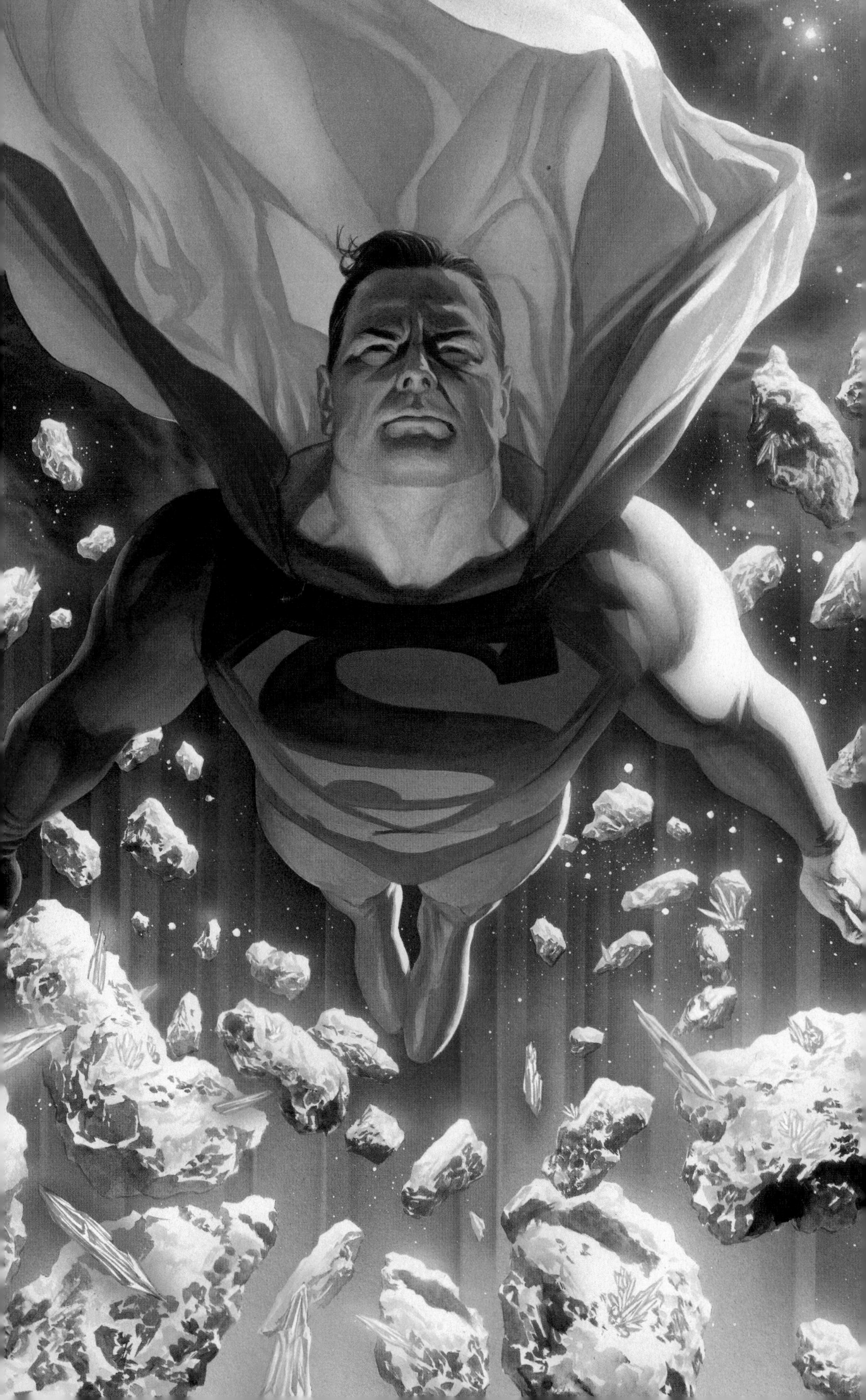

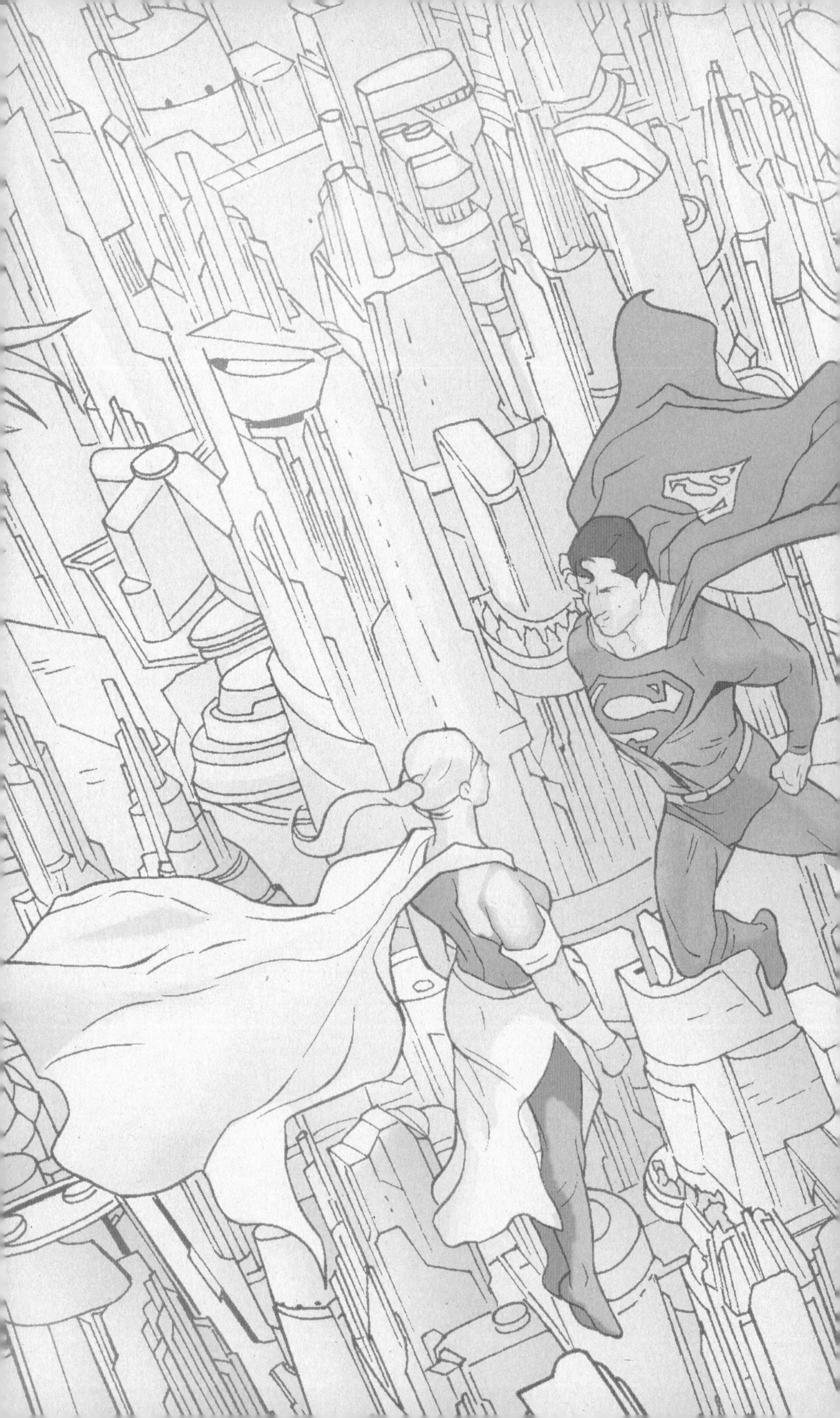

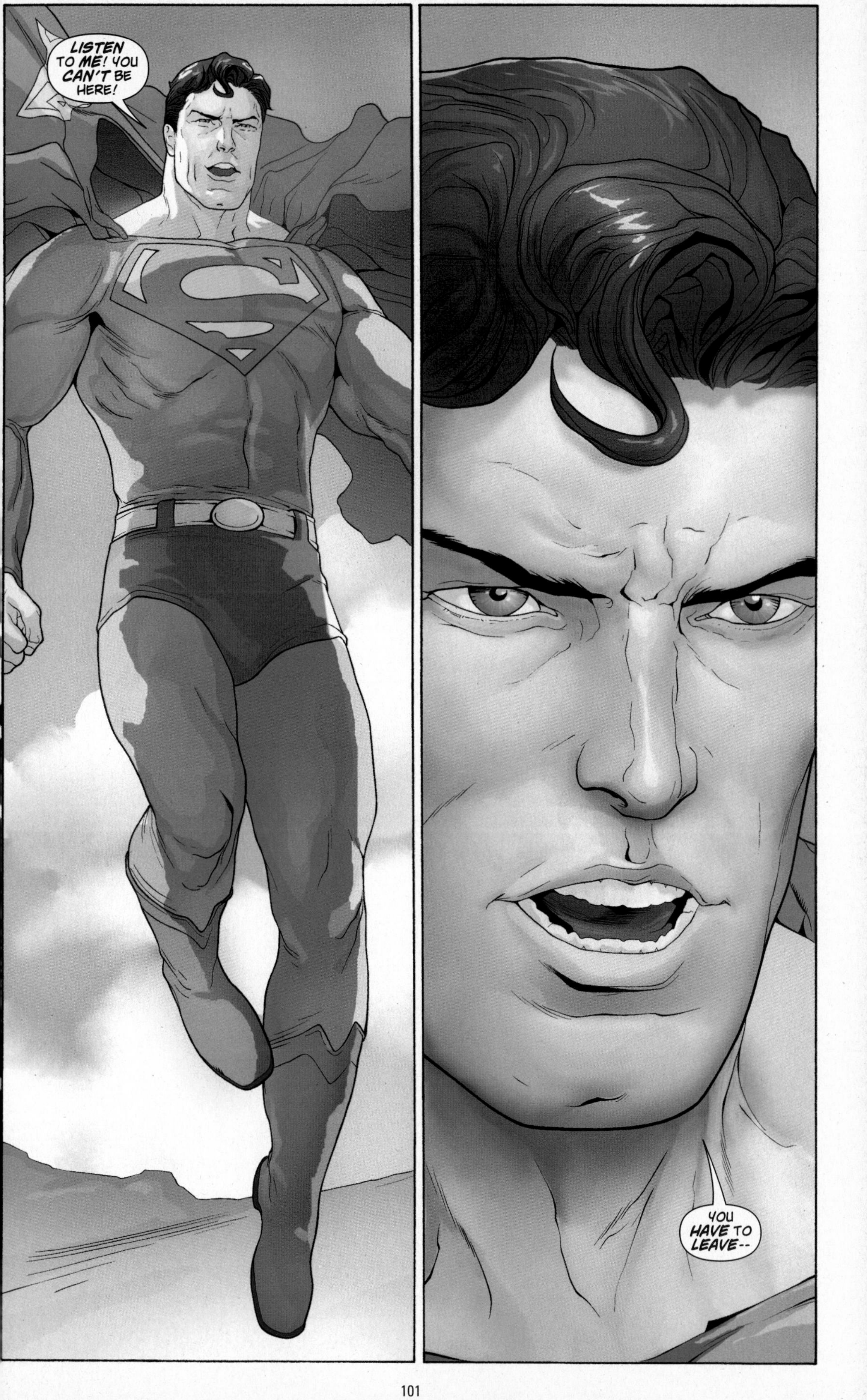
LISTEN TO ME! YOU CAN'T BE HERE!
YOU HAVE TO LEAVE--

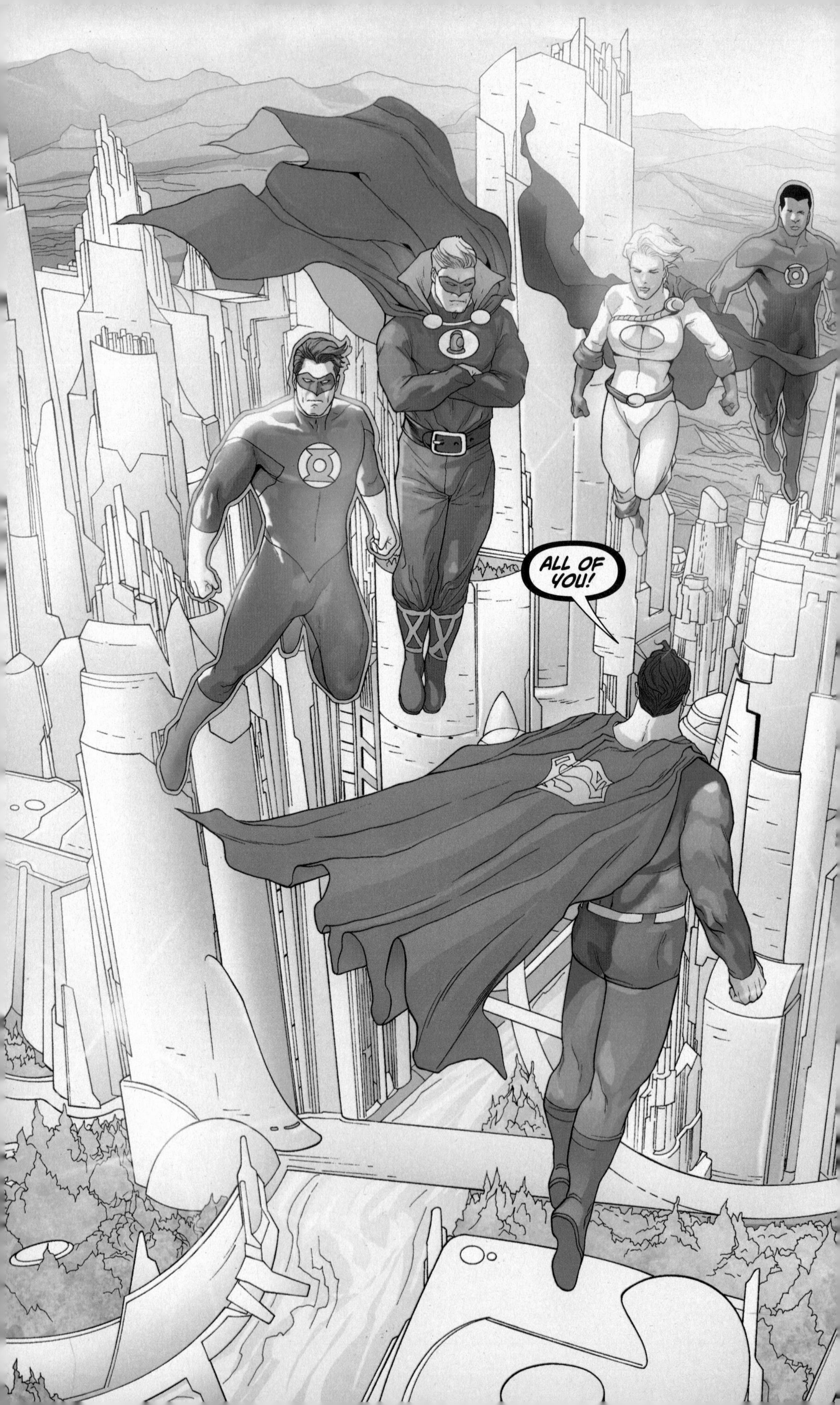
ALL OF YOU!

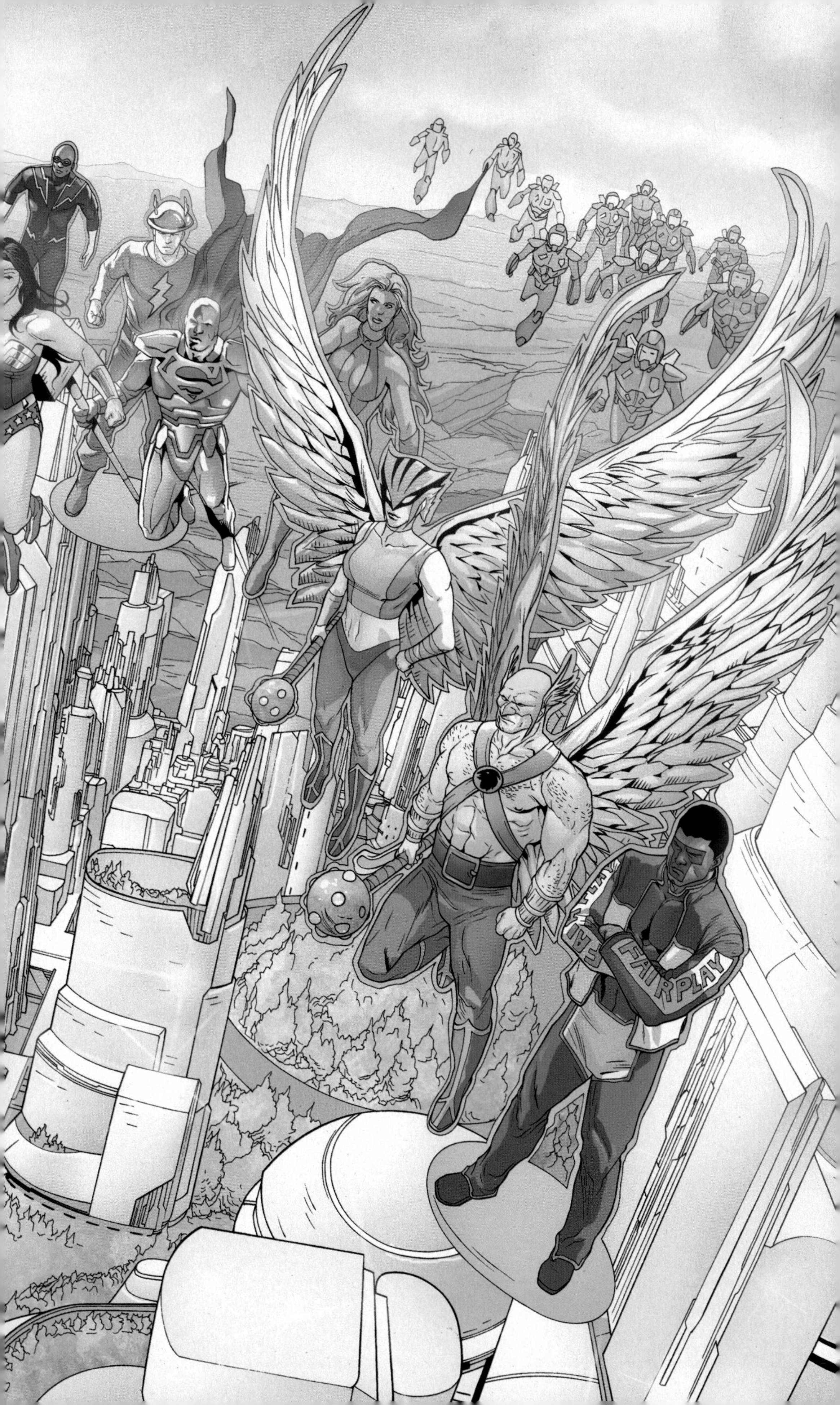
FAIRPLAY

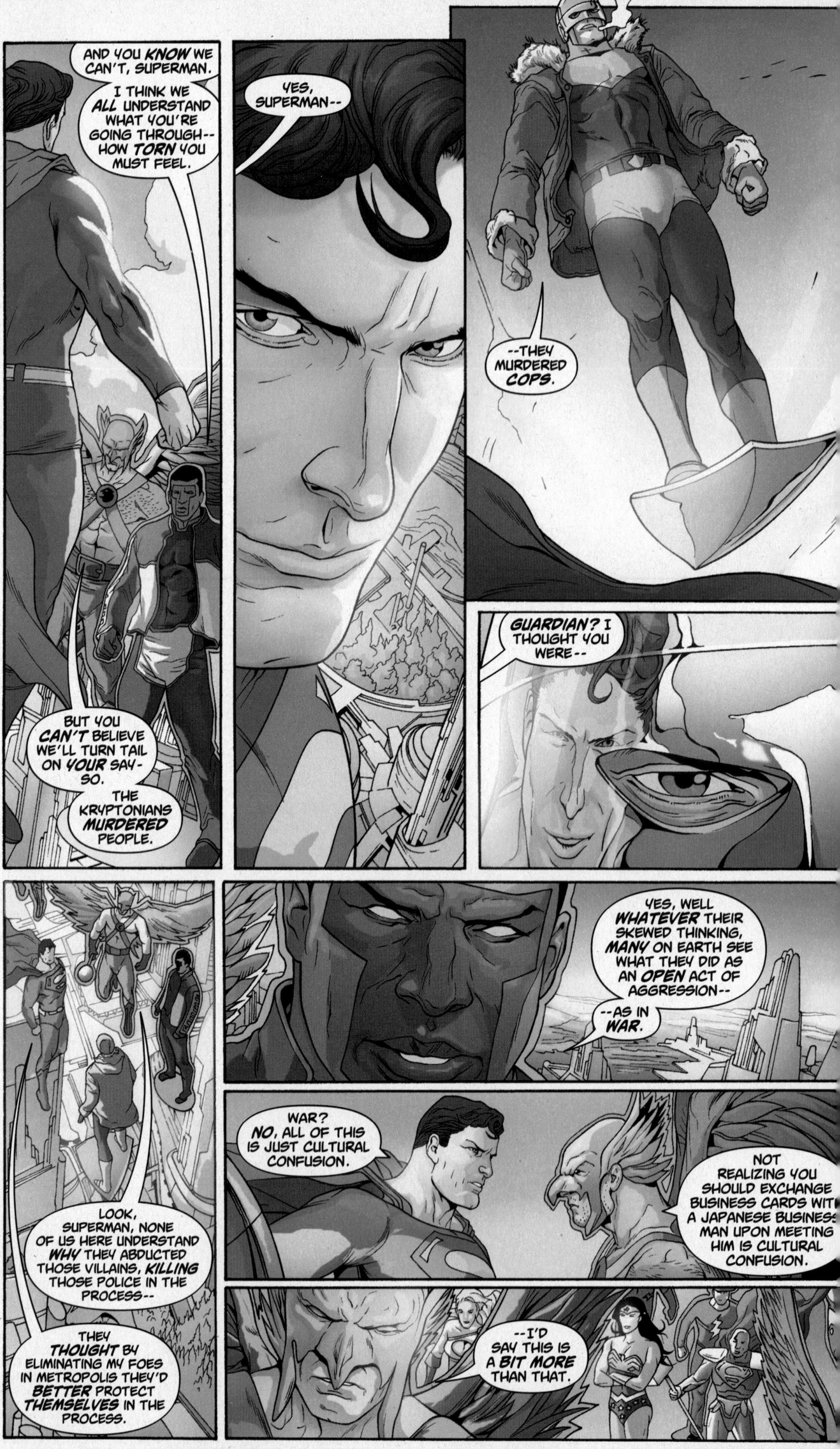

AND YOU KNOW WE CAN'T, SUPERMAN.
I THINK WE ALL UNDERSTAND WHAT YOU'RE GOING THROUGH-- HOW TORN YOU MUST FEEL.
BUT YOU CAN'T BELIEVE WE'LL TURN TAIL ON YOUR SAY-SO.
THE KRYPTONIANS MURDERED PEOPLE.
YES, SUPERMAN--
--THEY MURDERED COPS.
GUARDIAN? I THOUGHT YOU WERE--
LOOK, SUPERMAN, NONE OF US HERE UNDERSTAND WHY THEY ABDUCTED THOSE VILLAINS, KILLING THOSE POLICE IN THE PROCESS--
THEY THOUGHT BY ELIMINATING MY FOES IN METROPOLIS THEY'D BETTER PROTECT THEMSELVES IN THE PROCESS.
YES, WELL WHATEVER THEIR SKEWED THINKING, MANY ON EARTH SEE WHAT THEY DID AS AN OPEN ACT OF AGGRESSION--
--AS IN WAR.
WAR? NO, ALL OF THIS IS JUST CULTURAL CONFUSION.
NOT REALIZING YOU SHOULD EXCHANGE BUSINESS CARDS WITH A JAPANESE BUSINESS MAN UPON MEETING HIM IS CULTURAL CONFUSION.
--I'D SAY THIS IS A BIT MORE THAN THAT.

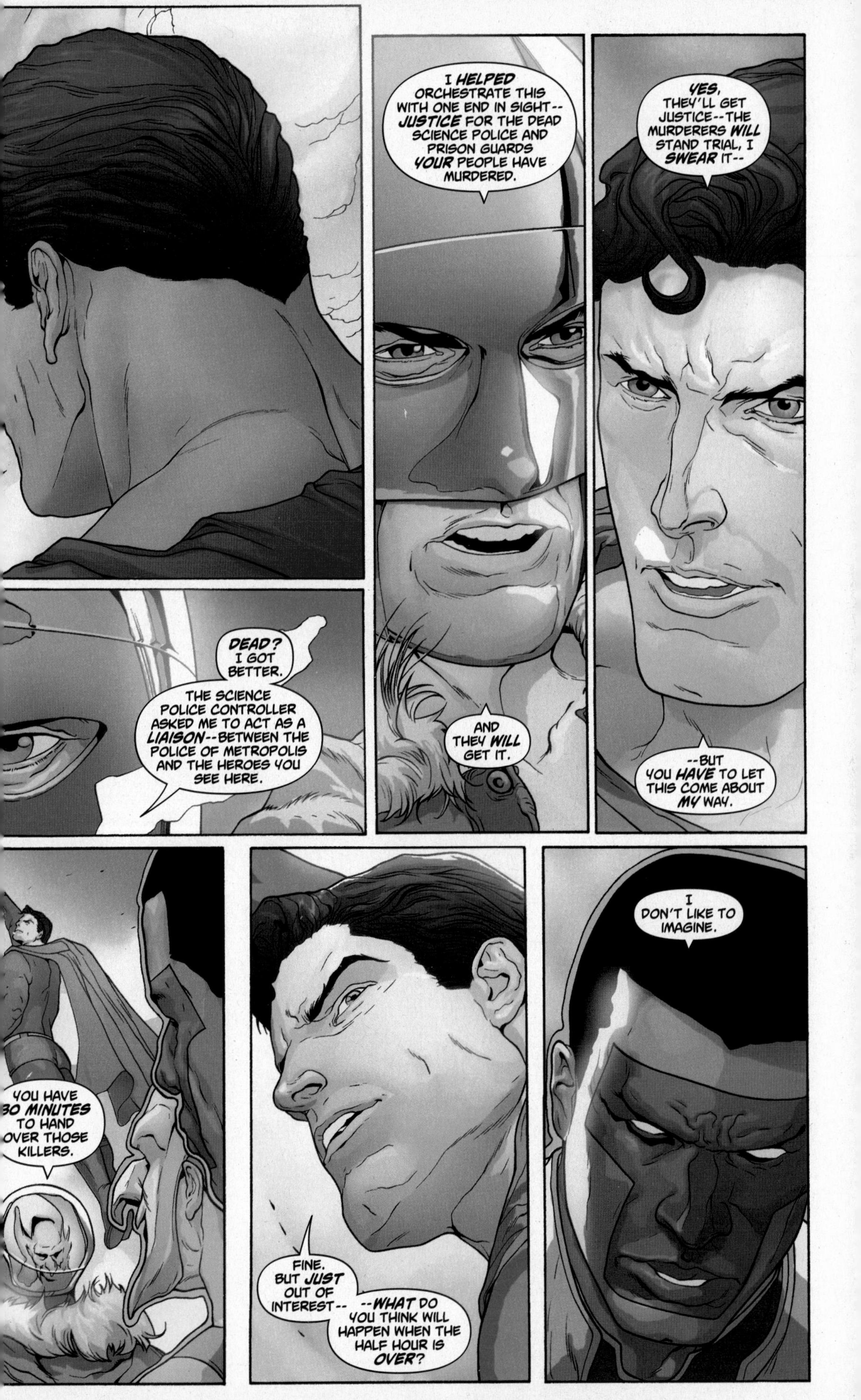
I HELPED ORCHESTRATE THIS WITH ONE END IN SIGHT-- JUSTICE FOR THE DEAD SCIENCE POLICE AND PRISON GUARDS YOUR PEOPLE HAVE MURDERED.
YES, THEY'LL GET JUSTICE--THE MURDERERS WILL STAND TRIAL, I SWEAR IT--
DEAD? I GOT BETTER.
THE SCIENCE POLICE CONTROLLER ASKED ME TO ACT AS A LIAISON--BETWEEN THE POLICE OF METROPOLIS AND THE HEROES YOU SEE HERE.
AND THEY WILL GET IT.
--BUT YOU HAVE TO LET THIS COME ABOUT MY WAY.
YOU HAVE 30 MINUTES TO HAND OVER THOSE KILLERS.
FINE. BUT JUST OUT OF INTEREST--
--WHAT DO YOU THINK WILL HAPPEN WHEN THE HALF HOUR IS OVER?
I DON'T LIKE TO IMAGINE.

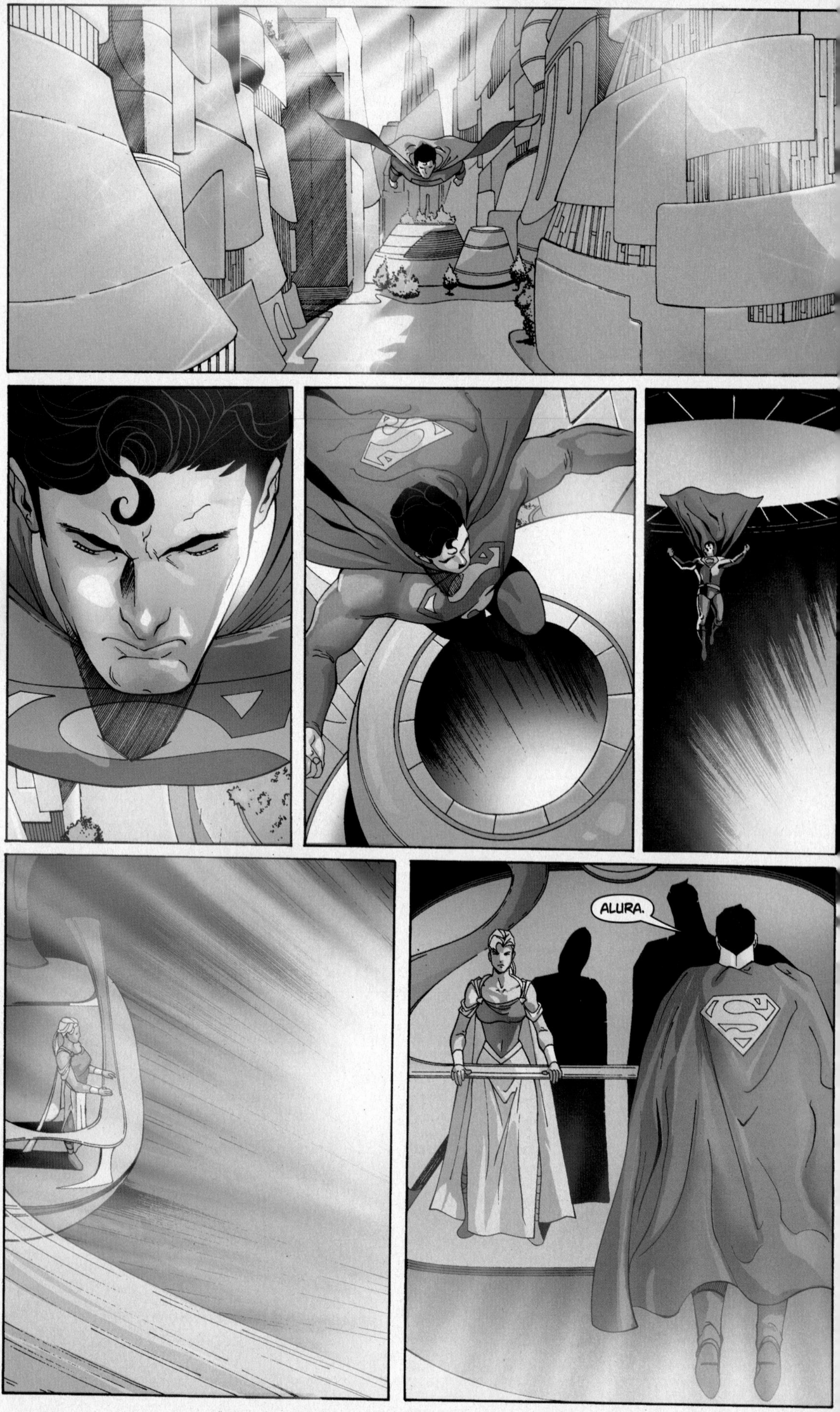
ALURA.

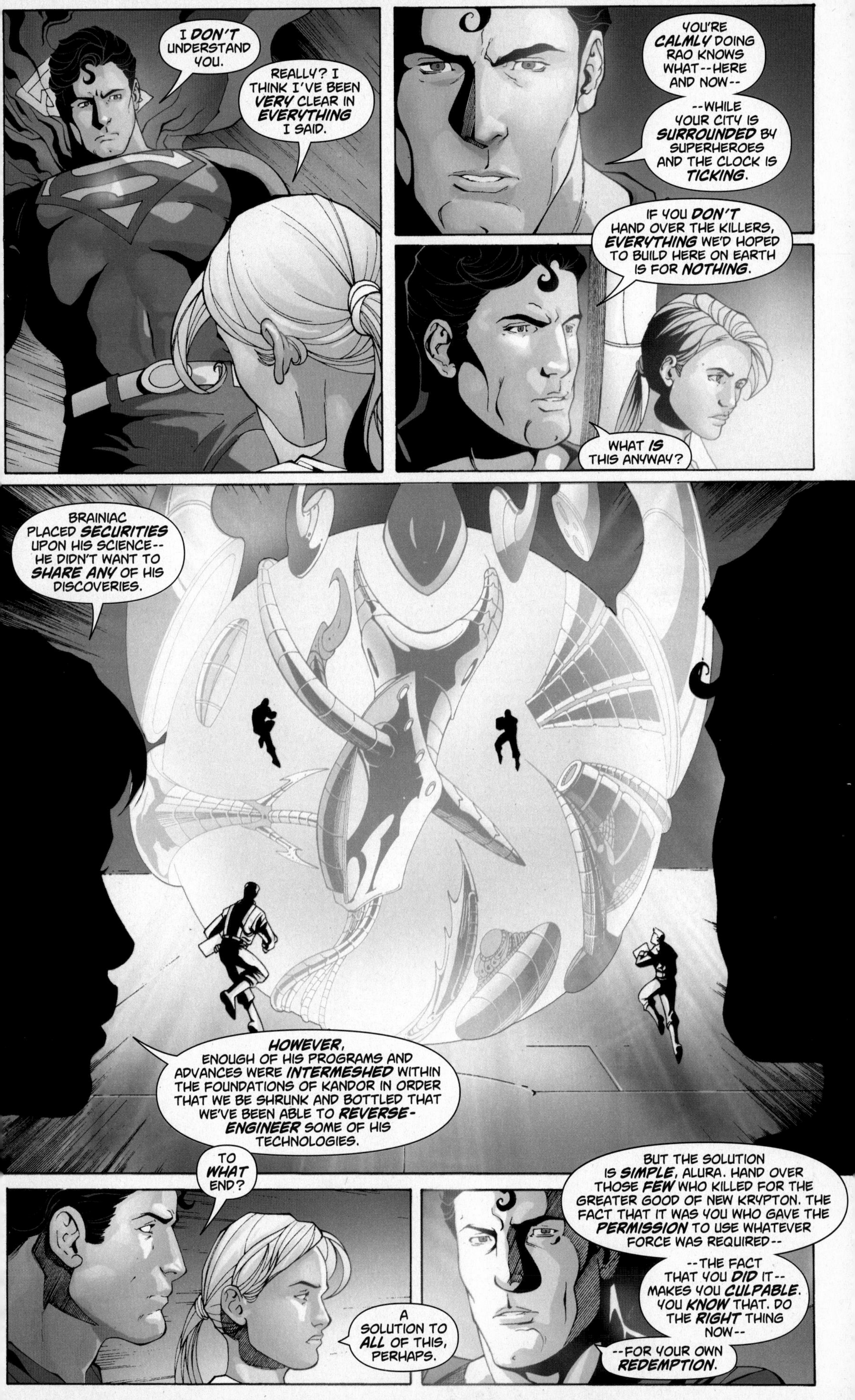

I DON'T UNDERSTAND YOU.
REALLY? I THINK I'VE BEEN VERY CLEAR IN EVERYTHING I SAID.
YOU'RE CALMLY DOING RAO KNOWS WHAT--HERE AND NOW--
--WHILE YOUR CITY IS SURROUNDED BY SUPERHEROES AND THE CLOCK IS TICKING.
IF YOU DON'T HAND OVER THE KILLERS, EVERYTHING WE'D HOPED TO BUILD HERE ON EARTH IS FOR NOTHING.
WHAT IS THIS ANYWAY?
BRAINIAC PLACED SECURITIES UPON HIS SCIENCE--HE DIDN'T WANT TO SHARE ANY OF HIS DISCOVERIES.
HOWEVER, ENOUGH OF HIS PROGRAMS AND ADVANCES WERE INTERMESHED WITHIN THE FOUNDATIONS OF KANDOR IN ORDER THAT WE BE SHRUNK AND BOTTLED THAT WE'VE BEEN ABLE TO REVERSE-ENGINEER SOME OF HIS TECHNOLOGIES.
TO WHAT END?
A SOLUTION TO ALL OF THIS, PERHAPS.
BUT THE SOLUTION IS SIMPLE, ALURA. HAND OVER THOSE FEW WHO KILLED FOR THE GREATER GOOD OF NEW KRYPTON. THE FACT THAT IT WAS YOU WHO GAVE THE PERMISSION TO USE WHATEVER FORCE WAS REQUIRED--
--THE FACT THAT YOU DID IT--MAKES YOU CULPABLE. YOU KNOW THAT. DO THE RIGHT THING NOW--
--FOR YOUR OWN REDEMPTION.

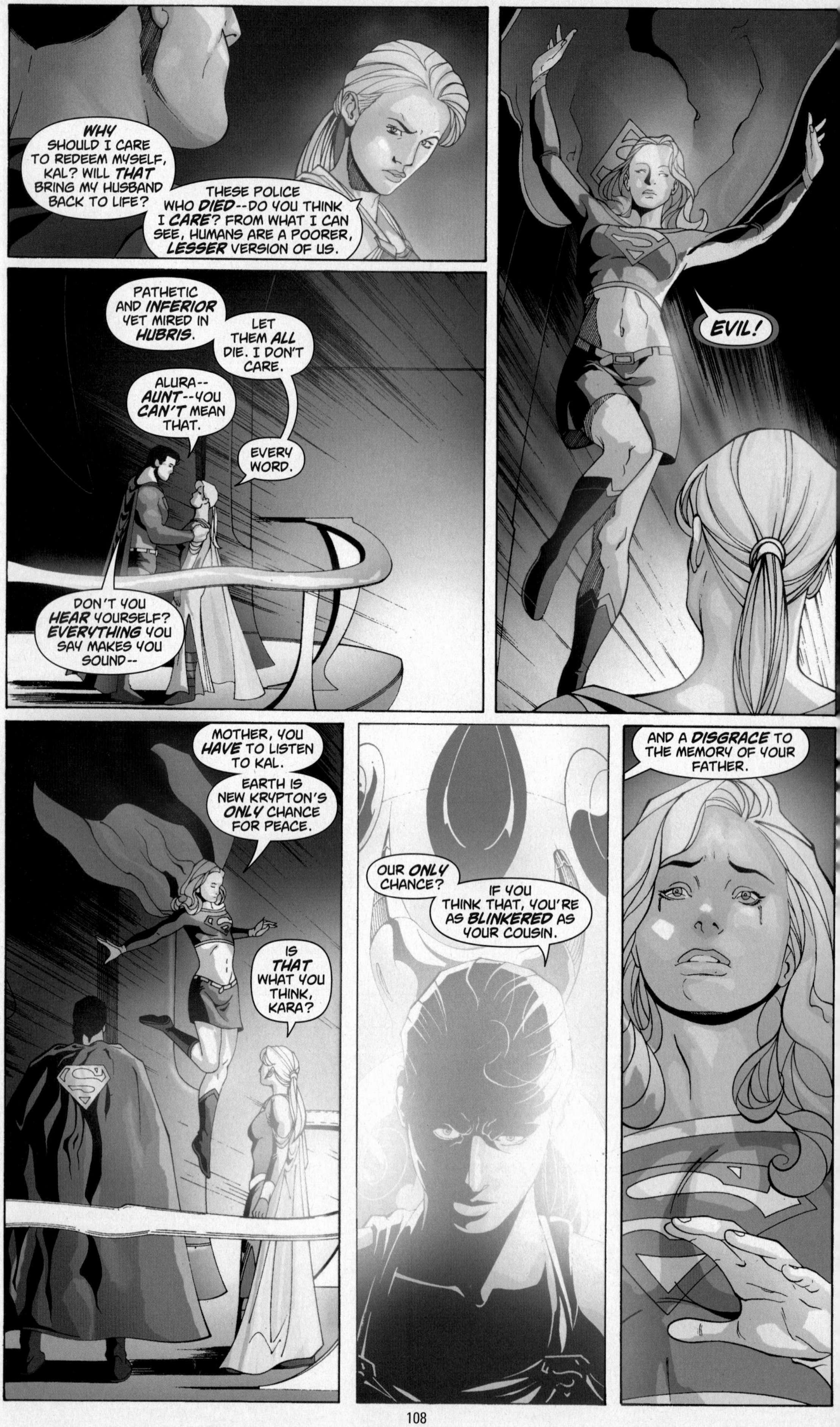
WHY SHOULD I CARE TO REDEEM MYSELF, KAL? WILL THAT BRING MY HUSBAND BACK TO LIFE?
THESE POLICE WHO DIED--DO YOU THINK I CARE? FROM WHAT I CAN SEE, HUMANS ARE A POORER, LESSER VERSION OF US.
EVIL!
PATHETIC AND INFERIOR YET MIRED IN HUBRIS.
LET THEM ALL DIE. I DON'T CARE.
ALURA--AUNT--YOU CAN'T MEAN THAT.
EVERY WORD.
DON'T YOU HEAR YOURSELF? EVERYTHING YOU SAY MAKES YOU SOUND--
MOTHER, YOU HAVE TO LISTEN TO KAL.
EARTH IS NEW KRYPTON'S ONLY CHANCE FOR PEACE.
IS THAT WHAT YOU THINK, KARA?
OUR ONLY CHANCE?
IF YOU THINK THAT, YOU'RE AS BLINKERED AS YOUR COUSIN.
AND A DISGRACE TO THE MEMORY OF YOUR FATHER.

ALURA, *DON'T* SPEAK TO HER *THAT* WAY.

I'LL SPEAK TO MY DAUGHTER *ANY* WAY I *CHOOSE* TO.

WELL, LET'S *NOT* FORGET THAT THE CLOCK--

YES, YES, I HEARD YOU THE *FIRST* TIME, IT'S TICKING.

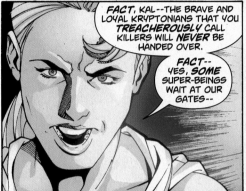

*FACT*, KAL--THE BRAVE AND LOYAL KRYPTONIANS THAT YOU *TREACHEROUSLY* CALL KILLERS WILL *NEVER* BE HANDED OVER.

*FACT*-- YES, *SOME* SUPER-BEINGS WAIT AT OUR GATES--

--BUT WE ARE SO *MUCH* MORE. AND SO *MANY*.

MOTHER, *PLEASE*--

I THOUGHT YOU *WORTHY* TO STAND BESIDE ME, DAUGHTER. *NOW* I SEE YOUR TIME ON EARTH--AS *LITTLE* AS IT'S BEEN--HAS MADE YOU *WEAK*.

LET ME SHOW YOU *STRENGTH*.

ALURA GESTURES-- HER HAND, A *SMALL* MOVEMENT, BARELY ANYTHING AT ALL--

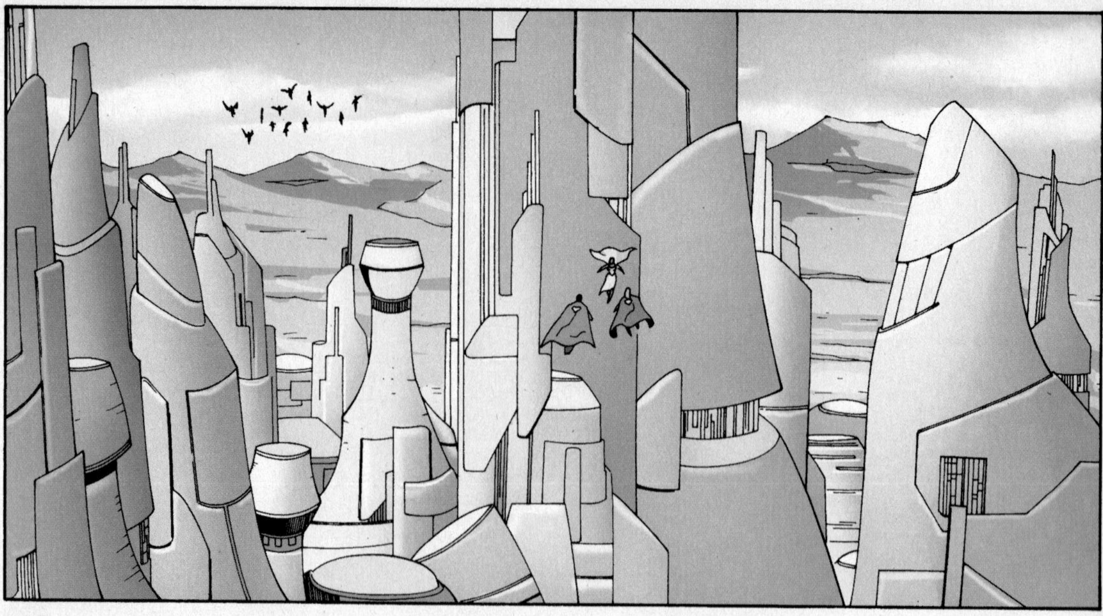

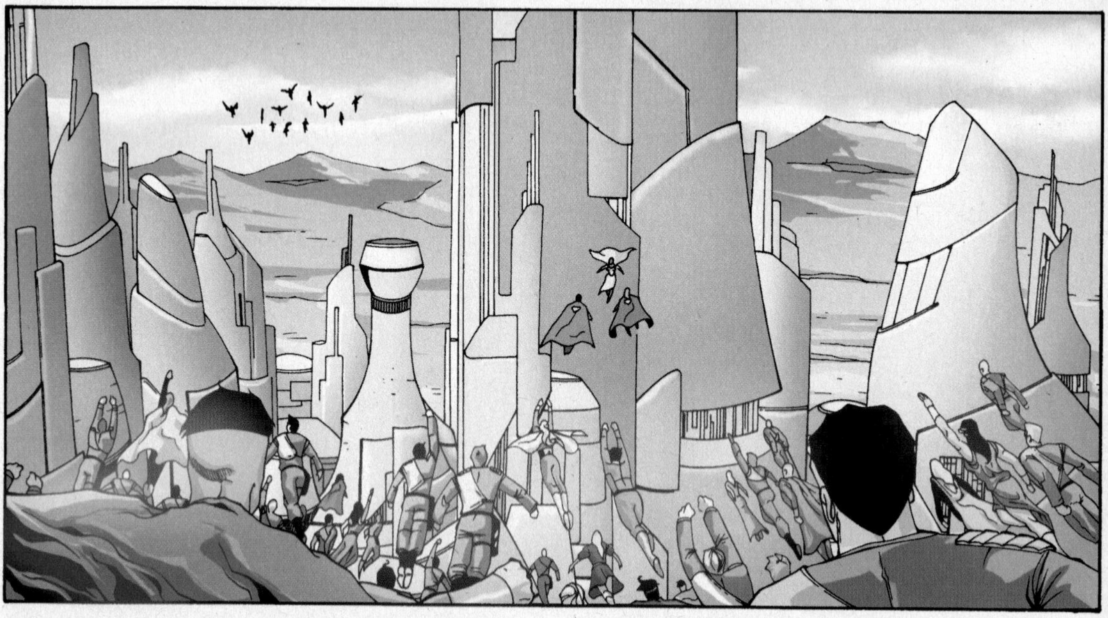

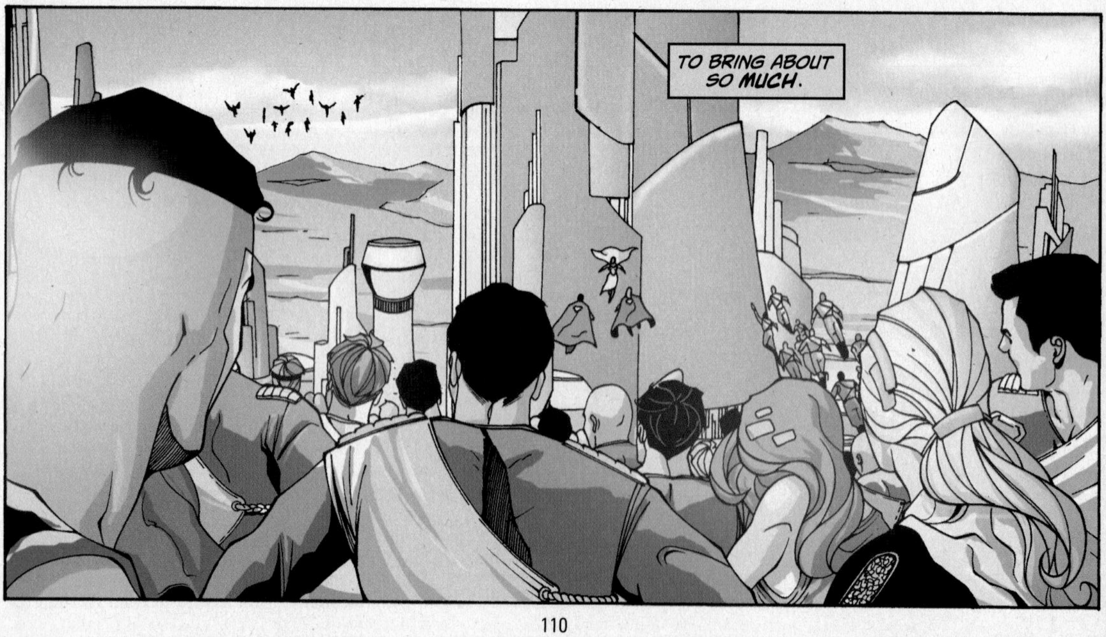
TO BRING ABOUT SO MUCH.

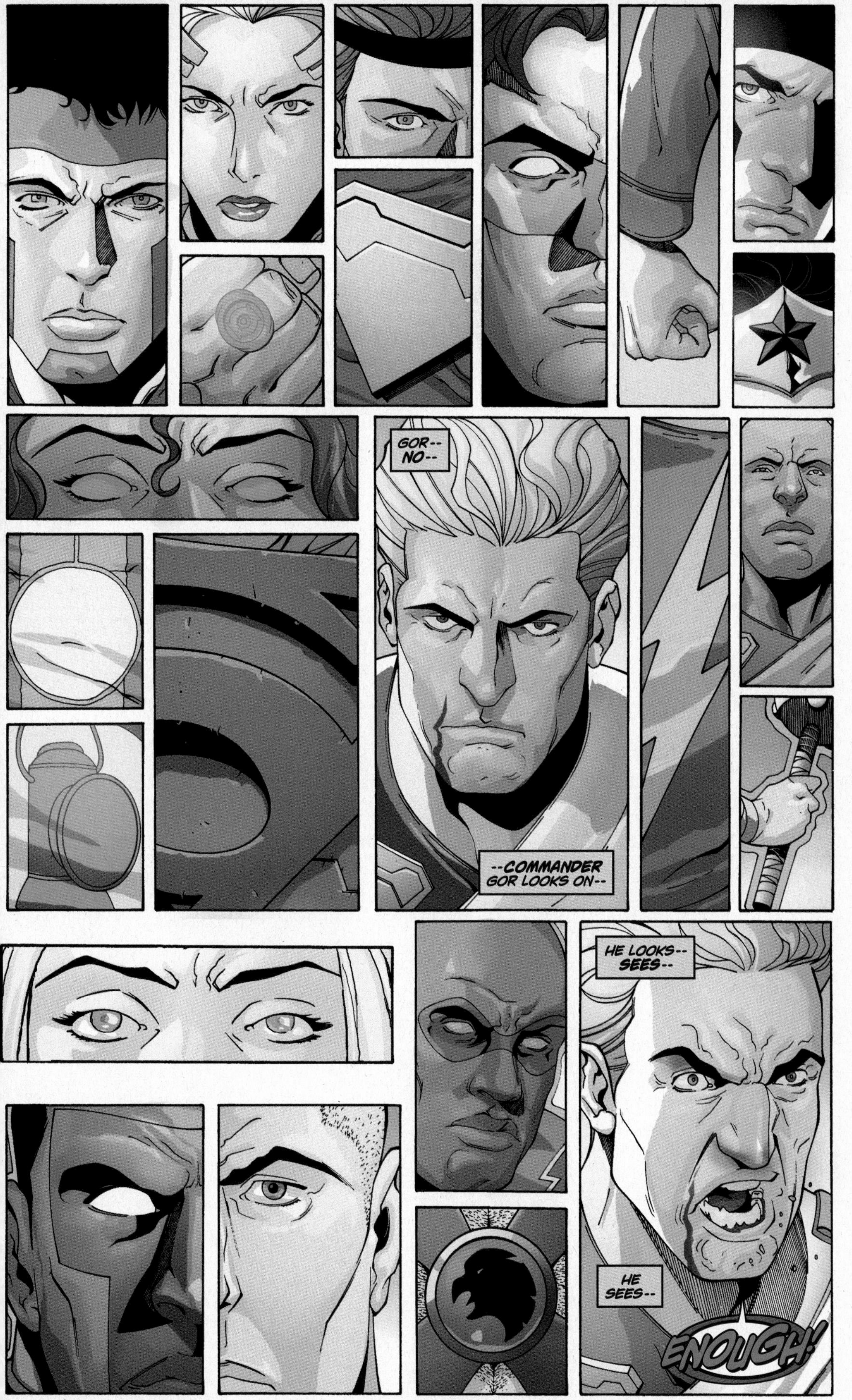
GOR--
NO--
--COMMANDER
GOR LOOKS ON--
HE LOOKS--
SEES--
HE
SEES--
ENOUGH!

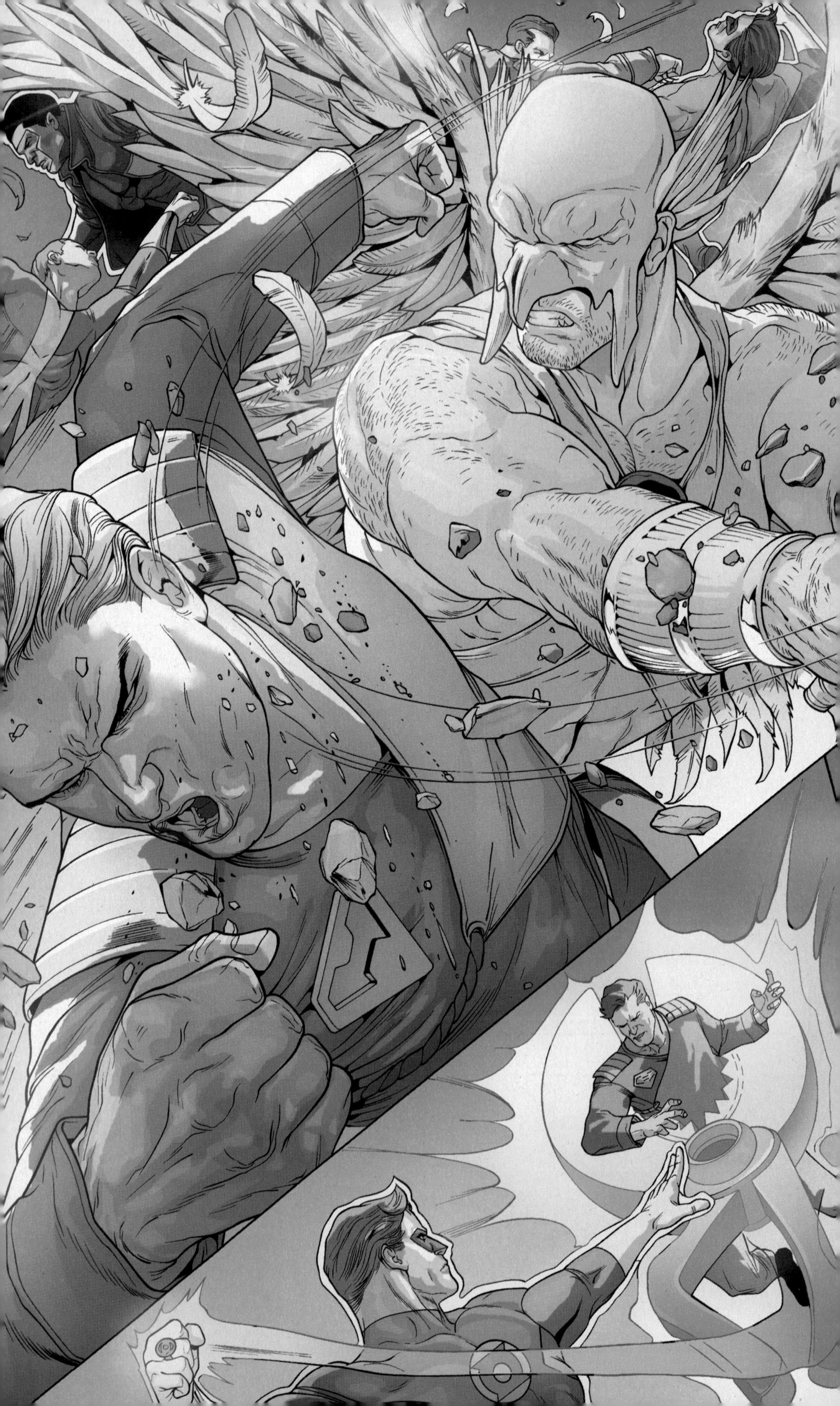

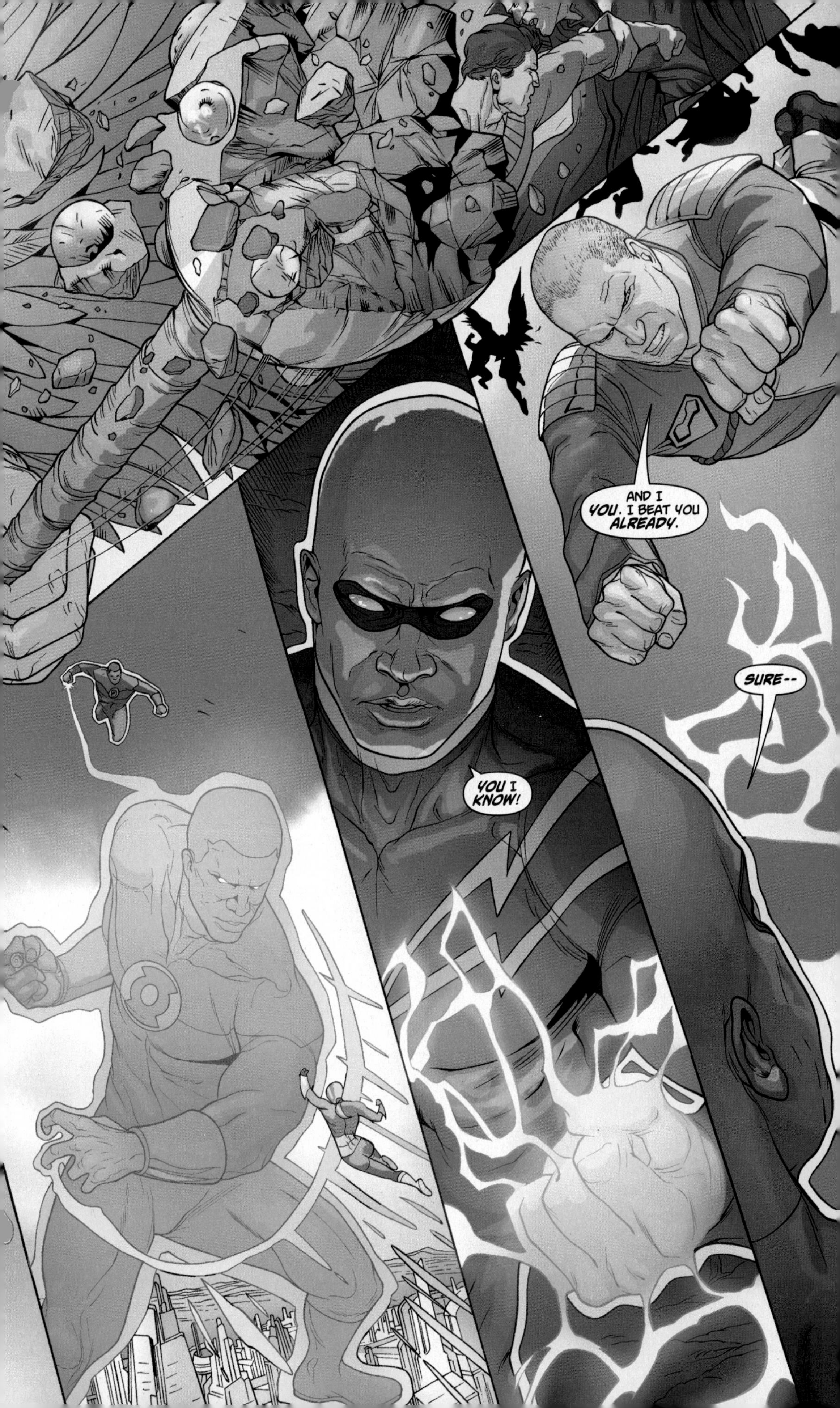
AND I YOU. I BEAT YOU ALREADY.
SURE--
YOU I KNOW!

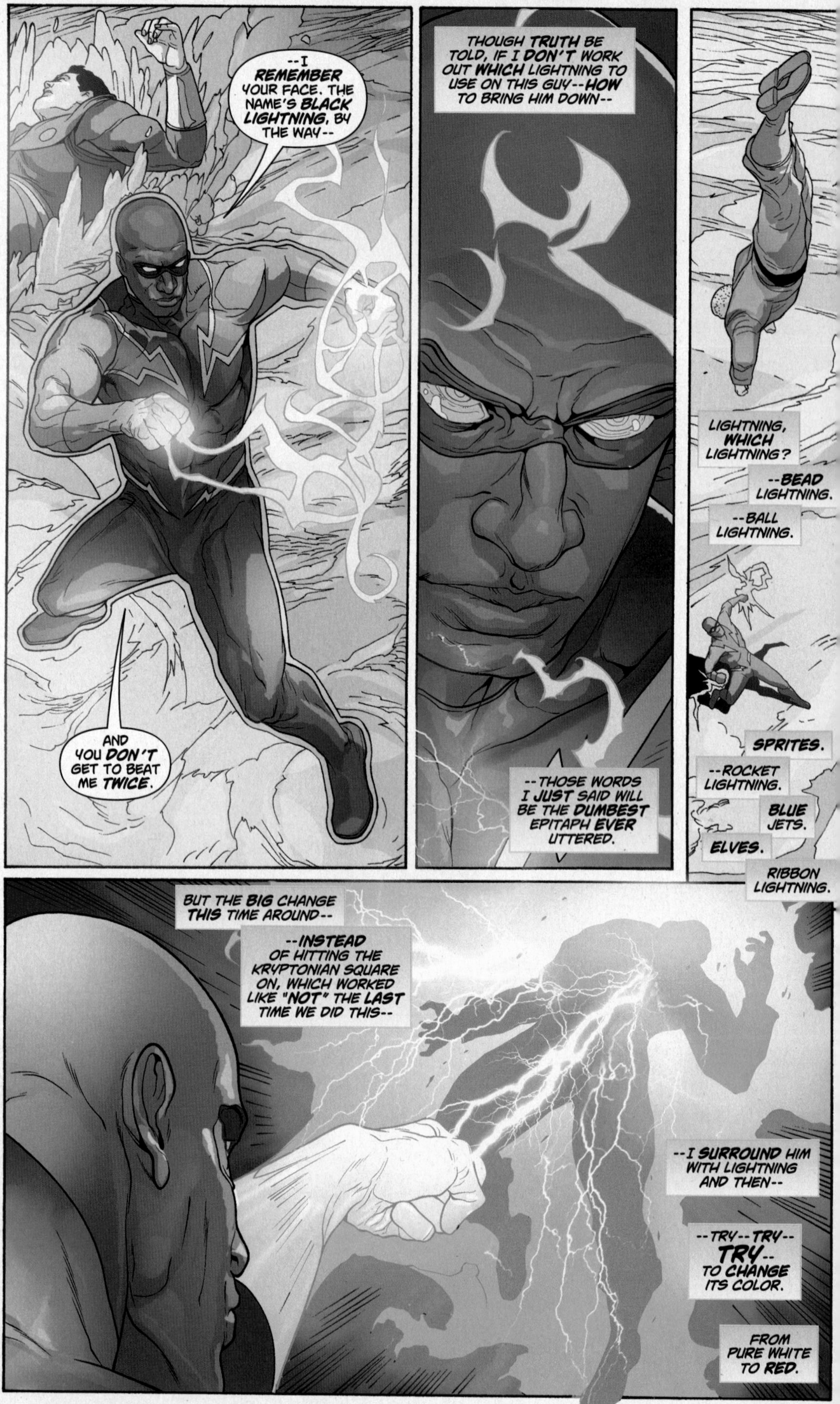
--I REMEMBER YOUR FACE. THE NAME'S BLACK LIGHTNING, BY THE WAY--
AND YOU DON'T GET TO BEAT ME TWICE.
THOUGH TRUTH BE TOLD, IF I DON'T WORK OUT WHICH LIGHTNING TO USE ON THIS GUY--HOW TO BRING HIM DOWN--
--THOSE WORDS I JUST SAID WILL BE THE DUMBEST EPITAPH EVER UTTERED.
LIGHTNING, WHICH LIGHTNING?
--BEAD LIGHTNING.
--BALL LIGHTNING.
SPRITES.
--ROCKET LIGHTNING.
BLUE JETS.
ELVES.
RIBBON LIGHTNING.
BUT THE BIG CHANGE THIS TIME AROUND--
--INSTEAD OF HITTING THE KRYPTONIAN SQUARE ON, WHICH WORKED LIKE "NOT" THE LAST TIME WE DID THIS--
--I SURROUND HIM WITH LIGHTNING AND THEN--
--TRY--TRY--TRY--TO CHANGE ITS COLOR.
FROM PURE WHITE TO RED.

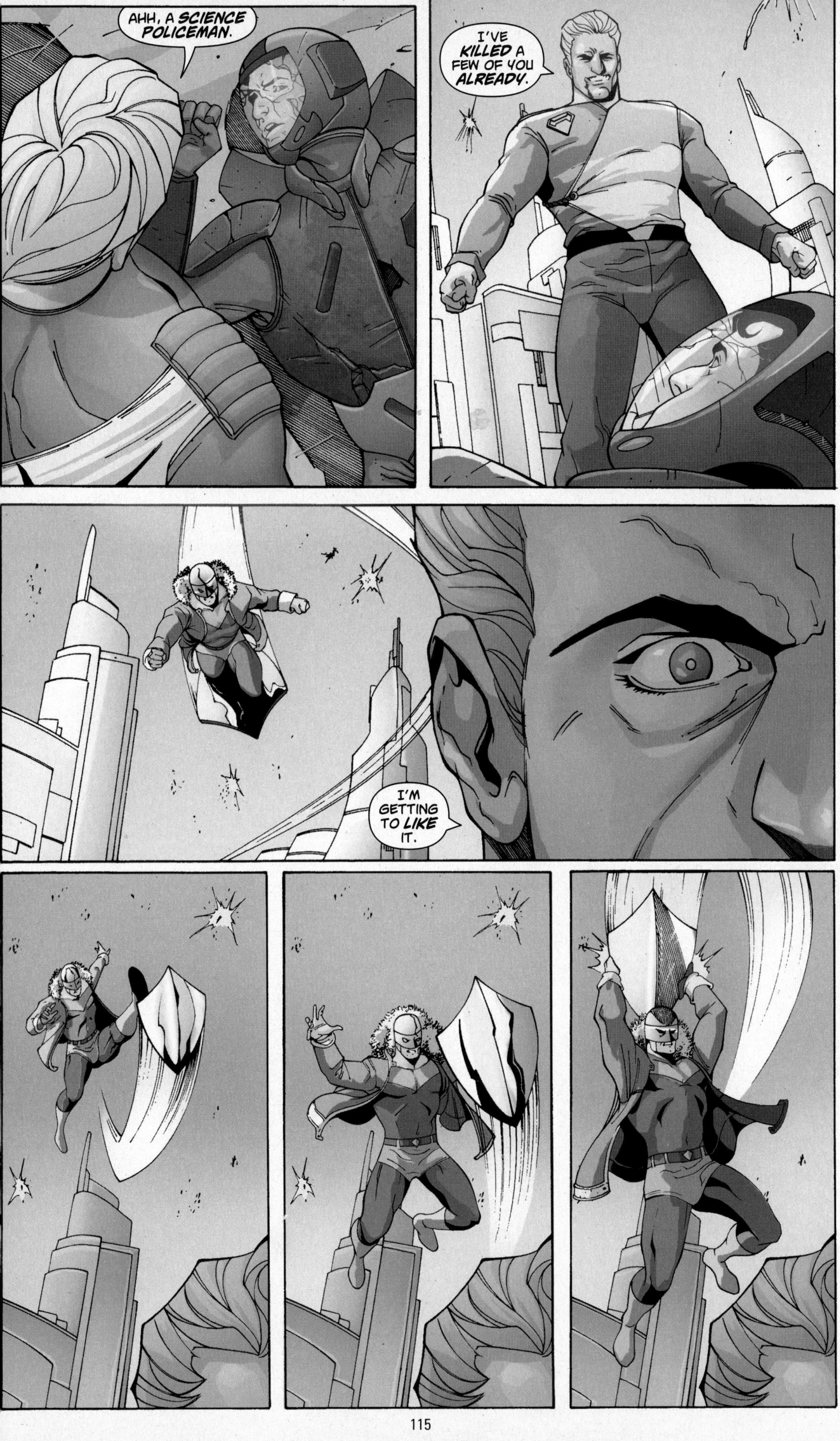

AHH, A SCIENCE POLICEMAN.
I'VE KILLED A FEW OF YOU ALREADY.
I'M GETTING TO LIKE IT.

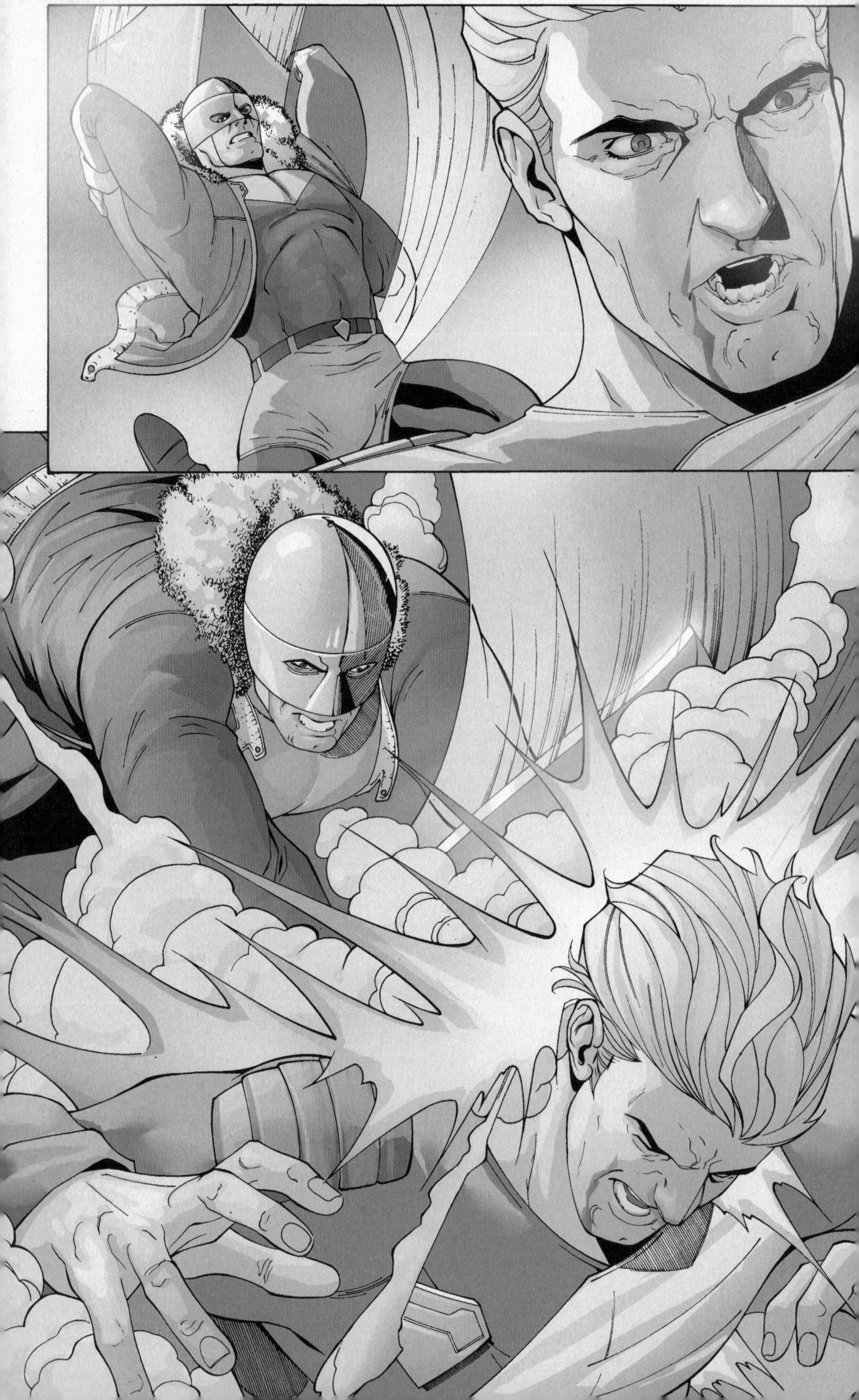

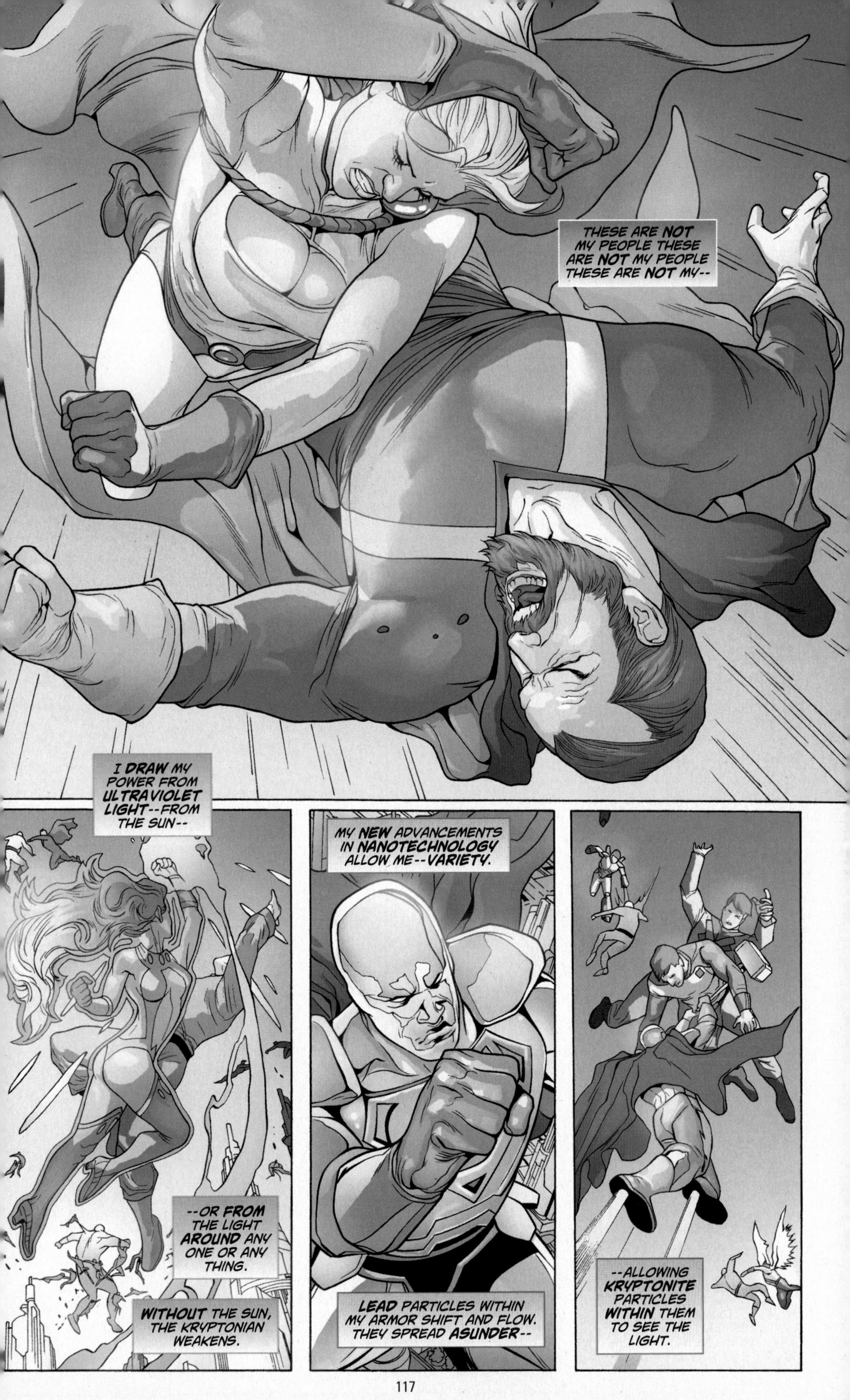
THESE ARE NOT MY PEOPLE THESE ARE NOT MY PEOPLE THESE ARE NOT MY--
I DRAW MY POWER FROM ULTRAVIOLET LIGHT--FROM THE SUN--
--OR FROM THE LIGHT AROUND ANY ONE OR ANY THING.
WITHOUT THE SUN, THE KRYPTONIAN WEAKENS.
MY NEW ADVANCEMENTS IN NANOTECHNOLOGY ALLOW ME--VARIETY.
LEAD PARTICLES WITHIN MY ARMOR SHIFT AND FLOW. THEY SPREAD ASUNDER--
--ALLOWING KRYPTONITE PARTICLES WITHIN THEM TO SEE THE LIGHT.

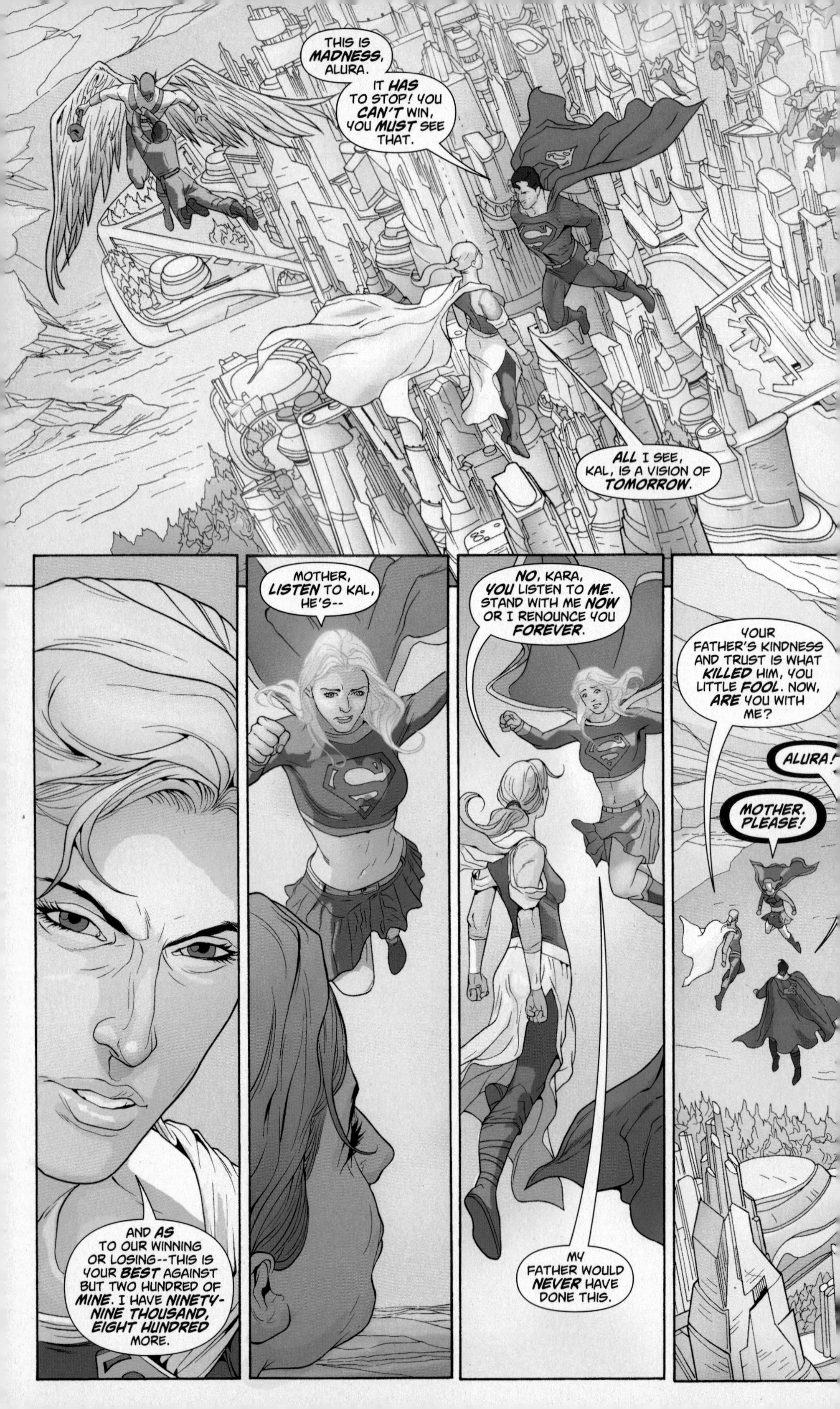
THIS IS MADNESS, ALURA.
IT HAS TO STOP! YOU CAN'T WIN, YOU MUST SEE THAT.
ALL I SEE, KAL, IS A VISION OF TOMORROW.
AND AS TO OUR WINNING OR LOSING--THIS IS YOUR BEST AGAINST BUT TWO HUNDRED OF MINE. I HAVE NINETY-NINE THOUSAND, EIGHT HUNDRED MORE.
MOTHER, LISTEN TO KAL, HE'S--
NO, KARA, YOU LISTEN TO ME. STAND WITH ME NOW OR I RENOUNCE YOU FOREVER.
MY FATHER WOULD NEVER HAVE DONE THIS.
YOUR FATHER'S KINDNESS AND TRUST IS WHAT KILLED HIM, YOU LITTLE FOOL. NOW, ARE YOU WITH ME?
ALURA!
MOTHER. PLEASE!

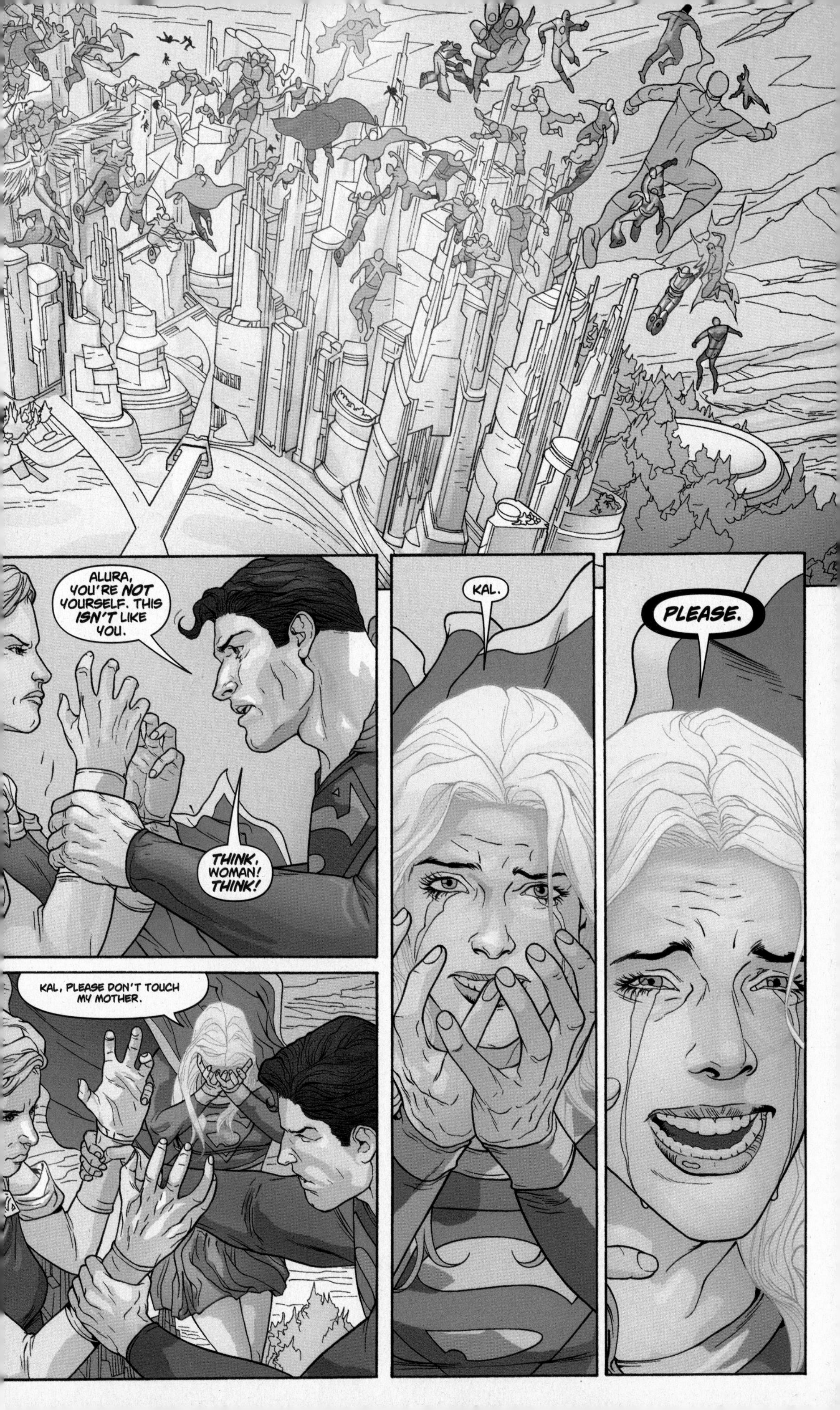

ALURA, YOU'RE NOT YOURSELF. THIS ISN'T LIKE YOU.
THINK, WOMAN! THINK!
KAL.
PLEASE.
KAL, PLEASE DON'T TOUCH MY MOTHER.

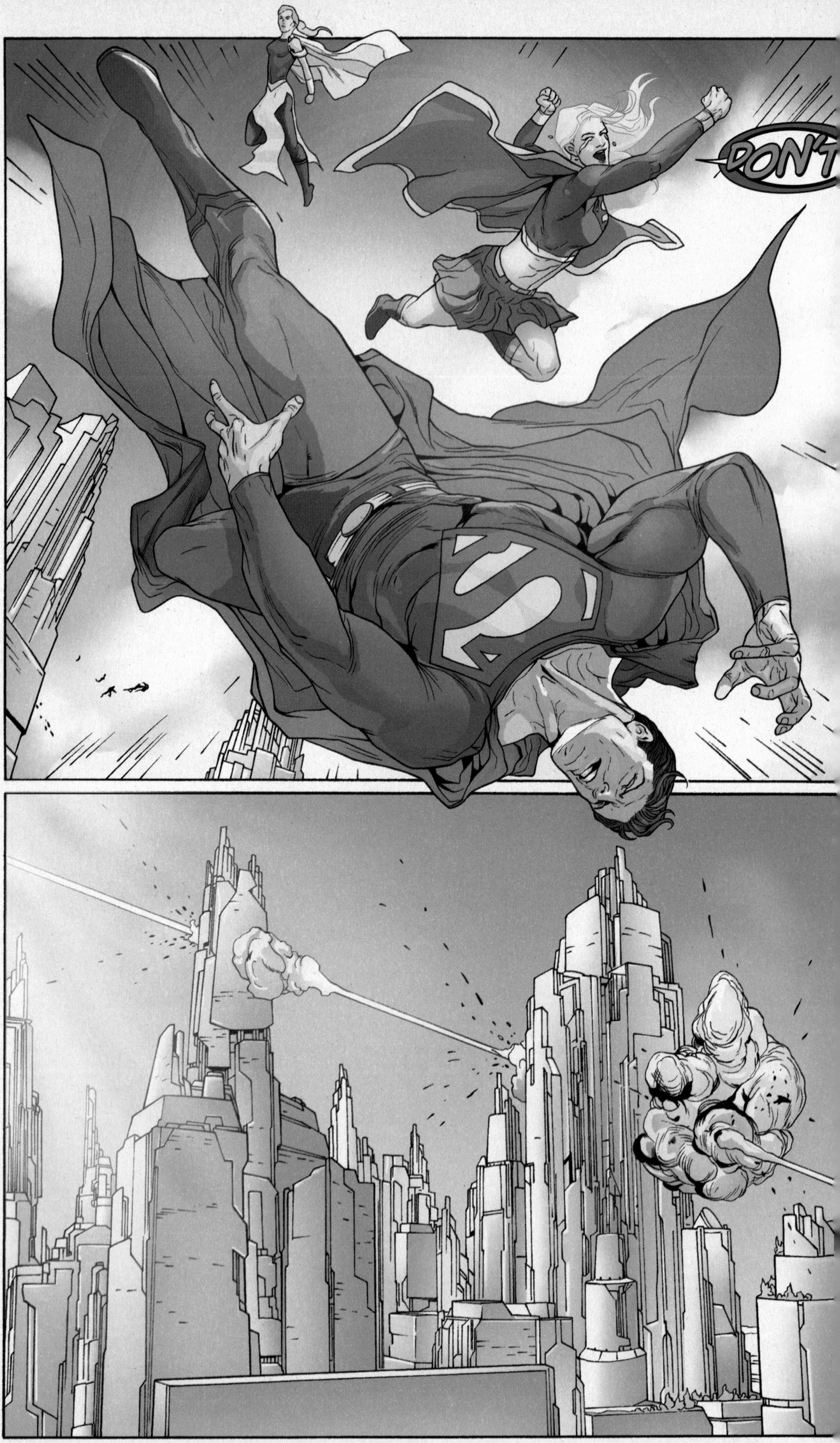
DON'T

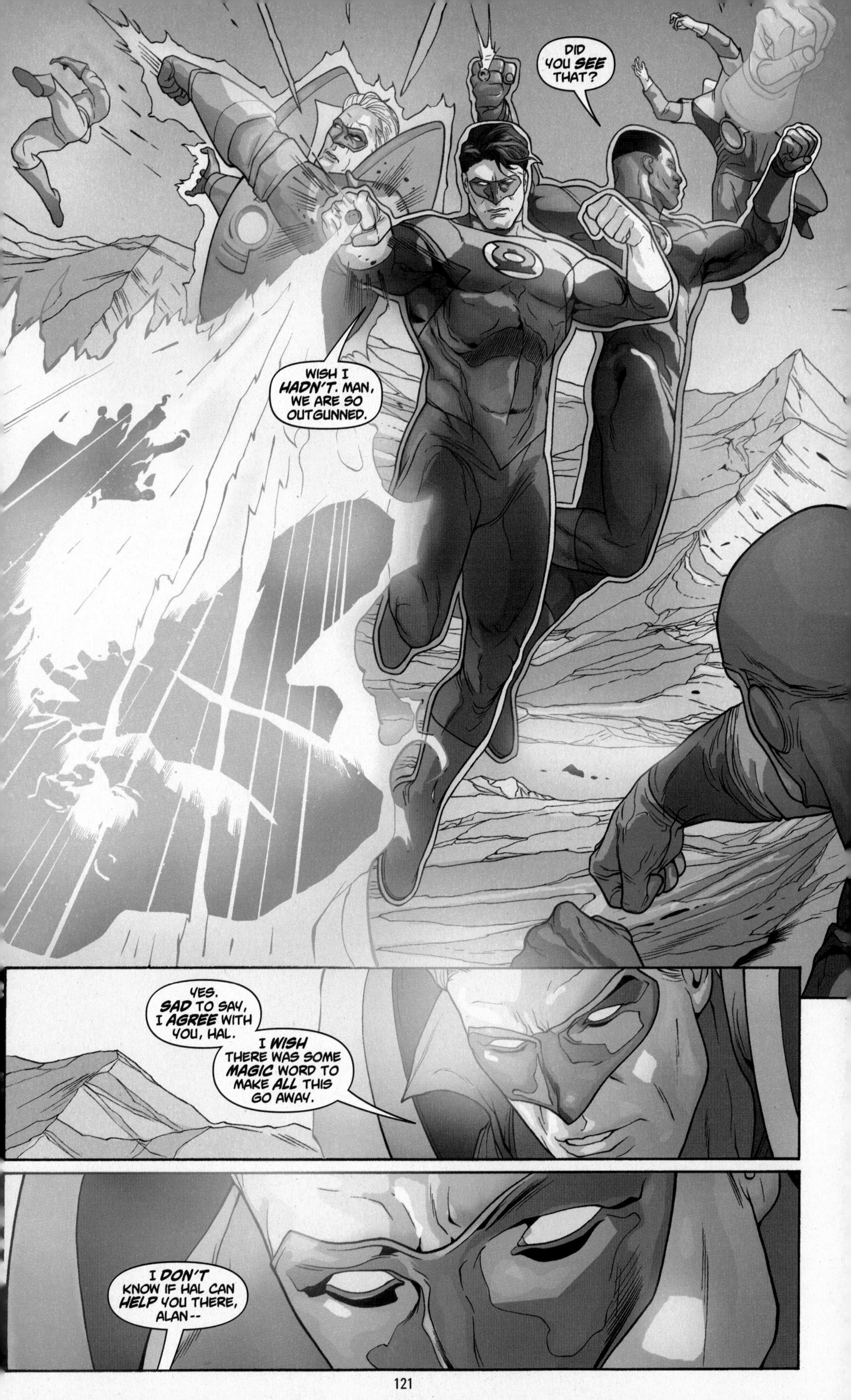

DID YOU SEE THAT?
WISH I HADN'T. MAN, WE ARE SO OUTGUNNED.
YES. SAD TO SAY, I AGREE WITH YOU, HAL.
I WISH THERE WAS SOME MAGIC WORD TO MAKE ALL THIS GO AWAY.
I DON'T KNOW IF HAL CAN HELP YOU THERE, ALAN--

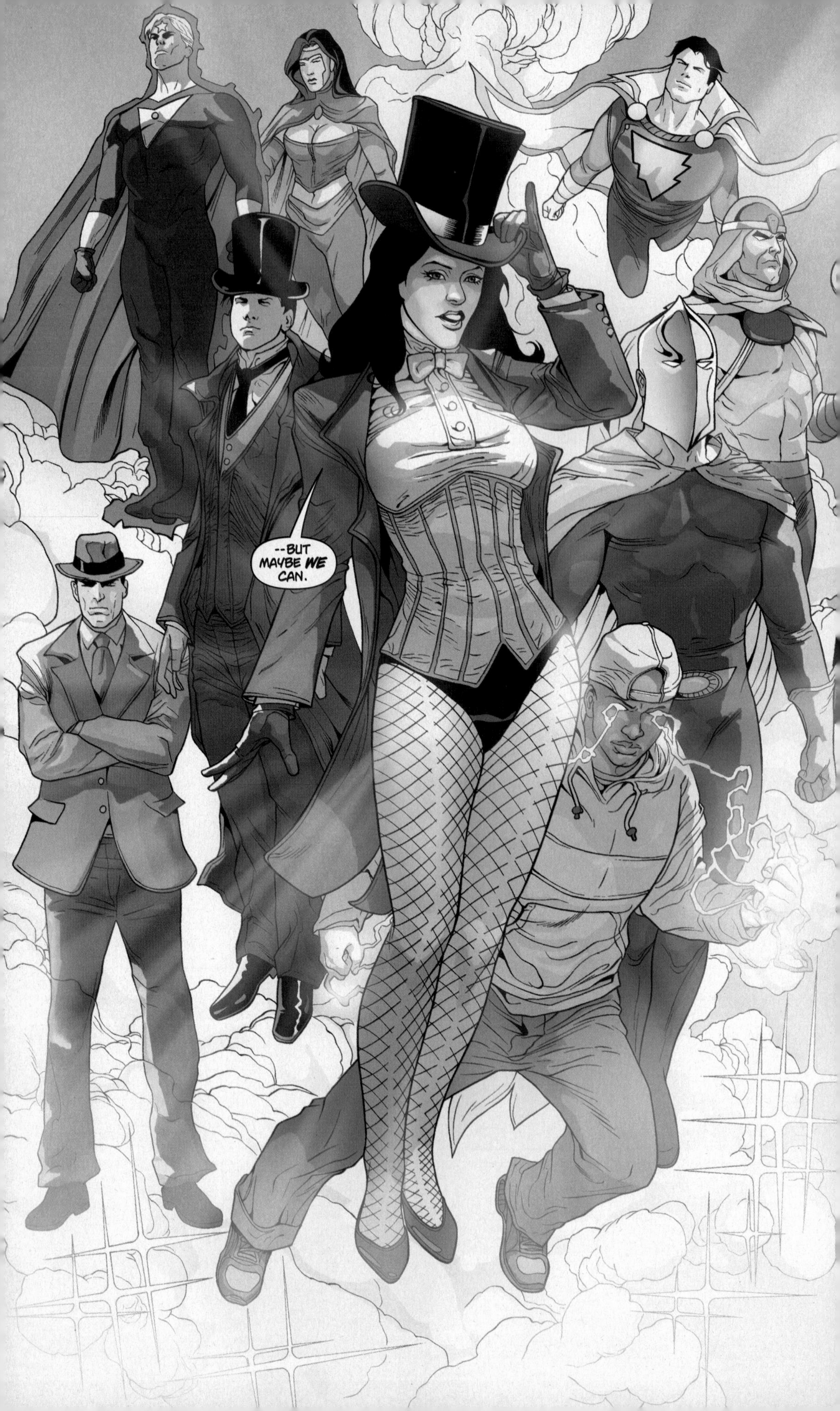
--BUT MAYBE WE CAN.

<BIRTH OF A NATION> ACTION COMICS 873 COVER ART BY **LADRÖNN**

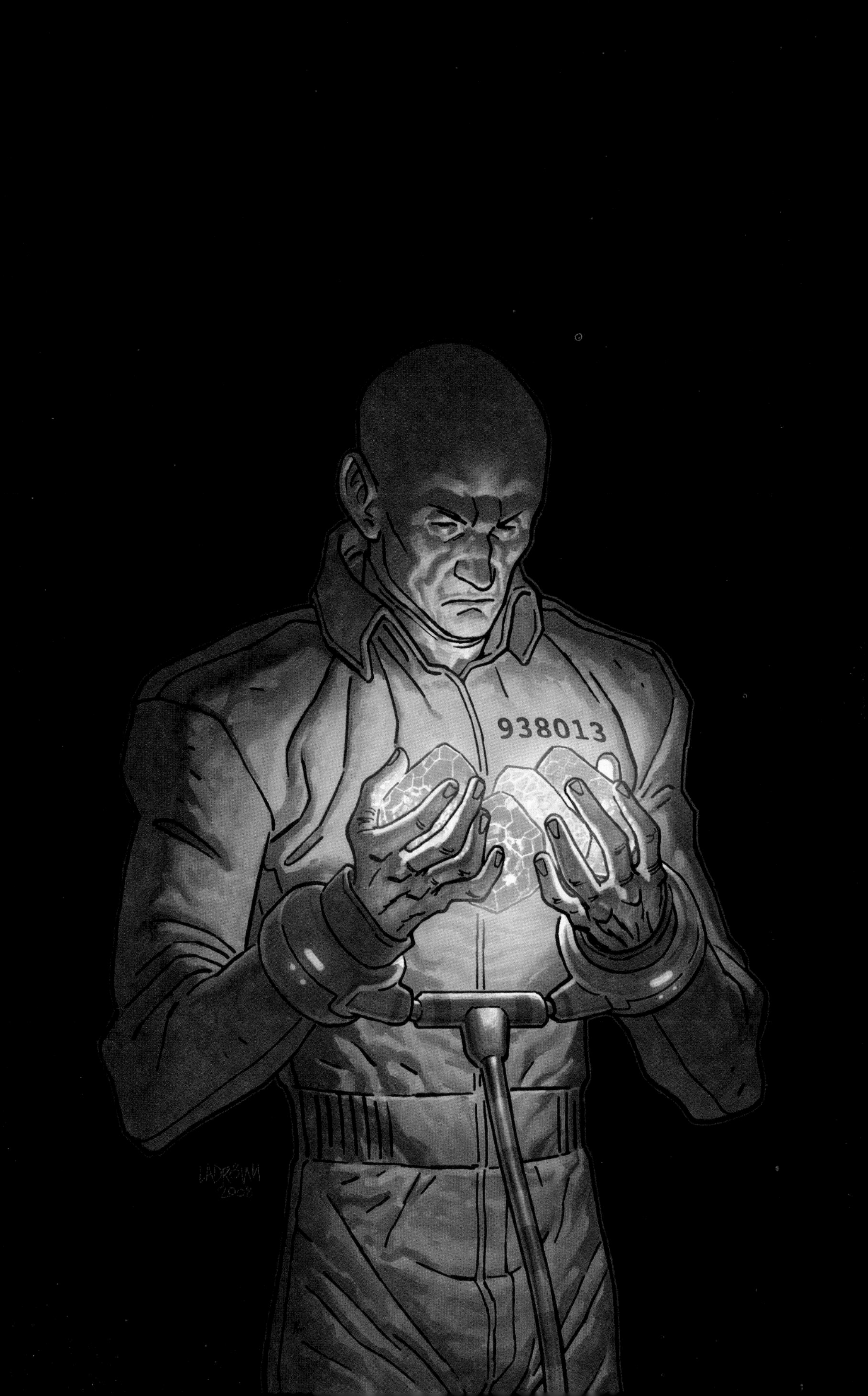
938013

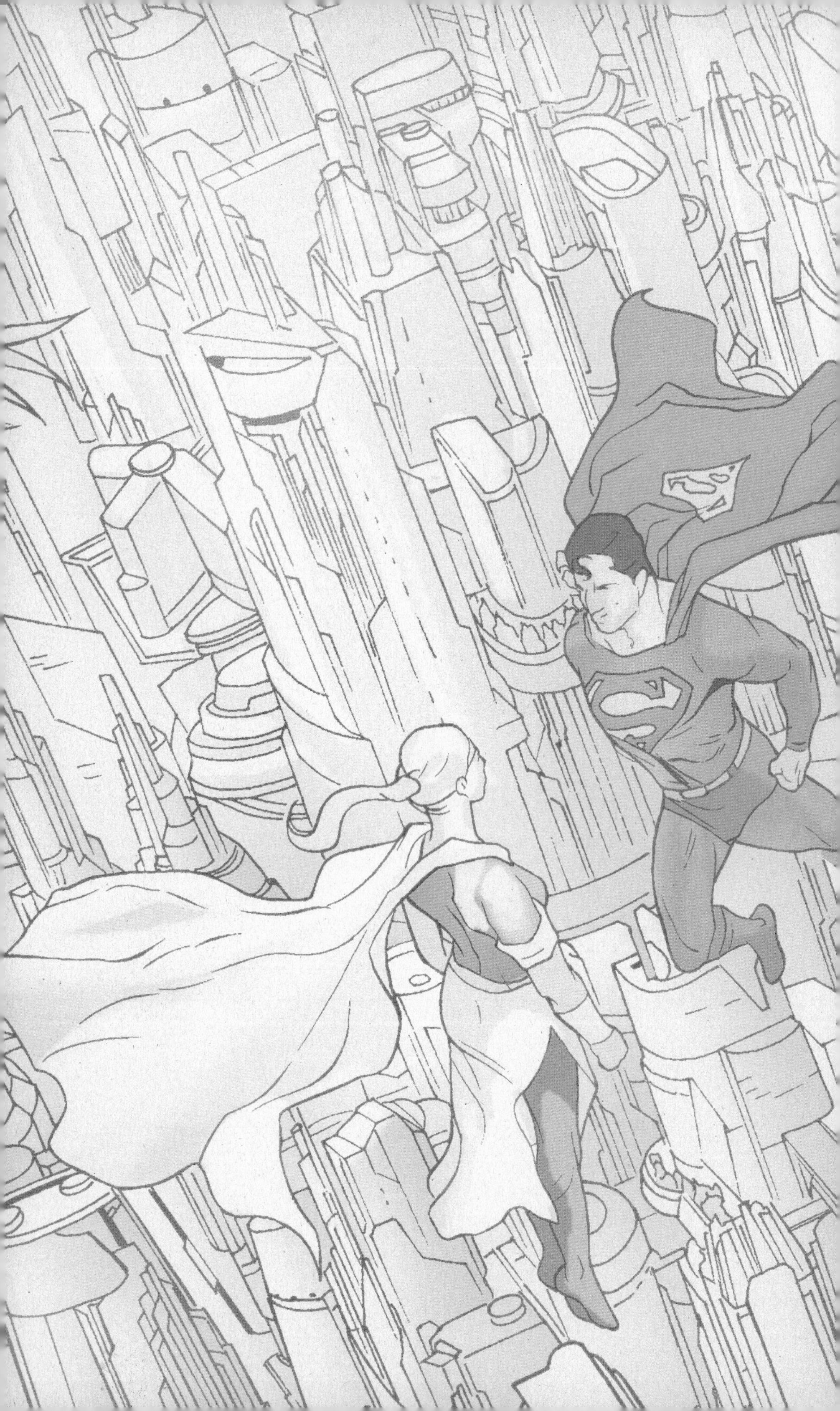

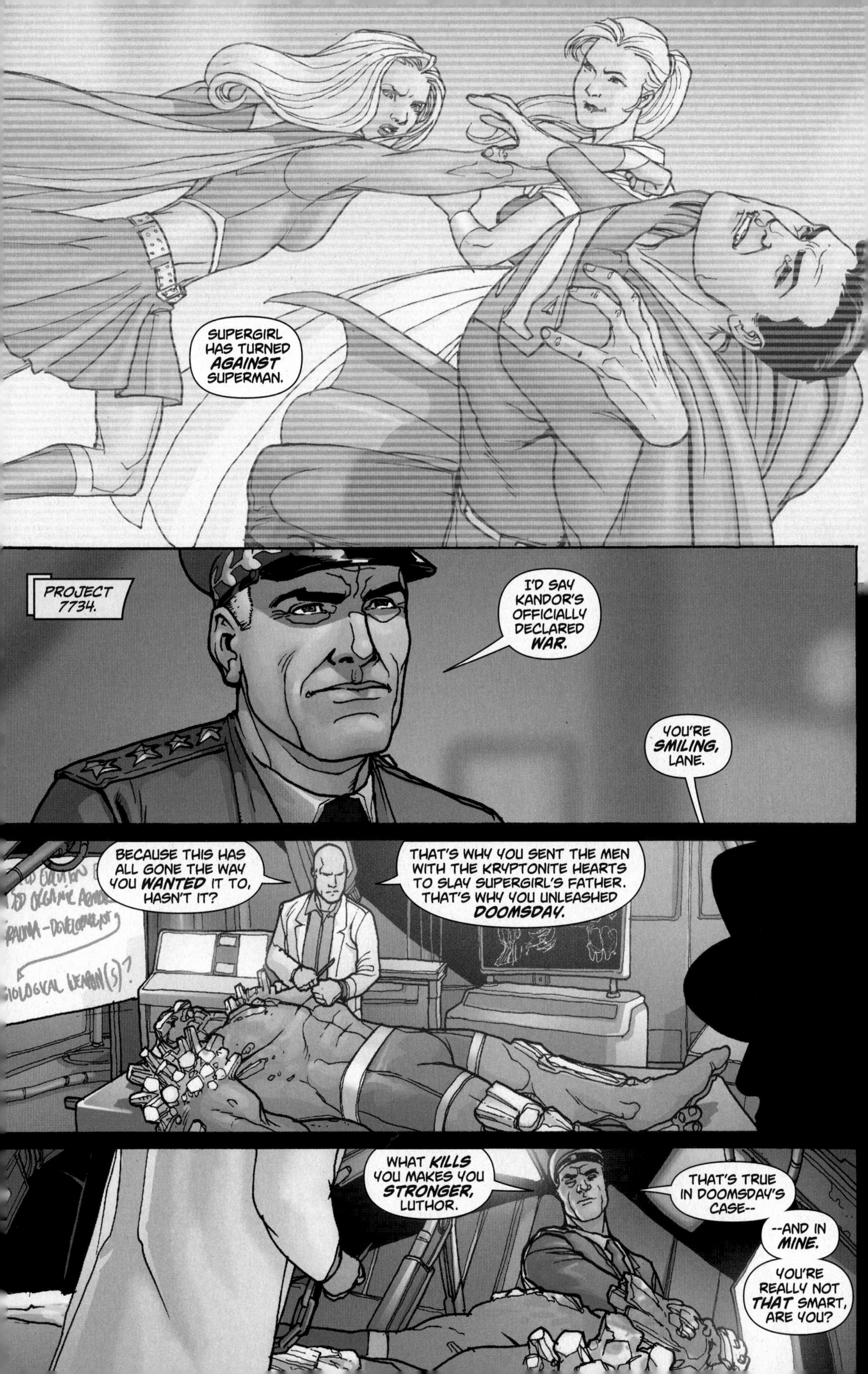
SUPERGIRL HAS TURNED AGAINST SUPERMAN.
PROJECT 7734.
I'D SAY KANDOR'S OFFICIALLY DECLARED WAR.
YOU'RE SMILING, LANE.
BECAUSE THIS HAS ALL GONE THE WAY YOU WANTED IT TO, HASN'T IT?
THAT'S WHY YOU SENT THE MEN WITH THE KRYPTONITE HEARTS TO SLAY SUPERGIRL'S FATHER. THAT'S WHY YOU UNLEASHED DOOMSDAY.
WHAT KILLS YOU MAKES YOU STRONGER, LUTHOR.
THAT'S TRUE IN DOOMSDAY'S CASE--
--AND IN MINE.
YOU'RE REALLY NOT THAT SMART, ARE YOU?

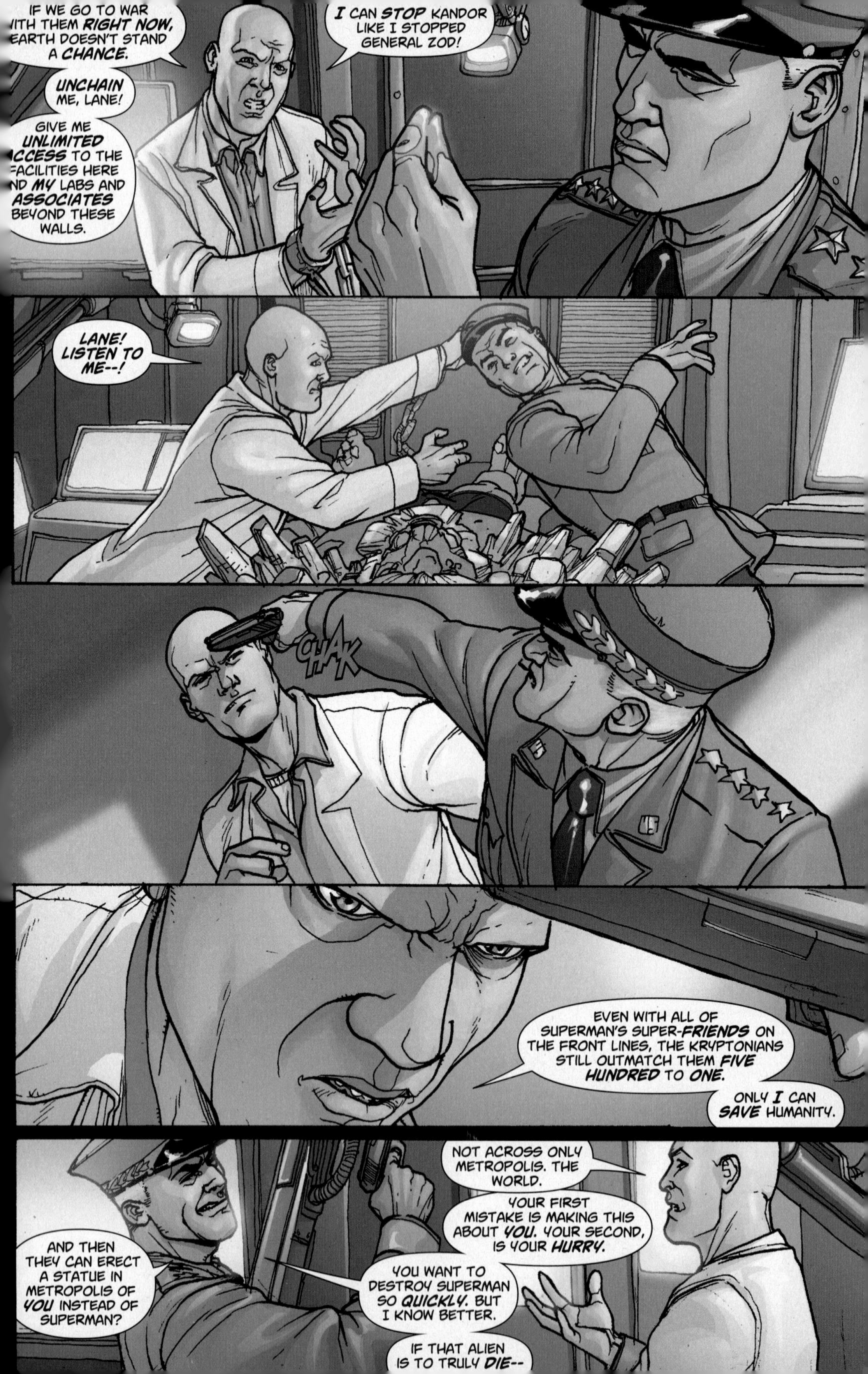

IF WE GO TO WAR WITH THEM RIGHT NOW, EARTH DOESN'T STAND A CHANCE.
UNCHAIN ME, LANE!
GIVE ME UNLIMITED ACCESS TO THE FACILITIES HERE AND MY LABS AND ASSOCIATES BEYOND THESE WALLS.
I CAN STOP KANDOR LIKE I STOPPED GENERAL ZOD!
LANE! LISTEN TO ME--!
CHAK
EVEN WITH ALL OF SUPERMAN'S SUPER-FRIENDS ON THE FRONT LINES, THE KRYPTONIANS STILL OUTMATCH THEM FIVE HUNDRED TO ONE.
ONLY I CAN SAVE HUMANITY.
AND THEN THEY CAN ERECT A STATUE IN METROPOLIS OF YOU INSTEAD OF SUPERMAN?
NOT ACROSS ONLY METROPOLIS. THE WORLD.
YOUR FIRST MISTAKE IS MAKING THIS ABOUT YOU. YOUR SECOND, IS YOUR HURRY.
YOU WANT TO DESTROY SUPERMAN SO QUICKLY. BUT I KNOW BETTER.
IF THAT ALIEN IS TO TRULY DIE--

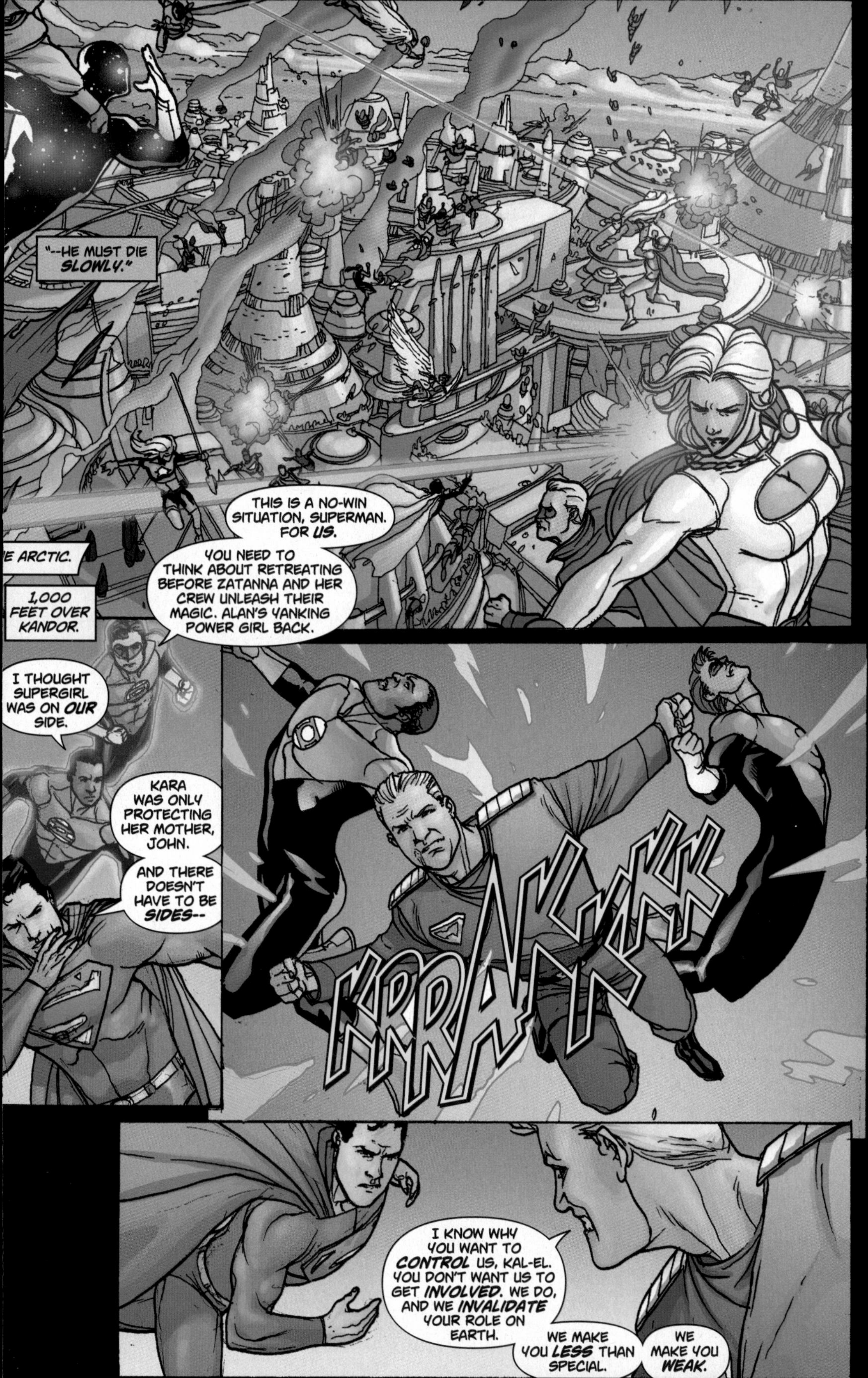
"--HE MUST DIE SLOWLY."
...E ARCTIC.
1,000 FEET OVER KANDOR.
THIS IS A NO-WIN SITUATION, SUPERMAN. FOR US.
YOU NEED TO THINK ABOUT RETREATING BEFORE ZATANNA AND HER CREW UNLEASH THEIR MAGIC. ALAN'S YANKING POWER GIRL BACK.
I THOUGHT SUPERGIRL WAS ON OUR SIDE.
KARA WAS ONLY PROTECTING HER MOTHER, JOHN.
AND THERE DOESN'T HAVE TO BE SIDES--
KRRAKKK
I KNOW WHY YOU WANT TO CONTROL US, KAL-EL. YOU DON'T WANT US TO GET INVOLVED. WE DO, AND WE INVALIDATE YOUR ROLE ON EARTH.
WE MAKE YOU LESS THAN SPECIAL.
WE MAKE YOU WEAK.

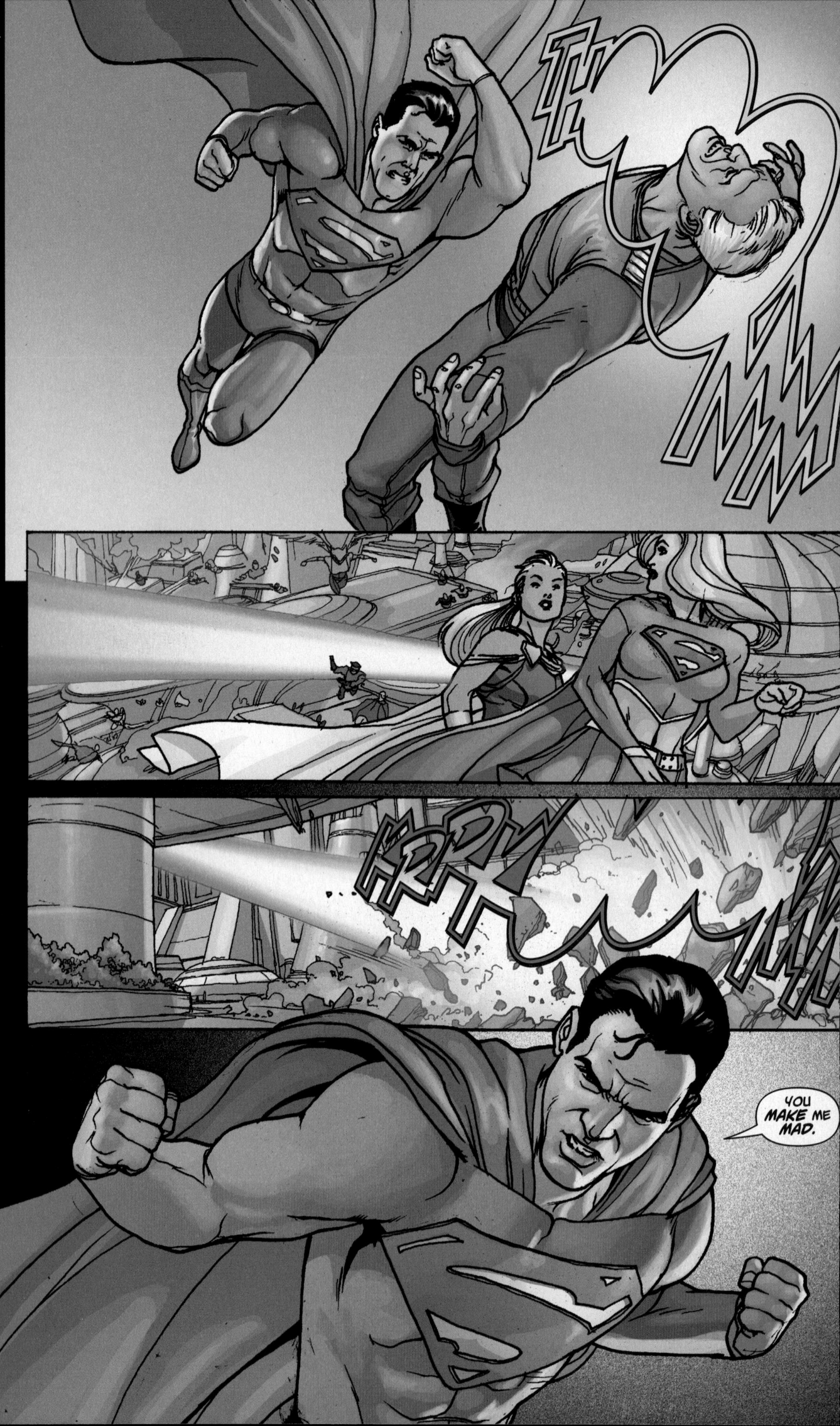
YOU MAKE ME MAD.

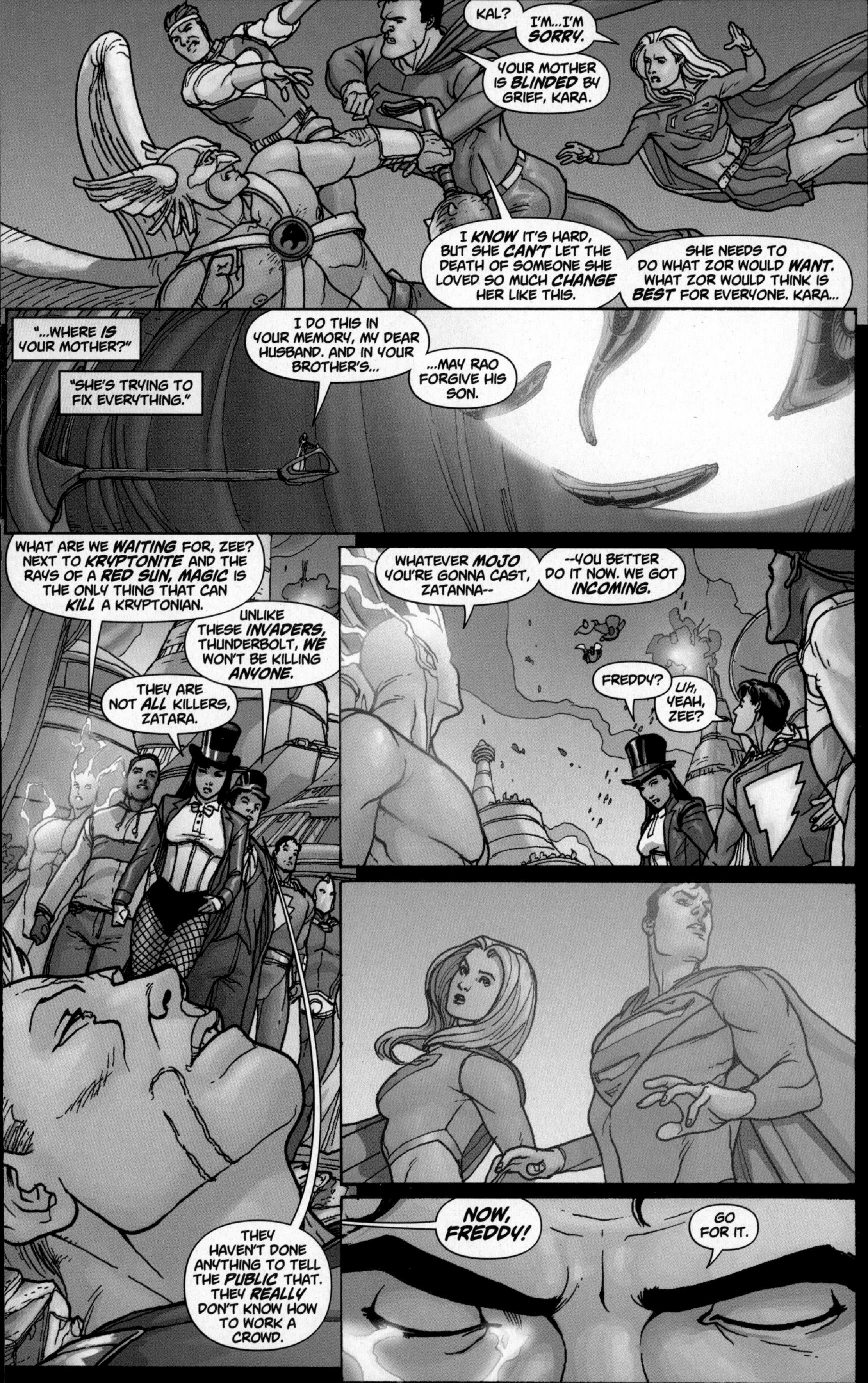
KAL?
I'M...I'M SORRY.
YOUR MOTHER IS BLINDED BY GRIEF, KARA.
I KNOW IT'S HARD, BUT SHE CAN'T LET THE DEATH OF SOMEONE SHE LOVED SO MUCH CHANGE HER LIKE THIS.
SHE NEEDS TO DO WHAT ZOR WOULD WANT. WHAT ZOR WOULD THINK IS BEST FOR EVERYONE. KARA...
"...WHERE IS YOUR MOTHER?"
"SHE'S TRYING TO FIX EVERYTHING."
I DO THIS IN YOUR MEMORY, MY DEAR HUSBAND. AND IN YOUR BROTHER'S...
...MAY RAO FORGIVE HIS SON.
WHAT ARE WE WAITING FOR, ZEE? NEXT TO KRYPTONITE AND THE RAYS OF A RED SUN, MAGIC IS THE ONLY THING THAT CAN KILL A KRYPTONIAN.
UNLIKE THESE INVADERS, THUNDERBOLT, WE WON'T BE KILLING ANYONE.
THEY ARE NOT ALL KILLERS, ZATARA.
THEY HAVEN'T DONE ANYTHING TO TELL THE PUBLIC THAT. THEY REALLY DON'T KNOW HOW TO WORK A CROWD.
WHATEVER MOJO YOU'RE GONNA CAST, ZATANNA--
--YOU BETTER DO IT NOW. WE GOT INCOMING.
FREDDY?
UH, YEAH, ZEE?
NOW, FREDDY!
GO FOR IT.

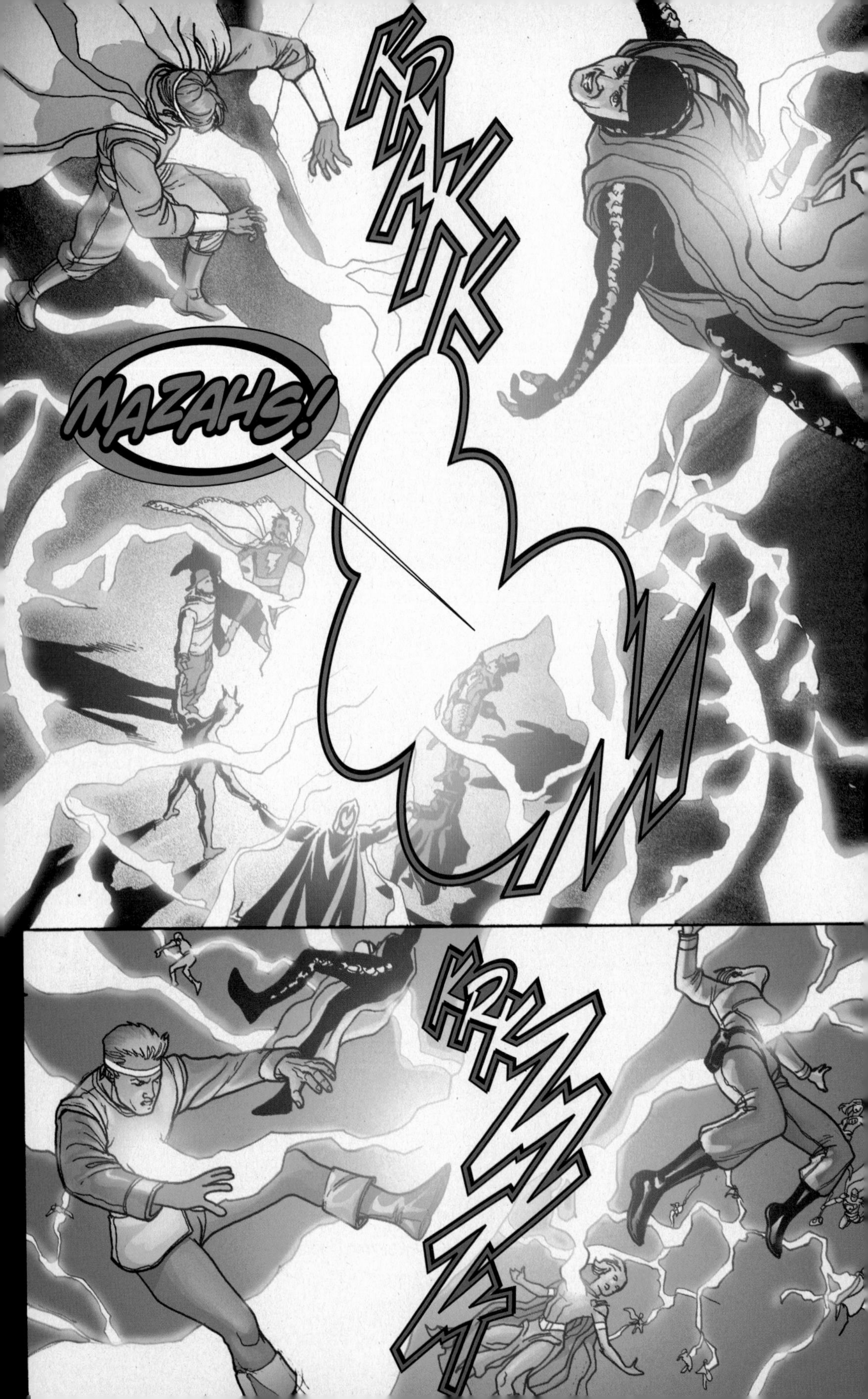
MAZAHS!

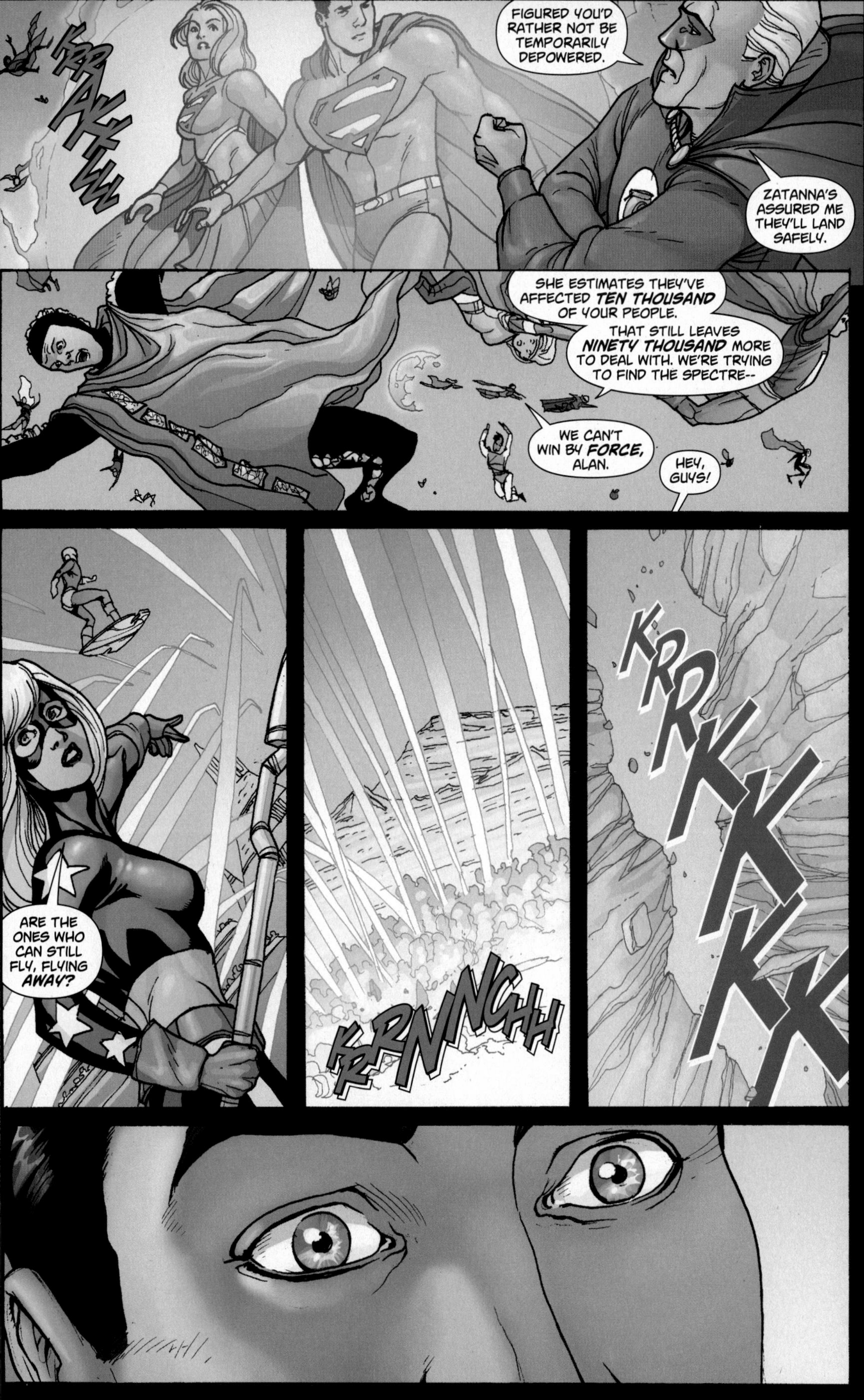

KRRAKKW
FIGURED YOU'D RATHER NOT BE TEMPORARILY DEPOWERED.
ZATANNA'S ASSURED ME THEY'LL LAND SAFELY.
SHE ESTIMATES THEY'VE AFFECTED TEN THOUSAND OF YOUR PEOPLE.
THAT STILL LEAVES NINETY THOUSAND MORE TO DEAL WITH. WE'RE TRYING TO FIND THE SPECTRE--
WE CAN'T WIN BY FORCE, ALAN.
HEY, GUYS!
ARE THE ONES WHO CAN STILL FLY, FLYING AWAY?
KRRNNGHH
KRRKKKK

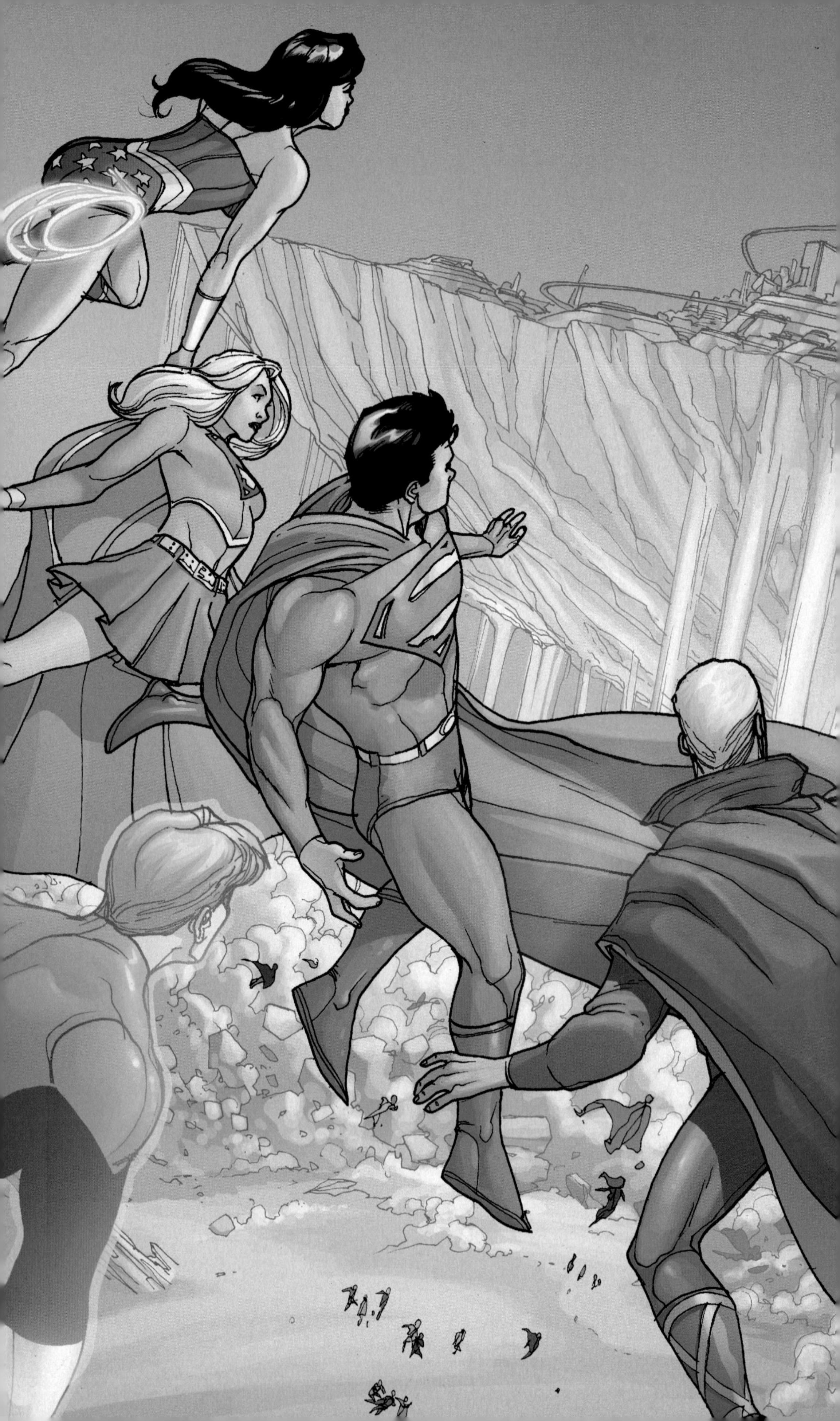

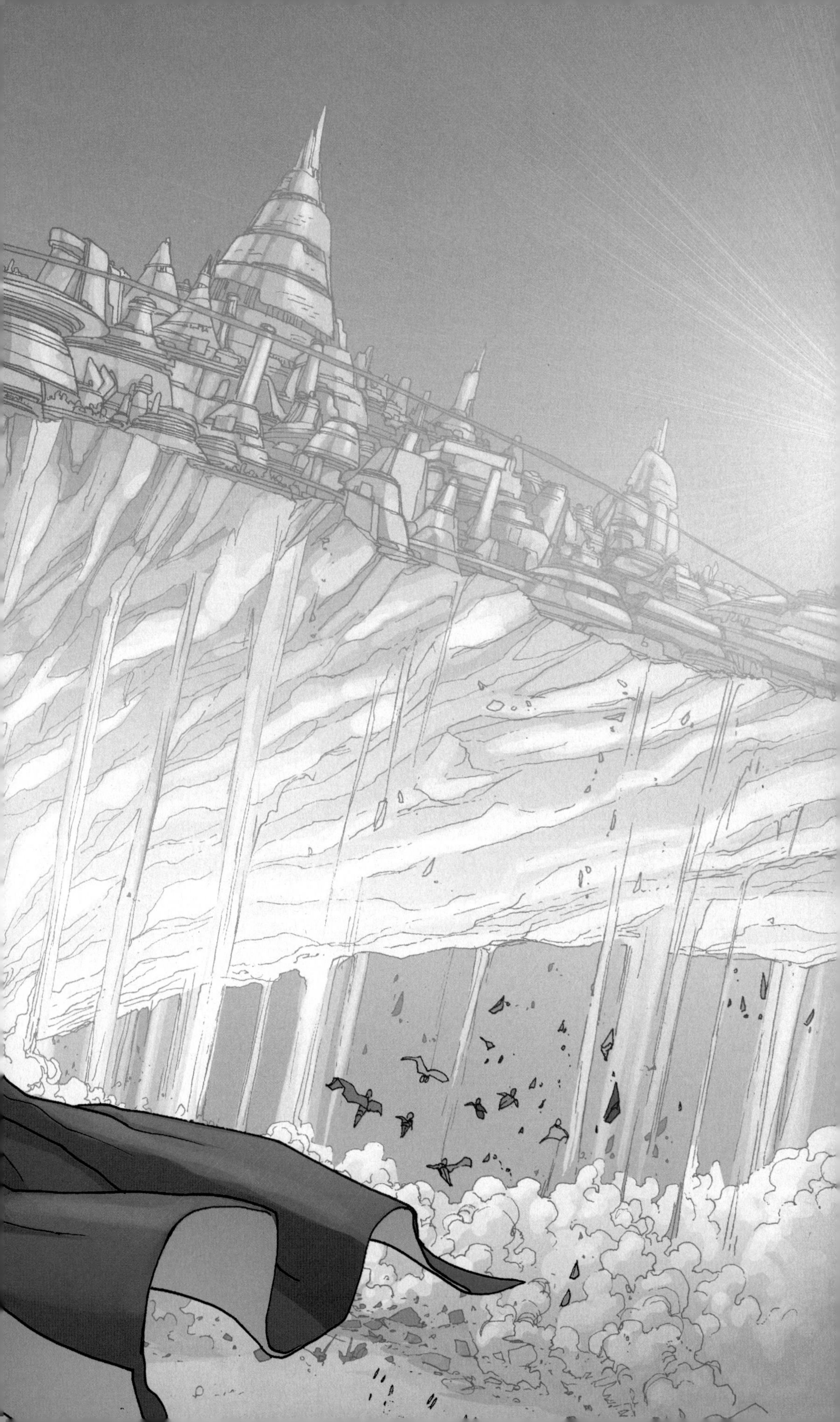

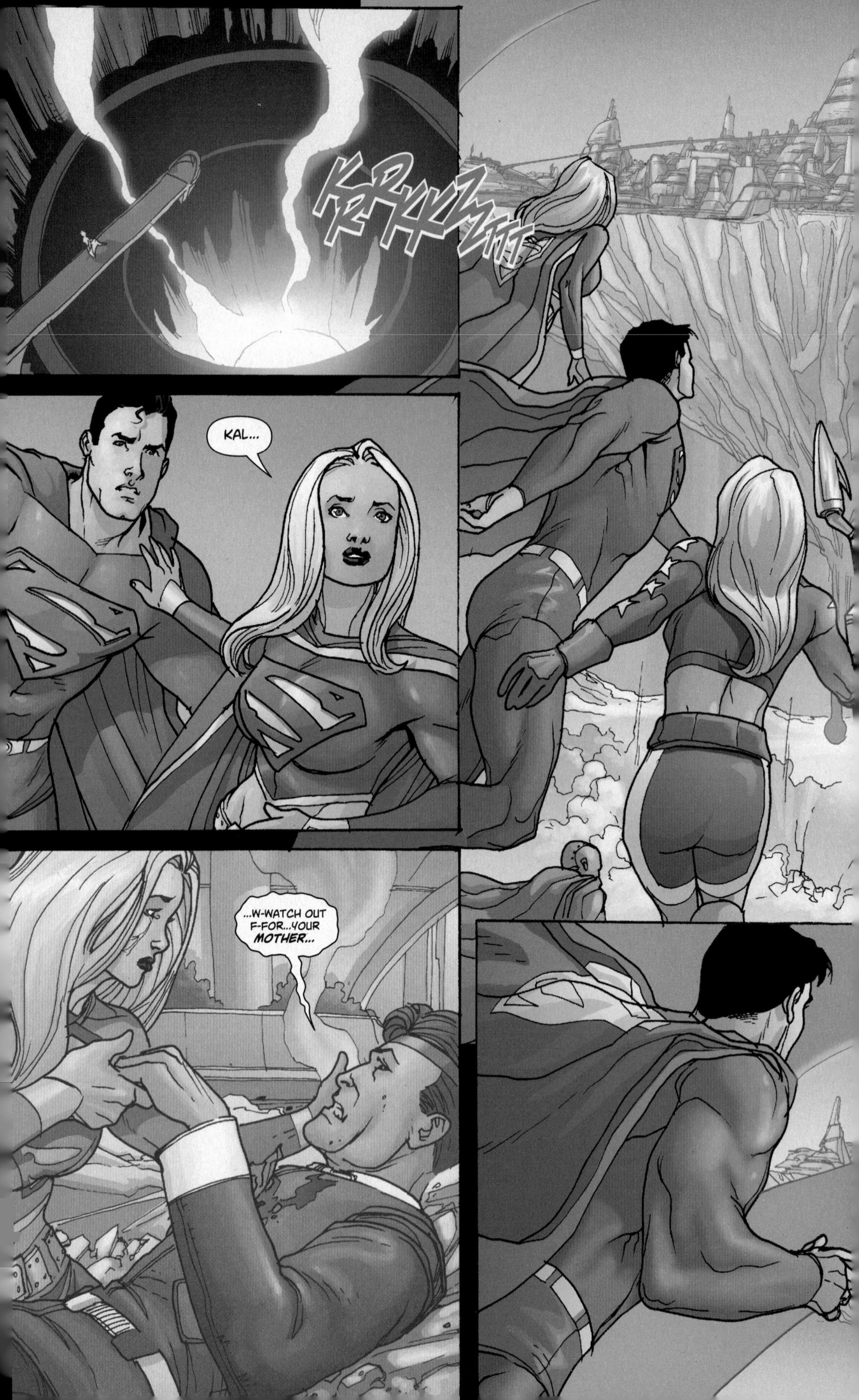
KRRAKZZTTT
KAL...
...W-WATCH OUT
F-FOR...YOUR
MOTHER...

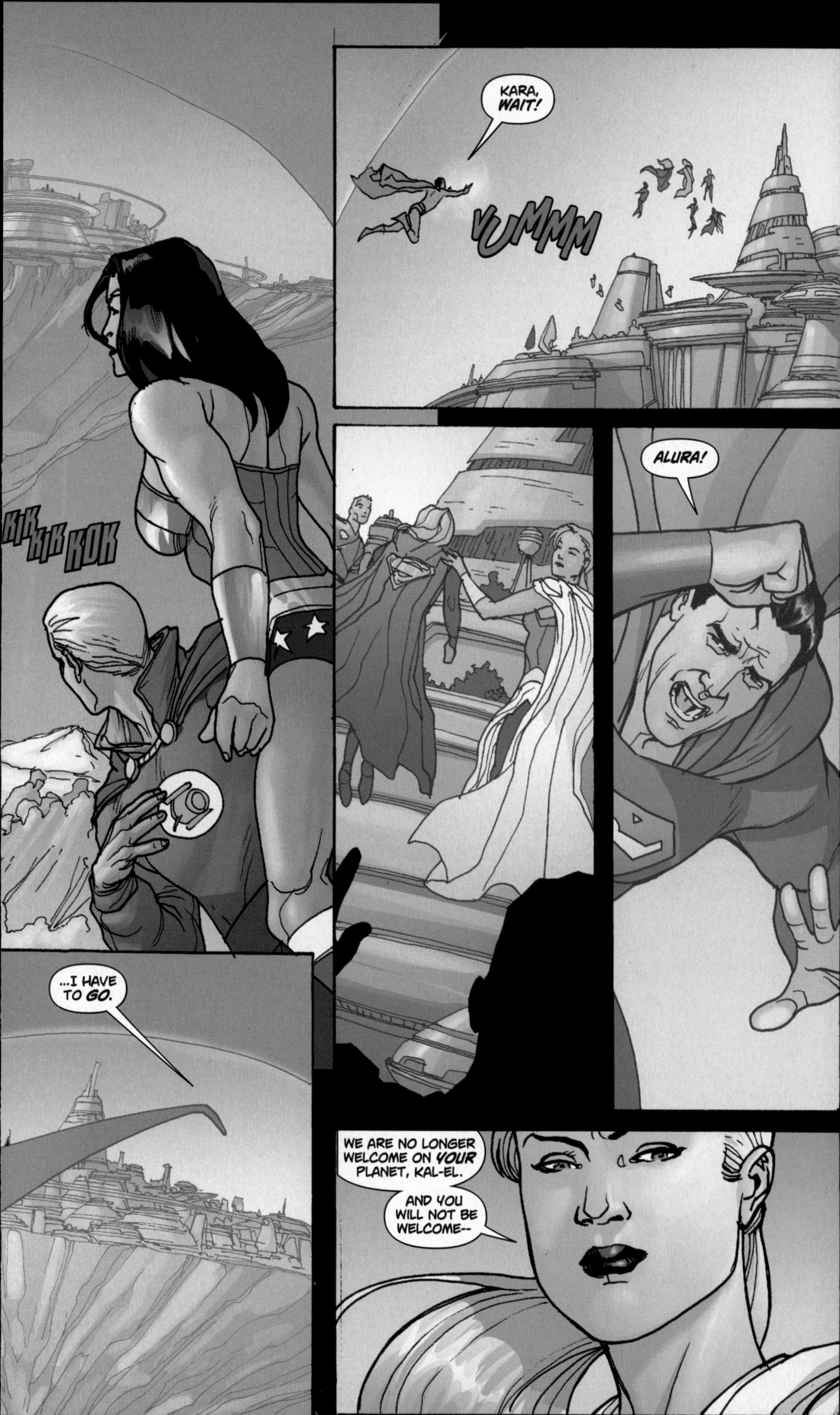
KIK KIK KOK
KARA, WAIT!
VUMMM
ALURA!
...I HAVE TO GO.
WE ARE NO LONGER WELCOME ON YOUR PLANET, KAL-EL.
AND YOU WILL NOT BE WELCOME--

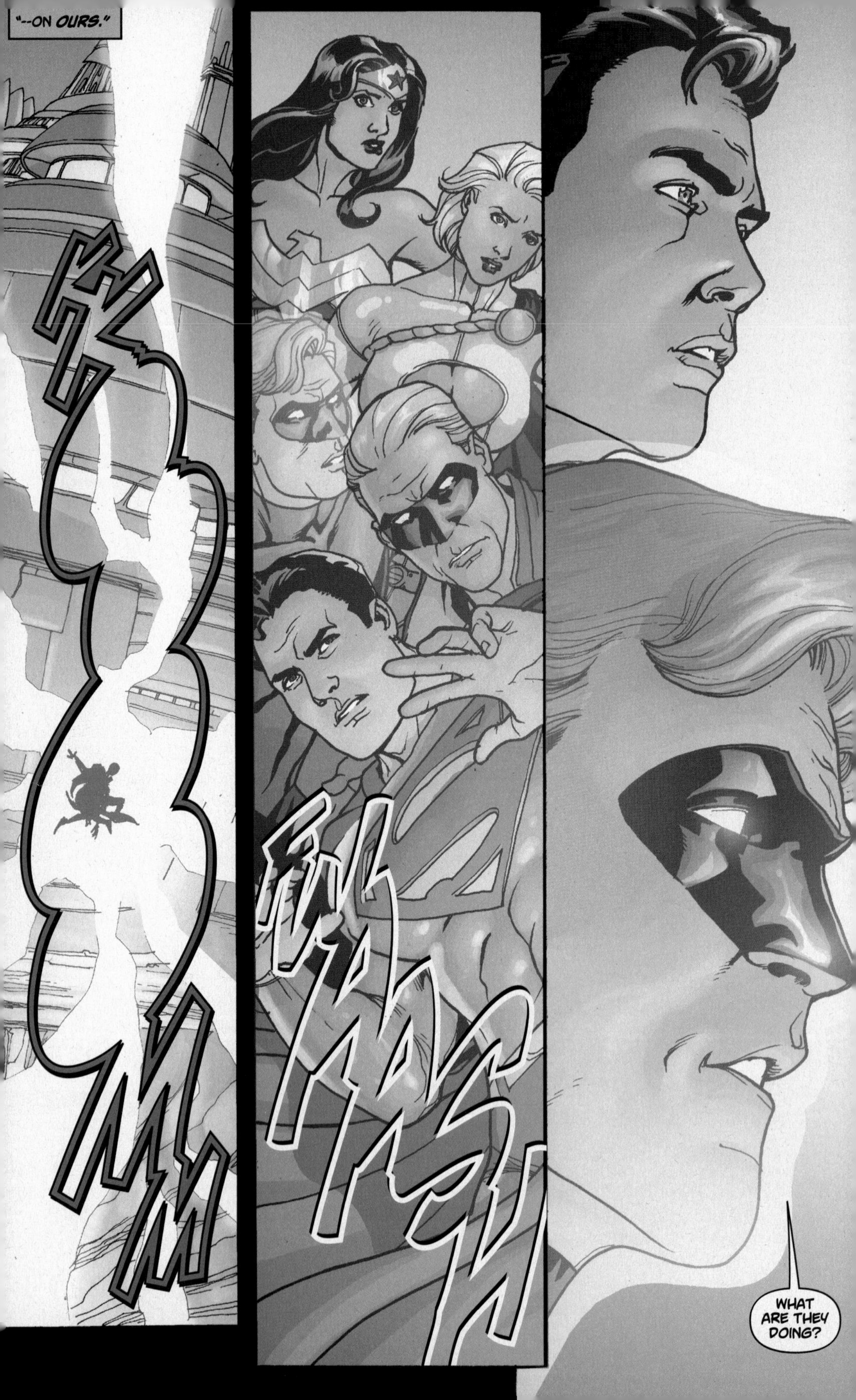
"--ON *OURS.*"
WHAT ARE THEY DOING?

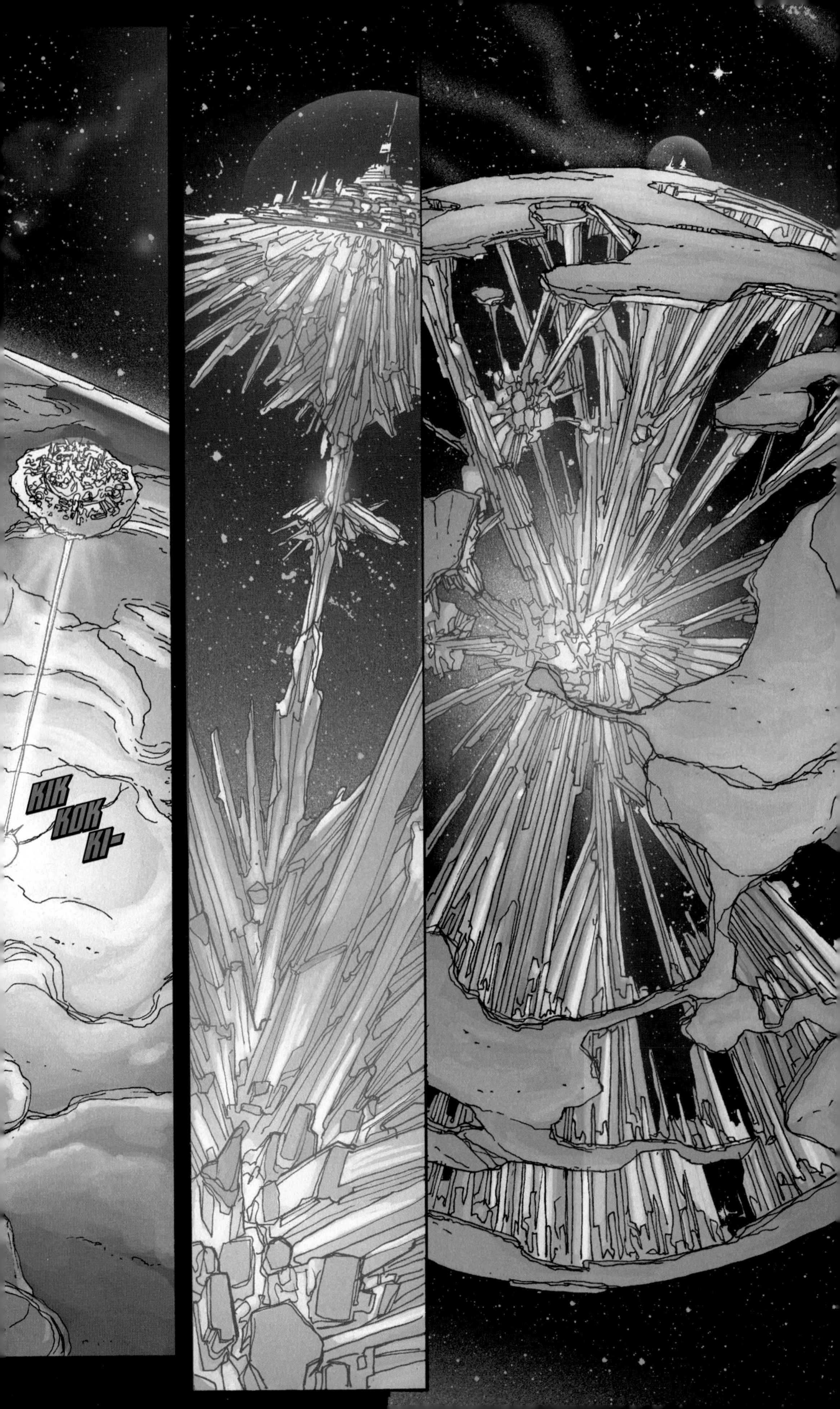
KIK
KOK
KI-

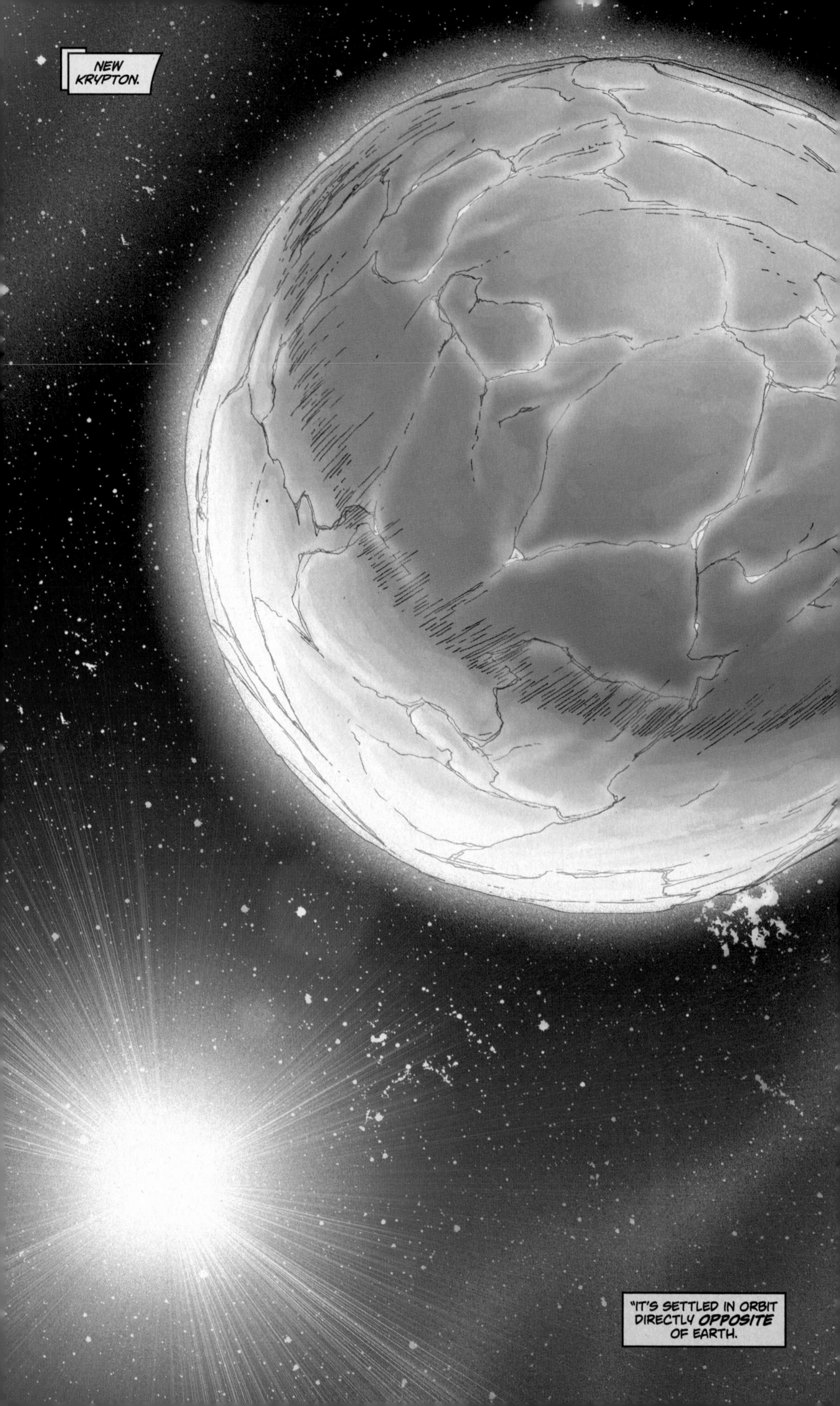
NEW KRYPTON.
"IT'S SETTLED IN ORBIT DIRECTLY OPPOSITE OF EARTH.

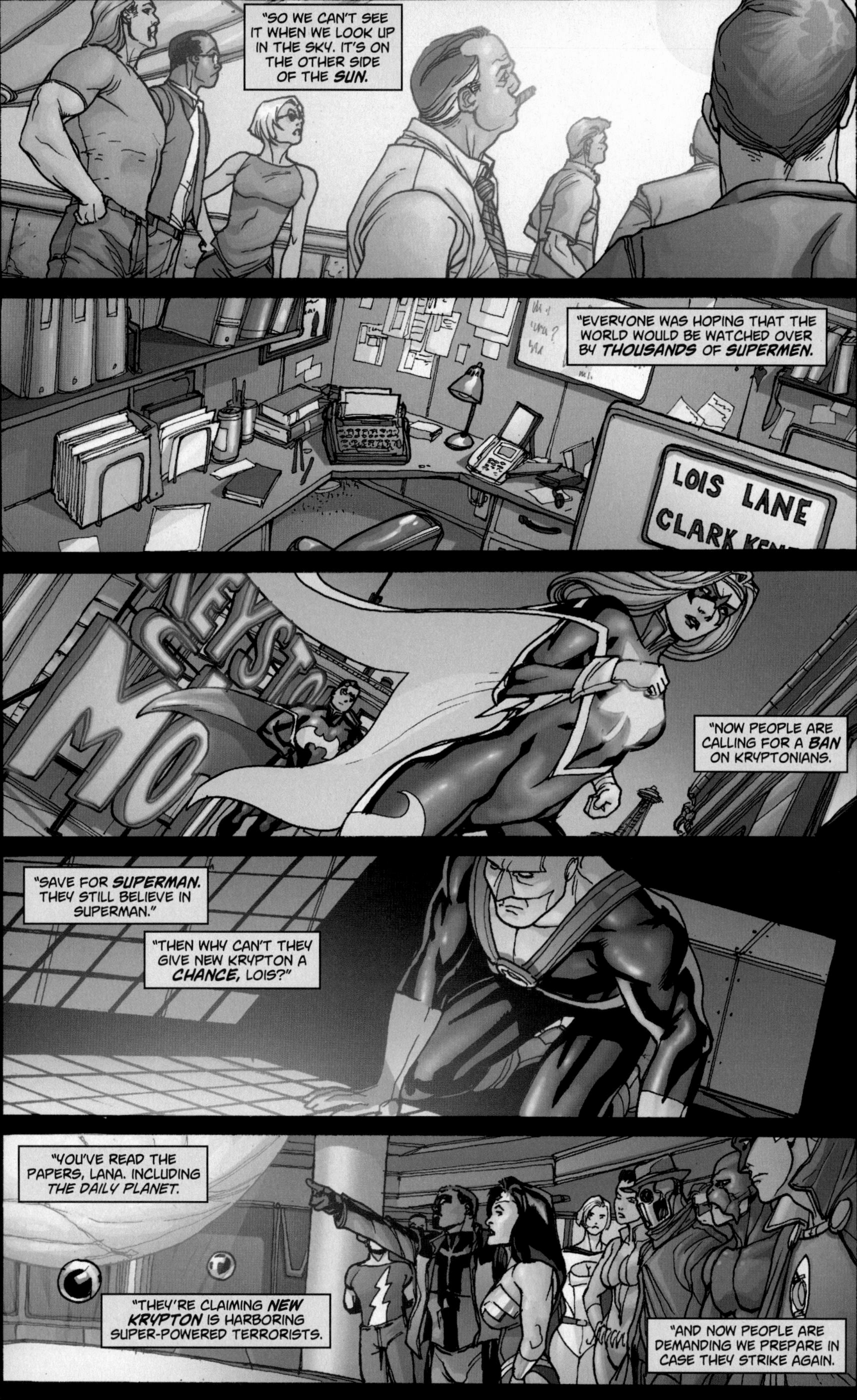
"SO WE CAN'T SEE IT WHEN WE LOOK UP IN THE SKY. IT'S ON THE OTHER SIDE OF THE SUN.
"EVERYONE WAS HOPING THAT THE WORLD WOULD BE WATCHED OVER BY THOUSANDS OF SUPERMEN.
LOIS LANE
CLARK KEN
"NOW PEOPLE ARE CALLING FOR A BAN ON KRYPTONIANS.
"SAVE FOR SUPERMAN. THEY STILL BELIEVE IN SUPERMAN."
"THEN WHY CAN'T THEY GIVE NEW KRYPTON A CHANCE, LOIS?"
"YOU'VE READ THE PAPERS, LANA. INCLUDING THE DAILY PLANET.
"THEY'RE CLAIMING NEW KRYPTON IS HARBORING SUPER-POWERED TERRORISTS.
"AND NOW PEOPLE ARE DEMANDING WE PREPARE IN CASE THEY STRIKE AGAIN.

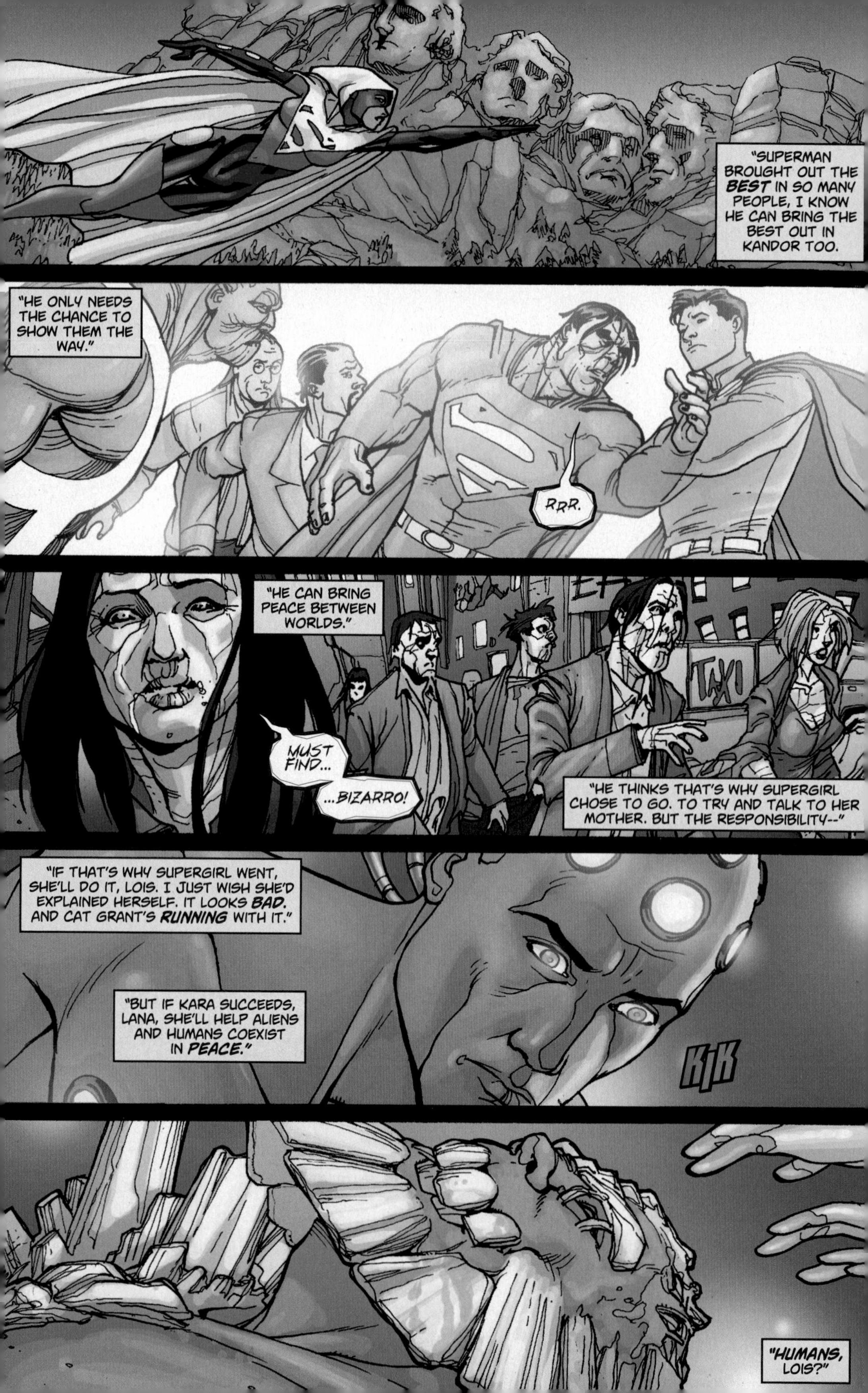
"SUPERMAN BROUGHT OUT THE BEST IN SO MANY PEOPLE, I KNOW HE CAN BRING THE BEST OUT IN KANDOR TOO.
"HE ONLY NEEDS THE CHANCE TO SHOW THEM THE WAY."
RRR.
"HE CAN BRING PEACE BETWEEN WORLDS."
MUST FIND...
...BIZARRO!
TAXI
"HE THINKS THAT'S WHY SUPERGIRL CHOSE TO GO. TO TRY AND TALK TO HER MOTHER. BUT THE RESPONSIBILITY--"
"IF THAT'S WHY SUPERGIRL WENT, SHE'LL DO IT, LOIS. I JUST WISH SHE'D EXPLAINED HERSELF. IT LOOKS BAD. AND CAT GRANT'S RUNNING WITH IT."
"BUT IF KARA SUCCEEDS, LANA, SHE'LL HELP ALIENS AND HUMANS COEXIST IN PEACE."
KIK
"HUMANS, LOIS?"

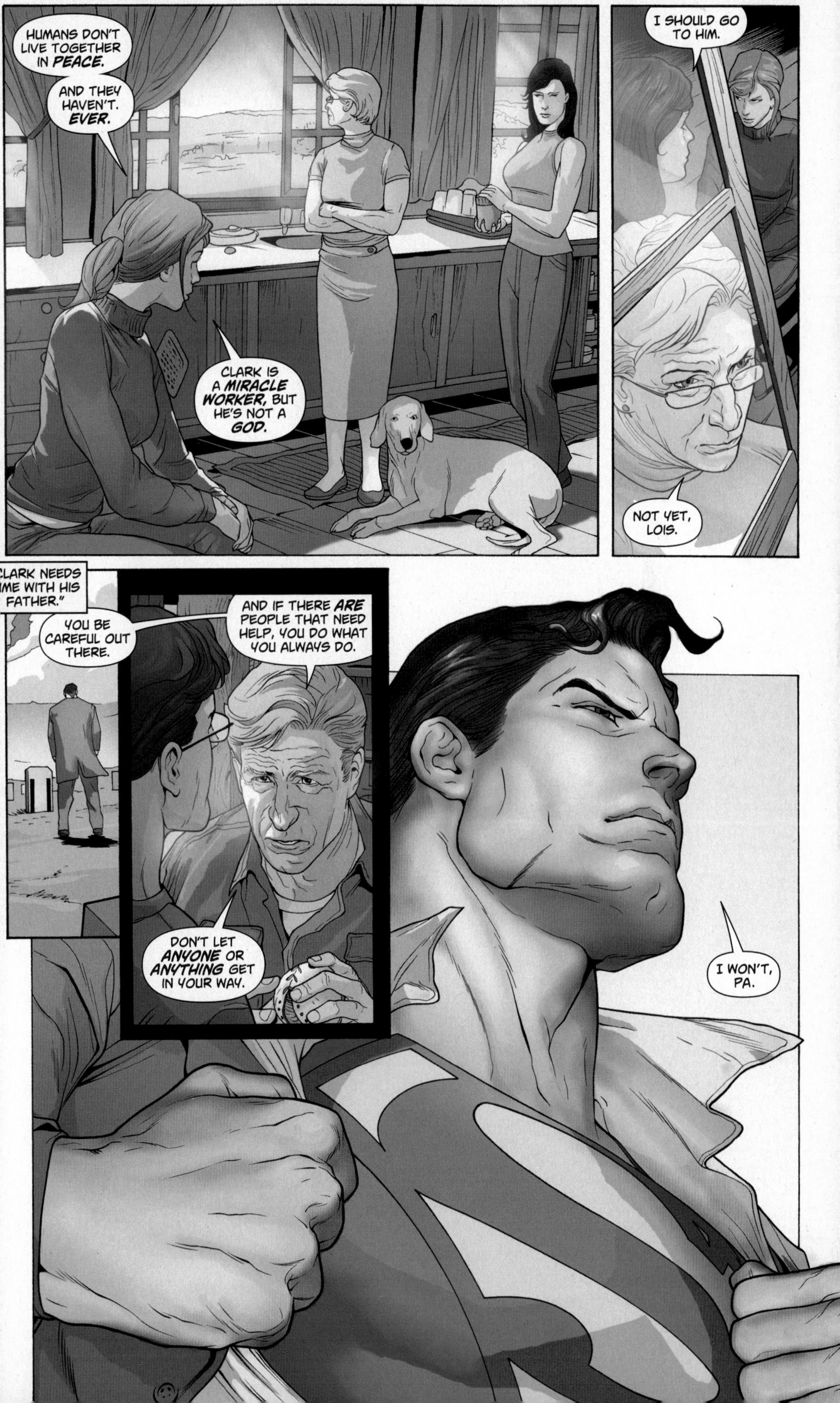
HUMANS DON'T LIVE TOGETHER IN PEACE.
AND THEY HAVEN'T. EVER.
CLARK IS A MIRACLE WORKER, BUT HE'S NOT A GOD.
I SHOULD GO TO HIM.
NOT YET, LOIS.
CLARK NEEDS ME WITH HIS FATHER."
YOU BE CAREFUL OUT THERE.
AND IF THERE ARE PEOPLE THAT NEED HELP, YOU DO WHAT YOU ALWAYS DO.
DON'T LET ANYONE OR ANYTHING GET IN YOUR WAY.
I WON'T, PA.

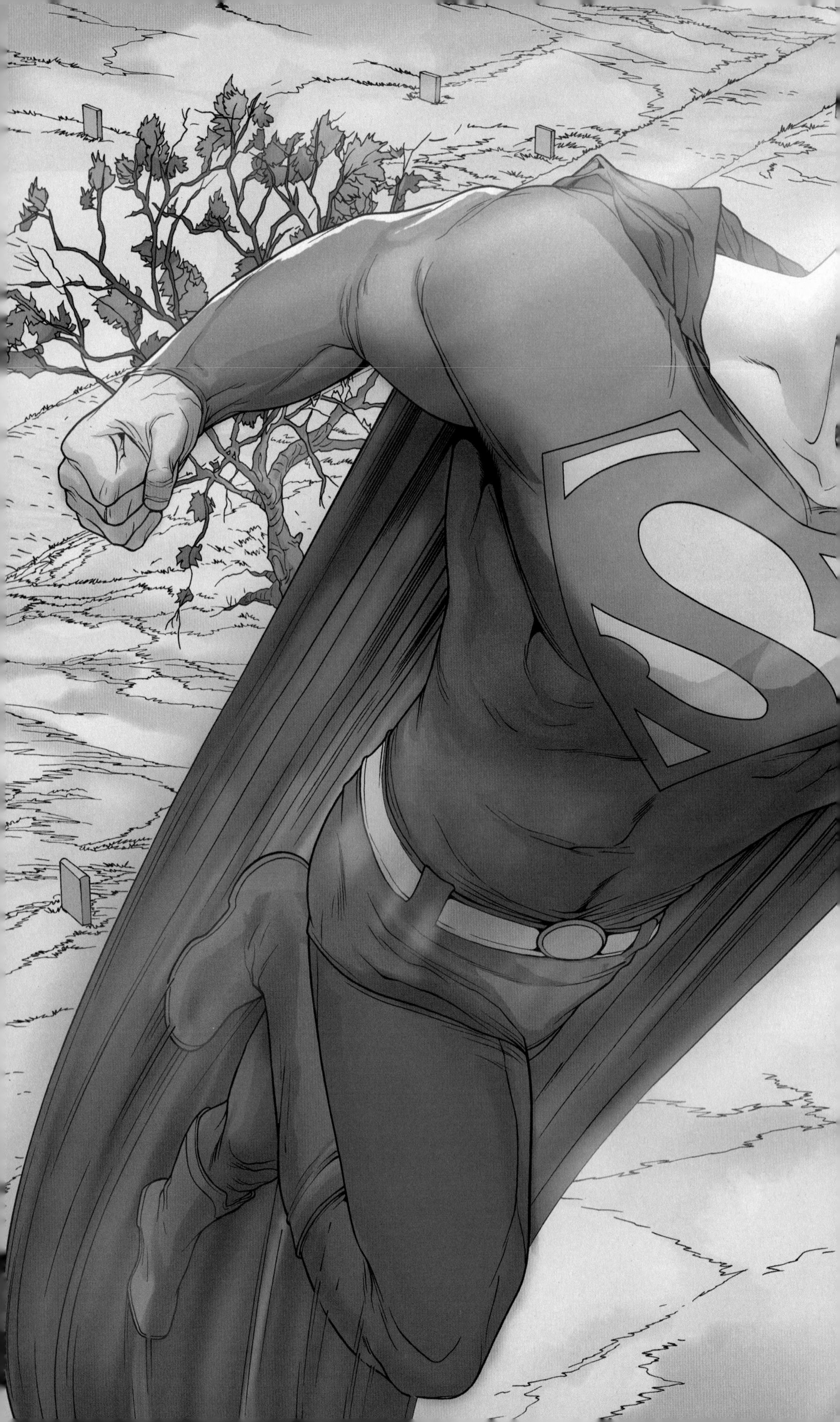

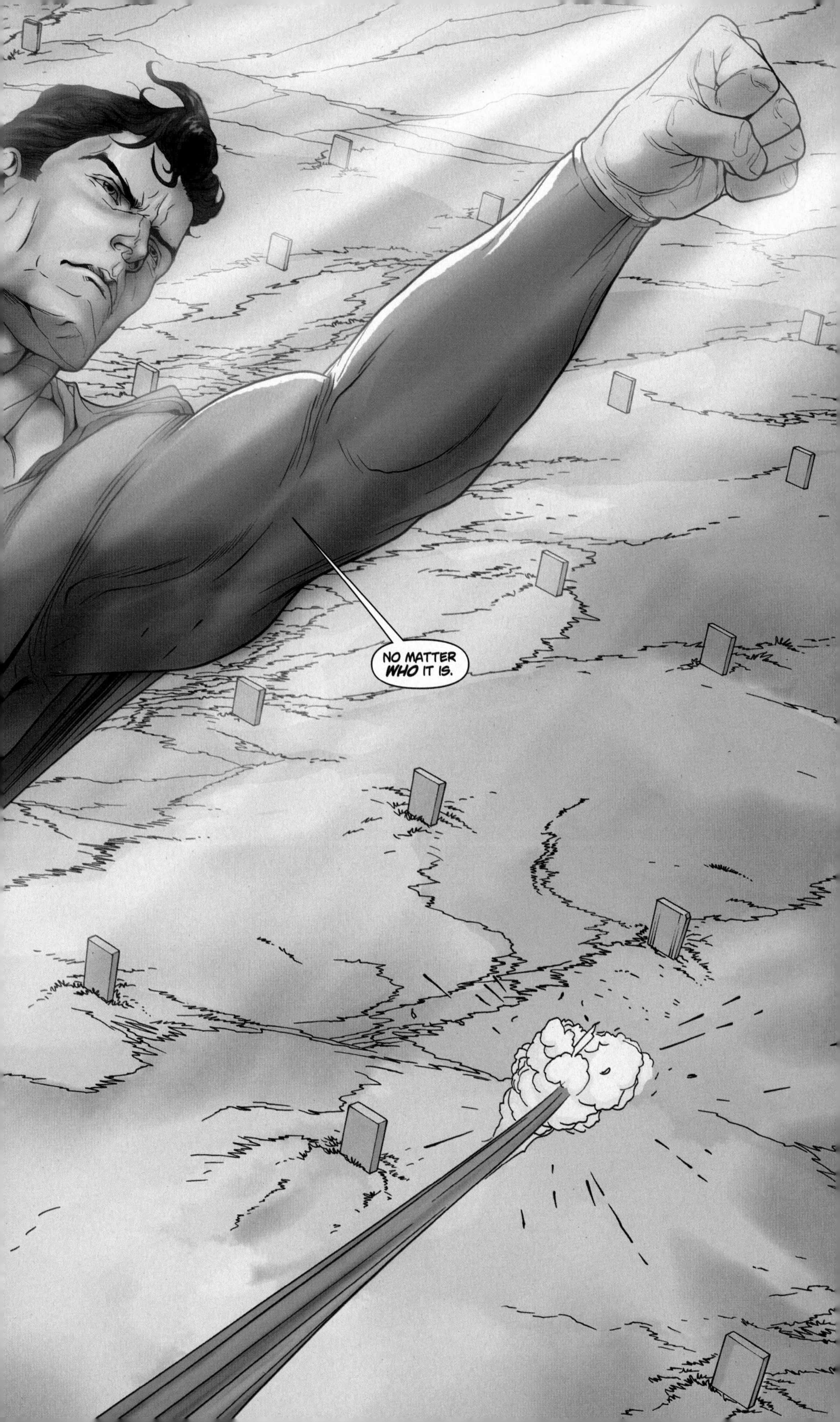
NO MATTER WHO IT IS.

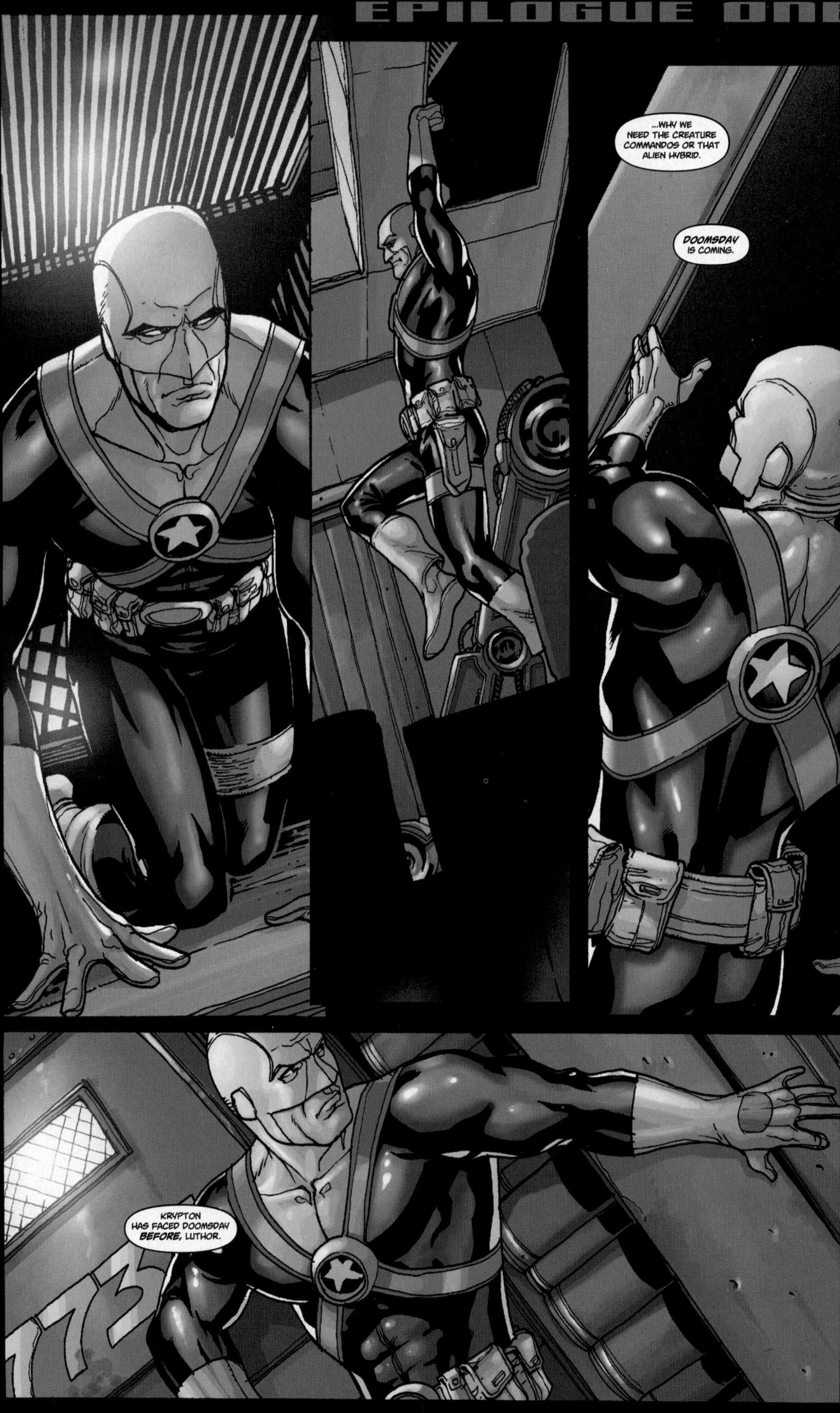
...WHY WE NEED THE CREATURE COMMANDOS OR THAT ALIEN HYBRID.
DOOMSDAY IS COMING.
KRYPTON HAS FACED DOOMSDAY BEFORE, LUTHOR.

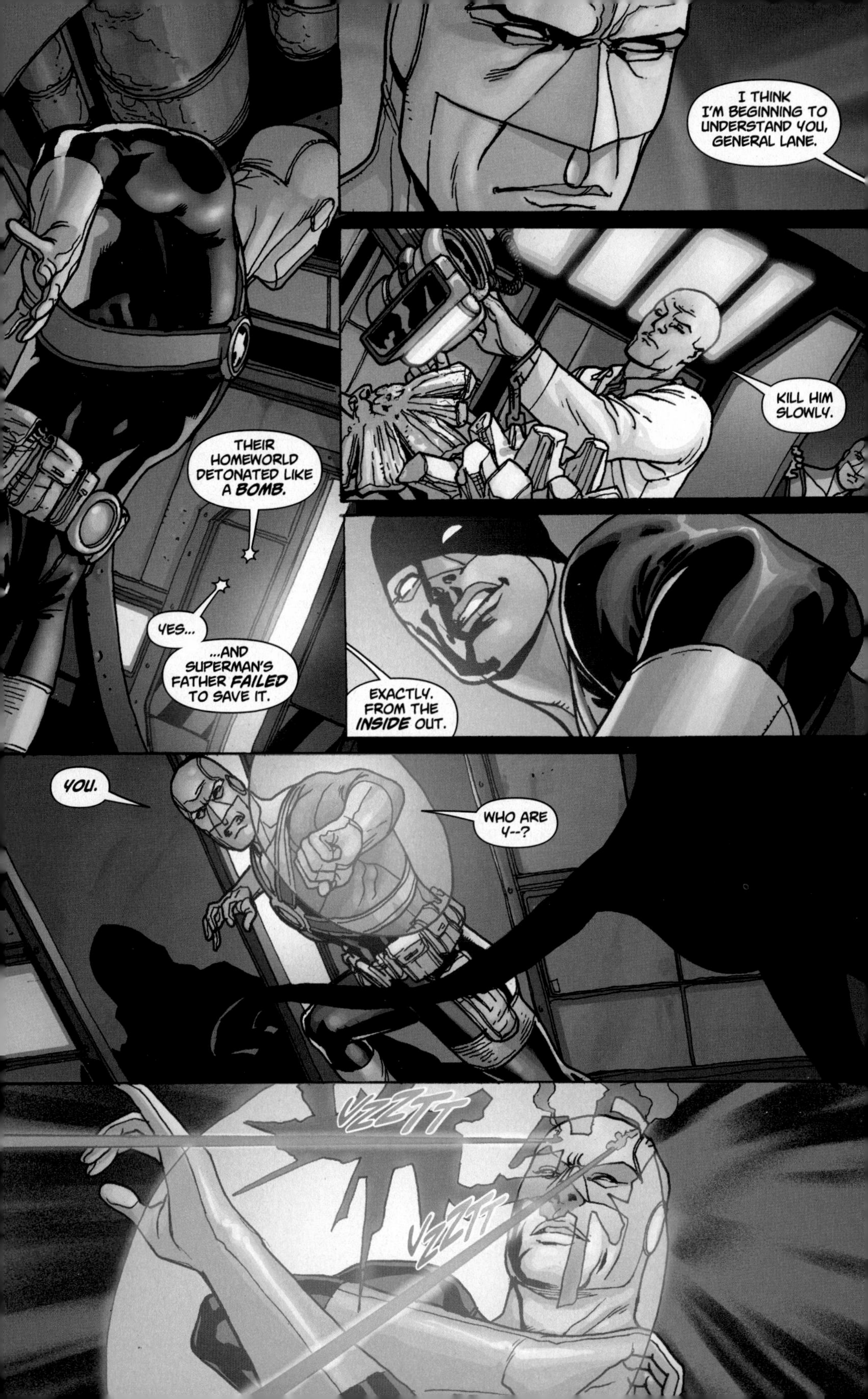
I THINK I'M BEGINNING TO UNDERSTAND YOU, GENERAL LANE.
KILL HIM SLOWLY.
THEIR HOMEWORLD DETONATED LIKE A *BOMB.*
YES...
...AND SUPERMAN'S FATHER *FAILED* TO SAVE IT.
EXACTLY. FROM THE *INSIDE* OUT.
YOU.
WHO ARE Y--?
VZZTT
VZZTT

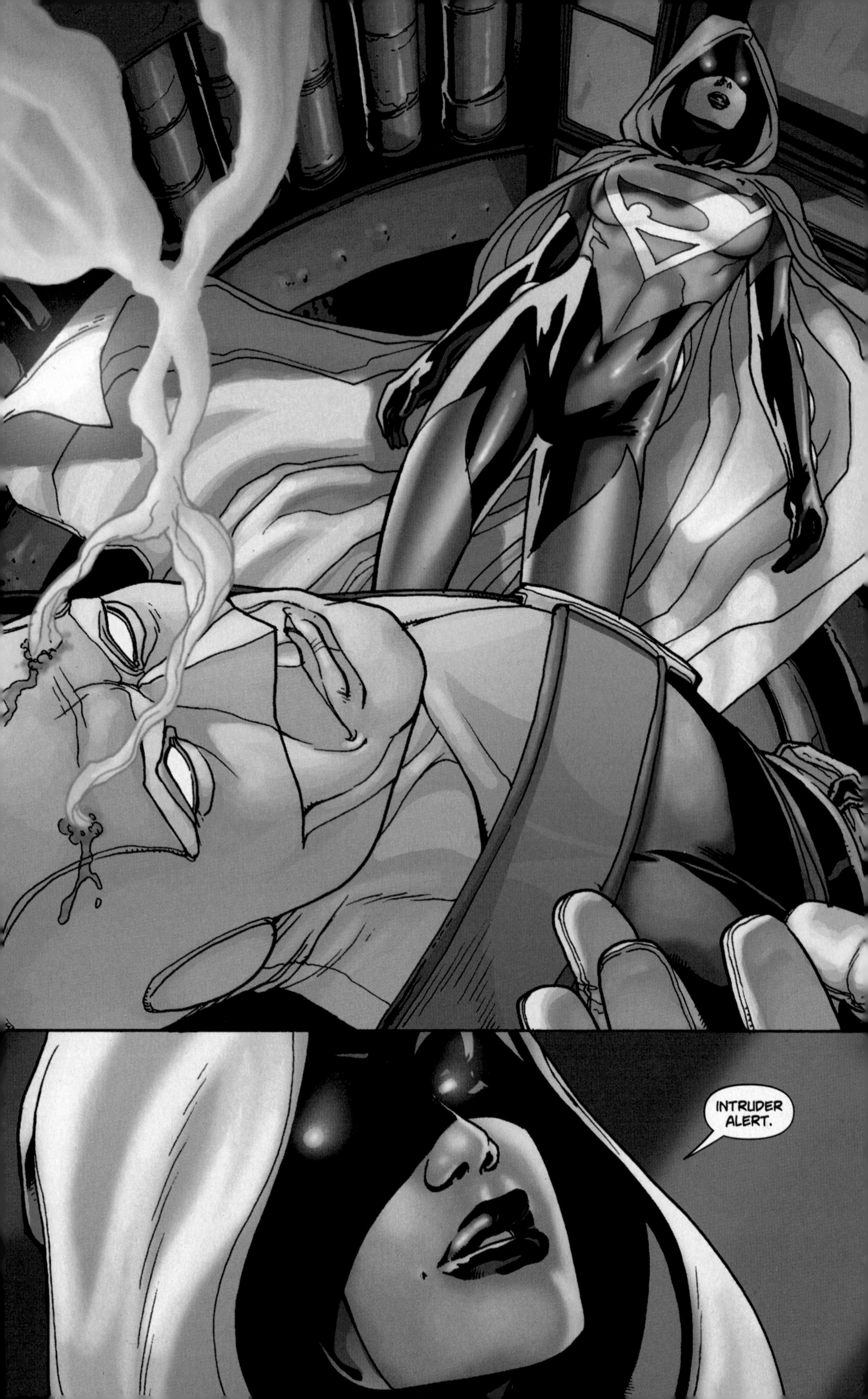
INTRUDER ALERT.

# EPILOGUE TWO

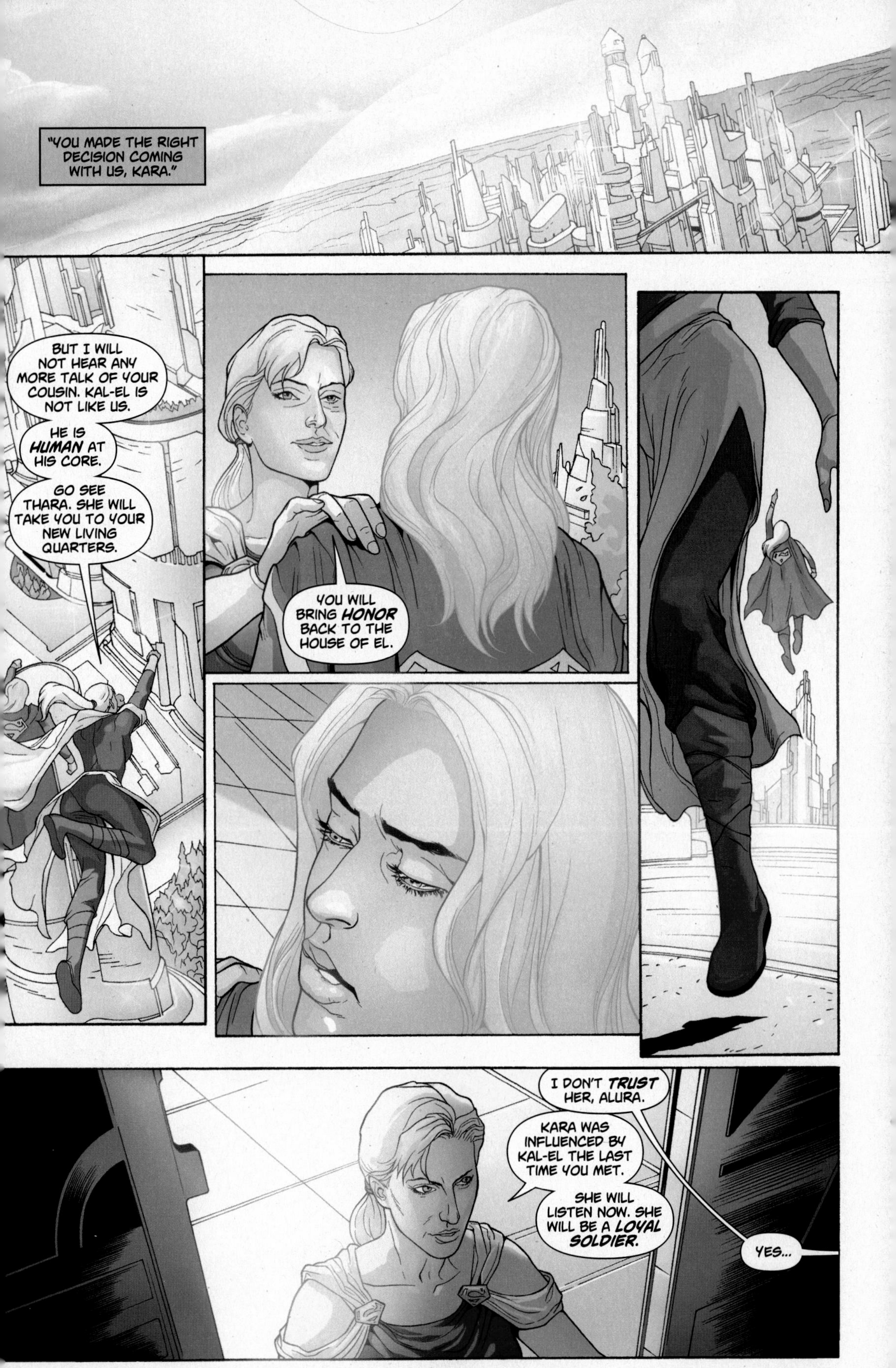

"YOU MADE THE RIGHT DECISION COMING WITH US, KARA."
BUT I WILL NOT HEAR ANY MORE TALK OF YOUR COUSIN. KAL-EL IS NOT LIKE US.
HE IS HUMAN AT HIS CORE.
GO SEE THARA. SHE WILL TAKE YOU TO YOUR NEW LIVING QUARTERS.
YOU WILL BRING HONOR BACK TO THE HOUSE OF EL.
I DON'T TRUST HER, ALURA.
KARA WAS INFLUENCED BY KAL-EL THE LAST TIME YOU MET.
SHE WILL LISTEN NOW. SHE WILL BE A LOYAL SOLDIER.
YES...

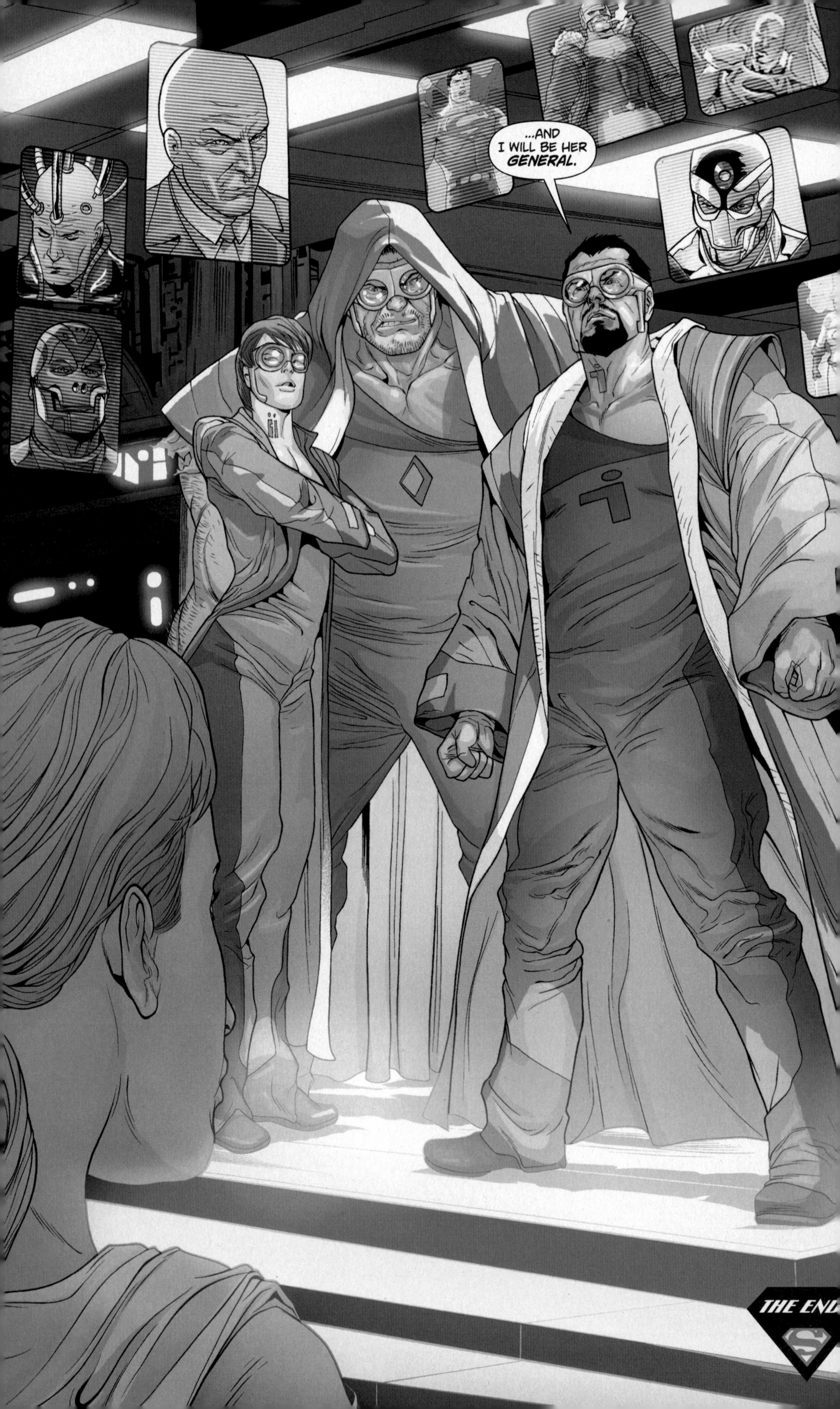
...AND I WILL BE HER GENERAL.
THE END

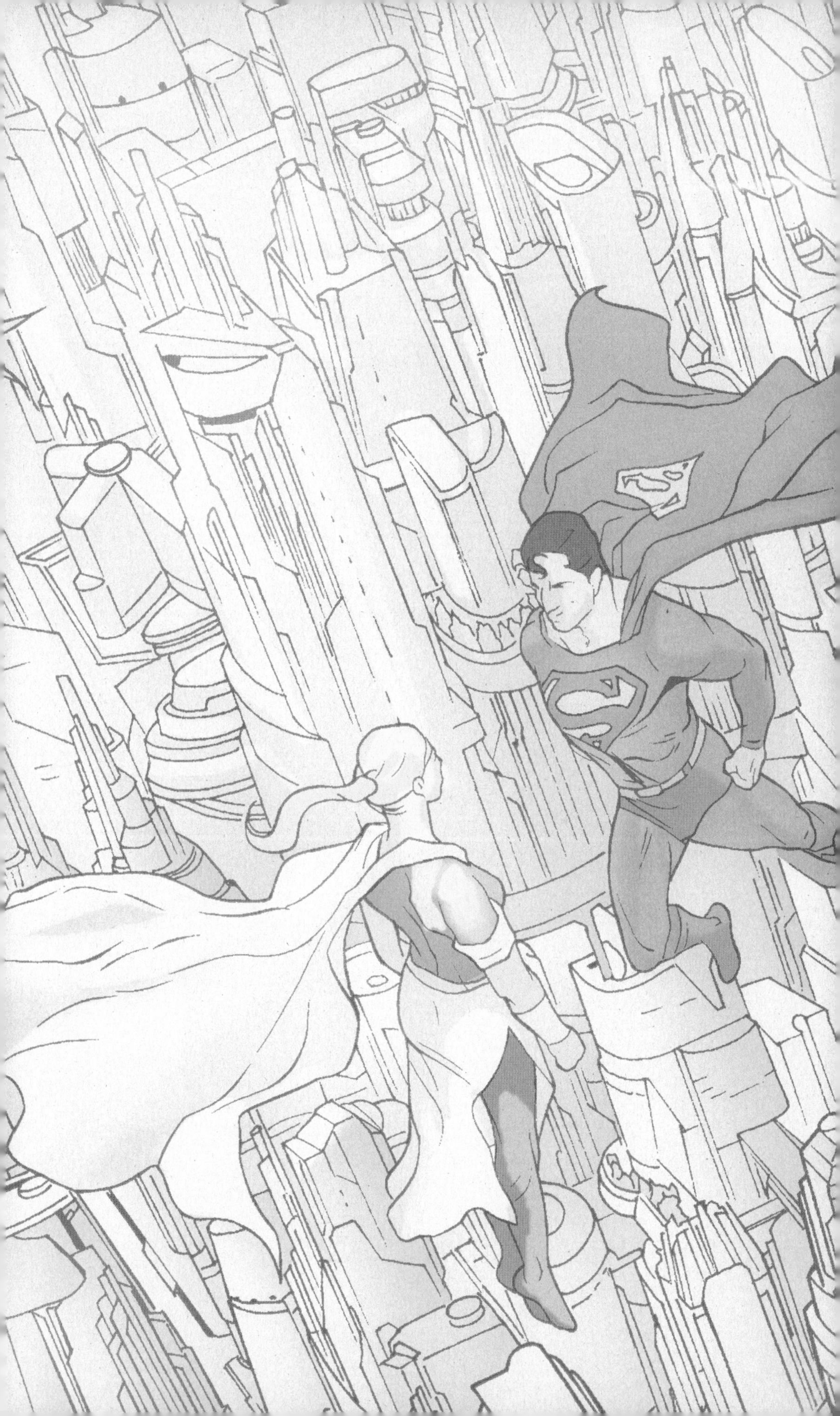

<SUPERGIRL 35 VARIANT> COVER ART BY **STEPHANE ROUX**

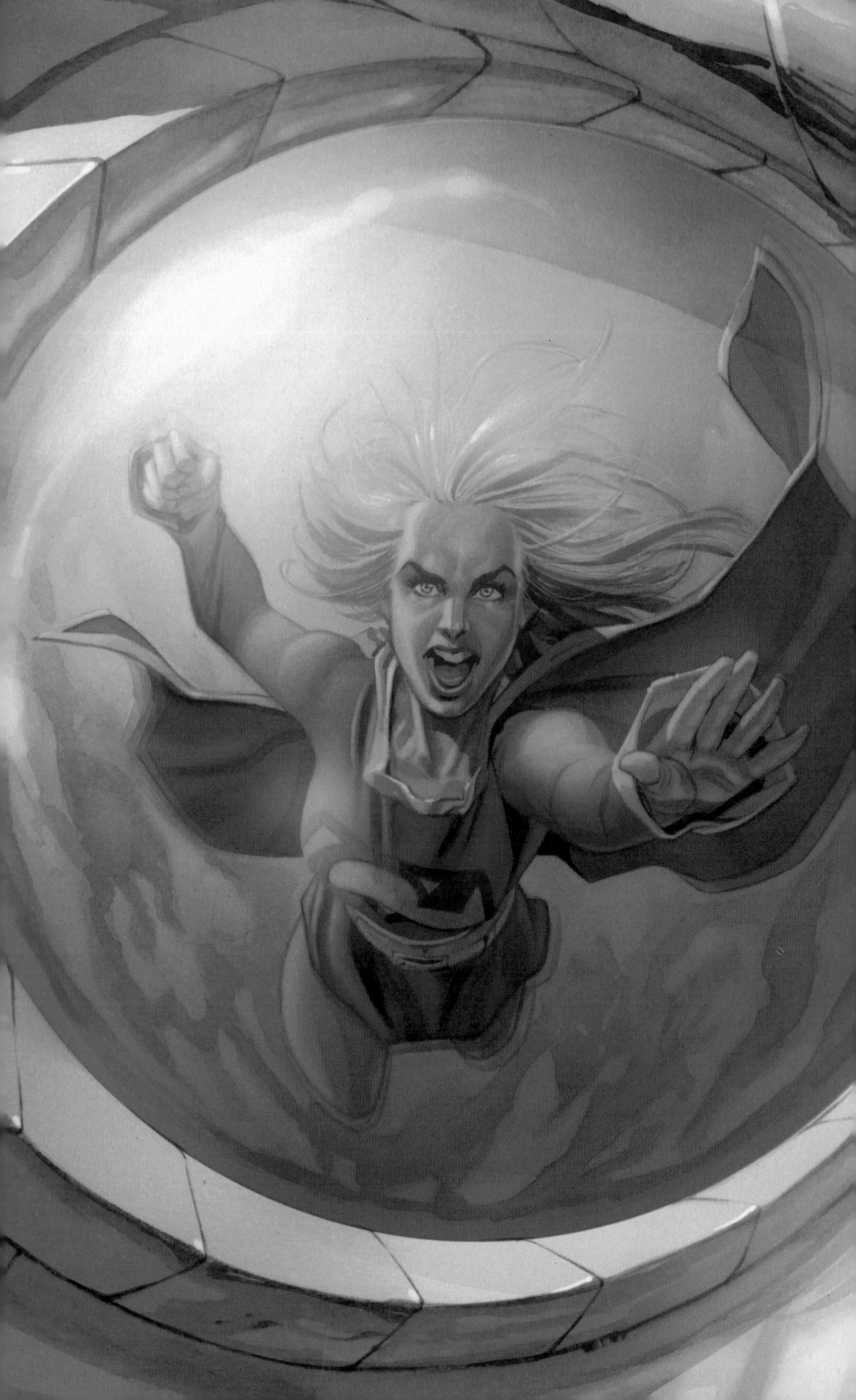

<SUPERMAN 682 VARIANT> COVER ART BY **RODOLFO MIGLIARI**

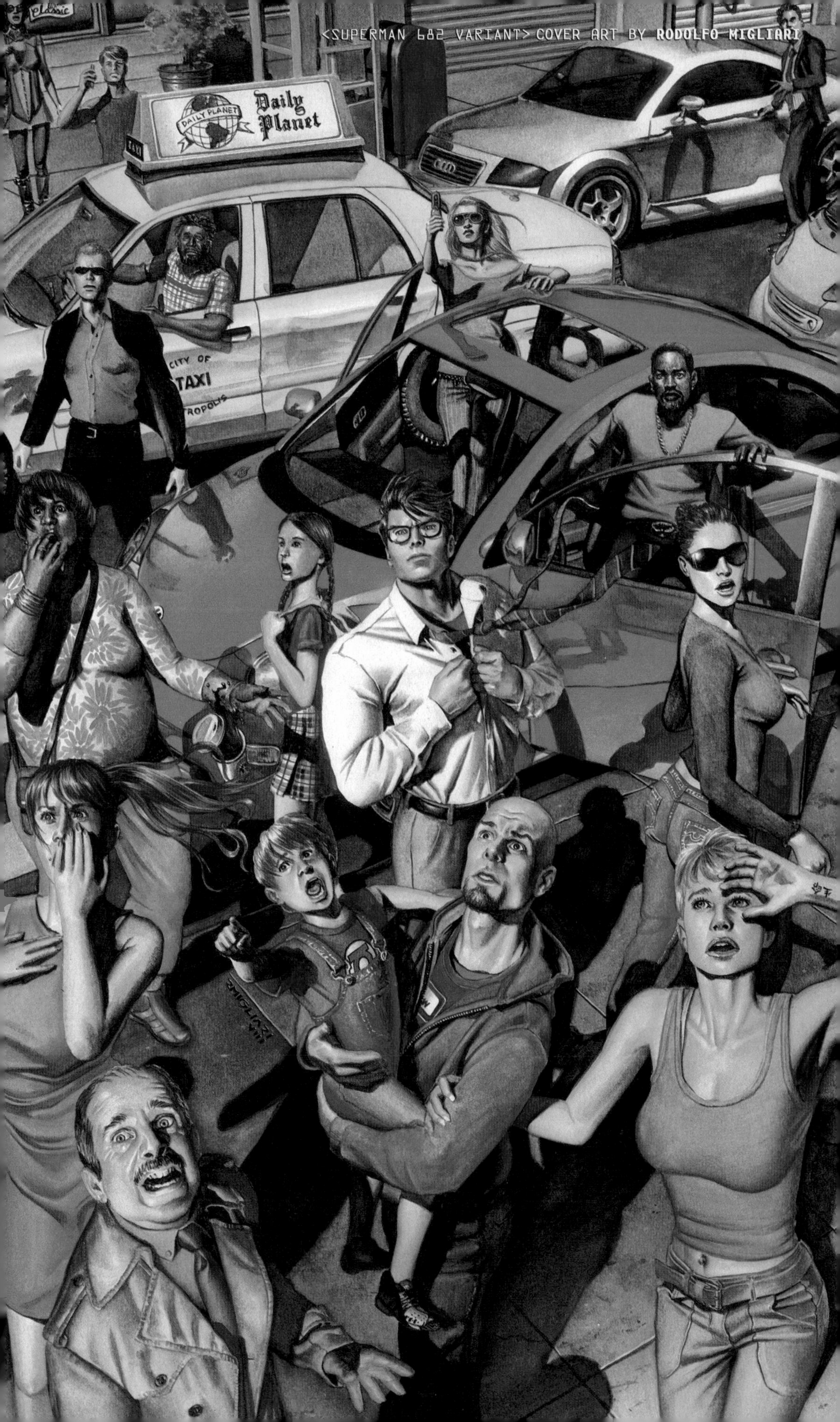
Daily Planet
DAILY PLANET
TAXI
CITY OF
TAXI

<ACTION COMICS 872 VARIANT> COVER ART BY **CHRIS SPROUSE** AND **KARL STORY** WITH **GUY MAJOR**

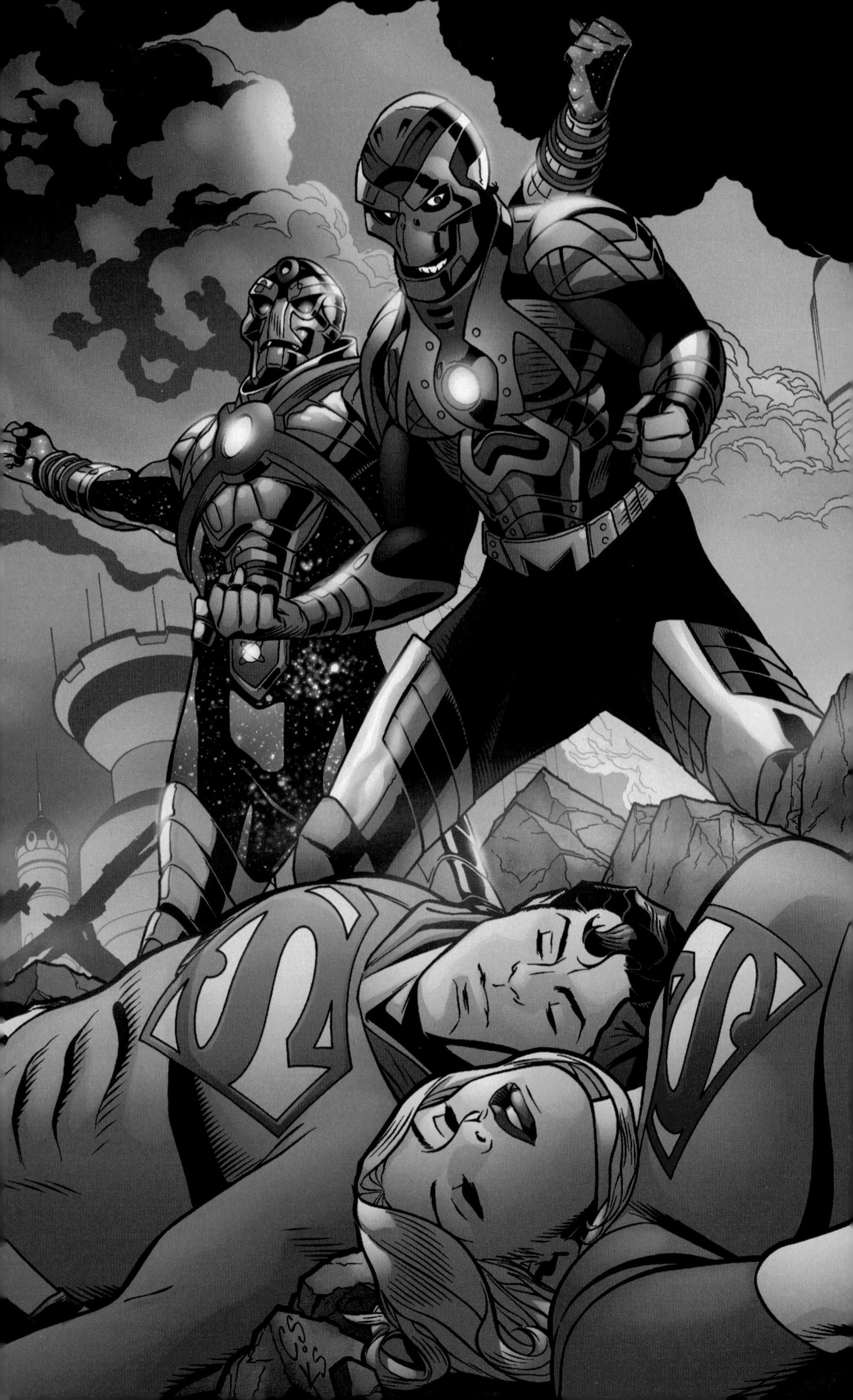

<SUPERGIRL 36 VARIANT> COVER ART BY **CHRIS SPROUSE** AND **KARL STORY** WITH **LAURA MARTIN**

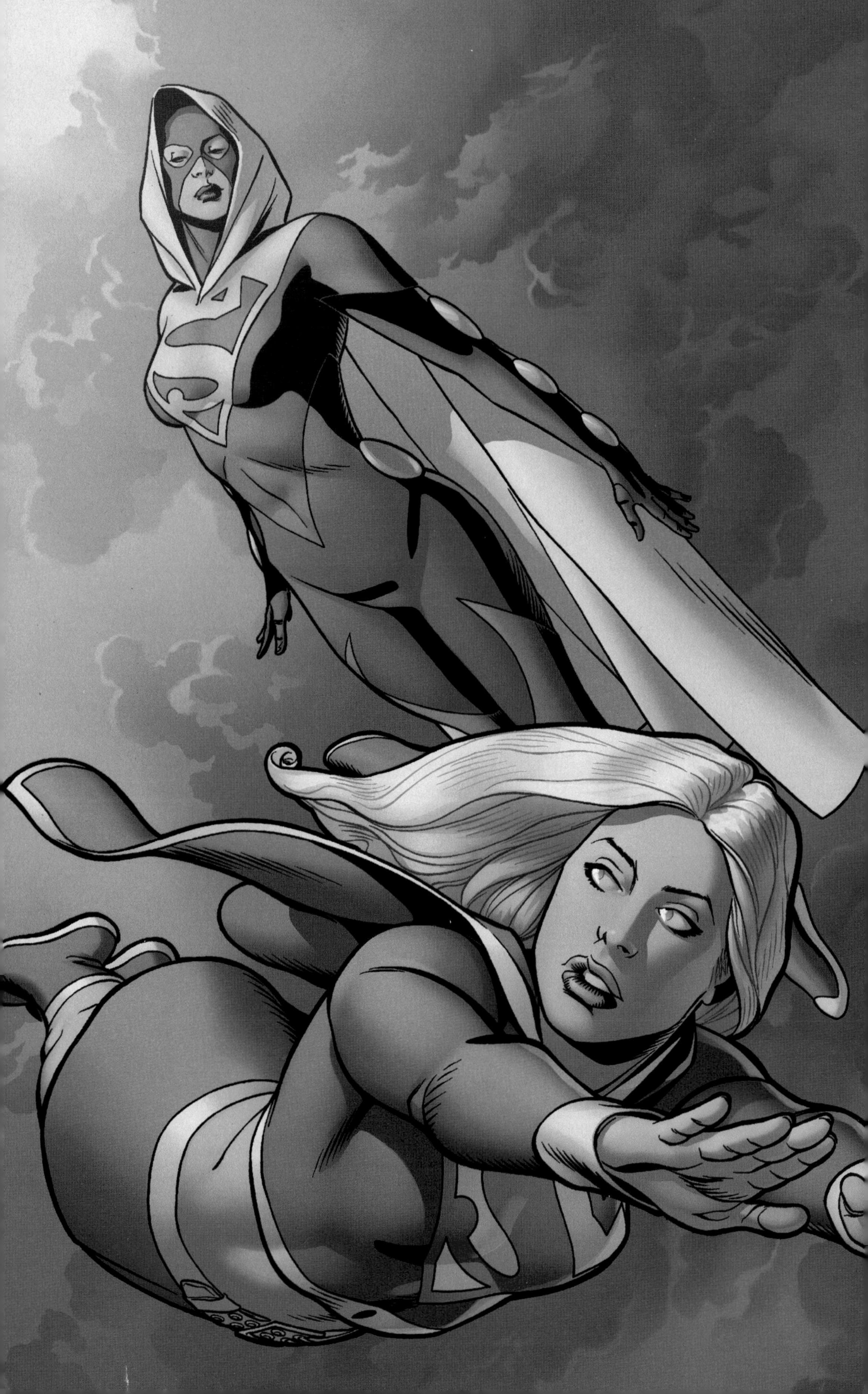

&lt;SUPERMAN 683 VARIANT&gt; COVER ART BY CHRIS SPROUSE AND KARL STORY WITH LAURA MARFIN

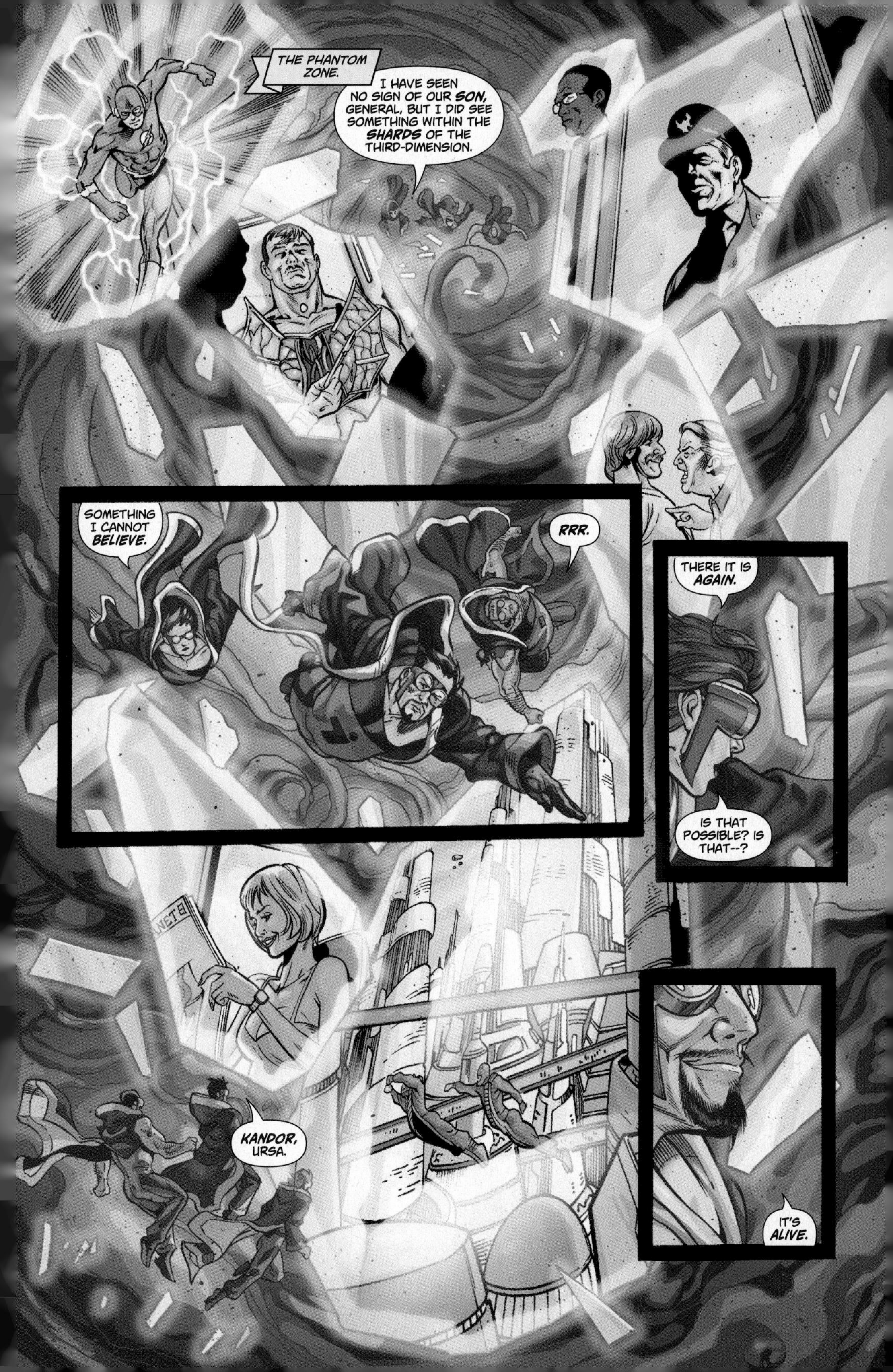
THE PHANTOM ZONE.
I HAVE SEEN NO SIGN OF OUR SON, GENERAL, BUT I DID SEE SOMETHING WITHIN THE SHARDS OF THE THIRD-DIMENSION.
SOMETHING I CANNOT BELIEVE.
RRR.
THERE IT IS AGAIN.
IS THAT POSSIBLE? IS THAT--?
KANDOR, URSA.
IT'S ALIVE.

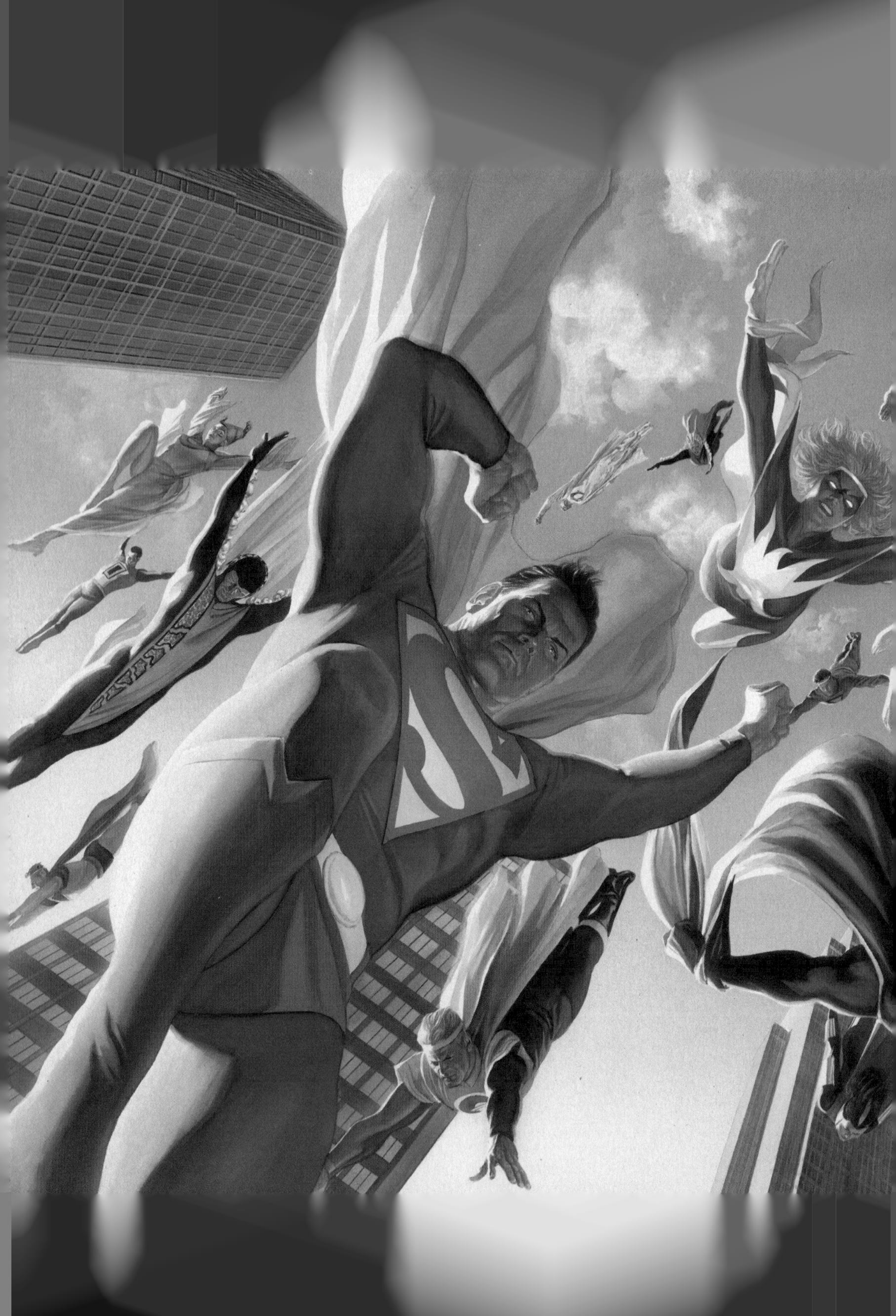

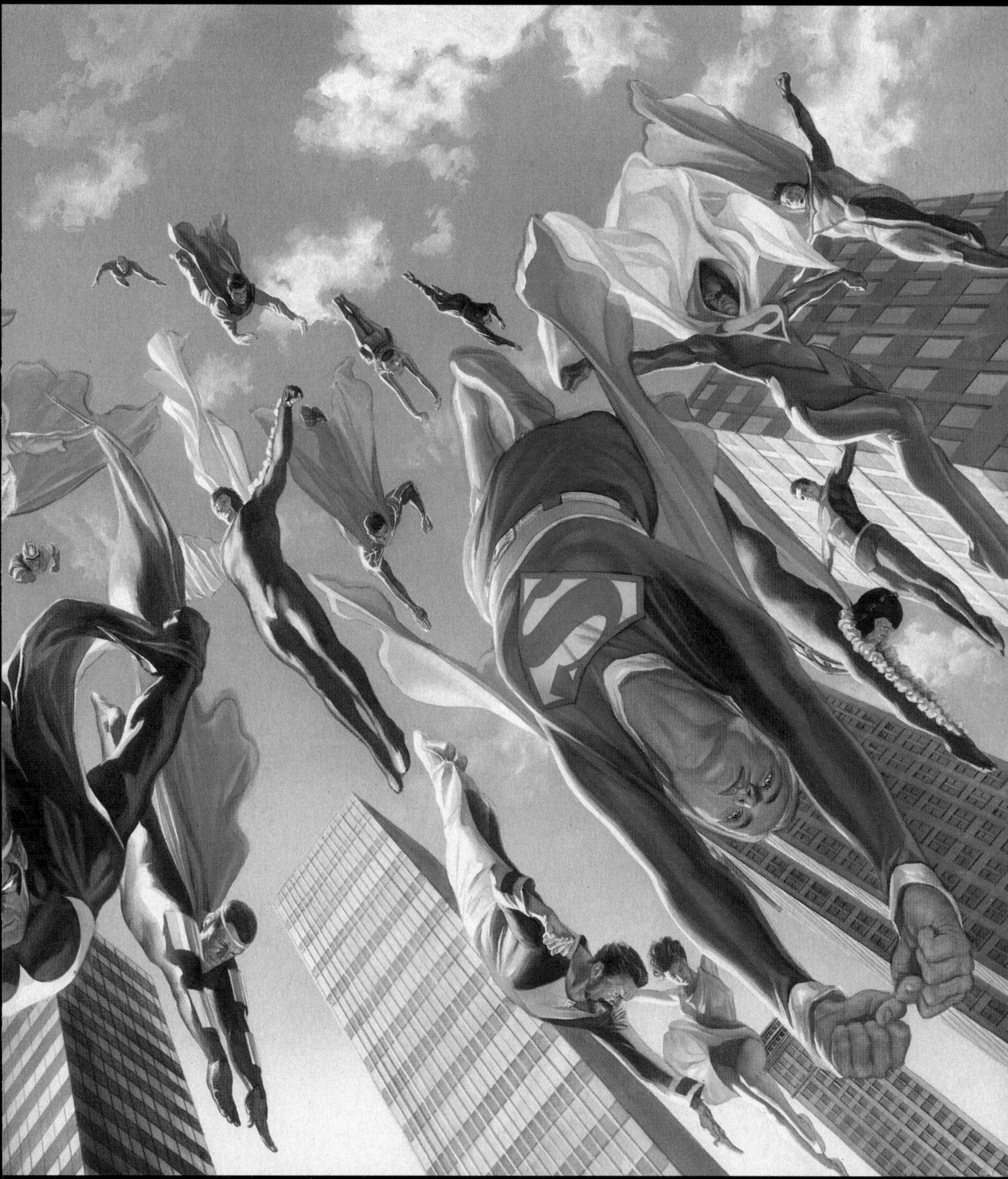

ORIGINAL COVERS TO <SUPERMAN 681, ACTION COMICS 871, AND SUPERGIRL 35>
BY **ALEX ROSS**

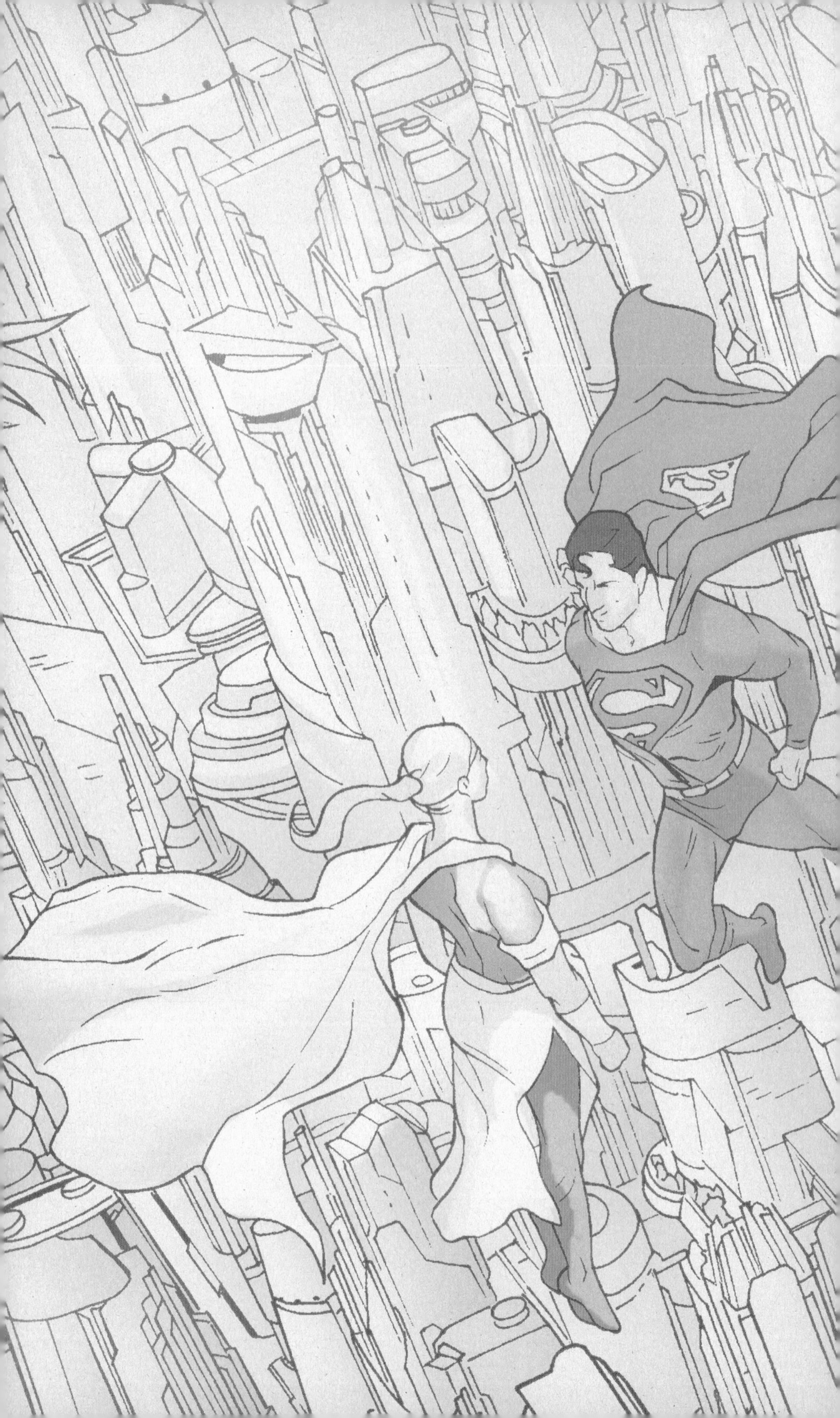

# MORE CLASSIC TALES OF THE MAN OF STEEL

SUPERMAN:
THE MAN OF STEEL
VOLS. 1 - 6

SUPERMAN:
BIRTHRIGHT

SUPERMAN:
CAMELOT FALLS
VOLS. 1 - 2

**JOHN BYRNE**

**MARK WAID
LEINIL YU**

**KURT BUSIEK
CARLOS PACHECO**

SUPERMAN:
OUR WORLDS AT WAR

SUPERMAN:
RED SON

SUPERMAN:
SECRET IDENTITY

**VARIOUS
WRITERS & ARTISTS**

**MARK MILLAR
DAVE JOHNSON
KILLIAN PLUNKETT**

**KURT BUSIEK
STUART IMMONEN**